Luxury and Gender in European Towns, 1700–1914

This book conceives the role of the modern town as a crucial place for material and cultural circulations of luxury. It concentrates on a critical period of historical change, the long eighteenth and nineteenth centuries, that was marked by the passage from a society of scarcity to one of expenditure and accumulation, from ranks and orders to greater social mobility, from traditional aristocratic luxury to a new bourgeois and even democratic form of luxury. This volume recognizes not only the notion that luxury operated as a mechanism of social separation, but also that all classes aspired to engage in consumption at some level, thus extending the idea of what constituted luxury and blurring the boundaries of class and status, often in unsettling ways. It moves beyond the moral aspects of luxury and the luxury debates to analyse how the production, distribution, purchase or display of luxury goods could participate in the creation of autonomous selves and thus challenge gender roles.

Deborah Simonton is an associate professor of British History at the University of Southern Denmark, Fellow of the Royal Historical Society and a visiting professor at the University of Turku, Finland.

Marjo Kaartinen is a professor of cultural history at the University of Turku and the director of the Turku Centre for Medieval and Early Modern Studies.

Anne Montenach is an associate professor of early modern history at Aix-Marseille University, CNRS, UMR 7303 TELEMME (13094 Aix-en-Provence, France).

Routledge Studies in Cultural History

For a full list of titles in this series, please visit www.routledge.com

4 **Genre and Cinema**
Ireland and Transnationalism
Edited by Brian McIlroy

5 **Histories of Postmodernism**
Edited by Mark Bevir, Jill Hargis, and Sara Rushing

6 **Africa after Modernism**
Transitions in Literature, Media, and Philosophy
Michael Janis

7 **Rethinking Race, Politics, and Poetics**
C. L. R. James' Critique of Modernity
Brett St Louis

8 **Making British Culture**
English Readers and the Scottish Enlightenment, 1740–1830
David Allan

9 **Empires and Boundaries**
Rethinking Race, Class, and Gender in Colonial Settings
Edited by Harald Fischer-Tiné and Susanne Gehrmann

10 **Tobacco in Russian History and Culture**
From the Seventeenth Century to the Present
Edited by Matthew P. Romaniello and Tricia Starks

11 **History of Islam in German Thought**
From Leibniz to Nietzsche
Ian Almond

12 **Israeli-Palestinian Conflict in the Francophone World**
Edited by Nathalie Debrauwere-Miller

13 **History of Participatory Media**
Politics and Publics, 1750–2000
Edited by Anders Ekström Solveig Jülich, Frans Lundgren and Per Wisselgren

14 **Living in the City**
Urban Institutions in the Low Countries, 1200–2010
Leo Lucassen and Wim Willems

15 **Historical Disasters in Context**
Science, Religion, and Politics
Edited by Andrea Janku, Gerrit J. Schenk and Franz Mauelshagen

16 **Migration, Ethnicity, and Mental Health**
International Perspectives, 1840–2010
Edited by Angela McCarthy and Catharine Coleborne

17 **Politics of Memory: Making Slavery Visible in the Public Space**
Edited by Ana Lucia Araujo

18 **Neutrality in Twentieth-Century Europe**
Intersections of Science, Culture, and Politics after the First World War
Edited by Rebecka Lettevall, Geert Somsen, and Sven Widmalm

19 **Americans Experience Russia**
Encountering the Enigma, 1917 to the Present
Edited by Choi Chatterjee and Beth Holmgren

20 **A Social History of Disability in the Middle Ages**
Cultural Considerations of Physical Impairment
Irina Metzler

21 **Race, Science, and the Nation**
Reconstructing the Ancient Past in Britain, France and Germany
Chris Manias

22 **Identity, Aesthetics, and Sound in the Fin de Siècle**
Redesigning Perception
Dariusz Gafijczuk

23 **Disease and Crime**
A History of Social Pathologies and the New Politics of Health
Edited by Robert Peckham

24 **Critical Perspectives on Colonialism**
Writing the Empire from Below
Edited by Fiona Paisley and Kirsty Reid

25 **Old World Empires**
Cultures of Power and Governance in Eurasia
Ilhan Niaz

26 **The Afterlife of Used Things**
Recycling in the Long Eighteenth Century
Edited by Ariane Fennetaux, Amélie Junqua and Sophie Vasset

27 **Holocaust Consciousness in Contemporary Britain**
Andy Pearce

28 **The Invention of Race**
Scientific and Popular Representations
Edited by Nicolas Bancel, Thomas David and Dominic Thomas

29 **Indigenous Networks**
Mobility, Connections and Exchange
Edited by Jane Carey and Jane Lydon

30 **Shadows of the Slave Past**
Memory, Heritage, and Slavery
Ana Lucia Araujo

31 **Expedition into Empire**
Exploratory Journeys and the Making of the Modern World
Edited by Martin Thomas

32 **Luxury and Gender in European Towns, 1700–1914**
Edited by Deborah Simonton, Marjo Kaartinen and Anne Montenach

Luxury and Gender in European Towns, 1700–1914

Edited by Deborah Simonton, Marjo Kaartinen and Anne Montenach

Routledge
Taylor & Francis Group
LONDON AND NEW YORK

First published 2015
by Routledge

2 Park Square, Milton Park, Abingdon, Oxfordshire OX14 4RN
52 Vanderbilt Avenue, New York, NY 10017

Routledge is an imprint of the Taylor & Francis Group, an informa business

First issued in paperback 2018

Library of Congress Cataloging-in-Publication Data

Luxury and gender in European towns, 1700–1914 / edited by Deborah Simonton, Marjo Kaartinen, and Anne Montenach.
pages cm. — (Routledge studies in cultural history ; 32)
Includes bibliographical references and index.
1. Luxury—Social aspects—Europe—History—18th century. 2. Luxury—Social aspects—Europe—History—19th century. 3. City and town life—Europe—History. 4. Sex role—Europe—History. 5. Social classes—Europe—History. 6. Luxury goods industry—Europe—History. 7. Europe—Economic conditions—18th century. 8. Europe—Economic conditions—1789–1900. 9. Europe—Social conditions—18th century. 10. Europe—Social conditions—1789–1900. I. Simonton, Deborah, 1948– II. Kaartinen, Marjo, 1964– III. Montenach, Anne.
HC240.L89 2014
330.94'02—dc23
2014017956

ISBN: 978-1-138-80316-9 (hbk)
ISBN: 978-0-367-20875-2 (pbk)

Typeset in Sabon
by Apex CoVantage, LLC

To our 'boys' and friends who make our lives luxurious

Contents

PART II
Metropole and Province

PART III
Class and Status

Figures

Tables

Tables

Preface

Deborah Simonton

In Europe today, most of the population lives in towns and women still make up the majority; thus the relationships between men and women and an understanding of masculinity and femininity are central to the idea of the city. As women constituted a significant majority in most towns, which were governed by men of a certain social order, the cultural dynamics of gender were and remain important. Towns were central to migratory patterns and crucial in the transmission of ideas across what came to be seen as the idea of Europe. Europe was identified as a place in the mind's eye, but boundaries shifted, nation-states were not fixed, and people identified as much with locality, region or principality as nationality. Thus, many people shaped their identities from urban culture. As places which fostered and disseminated key social, economic, political and cultural developments, towns were central to the creation of gendered identities and the transmission of ideas across local, national and transnational boundaries. This book is one of a series of publications from a European network of historians whose interests lie in examining the ways that the European urban experience was gendered over time and across borders. We also ask what influence gender has on the shape of towns themselves.

The research network Gender in the European Town: The Making of the Modern Town is interjecting gender into urban historiography and therefore altering perspectives on urban identity and development. The period from about 1600 is fundamental to how our modern cities have developed and shapes our contemporary understanding of towns and the way they work in cultural, spatial and gendered ways. The idea of the city is central to contemporary practices, which draw on ideas and imagined spaces of the past. Concentrating on the three-hundred-year period between 1650 and 1950 that traces the emergence, diversification and developing hegemony of the town in the history of Europe, this network interrogates the operation of gender in three distinct, but interrelated, areas of urban study: the economic, the political and the spatial.

The network examines the influence of gender on the shape of towns, on urban spaces and as a force for urban change through relational studies, which explore the subtle and changing nature and operation of power, patriarchy and privilege through the lens of the town, alert to the ways that these factors shaped and were shaped by gendered identities. This research explores relationships of gender, space, workplace, commerce, trade and sociability, and will promote a wider understanding of the issues of gender and urban experience. Asking new questions and exploring a range of towns, the network will contribute to a wider understanding of the spaces, places and dynamics that shape the contemporary urban European world. The scope and scale of this project will ultimately tell us a great deal more about the formation of urban identities and cultures, and help us to understand the European inflection of these developments over an important formative period. It will broaden our idea about the development and legacy of towns in this period and will help us to understand the contribution of gender to the culture of towns over time.

Acknowledgments

In 2006, a group of around thirty academics initiated the Gender in European Towns Network. Eight years on sees the publication of this volume, which is the third collaborative publication from this energetic group. We would like to thank this band of sisters and brothers for rising to the challenge and for providing such a fruitful and exhilarating milieu within which to work. A collection such as this relies on a huge amount of work from a large number of people. We would therefore wish to thank not only our contributors for their hard work and enthusiasm, but also the numerous individuals who gave us feedback personally and professionally, strengthening our ideas and arguments and making this a stronger and more coherent piece of work. Behind each piece of research are countless hours spent working in numerous archives and libraries. We are indebted to the staff at these institutions who helped us find our way through their troves of sources. Our invaluable map-makers, Farid Boumédiene, University of Limoges, and Edward Irvine, University of North Carolina, Wilmington, have provided immeasurable support in helping to render some of our luxury worlds more visible. We thank the editorial team at Routledge for their support and encouragement, as always, in bringing this project to its final published form.

We also thank network members and colleagues who attended colloquia held under the umbrella of the Gender in the European Town Network and the contributors to the Gender in the European Town Conference held in Odense in May 2013, which was supported by the Carlsberg Foundation, The Economic History Society, Letterstedska Foundation and Forskningsrådet for Kultur og Kommunikation as well as the Universities of Southern Denmark and Aarhus. We also wish to acknowledge the significant support from Det Frie Forskningsråd: Forskningsrådet for Kultur og Kommunikation of the Danish Agency for Science, Technology and Innovation and the Rektor's Fund of the University of Southern Denmark for substantial financial support for our networking activities. Many of our institutions also contributed important financial support, venues for meetings and travel to enable our research, writing and collaboration. Specifically, in September 2011 the UMR 7303 TELEMME (CNRS-Aix Marseille Université) hosted a workshop that was the origin of this book project; this meeting gave

Northern European colleagues a chance to enjoy hard work under the Provençal sun. We thank these institutions for this vote of confidence in the project.

Despite collaboration, research can be an isolated experience—we work with our sources, and as historians, trying to talk to and understand people who are usually dead and who cannot explain things to us. It is at these moments that colleagues, friends and family, who offered advice, support and helpful suggestions along the way, become ever more important. Importantly, the editors specifically wish to acknowledge the patience and understanding of our partners and families. We have dedicated this book to the men in our lives and our friends, without whom we would never have reached this point, and we offer them eternal gratitude for the underpinning support we need.

The authors and publisher would like to thank the following for assistance with and the permission to reproduce the images in this book: Museum of Copenhagen, Copenhagen, and Erhvervsarkivet i Danmark (The National Business Archive), Aarhus, Denmark; Pamela Fletcher and David Israel of the *London Gallery Project*, Bowdoin College, Brunswick, Maine, USA; Russell-Cotes Art Gallery and Museum, Bournemouth, England; Shetland Museum Photographic Archive, Scotland; Kim Downie and Special Collections & Museums, Aberdeen University Library, Scotland; Riksarkivet, Sweden; Eiker Arkiv, Drammen, Norway; Magyar Nemzeti Múzeum, Budapest, Hungary; and The British Museum, London.

1 Luxury, Gender and the Urban Experience

Marjo Kaartinen, Anne Montenach and Deborah Simonton

Luxury and Gender in European Towns, 1700–1914, conceives the role of the modern town as a crucial place for material and cultural circulations of luxury. The chapters in this volume concentrate on a critical period of historical change, the long eighteenth and nineteenth centuries. This period was marked by the passage from a society of scarcity to one of expenditure and accumulation, from ranks and orders to greater social mobility, from traditional aristocratic luxury to a new *bourgeois* and even democratic form of luxury. This volume recognises not only the notion that luxury operated as a mechanism of social separation but also that all classes aspired to engage in consumption at some level, thus extending the idea of what constituted luxury and blurring the boundaries of class and status, often in unsettling ways. This book asks what was acceptable and desirable luxury, according to gender, status, social class, life-course, time and space. It analyses in what ways the production, distribution, purchase or display of luxury goods could participate in the creation of autonomous selves and thus challenge gender roles.

This book is about urban practices of luxury. Therefore it moves beyond the moral aspects of luxury and the luxury debates, which have dominated much of early modern thinking and which have fascinated historians. By exploring the processes of production, distribution and consumption of luxury goods from a gendered perspective, and articulating a wide geographical spectrum, the chapters fill gaps in the rich historiography of material culture and luxury consumption. In order to interrogate the concept of luxury itself and its shifting meanings, this volume looks at specific political, social and cultural contexts on a European scale and investigates different local cultures of luxury. Towns were at the heart of these shifting paradigms. As a physical environment, and a social and spatial construct, the town comprises discourses about the meanings and perceptions of towns by its inhabitants and observers as well as the material fabric and objects which give the town a physical and symbolic shape. Modern European towns fostered commercial developments that meant that more goods and services were available to support the urban community. The growth of proto-industries, although often rural, had their birthplace in urban capitalism, which managed the circulation of raw materials and finished products. These were central to the growth of a wider commercial marketplace on a regional, national and even global scale, a marketplace that gave birth to luxury production and consumption. Therefore, the town constitutes a key site to observe and analyse the relationship between luxury and gender.

An important contribution of this book is its chronological and geographic coverage, which juxtaposes discussions of luxury and towns in much-researched Britain and France with developments in Scandinavia, the Mediterranean and Eastern Europe. Drawing on a range of sources, including official records such as censuses, tax records, post-mortem inventories, court records and guild records; receipts, bills and private account books; memoirs and letters; and a variety of materials from the burgeoning print culture like maps, novels, treatises, newspapers and magazines, and often reading across the grain, the authors illustrate the variety of materials that can be used to evaluate the production, marketing and consumption of luxury.

LUXURY DISCOURSES

This book offers an opportunity to view luxury not only as an object of consumption but also from the viewpoint of production and regulation of luxury. We do not propose to review the luxury debates and historiography in depth here. Nevertheless, a few comments that situate this volume are in order. As a malleable and dynamic concept, luxury 'can be understood as one of the basic categorising components of a society's grammar', as Christopher J. Berry has pointed out.[1] Luxury is an extremely complex social, historical and cultural construct which has to do with desirability, expensiveness, rarity, sensory enjoyment, refinement and pleasure(s), superfluity, magnificence and ostentation, but also with high quality, design and fashion, creativity and innovation or authenticity. Definitions and perceptions of luxury changed over time as well. During the period under scrutiny, luxury was not only a social and economic concern, but also a political issue.

The eighteenth century is now well known as a time of strong economic expansion in Europe, where towns of all sizes, and especially commercial centres, experienced significant growth in population and wealth. At the same time, people's lifestyles changed gradually, but dramatically. Given growth in what John Brewer and Roy Porter identify as a new 'world of goods', which they interpreted as the source of an alarming confusion of social conditions, many contemporaries denounced 'the scourge of luxury'.[2] By upsetting social markers and blurring the divisions between upper and lower classes, increased trade and consumerism certainly challenged the traditional values inspired by social hierarchies and sumptuary legislation. Many eighteenth-century authors viewed this phenomenon as a disease that had infected the entire society.

One relevant issue that emerged from these debates was the interest in finding a definition for 'luxury', a concept that was open to myriad interpretations but that mostly appears to be 'the code word for threatening social changes'.[3] Adam Ferguson, Professor of Moral Philosophy at the University of Edinburgh, reflected in 1767:

> We are far from being agreed on the application of the term *luxury*, or on that degree of its meaning which is consistent with national prosperity, or with the moral rectitude of our nature. It is sometimes employed to signify a manner of life which we think necessary to civilization, and even to happiness. It is, in our panegyric of polished ages, the parent of arts, the support of commerce, and the minister of national greatness, and of opulence. It is, in our censure of degenerate manners, the source of corruption, and the presage of national descension and ruin. It is admired, and it is blamed; it is treated as ornamental and useful; and it proscribed as a vice.[4]

Ferguson thus synthesized the opposing and shifting view of luxury as a vice (i.e., as corruption and excessive displays by the elite) to that of a 'refinement for the gratification of the senses', as previously expressed by Mandeville in his famous *Fable of the Bees* (1714), and also of a market.[5] In this process of 'de-moralization' of luxury, to quote Christopher Berry, luxury was increasingly seen as merchandise that was not only socially useful, but also good for business and human well-being.

As a result of the transport 'revolution' and increasing domestic and international trade, rising competition and the 'industrious' revolution with its growing production rates, some products that people still considered luxuries at the turn of the seventeenth century, such as sugar or drink ware and its paraphernalia for hot drinks, entered working-class homes in the eighteenth century. In the nineteenth and early twentieth centuries, further commercialization, better transport and the emergence of urban department stores as well as an increasingly vociferous bourgeois class intent on stamping their image on the century led to a further diversification of luxury items. Thus by the First World War, social constructions of luxury and their cultural meanings permeated all levels of society. However, these meanings operated differently and were inevitably variable in terms of class, nationality and status. As Woodruff Smith argued, 'as a word, as a concept, and a set of cultural practices, [luxury] has always had multiple meanings, few of which have been stable over time or unambiguous.'[6]

GENDER, LUXURY AND CONSUMPTION

This volume does not assume luxury as a feminine construct but looks at the ways in which luxury was gendered. As Samuel Fawconer suggests in his

1765 *An Essay on Modern Luxury*, the eighteenth-century understanding of luxury was not necessarily perceived as feminine:

> where the exteriours form our judgment of the man, and appearance in the vulgar eye passes for the only criterion of true worth: every one is ready to assume the marks of a superiour condition, in order to be esteemed more than what he really is.[7]

For those who wanted to moralize luxury, both sexes were guilty of the want of too much. Early modern Swedish and Danish sumptuary laws rarely distinguished between men and women while stipulating limits on luxury purchases, and, notably, Danish law was more concerned with feasts and food than with fashion.[8] However, many eighteenth-century authors highlighted two aspects that demonstrated the close links between luxury and femininity. First, luxury, now defined as any unnecessary object that created desire through the specific process of seduction and temptation, was thought to be more attractive to women because of their excessive desire for fashion, novelties and frivolities.[9] Second, luxury led to the development of *mollesse*, a physical phenomenon that led to effeminacy and hence to the emasculation of men and national decline.

Contemporaries quickly singled women out as purchasers of luxury items. Josiah Wedgwood, the Staffordshire potter whose wares became all the rage, including commissions from Catherine II, catered for all levels in society, both home and abroad. As a consummate promoter of his goods, he acknowledged: 'Few ladies, you know, dare venture at anything out of the common stile, 'till authoris'd by their betters—by the Ladies of superior spirit who set the ton.'[10] In English tracts from the period, contemporaries quickly began to blame women for the excesses of luxury. Bernard Mandeville wrote: 'I have shewn already that the worst of Women and the most profligate of the Sex did contribute to the Consumption of Superfluities, as well as the Necessaries of Life'.[11] Mandeville did not exclusively attack women for their profligate spending, but his discussions of men tended to situate them as victims of employers and others, including women, who conspired to relieve them of their money. Millinery and fashion came to be epitomised as a female world where women's purchases made victims of their husbands and their pocketbooks, as Louis-Sébastien Mercier wrote:

> What is spent on fashion today exceeds the expenses of the table and that for horses and carriages. The unfortunate husband can never calculate to what price these changing fantasies will climb; & he will need swift resources to fight off these unexpected whims.[12]

Thus women quickly came to be seen as idle, frivolous and irresponsible purchasers. This is an image that continued throughout the nineteenth century, and Emile Zola neatly juxtaposed the frivolous female consumer with the hardworking shop assistant in *Au Bonheur des Dames* (1883).[13] He also captured the impact of the department stores and their selling and promotion of luxury experiences, while pointedly criticising the practice of undercutting producers by insisting on buying from them at prices that made their work uneconomic. In this passage he characterises several female customers:

> Madame Marty, carried away by her rage for spending, took everything at *The Ladies' Paradise*, without choosing, just as the articles appeared; Madame Guibal walked about the shop for hours without ever buying anything, happy and satisfied to simply feast her eyes; Madame de Boves, short of money, always tortured by some immoderate wish, nourished a feeling of rancour against the goods she could not carry away . . . The idea of getting goods below cost price awoke in them all the greed felt by women, whose enjoyment as buyers is doubled when they think they are robbing the tradesman.[14]

However, men were also important shoppers and this created anxiety for moralists, who threatened luxury-consuming men with succumbing to effeminacy. Luxury and effeminacy denoted individual and national degeneracy, and submission to female charms and conspicuous consumption was perceived as undermining manly virtue. Michele Cohen has argued that effeminacy was a dominant metaphor for 'problematic gender boundaries for men' and conflated with 'luxury', it was used to criticize many social evils.[15] The British, especially, linked the critique of luxury to the French, and believed French style and the desire for imported luxury goods was damaging both economic and military strength. National patriotic political discourse drew on women in luxury trades, condemning 'Frenchness' in millinery, mirroring discourses in electoral politics. The critique was both economic and political in the final analysis, with 'luxury' identified as French, and adherence to sober 'English' goods a central part of national identity. The Society for the Encouragement of the Arts, Manufactures and Commerce, founded in 1754, promoted British culture over French, and awarded prizes to women for their 'nationalist' endeavours. Mrs Williams, awarded a prize in 1784 for breeding silkworms, hoped '[t]hat my poor endeavours may one day prove beneficial to my country.'[16] Cultural disintegration and commercial imperatives went hand in hand.

National good and the importance of competitiveness in commerce gradually undermined sumptuary legislation in the eighteenth century, and the critique of luxury shifted to accommodate commercial imperatives. So, contemporary critiques of luxury had altered by the end of the eighteenth century, encapsulated by Adam Smith's argument that individual greed and acquisitiveness were necessary prerequisites for the stimulation of the economy, and one of the last Scottish laws regulating dress, in fact, controlled imports from the continent which it was believed were hurting Scottish commerce.[17] In this respect, the wider ability of people to consume items deemed luxurious was seen as a positive factor, so that by the nineteenth century *laissez faire* economics valorised the consuming habits of the populace as stimulus to production and commerce.[18] At the same time, luxury, when conceived as the incarnation of good taste, was seen by romantic artists and dandy writers such as Baudelaire as the driving force behind moral and aesthetic sensibility.[19]

METROPOLE AND PROVINCE

The history of consumption and material culture has closely associated luxury with city life, as a place of fancy, novelty and display. This certainly is what contemporaries thought of luxury because it was believed that metropolises especially fed a need for self-presentation through ostentation; anonymity and the desire to distinguish oneself 'opened the possibilities of fantasy and self-fashioning'.[20] This was, of course, done by dressing up and deploying various luxury items on one's person, parading on new urban promenades, on well-kitted-out horses, with refined carriages or the novelty of new motor cars. As Fawconer wrote: '[I]t is observable, that luxury generally abounds, in proportion to the populousness of the capital city. . . . In so large and populous a city, the generality of the inhabitants must be entire strangers to each other'.[21]

The case studies in this volume focus on towns that were vibrant centres of luxury production, trade and consumption. Their economies were profoundly shaped by what was understood as luxury, both through production of goods and commercial trading in luxury items, across the two centuries studied here. Writing on Drammen, Paris, Vyborg, Grenoble, Copenhagen, Barcelona, London, La Rochelle, Aberdeen, Budapest and Colchester, the authors demonstrate the importance that the 'urban' had to the conceptualization of luxury and, symbiotically, the impact that luxury discourses had on the town. The size and importance of these towns differed from each other and across time: from playing significant roles in world politics and international trade, like London and Paris, to important local centres such as Aberdeen, Budapest, Barcelona or Copenhagen, to small quiet provincial towns like Vyborg. The small size or the provincial nature of towns did not necessarily mean lack of vibrancy. For example, nineteenth-century Vyborg grew enormously, from fewer than 3,000 inhabitants to a town of more than 32,000 in 1900. At the same time, global and imperial goods played a role in generating expectations and redefining the meanings and access to luxury. Many towns like Copenhagen and Aberdeen had harbours that were significant to their local and national economies, while the likes of London and La Rochelle were significant players in international commerce.

Whatever their geographical position however, luxury trades signalled transition, exchange, and very often long-distance trade. While provincial elites, such as the Hackman merchant family in early nineteenth-century

Vyborg, studied by Ulla Ijäs, made good use of the vicinity of St Petersburg, Swedish aristocrats commissioned luxury items from Paris through their relatives, friends and even the diplomatic circle. As shown by Johanna Ilmakunnas, shopping was both a male and female activity among the Swedish aristocracy. More generally, shopping was couched in leisure discourses, and the shop increasingly emerged as a new social space during the eighteenth century as part of the development of polite and sociable society. It was a place to see and be seen and it filled some of the same functions as visiting and promenading. Indeed, shopping often was not about purchasing at all, but about the act of visiting shops, checking out fashion and new trends and showing off. Shopping was more than just marketing or buying; the new emporiums conjured up the image of luxury and were places to see and be seen, as Kemille Moore demonstrates for London's West End. Shoppers were often seeking something desirable, not something essential, and their motives and approaches to shopping varied, as the quote from Zola above shows.

The mercantile empires and growing international trade contributed to notions of luxury and the exotic, images conjured by goods brought back to ports and dispersed across European urban centres from China, Japan and India.[22] The exotic luxury products were a key area in the economic growth in the period discussed here. But it certainly came with a price: It was often noted how very unpatriotic it was to support the trade of foreign luxuries such as china, silk or coffee.[23] Regulations of foreign trade were attempted in many places in the period under study here, but these efforts were always met with the fact that, as mentioned above, in many senses luxuries had become necessities—silk was an absolute necessity for the elite woman, and even the working-class women and men of the later eighteenth century were desperately addicted to coffee. Failed coffee prohibitions in eighteenth-century Sweden (the first ban commenced in 1756, the last in 1817) serve as good examples of futile governmental regulation against the overpowering need to buy and enjoy the luxury product under ban. Illicit trade grew to such an extent that it had to be given up: The consumers needed their cup of 'brown' and they minded very little about the illegal nature of their great pleasure. As Ilmakunnas argues, the Swedish aristocracy took very little notice of these bans and quite freely smuggled French luxuries into the country. Without doubt these included a number of exotics as well. Such items as monkeys were still considered highly fashionable under Russian rule in the Finnish nineteenth-century provincial town of Vyborg, where the wealthy Hackman family tried their best to invest in high quality luxuries and lived according to their class, even in their purchase of pets.

Whereas luxury has been perceived, by contemporaries as well as by historians, as generated by cities, the taste for luxury was not completely ignored in the countryside. Recent research has thus shown that new goods imported from the city found their way into Frisian or Tuscan rural homes, respectively, from the seventeenth and the eighteenth centuries onwards. However, this significant revision of the stark contrast between a civilised town and a barbaric countryside still deserves further investigation for other parts of Europe.[24] Belén Moreno explicitly examines the differences between country and urban consumption in her chapter on women of eighteenth-century Barcelona, which shows that the place of residence had great impact on the consumption needs. Owning luxury items in the countryside, even in rural towns, was far less usual than in Barcelona: There was no need for such displays to identify the individual because people already knew each other. Dress would have made no difference. But, at the same time, for the elite the town was a place where middling-sort women acquired their luxuries, and the country where they displayed it. This factor also becomes evident in Jon Stobart and Mark Rothery's chapter on the consumption patterns of Edward and Mary Leigh, English siblings who lived both in town and country. In a very different context, namely the late nineteenth-century growing urbanisation of Europe, Stana Nenadic's exploration of international exhibitions and the promotion and display of exotic luxury goods points out the ways in which rural female knitters, for example, were turned into interesting exotic displays in their own right. In this way the everyday was made into a sentimentalist and consumerist notion of rural life in a new kind of urban, if artificial, setting. Thus international exhibitions both displayed the latest commodities and played with ideas of new urbanity and its counterparts, the rural idyll.

MARKETS AND OPPORTUNITIES

A key aim of this book is to interrogate 'the invention, making and buying' of luxury, and to explore luxury markets and urban practices.[25] Since the seminal collective work published in 1982 by Neil McKendrick, John Brewer and J. H. Plumb, there has been a copious and vigorous literature on consumption and luxury, which has developed, refined, interrogated and challenged McKendrick's controversial notions of 'consumer society', 'consumer revolution' and 'mass consumption'.[26] As the Further Reading shows, the focus of most research on luxury has been embedded in the historiography of consumption and frequently focused on the elite. Taking an important new tack is the work of Maxine Berg, who has explored the economy of 'semi-luxury', fashionable consumer goods during the eighteenth century'.[27] Thus she produced a more holistic approach to the issues of luxury, acknowledging the importance of invention as well as imitation, and recognising the role of middling classes in not only promoting and stimulating demand for these goods, but also consequently driving forward production. Her juxtaposition of multiple historiographies, especially the grand narratives of the industrial revolution to the consumer one, and her identification of the importance of global connections in understanding eighteenth-century consumption were vital to opening up issues of luxury, and ultimately luxury and gender.

Whereas in 1982 McKendrick highlighted female consumer choice as a factor in the increasing demand for goods and especially luxury items, it was only eleven years later that gender explicitly appeared as a central factor in the historical analysis of consumption.[28] This has been followed by further enquiries into male shopping and is taken up here by several case studies. While men seem to disappear as consumers in the nineteenth century, '[r]ecent scholarship has . . . challenged the notion of a "Great Masculine Renunciation," in which nineteenth-century middle-class Englishmen adopted sober, unadorned business-oriented dress in an attempt to gain sociopolitical legitimacy.'[29] As Brent Shannon has argued, the retail expansion in the nineteenth century was accompanied by the creation of male-friendly spaces, while middle-class masculinity had become highly contested, so that for many men 'fashion became a highly visual means by which to subvert the rigid and confining dictates of proper masculine behavior.'[30] Of significance is that few authors have yet grasped the links between gender, production and consumption. Additionally, much of the research is still highly tied to national narratives, albeit producing important studies, such as work by Leonora Auslander, Natacha Coquery and Daniel Roche for France.[31] Other areas are less well covered, but as the Further Reading shows, the research is expanding. These worlds of urban luxury were gendered at every level: production, distribution and acquisition, and this is the diversity that this book brings to the understanding of luxury and gender.

Before consumers could enjoy the world of goods, they had to be produced. In contrast to many quotidian goods, luxury items often derived from imported materials, or were themselves imported as in the case of the exotic. They were distributed, promoted and displayed using many techniques, from modest advertisements in the increasing number of local newspapers and trade cards to the grand international exhibitions. Luxury trades were competitive, and imitation was rampant. Entrepreneurs undertook numerous devices to enhance the attraction of their goods, and producers like Wedgwood recognised that luxury items for the elite could be modified and produced for the middling and ultimately the lower orders. Production, promotion and distribution were met with gendered responses in urban societies, and questions of work distribution, gender roles, propriety, materiality, class and wealth all came into play. Towns tended to be built on a foundation of corporatism. Michael Sonenscher's discussion of French *compagnonnages* and Robert Darnton's essay 'The Great Cat Massacre' identify the importance of rituals in creating symbolic inequalities in order to establish barriers to protect workers' fragile claims to their work.[32] Custom and control in the workshop, divisions of labour and the political and economic life of many towns shaped the ways in which men and women operated to find their niches in urban economic life.

The industrial revolution, which reshaped urban worlds in Europe, brought shifting workplace dynamics and influenced newer approaches to urban economic relationships and power structures. It also provided new goods and heightened expectations as luxury goods shifted in the face of new marketing practices such as the department store in the nineteenth century, which created 'dream worlds' for people throughout the social structure.[33] The town remained at the hub of global and domestic markets within this growing global economy, with its tantalising array of goods to tempt the emergent middle classes and permeated into the worlds of labouring people. The discourses changed, and indeed the meanings and accessibility to luxury goods shifted, but underpinning the worlds of production, distribution and consumption, luxury was a fundamental part of the economic developments of this period. It especially moulded local urban economies. While women are often depicted as consumers, in fact they were often the 'hands' making the goods, selling through small shops as well as in larger department stores. However, the dynamics of paid work and perceptions of the male as the key producer, capitalist and owner of ships and shops inflect the gendered character of the luxury trades. This attribution of roles was not static and the shifting urban paradigms influenced economic relationships and power structures, while the emergence of bourgeois notions of rights, individuality and gender became ever more powerful in shaping not only gender but also the interplay with consumption and the strategies of men and women to claim their place in this shifting economy.

The book explores the ways in which the production of luxury was a concern for both male and female workers. It also points out the gendered processes of luxury production and trade—even illegal trade. Historians have shown a growing interest in the history of the retail trades and the complexities of retail circuits, both formal and informal, augmented here and elsewhere by Anne Montenach.[34] Custom and corporatism created hurdles for female producers, just as Moore illustrates for late nineteenth-century art markets, where exhibition spaces, academies and the idea of 'appropriate' media for female artists created barriers. Significantly, these chapters also show how such gendered obstacles could be successfully negotiated, and how female agency played an important role in shifting the paradigms of the crafts. Moore thus also shows that London's West End emerged as a suitable playground for turn-of-the-century women, creating a modern space of luxury. Here women were able to both create luxuries, i.e., artworks, and consume them. Women's strong input to urban economies is evident not only in cities that are exceptional in many ways such as London, but also in more modestly sized towns such as Aberdeen, La Rochelle or Colchester, explored in Deborah Simonton's chapter on the control of the needle. It shows how commercial needle trades were extremely urbanized in the eighteenth century, and how skilled these women were in conducting their city businesses. She discusses the tensions and gender of milliners and *modistes* in Britain and France, positioning the work of these skilled women against the tensions that their productivity raised among established and guilded male needleworkers like tailors. Montenach's chapter examines how the smuggling of calicos (patterned cotton fabric) was organized and gendered in Dauphiné and points out how inventive women were in these illicit markets. Bourgeois women could also play important roles in distribution. Carol Gold talks about the strong trading input of major female merchants in Copenhagen, including overseas shipping. As these chapters argue, women had a role of their own in the town, and not only in the shadows of men.

CLASS AND STATUS

If luxury was a central issue in eighteenth- and nineteenth-century political and economic thought, it also had to do, more practically, with the meaning of goods and their social function. As shown by anthropologists, consumption is essentially social and relational, and things play an important part in the construction of identity. Within what has been analysed as an 'information system', luxury goods are used as 'incarnated signs' and as 'social valuables' in the manifestation and reproduction of status.[35]

One of the arguments of this book is that the notions of luxury and necessity went hand in hand, and not only in the sense that they were perceived as different ends of the spectrum. On the one hand, *luxuria* was one of the seven deadly sins and linked to vices such as sensuality, vanity, and arrogance, and on the other, luxury was a necessity to the elite to enable them to confirm their status in urban society. Necessities are usually not considered luxuries, but the definition depended on the definer. The aristocrat had to cover her body with luxurious fabrics and precious stones and fill her townhouse with the world of luxury goods, from clavichords to silver snuffboxes. However, a fresh glass of milk could be luxury for the urban poor. Hanne Marie Johansen in this volume studying the urban poor in the Norwegian town of Drammen challenges the notion of luxury. Luxuries could be items that were 'nice to have', usually positioned against the shifting sands of 'necessity'. For a civil servant's wife a bottle of milk or dozen eggs hardly constituted luxury, but for her washing woman living in the poorer quarters, these were luxuries, and important sources of additional income if sold to others. The poverty of the princess of blood Marie-Fortunée d'Este, Princesse de Conti, demonstrated by Aurélie Chatenet-Calyste is in stark contrast with the poverty of the industrial workers, studied by Johansen, who shows how small pleasures were considered luxuries. This volume makes the strong argument that luxury was perceived and practised as a social necessity for people in the upper echelons of society, especially the aristocracy. Therefore, many were forced to spend staggering amounts of money on expensive items designed to make a suitable impression. So strong was the necessity for appropriate consumption among aristocratic circles that Princesse de Conti, with an annual income of 180,000 *livres*, was considered poor among her peers after her divorce, as she was unable to purchase fashionable luxuries in the range expected or from the sellers favoured by the court circles. The obligation for expenditure aimed at keeping up a certain lifestyle in order to retain status and power is further demonstrated in Zsuzsa Sidó's examination of luxury as an obligation in the form of the aristocratic 'national costume' in nineteenth-century Budapest. Concentrating on Swedish aristocrats purchasing in Paris, Ilmakunnas shows that they broke Swedish sumptuary laws with impunity in order to buy goods that played a role in establishing their status. Because luxury was necessary and desirable at the same time, various bans on luxury items invariably failed.

One of the strong arguments in this book is that elite consumption had much less to do with gender than with social rank. From this perspective, the perception of consuming men as effeminate was not shared by everyone. As it was necessary for elite men to consume according to their estate, they put great effort in acquiring luxuries and spent significant amounts of their wealth in various kinds of luxuries. Luxury was for them an investment in their own and their children's future and a demonstration of that wealth in their present. Further, interestingly, the purchasing patterns of elite women such as Mary Leigh studied by Stobart and Rothery, and Marie Hackman discussed by Ijäs, show that when through inheritance or widowhood elite women acquired the role as the head of the household, their consumption patterns very strongly followed those of elite men. It now became their turn to consume according the rank. Importantly, as shown by these last examples, age is a factor that affects consumption. In many cultures it was the youth that had to display modesty, as Moreno Claveriás points out, and the married were expected to display all the glory of wedded partnership—for example, in their jewellery. Marriage status naturally was important in other ways too: When getting married, it was the man's duty to furnish the house displaying proper wealth and taste, and during the marriage both spouses were expected to put effort into maintaining the status of the household. Thus old age did not necessarily mean withdrawal from worldly pleasures.

Through specific case studies, while not directly comparative, this volume casts light on the complexity of the interplay of gender and luxury. It highlights shared themes and subtle, as well as significant, differences, thus facilitating discussion and opening the way to future research. The chapters reflect how the gendered experience and practices of luxury informed and were informed by the urban environment. The authors examine how forms of production and commercialization introduced by the culture of luxury affected urban communities. This book articulates the opportunities that men and women had to participate in the market, both legal and illegal, high status or proletarianized, and how labour segmentation, competition and conflicts affected gender construction. It asks what the geography of luxury consumption, scrutinized at a local, regional, national or international scale, tells us about the relationship of male and female individuals to the town or about their knowledge of the urban environment and luxury markets. Thus, the book raises questions about the language, production, representations and experiences of luxury, and their implication both in the construction of the individual urban subjects and in the shaping of the European urban societies. The authors pay particular attention to the complexity of its creation and definition according to various social groups and historical contexts. By putting in perspective female and male identities as producers, sellers or consumers, this book attempts to challenge gender stereotypes and to open new topographies in the gendering of towns.

NOTES

1 Christopher J. Berry, *The Idea of Luxury: A Conceptual and Historical Investigation* (Cambridge: Cambridge University Press 1994), 38.
2 John Brewer and Roy Porter, eds, *Consumption and the World of Goods* (London: Routledge, 1993). For an overview of the European debate on luxury, especially in England, France and Germany between the eighteenth century and the turn of the twentieth century, see Maxine Berg and Elizabeth Eger, 'The Rise and Fall of the Luxury Debates', in *Luxury in the Eighteenth Century: Debates, Desires and Delectable Goods*, ed. Maxine Berg and Elizabeth Eger (Basingstoke: Palgrave Macmillan, 2003), 7–27.
3 Sara Maza, *The Myth of the French Bourgeoisie: An Essay on the Social Imaginary 1750–1850* (Cambridge, MA: Harvard University Press, 2003), 54.
4 Adam Ferguson, *An Essay on the History of Civil Society* (Edinburgh: A. Millar, 1767), 375.
5 Bernard Mandeville, *The Fable of the Bees, or Private Vices, Publick Benefits*, 3rd ed. (London: J. Tonson, 1724). Mandeville's book is often taken as a starting point in the luxury discourses.
6 Woodruff D. Smith, *Consumption and the Making of Respectability, 1600–1800* (New York: Routledge, 2002), 63.
7 Samuel Fawconer, *An Essay on Modern Luxury: Or, An Attempt to Delineate Its Nature, Causes, and Effects* (London: James Fletcher and J. Robson, 1765), 6–7.
8 Leon Jespersen, 'Statuskonsumtion og luksuslovgivning i Danmark och Sverige i 1600-tallet—en skitse', in *1600-talets ansikte*, ed. Sten Åke Nilsson and Margareta Ramsay (Copenhagen: Gyllenstiernska Krapperudstiftelsen, 1997), 169–95.
9 Jennifer Jones, *Sexing la Mode: Gender, Fashion, and Commercial Culture in Old Regime France* (Oxford: Berg, 2004), 145–50.
10 Josiah Wedgwood to Thomas Bentley, 9 February 1778, in Neil McKendrick, 'Josiah Wedgwood and the Commercialization of the Potteries', in *The Birth of a Consumer Society: The Commercialization of Eighteenth Century England*, ed. Neil McKendrick, John Brewer and J.H. Plumb (London: Hutchinson, 1982), 100–45.
11 Mandeville, *The Fable of the Bees*, 250–1.
12 Louis-Sébastien Mercier, *Le Tableau de Paris*, vol. 1 (Hamburg: Virchaux & Compagnie, Libraires, 1781), 290.
13 Émile Zola, *The Ladies' Paradise [Au Bonheur des Dames]* (London: Sovereign, 2013). On the moral views of luxury in the nineteenth century, see Matthew Hilton, 'The Legacy of Luxury; Moralities of Consumption Since the Eighteenth Century,' *Journal of Consumer Culture*, 4, no. 1 (2004): 101–23.
14 Zola, *Ladies' Paradise*, 74–6.

15 Michele Cohen, *Fashioning Masculinity: National Identity and Language in the Eighteenth Century* (London: Routledge, 1996).
16 *Transactions of the Society of Arts*, ii (1784), 169, 171.
17 National Archives of Scotland, Act for encouraging trade and manufactories [Scotland 1681].
18 As Hilton argues, however, the moral debate also shifted, but did not go away. Hilton, 'The Legacy of Luxury'.
19 Alain Rey, 'Luxe, le mot et la chose', in *Le luxe en France du siècle des Lumières à nos jours*, ed. Jacques Marseille (Paris: Association pour le développement de l'histoire économique, 1999), 17–23.
20 Maxine Berg, 'Luxury, the Luxury Trades, and the Roots of Industrial Growth: A Global Perpective', in *The Oxford Handbook of the History of Consumption*, ed. Frank Trentmann (Oxford: Oxford University Press, 2013), 181.
21 Fawconer, *Essay on Modern Luxury*, 6–7.
22 Anne E. C. McCants, 'Exotic Goods, Popular Consumption, and the Standard of Living: Thinking about Globalization in the Early Modern World', *Journal of World History* 8, no. 4 (2007): 433–62.
23 Fawconer, *Essay on Modern Luxury*, 40.
24 Dominique Margairaz, 'City and Country: Home, Possessions, and Diet, Western Europe 1600–1800', in *The Oxford Handbook of the History of Consumption*, ed. Trentmann, 192–210.
25 Quote from Maxine Berg, *Luxury and Pleasure in Eighteenth-Century Britain* (Oxford: Oxford University Press, 2005), 15.
26 Neil McKendrick, 'The Consumer Revolution in Eighteen-Century England,' in *The Birth of a Consumer Society*, ed. McKendrick, Brewer and Plumb, 9.
27 Berg, *Luxury and Pleasure*; Maxine Berg and Helen Clifford, *Consumers and Luxury* (Manchester: Manchester University Press, 1999); Berg and Eger, *Luxury in the Eighteenth Century*.
28 McKendrick, 'The Consumer Revolution', 20, 23; Amanda Vickery, 'Women and the World of Goods: A Lancashire Consumer and Her Possessions, 1751–1781', in *Consumption*, ed. Brewer and Porter, 274–301; Jan de Vries, 'Between Purchasing Power and the World of Goods: Understanding the Household Economy in Early Modern Europe', in *Consumption*, ed. Brewer and Porter, 85–132. For a recent overview, see Renata Ago, 'Le genre de la consommation à l'époque moderne', in *Genre, femmes, histoire en Europe*, ed. Anna Bellavitis and Nicole Edelman (Paris: Presses universitaires de Paris Ouest, 2011), 37–50.
29 Brent Shannon, 'ReFashioning Men: Fashion, Masculinity, and the Cultivation of the Male Consumer in Britain, 1860–1914,' *Victorian Studies* 46, no. 4 (2004): 598.
30 *Ibid.*, 599. See also, Amanda Vickery, *Behind Closed Doors. At Home in Georgian England* (New Haven and London: Yale University Press, 2009); Christopher Breward, *The Hidden Consumers: Masculinities, Fashion, and City Life, 1860–1914* (Manchester: Manchester University Press, 1999); Laura Ugolini, *Men and Menswear: Sartorial Consumption in Britain, 1880–1939* (Aldershot: Ashgate, 2007).
31 Leora Auslander, *Taste and Power: Furnishing Modern France* (Berkeley: University of California, 1996); Natacha Coquery, *L'hôtel aristocratique: le marché du luxe à Paris au XVIII*[e] *siècle* (Paris: Publications de la Sorbonne, 1998); Natacha Coquery, *Tenir boutique à Paris au XVIII*[e] *siècle. Luxe et demi-luxe* (Paris: Éditions du Comité des travaux historiques et scientifiques, 2012); Daniel Roche, *A History of Everyday Things: The Birth of Consumption in France, 1600–1800*, trans. Brian Pearce (Cambridge: Cambridge

University Press, 2000); Victoria De Grazia, ed., *The Sex of Things: Gender and Consumption in Historical Perspective* (Berkeley: University of California Press, 1996). See the Further Reading for other publications which have moved forward the discussions of luxury and consumption.

32 Michael Sonenscher, 'Mythical Work: Workshop Production and the *Compagnonnages* of Eighteenth-Century France', in *The Historical Meanings of Work*, ed. Patrick Joyce, (New York and Cambridge: Cambridge University Press, 1989) 50; Robert Darnton, *The Great Cat Massacre and Other Episodes in French Cultural History* (London: Penguin Books, 1991).

33 Rosalind Williams, *Dream Worlds: Mass Consumption in Late Nineteenth-Century France* (Berkeley: University of California Press, 1982).

34 Anne Montenach, 'Legal Trade and Black Markets: Food Trades in Lyon in the Late Seventeenth and Early Eighteenth Centuries', in *Female Agency in the Urban Economy, Gender in European Towns, 1640–1830*, ed. Deborah Simonton and Anne Montenach (New York: Routledge, 2013), 17–34. For example, for Britain, see John Benson and Laura Ugolini, eds, *A Nation of Shopkeepers: Five Centuries of British Retailing* (London: I.B. Tauris, 2003), Jon Stobart, *Spend, Spend, Spend! A History of Shopping* (Stroud: The History Press, 2008); for Europe see Geoffrey Crossick and Serge Jaumain, eds, *Cathedrals of Consumption: The European Department Store, 1850–1939* (Aldershot: Ashgate, 1999), Geoffrey Crossick and Heinz-Gerhard Haupt, eds, *The Petite Bourgeoisie in Europe, 1914. Enterprise, Family and Independence* (London: Routledge, 1995), as well as others on the department store phenomenon. On second-hand and alternative retail practices, see Laurence Fontaine, ed., *Alternative Exchanges: Second-Hand Circulations from the Sixteenth Century to the Present* (New York: Berghahn Books, 2008) and Beverly Lemire, 'Consumerism in Preindustrial and Early Industrial England: The Trade in Secondhand Clothes', *The Journal of British Studies* 27 (1988): 1–24.

35 Mary Douglas and Baron Isherwood, *The World of Goods: Towards an Anthropology of Consumerism* (Harmondsworth: Penguin, 1978), 1–62.

Part I

Markets and Opportunities

2 Milliners and *Marchandes de Modes*
Gender, Creativity and Skill in the Workplace

Deborah Simonton

On 22 March 1757, Ann Buchanan wrote to Janet Muschet, milliner of Edinburgh,

> My Dr Jannie,
> I had the Favour of yours this day eight days and is glad to see business is going on so well with you, . . .
> I return you my most sincere thanks for your ready agreeing in taking me in partners with you, & your beloved spouse; I indeed look on it as a favour that I never can repay O how happy will I be my d[ea]r with you both and I hope you shall have no reason to be otherwise with me—they were told at home that it was Lady Polmaise that first made the proposal of taking me in with you; so in case they be writing anything of it to you; Don't say any thing that it was myself; I will long for the time when I shall be with you; . . .[1]

Several important pieces of information emerge from this letter. Ann came from a genteel background, based at Polmaise in Clackmannanshire, Scotland, with familial links to landed gentry, the Murrays of Touchadam and Polmaise. She also indicated her determination to go into business and in particular to go into partnership with two other women. The connection with Janet Muschet came from familial links, and 'your beloved spouse' was her cousin, Cicely Murray.

The same themes are redolent in the novel *Kirsteen* by Margaret Oliphant, set in 1804. Kirsteen came from Highland gentry, while the novel turns on her determination to make her own decisions, using family to become a partner in a high-class millinery shop in London. Both Kirsteen and Ann used their genteel origins and social standing to further their business. In dealing with some presumptive young women, Kirsteen refused them because they were 'commoners'. This led her employer, Miss Jean, to offer partnership partly because of her skill and invention with fabrics but especially because of her 'quality':

> 'Miss Kirsteen, that was a clever thing you did today.'
> 'What was the clever thing?' asked Kirsteen surprised.

> 'Just to turn those leddies over in that prideful way to me, as if they were not good enough to trouble our heads about . . . I could never have gotten the better of those leddies like you—I see it all, Miss Kirsteen, nobody clearer. Ye're just a gentlewoman ye see, Miss Kirsteen, and that's above a common person, whatever anybody may say . . . It makes a great deal of difference; it gives a freedom in treating them that I cannot help feeling are my superiors. Well; this is just what I have to propose. . . . It's just this Miss Kirsteen; that you and me, we should enter into partnership and carry on the business together. And I think,' said Miss Jean with modest confidence and a triumphant light in her eyes, 'that between us we could just face the world'.[2]

These stories, one real and the other fictional, provide a window into the worlds of fashion, luxury, consumption and trade. In the eighteenth-century town, women frequently sat at the centre of the luxury trades as the dressmakers and milliners to the town. They also sat at the centre of several different points of custom, control and opportunity. Milliners, or *modistes*, and *marchandes de modes*, or fashion merchants, like Buchanan, represented the top end of the needle trades, often not 'making' anything but serving as the premier 'fashionistas', decorating clothing and hair and assembling hats and other decorative items. However, they sometimes made dresses, especially the newest fashion, the mantua, introduced from the end of the seventeenth century. It was a loose-fitting garment often described as 'blown together', which disguises the high-quality skill and expertise required. Mantuamakers similarly played a significant role in the creation and promulgation of fashion, though they covered a wide spectrum, from the fashionable end to the small-town dressmaker. An army of seamstresses, or couturiers, ribbon weavers, lacemakers and staymakers supported these trades and produced many of the goods they utilised.[3]

Focusing on the top end of the needle trades, this chapter examines their influence on urban fashion industries and on the gender debates that permeated the competition between men and women in corporate towns where artisan solidarity was under challenge. Despite great swathes of rurality, many towns expanded rapidly during the eighteenth century, building a new dynamic, commercial world reliant less on older corporate structures of guilds and more on merchant classes and the accompanying professional middle classes. This discussion is based on the urban economies of three medium-sized eighteenth-century towns, each of between c. 10,000 and 25,000 population: Aberdeen (Scotland), Colchester (England) and La Rochelle (France), rather than big conurbations like Paris, studied by Clare Crowston, Jennifer Jones and Daniel Roche, or London, examined by Amy Erickson, or even larger towns like Rouen, discussed by Daryl Hafter, or Nantes, discussed by Nancy Musgrave, both c. 80,000 population.[4] The vibrant urban context is important since it provided the backdrop to the luxury trades and delivered consumers who gobbled them up. Certainly many villages had seamstresses, and sometimes tailors, who made up or altered clothes, but this was small scale and usually local. The growth of millinery and mantuamaking, in addition to reflecting changes in the trades themselves, built on growth in demand, largely from middling and elite consumers. Letters and account books make it obvious that these purchasers sought out fashion, and to them fashion simply did not exist in the parochial rural world—it was urban and cosmopolitan, not rural and parochial. Thus high-class needle trades were pre-eminently urban.

THE URBAN CONTEXT

The urban context also meant changes in the ideas of towns, with many developing a self-image that fostered a drive for status, sociability and civility. The economic base was one important factor helping to shape the culture and identity of a town, while the enhanced awareness of other towns, as well as of wider society, 'encouraged a more positive formulation of civic consciousness amongst those who participated in such activities'.[5] Display and the image of the town came to have new meaning, projecting an identity derived from a newer bustling commercial culture situated in part in *laissez faire* ideas that overlay and mingled with older ideas of status and standing that were personal and linked to corporate identity through artisanal traditions and honour.

In this context guild traditions were under stress, as commercial culture undermined their status. Recently the study of guilds and their role in controlling and managing urban economies has taken on a new lease of life, as scholars revisit and re-examine the structures, purposes and effectiveness of guilds. The interaction of guilds, towns and gender in eighteenth-century Europe has drawn less attention, despite notable work by Amy Erickson, Sheilagh Ogilvie, S. D. Smith, Clare Crowston and Daryl Hafter.[6] Guilds were clearly under attack during the century for what was seen as their role in hampering progress. They had become even more exclusive, reluctant to admit men to mastership and even more jealously guarded their privileges. Thus in protecting guildsmen's rights, women as the epitome of untrained labour came in for particular attention. They were generally denied access to political institutions and civic life; their exclusion from the right to pass on guild privileges was limited in the same way. At the same time, therefore, women's position within the guilds became even more vulnerable.

This chapter draws on evidence from three towns, which, although situated in various commercial contexts, demonstrate how complex the pattern of demographic and commercial growth was. But they also reflect similarities in how gender operated in the high-class needle trades. Aberdeen grew rapidly, benefiting from commercial expansion, yet did less well in the second half of the century than Glasgow, which had readier access to Atlantic markets. La Rochelle, one of the key Atlantic trading ports, recovered from the wars of religion and enjoyed renewed prosperity as one of the leading harbours for trade with the New World based on hides, sugar and, ultimately, slaves. Nevertheless, it suffered shifting trading fortunes after the Seven Years' Wars, and especially after the crackdown on the slave trade. Colchester experienced the decline of the woollen industry, political infighting and abuse of political offices, and the collapse of its corporation. Yet, it too shared in the rise of domestic consumption and the emergence of what William Blackstone called, 'the polite and commercial people'.[7] All had good links with their rural hinterlands, which provided markets and goods as well as wider networks of trade than previously, and all had port and road links that gave them access to non-local and non-domestic trade. They also shared in the spread of ideas and growing urban literacy; Aberdeen, for example, was a primary centre of the Scottish Enlightenment. All three had a newspaper after the middle of the century. The *Aberdeen Journal* began in 1747. Colchester shared the *Chelmsford and Colchester Chronicle* (from 1764) and relied on the Suffolk-based *Ipswich Journal* (from 1720). La Rochelle had *Affiches de la Rochelle* from 1772, with various title changes during the Revolution. Like many other towns, they embarked on 'modernising' building schemes, such as the redevelopment of the town centre of Aberdeen, with new merchant's townhouses, a new Town Hall in 1754 and paving and lighting projects. In 1773, Samuel Johnson described Aberdeen as having 'all the bustle of prosperous trade, and all the shew of increasing opulence'.[8] These activities were mirrored in Colchester, which Daniel Defoe described as 'fair and beautiful' with 'an abundance of good and well-built houses'.[9] Colchester created 'distinctive Georgian vistas in the central areas of the town', gained its first theatre in 1764, and from 1783 vigorously implemented paving schemes and the 'removal of nuisances'.[10] The fortifications of La Rochelle were rebuilt in 1685, the Tour de l'Horloge was given a prestigious new belfry in 1746 and the town fathers built the magnificent Hôtel de la Bourse in 1764 to promote and celebrate its commercial wealth, adding new Law Courts in 1789. Notably much of the innovation and implementation of urban renewal relied on the resources and intervention of the middle classes. These were precisely the people who shaped the gendered structures of towns through their reinterpretation of status and reputation. A 'dizzy sense of opportunity' from the growth of trade provided new prospects, with spinoffs for others like officials, lawyers and doctors who serviced the trading community.[11]

MILLINERS, *MODISTES* AND *MARCHANDES DE MODES*

Several debates, constructed first around luxury and secondly around commercial competition, and ultimately situated in Enlightenment discourses on female nature, converged on the high-status needle trades. Needle trades were especially important to women; however, during the century significant changes in female fashion altered the scope and scale of the trades and created opportunities for women to play a much larger role. Shifting fashion not only resulted from the emergence of the mantua, but also the rococo aesthetic of the 1730s and 40s, which introduced a vogue for profuse trimmings and accessories, while overseas influences brought fine cloths and other goods that facilitated decoration. Industrial developments in the metalworking trades also promoted the use of buckles and buttons. In the late 1760s high, padded hairstyles became fashionable, and milliners decorated them with everything from ribbons, flowers and feathers to birdcages and miniature ships. They created a new fashion of wide-brimmed hats when Marie-Antoinette's hair fell out during her first pregnancy in 1778.

These trades, but especially the milliner, benefited from the growing luxury trades, demand for decoration and changing fashions. By mid century, from Sweden in the north to Britain and France, millinery and mantuamaking had become highly feminised. Apprenticeship records underline the gendered division of these trades in a pronounced fashion (Table 2.1); fifty-six per cent of apprentice mistresses in research on the English counties of Essex and Staffordshire were mantuamakers or milliners.[12] In 1747 Robert Campbell, author of an apprenticeship guide, called millinery 'no Male Trade', saying that 'the Fair Sex . . . are generally bound to this Business', while the mantuamaker was 'Sister to the Taylor'.[13] Joseph Collyer, a few years later, also presumed the milliner was a woman, as did *The Book of English Trades*.[14]

Thus women became the milliners and *marchandes de modes* of European towns, producing the high-class haberdashery and dresses which fashion demanded. Indeed, they were often at the forefront of setting fashion, like Rose Bertin, milliner to Marie Antoinette. Millinery held a special place for enterprising women, because it was a good trade where they could make names for themselves in mercantile communities. Those at the top end, in specialist sewing trades, could achieve status and position. It was skilled and offered scope, attracting women with capital and some social standing. In addition to being a tradeswoman who made fashion accessories and embellished the garments of the aspirant middle classes, the milliner was also a businesswoman who sold a wide range of fashionable imported goods. Her counterpart, the mantuamaker, made up gowns and was often unable or

Table 2.1 Children apprenticed to skilled needle trades, 1700–1799.

	Girls	Boys
Apprenticed to tailors	11	1071
Apprenticed to milliners	134	2
Apprenticed to mantuamakers	217	1
Apprenticed to couples	49	38

Source: Simonton, 'Education and Training', Table A5.6.10.

not allowed to sell fabric. By the end of the century, *marchandes de modes* dominated the fashion industry and dictated tastes, not just in France but also throughout Europe.

Milliners played a crucial and sometimes controversial role in the fashion industries. An eighteenth-century woman's fashion sense was demonstrated not by the cut of her clothes, which remained fairly static, but by the choice of trimmings and accessories, supplied by milliners whose influence was supreme. In the story of Kirsteen, her ability to visualise and design garments and accessories was fundamental to her success in the trade. As Miss Jean said,

> I could never have struck out yon invention of yours for Lady Chatty with the silver gauze—though I saw it was just most beautiful when ye did it. . . . Ye . . . will get cleverer and cleverer as ye get more knowledge of the world.[15]

Chrisman-Campbell explained the importance of creativity in such work:

> In eighteenth-century portraits and fashion plates, the gowns themselves are barely visible under the profusion of feathers, ribbons, tassels, lace, artificial flowers and other ornaments, worn with the ubiquitous head-dress, fan and gloves. . . . [and] eighteenth-century dress trimmings were often even more expensive than the fabrics onto which they were sewn.[16]

In Aberdeen, Isabella Morison assured her customers that work would be produced in the most 'fashionable manner', while John Mitchell's daughter sold 'all kinds of MILLINERY GOODS, of the newest fashions'.[17] In drawing a link to the fashionableness of their skills and products, these women used any device they could to claim style, elegance and association with polite society, often linked to the 'fashionable' metropolis. A common 'shorthand' for Aberdeen women was to claim a link with London or Edinburgh, the centre of their political and social universe. Thus, Morison drew attention to the fact she had served a five-year apprenticeship in London. 'She hopes her customers will find her properly qualified' (See Figure 2.1).[18] Thus the creative abilities of these women were essential to their trading position, and they recognised the commercial importance of aligning themselves with urban centres of fashion.

Yet, their critics often projected an image of unskilled workers, assisting men, who had to do no more than exercise their 'fancy'. In 1761 de Garsault, writing on tailors and the sewing trades, described the *marchande de modes* thus:

> One should not place the *Marchande de modes* here among the arts of working with clothes if these women were not put in a position to construct some portions of clothes which ought naturally to have be the province of the Seamstress: they are not guild members and work only

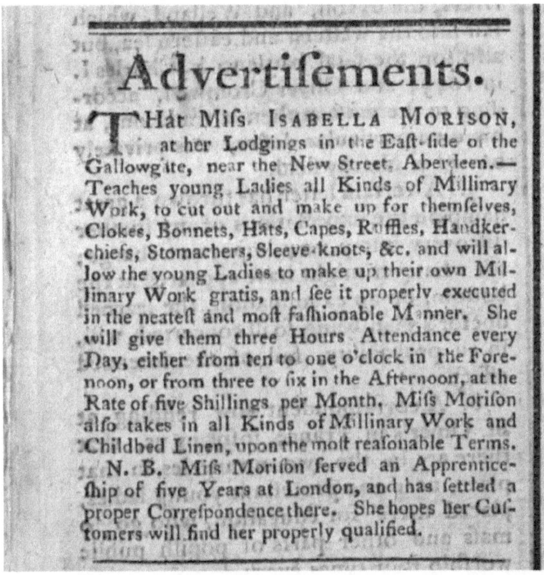

Advertiſements.

THat Miſs Isabella Morison, at her Lodgings in the Eaſt-ſide of the Gallowgate, near the New Street, Aberdeen.— Teaches young Ladies all Kinds of Millinary Work, to cut out and make up for themſelves, Clokes, Bonnets, Hats, Capes, Ruffles, Handkerchiefs, Stomachers, Sleeve-knots, &c. and will allow the young Ladies to make up their own Millinary Work gratis, and ſee it properly executed in the neateſt and moſt faſhionable Manner. She will give them three Hours Attendance every Day, either from ten to one o'clock in the Forenoon, or from three to ſix in the Afternoon, at the Rate of five Shillings per Month. Miſs Moriſon alſo takes in all Kinds of Millinary Work and Childbed Linen, upon the moſt reaſonable Terms.

N. B. Miſs Moriſon ſerved an Apprenticeſhip of five Years at London, and has ſettled a proper Correſpondence there. She hopes her Cuſtomers will find her properly qualified.

Figure 2.1 Isabella Morison advertising her skills, *Aberdeen Journal*, 18 September 1769.

> in the shadow of their husbands, which, . . . must be members of the Merchants Merciers guild: they call what they do a skill and this skill is principally to assemble and garnish the coiffures, dresses, skirts, etc.; that is to say, to sew and arrange on them the amenities that they and ladies constantly invent according to daily fashion.[19]

In Britain, *The Book of Trades* allowed that '[i]n the milliner taste and fancy are required, with a quickness in discernment, imitating, and improving upon, the various fashions, which are perpetually changing in the higher circles'. There is a sense in which commentators did not see artisanal skill as part of her trade; yet, the author also thought that few tailors knew 'how to cut out with any degree of skill'.[20] In a similar tone, in 1785 the *Encyclopédie méthodique* claimed, 'Her art is not to make anything; it consists of ingeniously providing new results, varied and gracious ornaments of all the frivolous productions of the other arts and particularly that of *passementerie*'.[21] These critiques, based on a gendered notion of skill and workers, were crucial as women sought to establish themselves as legitimate businesswomen in the urban commercial economy.[22]

MILLINERS, *MARCHANDES DE MODES* AND MEN

Strong traditions of skilled male needle workers persisted across Europe, and they made men's, women's and children's clothing, like *tailleurs d'habits* in La Rochelle and tailors in Colchester and Aberdeen. Despite the overtly feminine image, men commanded the trades of dressmakers, milliners and *modistes* for much of the century. Thus, women's commercial sewing brought them into competition and conflict with them; especially mantuamakers challenged the prerogatives and privileges of tailors. As Jones explained:

> Three of the most important rivalries in the fashion trades occurred between female seamstresses (*couturières*) and male tailors (*tailleurs*) . . . In addition a new category of female fashion merchants, the *marchandes de modes*, challenged the monopoly of several groups of clothing workers, including seamstresses, tailors, linen drapers, and hairdressers.[23]

Many men held their positions as members of tailors' and associated guilds, and there is no doubt that they played a 'gatekeeping' role, but one that was not all encompassing. As Erickson has shown for London, often guild members practised trades no longer associated with their original *métier*, and many of the milliners she discusses were in the Clockmakers Guild, even if still in tiny numbers.[24] What is unknown is how many women practised without admission to guilds. Women had long sewed for a living, but often were restricted to women's undergarments and children's clothing. The incursion of women into this male preserve with the shift in dressmaking to the mantua, and the heightened importance of millinery, led to tensions and battles that were highly important to urban commercial development. Across Europe, male guilds tried to control or exclude women from what they saw as encroaching on their position and prerogatives.

In England, a lack of solidarity ended in reducing the power of the guilds involved and led eventually to demands that women join the guilds. In Oxford, staymaking and boning was a masculine occupation; however, with the arrival of the mantua, which required little fitting, women became the mantuamakers. Ironically, male response was to try to force them to join the guild, which they refused to do. Similarly in York, the old established drapers' companies lost the battle to keep women from setting up as mantuamakers, dressmakers and milliners. In Prussia, this same dispute was couched in terms of proper spheres of work, with women's place defined as domestic and her work as not really work. In these cases, where technical skill was no obstacle, male guilds tried hard to create one.[25] One strategy employed in Aberdeen was not to exclude women, but to limit the amount of cloth they could use or the persons they could clothe.

The nineteenth-century historian of the Aberdeen Incorporated Trades, Ebenezer Bain, noted, 'The tailors claimed the monopoly of making all kinds of garments, both male and female, and, . . . it was only after a keen struggle that the craftsmen granted women even the partial privilege of making certain articles of female attire'.[26] He declared it a 'very knotty problem' for the tailors, which 'filled them with dismay'.[27] The attempts to control female mantuamakers certainly came about partly because of the shift in fashion, but the tailors also fought to retain their privileges in the face of men who were outside their control and who had not 'properly' served their time as apprentices and journeymen with a freeman of the guild. In 1768, the journeymen rebelled against their low wages and long hours, but the masters held firm, but again in 1797 they struck against the control and autocracy exercised by the master tailors.[28] This tension then was also part of the shifting character of the town, whereby enterprising men could create niches in the economy in the face of corporate pressure. Indeed, by the end of the century the workingmen of the town began to challenge the Merchant Company and insist on their rights to a role in town government.[29]

When women first started 'encroaching', the tailors turned to the magistrates, who declined to interfere on the ground that 'the application by a female for liberty to make mantles was "unprecedented"'. After prosecuting several women for encroaching on the tailors' privileges, a compromise allowed women to make mantuas and, in some instances, petticoats, 'but on no consideration whatever were they to import or deal in stays and other articles of female attire'. In fact, there was a voluminous correspondence on the subject, suggesting real reluctance to give up any of their privileges. The case of Rachel Baxter forced their hand, and on 30 May 1717, she was granted the freedom of the burgh for mantuamaking on condition that she only gained the privilege of mantuamaking 'and no ways make stays, or import the same to sell from any other place'. She could take only female apprentices and servants who were registered like other apprentices. In addition to the guild fees, she paid an extra sum of money to the boxmaster of the tailors, for 'banqueting money' to 'tolerate' her sewing activities. They also 'hereby declared that this presents to be no precedent to any woman in tyme coming'. However, more women came forward, and the tailors responded simply by gradually raising the 'toleration' fees they demanded from the women, so that in April 1734 it was thirty pounds Scots for the daughter of a burgess, and four pounds sterling for unfreemen's daughters, a hefty charge and not one easily paid by a poor woman.[30] The fact that burgesses' daughters were singled out is typical of a town in which the merchant burgesses maintained economic and political control, but it also suggests the gentility of the women applying. What is clear is that women won the right to make women's clothes and that these rights were not restricted to widows or to women with a connection to the guild, since daughters of 'unfree' men were allowed to practice the trade. But as Bain explained, they were

> compelled to come within the jurisdiction of the craft, but they were not admitted to full membership. The women were simply granted a 'toleration' to make certain classes of clothes, and even in granting this privilege the tailors of Aberdeen were, we believe, the only craftsmen in Scotland who allowed females to share in their special privileges. [31]

It is notable that women who seemed most to challenge the tailors were those moving into dressmaking. Nevertheless, mantuamakers had clearly won the day, because in 1767 the Council gave a bursary to Elizabeth Strachan, fifteen-year old-daughter of a deceased Baillie, and agreed to continue it a further year 'since she is apprenticeship to one of the town's first mantuamakers' and had about eighteen months further to finish her apprenticeship.[32]

Milliners seem to have been tolerated from the outset. In the last half-century, at least 19 women operated as milliners and mantuamakers in Aberdeen, as did William Mitchel—who advertised on the same day as John Mitchel's daughter from a separate address.[33] By 1824, 66 milliners, mantuamakers and dressmakers advertised in the first Aberdeen Directory.[34] In Colchester, a similar situation existed. Between 1753 and 1800, 20 milliners practiced, including the three firms of Reeve, Prior and Gibbon, which between them took at least 30 apprentices, some of who, including the Woods sisters, set up their own businesses.[35] These were long-standing and well-established firms consistent with the potential recognised by commentators for women to carve out a niche in the commercial world.

French towns demonstrate a different dynamic. Women's guilds existed in Paris and Rouen, and between 1652 and 1776 a few provincial guilds emerged while women sometimes joined men's guilds.[36] Crowston argues that guildswomen strongly supported the corporate system, which gave them concrete economic benefits and better legal rights, and they used the privileges and structures to protect their trade. In female guilds, they gained a corporate identity and a notion of female honour that derived from the female nature of their trades and the independence that it allowed them to enjoy. These women scorned the skills of women who worked in patriarchal workshops, and took pride in their legal and professional autonomy, much as male tailors did.[37] And yet, women did not regularly join corporations, and many towns like Lyon, Nantes and La Rochelle did not have women's guilds. In Clermont-Ferrand, after the abolition of corporations in 1776, needlewomen proudly declared themselves free of guild control and resisted tailors' attempts to bring them into their corporation, as they had in England and Bologna, Italy.[38]

La Rochelle had no all-female guilds, but in small numbers they had a presence in the *modistes*, *merciers* and tailoring guilds. In 1760, Helen Poupelin applied to the *modistes* to open a linen and *marchande de modes* boutique, the only woman among the four extant records. Among thirty-eight *merciers*, three women gained permission to practice, all in the 1780s. Records of the *tailleurs* were similarly overwhelmingly male, yet as the century progressed, several women gained admission. A list of 1671 included Maria Moyne amongst the men, while seven widows, indicated only by their deceased husbands' names, were appended at the end. Regulations in 1753 allowed widows to continue as tailors, with some restrictions, and it is clear they did so.[39] However, timing is important: While some women were admitted before Turgot's abolition of the guilds in 1776, like Elizabeth

Table 2.2 Admissions to the Tailors' Guild, La Rochelle, 1777–1789, by sex and marital status.

Gender and civil status	Number
Men alone	65
Single women	5
Married women	15
Widowed women	17
Women, not specified	7
Male/female partnerships	6
Female partnerships	2
Total men	71
Total women	55

Robert on 27 June 1707, most entered later. The royal Edict of 1777 reinstated but significantly reformed the guilds, with the intention of opening them to others, including men and women who had not been able to meet the tight guild controls before. Thus in 1777, a flood of enterprising women, single, married and widowed, applied and gained admission, as an extant list from 1788 shows.[40] This suggests that numerous women had been working 'informally' without rights of membership, some probably with husbands (Table 2.2). Men's marital status is only identifiable when they were admitted with their wives; women on the other hand were largely identified by civil status. Notably, however, while widowed and married women dominated the female admissions, fourteen of the women were single or their civil status was unspecified. It is hard to tell if male resistance persisted, since virtually none of the documentation comments. The regulations employed explicitly male language, and the lists were quixotically labelled as '*messieurs*' even when women were listed. As in other towns, admission brought income to the tailors' guild and allowed them some control over what needlewomen were doing. The fact that there is a second small bulge in female admissions in 1783 suggests that there may have been another 'crackdown' on unregistered practitioners.

TRAINING, SKILL AND EXPERTISE

This debate over control of the needle shows how status and exclusivity were important in artisanal trades, not straightforward expertise in the technology or even gender. Women already had a close association with the tool. Indeed, sewing was seen as the pre-eminent female prerogative, closely identified with their role as wives and mothers, linked to their feminine identity, and identified as a proficiency that was essential to women of all classes. Enlightenment discourses defining female nature and proper roles suggest that clothing production was particularly appropriate work for women, at a time when gendered discourses about work and notions of female modesty coincided to shape a view of women's 'natural right' to work in the clothing trades.[41] In Paris, seamstresses utilised 'an altogether novel argument', claiming production should not be organised according to the sex of the producer, but the sex of the consumer.[42] Yet in the examples of Aberdeen and La Rochelle, such rhetoric was absent as men claimed their right to the 'skilled' and lucrative bespoke trades. The tension was about territory, the notion of controlled training through apprenticeship and ultimately the status of the work and the worker.

The simple fact of being female was enough to be seen as not skilled. For example, the *Book of Trades* claimed that in lacemaking,

> much *art and ingenuity are not necessary*; . . . Lacemaking, therefore, is confined to the hands of indigent women and young girls who, *by their skill and dexterity*, raise the value of the materials, originally of little worth, to almost any sum [my emphasis].[43]

Thus, their skill was both denigrated and praised, but the implication is that it was natural, female and certainly not of the order of male skill since it lacked 'art and ingenuity'. However, while needlework was seen as something to be learned at home, utilising women's 'natural' abilities, sewing was taught in fashionable boarding schools to charity schools. Thus, it *did* have to be learned, but for females it was seen to operate outside the recognised structure of artisanal training, that is, apprenticeship. However, most milliners *did* serve apprenticeships, and many women used the apprenticeship system precisely to attach credit and legitimacy to their trade. Millinery, and to a lesser extent mantuamaking, drew the highest apprenticeship fees paid by girls and their families. For example, the Colchester milliners described above took a string of apprentices between 1753 and 1800, with fees ranging from £20 to £52. The average premium in 1750 for children in Essex and Staffordshire was £14, rising to £25 by 1800; in this respect milliners' apprentices paid over the average. Since 60 per cent of children were apprenticed with £10 or less, the relative prestige of millinery becomes apparent. Additionally, mistresses had to pay 6 pence in the pound for premiums up to £50 and 1 shilling in the pound for those over £50.[44] Mantuamakers as a group encompassed a broader range of sewing, not limited to the high-status seamstress, and average apprenticeship premiums were lower, £12, as was their capitalisation. Campbell stressed the need for parents to be able to provide adequately for their daughters, since despite 'vast profits' made by the mistresses, they 'yet give but poor, mean Wages to every Person they employ under them'.[45] For the top end of the trade and the well-capitalized employer, it could be a good business enterprise, and clearly women who owned and ran the ateliers were better situated than employees and apprentices.

Apprenticeship was important not only for teaching skills, but also for gaining credibility in the trades. Thus Aberdeen milliner Isabella Morison advertised that she 'had served an Apprenticeship of five years in London and has settled a proper correspondence there' (Figure 2.1).[46] The significance of apprenticeship is demonstrated by the fact that in Essex and Staffordshire 65.5 per cent of all female apprentices trained as milliners or mantuamakers.[47] Similarly, from 1675 apprenticeship was required to enter the Parisian *maîtresses couturières* guild, which enabled them 'to make Skirts, Dressing Gowns, Mantuas, Skirt Bodices and other clothes . . . for persons of their sex'.[48] Those who completed apprenticeships had the best chance of regular employment and of the best jobs. In La Rochelle, the rush of women to join the tailors' company after 1777 strongly suggests a desire for public acknowledgment of their skills and right to trade, and recognition that it added a veneer of credibility and status to their profession.

BUSINESSWOMEN

These 'workers' challenge a 'working-class' notion of working women. Few if any British girls sent to the trade were poor, and the level of training fees was such that only middling and elite families could afford them. Millinery was recommended to girls of good family, including gentry and tradesmen's families, as 'a most genteel Business for Young Maidens that are proficient at their needle'.[49] Contemporaries such as Campbell thought women could begin business with capital ranging from £100–£1000, suggesting not only a need for financial resources to put into the business but also the support of friends and family. Ann Buchanan and Kirsteen came from Scottish gentry families, and Buchanan explicitly commented,

> Mama and Grandpapa is very well pleased with the proposal and is willing to give as much credit as is needed; so I hope there is no fear of my getting Employment as I have so many relations; for there's all the Kier folk, Lady Helen Colquhoun; Lady Grace Campbell; Mrs Smalet and many my Dr that is needed to name.[50]

Many middling and gentry girls were raised with the expectation that they would have to support themselves, and the high-end needle trades were an acceptable option. Joseph Collyer explained,

> The girl, designed for this employment, ought to have a genteel person, be capable of ready address; she too should write a tolerable hand, understand the first rules of arithmetic, work quick and well at her needle, and have some fancy and imagination. These qualifications, joined

> to strict modesty and justice, will hardly fail of procuring, in this branch of business, a comfortable and genteel support; and I know none fitter for the daughters of numerous families, where the parents live handsomely, yet have no fortunes to leave their children.[51]

Thus, painter William Hogarth's sisters, Ann and Mary, became milliners, and author Lawrence Sterne recommended it as an appropriate opportunity for his sister. Aberdonian Isabella Morison, like others who advertised in the *Aberdeen Journal*, offered needlework lessons encompassing a vast array of skills, thus suggesting a keen demand for such teaching. In this respect, 'milliners acted as a bridge between classes, and sometimes within classes'.[52] They had access to those above them in status, even sharing tea with them, though the gentry usually kept the boundaries of class firmly in mind (see Figure 2.2).[53]

Figure 2.2 The Milliner in her Shop, *Book of English Trades*, 44.

Across Britain, high-end milliners built strong firms. In the High Street, Colchester, Lucia Reeve and her sisters operated a large millinery firm for some twenty years from 1761, sometimes styling the business 'Lucia Reeves and Co'.[54] This firm was typical of the conscientiously run high-status concern. Mary Gibbon took apprentices in Colchester from 1753 to 1761, one of whom was Elizabeth Reeve, while two were the Woods sisters. These sisters later succeeded Lucia Reeve in her business, and then they joined forces as Reeves and Wood. Gibbon disappeared from the Essex records, and from May 1763 a 'Mary Gibbon' began taking millinery apprentices in Bath Spa, apprenticing ten by December 1773. Ann and Hannah Prior began taking registered apprentices in 1786 and continued until 1803.

PARTNERSHIP

Partnerships were important to many women in business, since sharing costs gave them an edge in the business world, as well as the potential for successful independence. Partnerships were a time-honoured way for couples to operate, and female partnerships shared many of the same advantages. They halved rent, servants and other costs connected with managing a concern. In Aberdeen, milliners Misses Ramsay and McKenzie worked in a partnership upstairs from Miss Forbes, also a milliner, and in Edinburgh at least 140 single women ran businesses, often in female partnerships.[55] Similarly, as the two extracts which opened this chapter showed, Ann Buchanan welcomed partnership, while combining with Kirsteen was seen as enhancing Miss Jean's business. Frequently relatives, often sisters, lived together sharing expenses. The large and successful Colchester firm run by Lucia Reeve and her sisters and followed by the sisters Wood is a prime example. Networks of women were obvious in these trades. The Woods sisters were trained by Mary Gibbon, took over the Reeves' business, and ultimately worked in partnership with them. Similarly, Nicola Phillips identified sisterly and female networks of tradeswomen and clients who frequently supported each other, with a particularly high incidence in millinery.[56] In contrast, Sanderson's research on Edinburgh, while demonstrating the importance of partnership, showed only a handful of sisters working together, and in La Rochelle only *Madame* Dumaine and *Mesdemoiselles* Mesnier (1783) and Louise Bourdier and Jeanne la France (1788) were admitted as *tailleurs d'habits* together, suggesting working partnerships.[57]

The family connections of Edinburgh milliners Ann Buchanan, Cicely Murray and Janet Muschet are indicative. Cicely worked in partnership with Janet in the 1750s, and Cicely's cousin Ann joined them in 1757. Cicely then left and married, but wrote to her brother John Murray in 1758 that Janet 'had used her' and showed 'such ingratitude'. When Ann and Janet had a serious quarrel, the family was drawn in, and Cicely, contradictorily, was then critical of Ann's 'behaviour'. Ann wrote to her uncle, Dr Adam Murray, in 1758, describing how badly she was used by Janet and complained that she was being treated quite differently than Cicely had been:

> I really Don't know what she means By her Behaviour to me; I have done all that is possible I can for the Business, But I fancy she imagined when I came that I was to run and serve her; in everything Even to the making ready her Meat and putting on her fire in the morning, She thinks herself on a quite Different footing with me then she was with Mrs Lindsay for she behaves to me as I were far below her, and that I should not go out of the Door without asking her lieve.[58]

She may have chosen her correspondent unwisely, because Muschet also wrote to 'My Dearest Doctor' complaining about Buchanan. Ultimately Ann went back to the partnership—the reasons are not clear, but it may have been the best option for a single woman. In 1760, Muschet married her 'dear' doctor, Adam Murray, brother of the laird of Polmaise, but died a year later. A family network clearly underpinned this partnership, with money, support and probably pressure, as the letters suggest. Notably, historians' notion of collaborative and supportive female networks frequently obscures the level of rancour, dispute and competition that could exist in partnerships.

Given the close link between the trades, and the fact that women often joined tailors' guilds, it should not surprise us that tailors and milliners or mantuamakers worked together. Indeed, given the gendered association of female milliner to male tailor, often husbands, like Samuel Phillips in Colchester, were tailors, while it is probable that wives, like milliner Sarah Wilder Phillips, operated independently or in a roughly equal partnership with them, in a gendered division of labour that rested on the identity of the trades. For example, in May of 1767, they advertised in the *Ipswich Journal*:

> At the 'Eagle and Child' he sells Woollen and Linnen Drapery, Mercery, Millinery, Hosiery and Haberdashery Goods and has no concern with the old Stock, 'but we have laid in a fresh Stock of such Goods as we hope will give Satisfaction'. All sorts of Millinery 'will be made up by Mrs Phillips, and an able Hand from London. The Tayloring Trade continued as usual'.[59]

Similarly, Daniel Blyth and Mary Brown Blythe, working in Colchester between 1765 and the 1780s, operated together as a perukemaker and milliner. She ran the mercery, linen drapery and haberdashery alongside her millinery, while he made wigs. And widowed milliner Mary Marsden Waynman married a draper. In La Rochelle, six wives and husbands were admitted together, including François Sicher and 'his wife', and Antoine Barbe and Marie-Anne Bajot, 'his wife', in 1788.[60] It was not uncommon, however, for couples to work in different trades. Martha Gibson Hedge was a milliner while her husband was a clockmaker and jeweller in Colchester; Christopher Gibbon was a minister, despite signing one of the indentures, while Lucia Reeve's husband was a musician.[61]

FINAL THOUGHTS

The debate over the needle trades demonstrates how status and exclusivity were important in artisanal trades, while skill was a contested terrain. In practice, milliners were highly skilled, but they were valued most for their style, imagination and invention. Their ability to be creative, to keep up with the times or even to stay ahead of them was their stock in trade. They benefited from their urban setting, where the flow of commerce and information helped them conduct businesses. They operated in synergy with the polite and sociable urban society of the eighteenth century like Aberdeen, La Rochelle and Colchester, where the dizzy sense of opportunity extended to entrepreneurial and fashion-conscious businesswomen.[62] Apprenticeship data, newspaper advertisements and insurance records clearly indicate that the better needle trades, catering to the luxury end of the market, did offer a genuine occupation and good future for some women; the simple fact that they required training was an added boost to their reputation and helped open the door to independence. They certainly did not work solely in the 'shadow of their husbands'.[63]

They fostered luxury and were both praised and criticised for it, thus they also needed a keen eye for their reputation. Chrisman-Campbell commented that they had 'no status or reputation to lose', but on the contrary, one of their strengths was their probity and chastity, and their vulnerability lay, in part, on their being seen as 'fair game'.[64] Some of the slanders about milliners—and they were stock figures in comedies of manners—rested on their overt presence in the business world and their vulnerability. But the critiques of luxury could rebound on them as well. They dressed as well as their clients, and their style and elegance was their *entrée*, not only to a good trade but also to the growing luxury trades of these vigorous commercial towns. Thus gender, creativity and skill shaped the interaction between milliners and their towns.

NOTES

1 Ann Buchanan to Janet Muschet, 22 March 1757, Stirling Council Archives (SCA), Murray of Polmaise Collection, PD189/2/337.
2 Margaret Oliphant, *Kirsteen*, ed. Anne M. Scriven (Glasgow: ASLS, 2010), 215–16.
3 The terms are nationally specific: 'Milliner' is not used in France and *marchande de modes* is rarely used in Britain. On terminology, see Montenach in this

volume and Kimberly Chrisman Campbell, 'The Face of Fashion: Milliners in Eighteenth-century Visual Culture', *British Society for Eighteenth Century Studies Journal*, 25 (2002): 158. On the development of the mantua, see Avril Hart, 'The Mantua: Its Evolution and Fashionable Significance in the Seventeenth and Eighteenth Centuries', in *Defining Dress as Object, Meaning and Identity*, ed. Amy de la Haye and Elizabeth Wilson (Manchester: Manchester University Press, 1999), 93–103.

4 The population of Aberdeen was about 16,000 in mid century, the population of La Rochelle about 18,000 and the population of Colchester around 11,000.

5 Rosemary Sweet, *The Writing of Urban Histories in Eighteenth-Century England* (Oxford: Oxford University Press, 1997), 274.

6 Clare Crowston, *Fabricating Women, The Seamstresses of Old Regime France, 1675–1791* (Durham: Duke University Press, 2001); Jennifer Jones, *Sexing La Mode: Gender, Fashion and Commercial Culture in Old Regime France* (Oxford: Berg, 2004); Amy Louise Erickson, 'Eleanor Mosley and Other Milliners in the City of London Companies, 1700–1750', *History Workshop Journal* 71 (2011): 147–72; Daryl Hafter, *Women and Work in Preindustrial France* (University Park: The Pennsylvania State University Press, 2007). See also Nicola Phillips, *Women in Business, 1700–1850* (London: The Boydell Press, 2006); Chrisman Campbell, 'Face of Fashion', 2; Louisa Cross, 'The Display and Trading of Fashionable Dress and Its Impact on Women in Scotland's Growing Urban Centres, c. 1780–1825', in *Women in Eighteenth-Century Scotland, Intimate, Intellectual and Public Lives*, ed. Katie Barclay and Deborah Simonton (Farnham: Ashgate, 2013): 233–52; Daniel Roche, *The Culture of Clothing: Dress and Fashion in the Ancien Régime* (Cambridge: Cambridge University Press, 1994); and Elizabeth Musgrave, 'Women and the Craft Guilds in Eighteenth-Century Nantes', in *The Artisan and the European Town*, ed. Geoffrey Crossick (Aldershot: Scolar Press, 1997), 151–71.

7 William Blackstone, *Commentaries on the Laws of England*, ed. Edward Christian, 13th ed. (London: A. Strahan, 1800), III, 326.

8 R. W. Chapman, *Johnson's Journey to the Western Isles of Scotland and Boswell's Journal of a Tour to the Hebrides* (Oxford: Oxford University Press, 1924), 12–13.

9 Daniel Defoe, *A Tour Through the Whole Island of Great Britain* (1724–6), vol. 1 (London: JM Dent & Co., 1962), 16.

10 Shani D'Cruze, *A Pleasing Prospect, Social Change and Urban Culture in Eighteenth-Century Colchester* (Hatfield: University of Hertfordshire Press, 2008), 26.

11 T. C. Smout, *A History of the Scottish People, 1560–1830* (London: Fontana, 1969), 339–40.

12 Apprenticeship, its fees, terms of service and gendered character are drawn out in Deborah Simonton, *The Education and Training of Eighteenth-Century English Girls* (PhD diss., University of Essex, 1988), and 'Apprenticeship: Training and Gender in Eighteenth-Century England', in *Markets and Manufactures in Early Industrial Europe*, ed. Maxine Berg (London: Routledge, 1991), 227–58.

13 Robert Campbell, *The London Tradesman* (London: T. Gardner, 1747), 206, 208.

14 Joseph Collyer, *The Parents' and Guardians' Directory* (London: R. Griffiths, 1761), 194–6; *The Book of English Trades and Library of the Useful Arts* (London: J. Souter, 1818), 222–25.

15 Oliphant, *Kirsteen*, 214–15.

16 Chrisman Campbell, 'Face of Fashion', 158–59.

17 *Aberdeen Journal*, 18 September 1769, 3 October 1758.

18 Ibid., 18 September 1769.
19 M. de Garsault, *l'Art du tailleur*, in *Descriptions des arts et métiers* (Paris: Saillant & Nyon, 1761), 54.
20 *Book of English Trades*, 47, 82, 84–85.
21 J. M. Roland de la Platière, *Encyclopédie méthodique: manufactures, arts et métiers* (Paris: Panckoucke Libraire, 1785–1790), I, 133.
22 See Deborah Simonton, *A History of European Women's Work, 1700 to the Present* (London: Routledge, 1998), 76–84.
23 Jones, *Sexing La Mode*, 80.
24 Erickson, 'Eleanor Moseley', 150–53.
25 S. D. Smith, 'Women's Admission to Guilds in Early-Modern England: The Case of the York Merchant Tailors' Company, 1693–1776', *Gender & History* 17 (2005): 99–126; Mary Prior, 'Women and the Urban Economy: Oxford, 1500–1800', in *Women in English Society, 1500–1800*, ed. Mary Prior (London: Methuen, 1985), 93–117; Jean Quataert 'The Shaping of Women's Work in Manufacturing Guilds, Households and the State in Central Europe, 1648–1870', *American Historical Review* 90 (1985): 1122–48.
26 Ebenezer Bain, *Merchant and Craft Guilds, A History of the Aberdeen Incorporated Trades* (Aberdeen: J & JP Edmond & Spark, 1887), 253.
27 Ibid., 256.
28 Ibid., 259–60.
29 For example, see *Aberdeen Journal*, 26 May, 23 and 30 June, 1 December 1783.
30 Bain, *Merchant and Craft Guilds*, 256–59.
31 Ibid., 259.
32 Aberdeen City Archives (ACA), Council, Baillie and Guild Registers, 19 December 1767.
33 *Aberdeen Journal*, 3 October 1758.
34 *A Directory for the City of Aberdeen and Its Vicinity, 1814–5* (Aberdeen: D. Chalmers & Co. 1824), 1–100.
35 Simonton, *Education and Training*, Appendix 5.8.
36 The structure of guilds is relatively complicated, and indeed so is women's inclusion. See the discussion in Clare Crowston, 'Women, Gender and Guilds in Early Modern Europe', *IRSH* 53 (2008), supplement: 19–44; Simonton, *History of European Women's Work*, 47–56; and Erickson, 'Eleanor Mosley'.
37 Crowston, *Fabricating Women*, 408–9.
38 Dora Dumont, 'Women and Guilds in Bologna: The Ambiguities of "Marginality"', *Radical History Review* 70 (1998): 4–5.
39 Archives municipales de La Rochelle (AMLR), HH 14: Corporations. Merciers. Modistes; HH 18: Tailleurs: *Reglements et statuts des maîtres tailleurs d'habit, marchandes drapiers et chaussetiers de la ville de La Rochelle*, Mesnier, Imprimeur du Roy, 1753, art. XX.
40 AMLR, HH 18: *Tableau des Maîtres Tailleurs & Frippiers en neuf & en vieux de la Communauté de la Ville de la Rochelle, pour l'année 1788*, A la Rochelle, chez P. L. Chauvet, libraire imprimeur du Roi, 1788.
41 Jones, *Sexing La Mode*, 96–101.
42 Ibid., 82.
43 *Book of English Trades*, 41–42.
44 Simonton, *Education and Training*, chapter 5B.
45 Campbell, *London Tradesman*, 336, 208.
46 *Aberdeen Journal*, 18 September 1769.
47 Simonton, *Education and Training*, Appendix 5. Data is for 'trade' apprentices and does not include charity or poor law apprentices.
48 Crowston, *Fabricating Women*, 190.

49 *A General Description of the Trades Digested in Alphabetical Order* (London: T. Waller, 1747), 149.
50 Ann Buchanan to Janet Muschet, 22 March 1757, SCA, Murray of Polmaise Collection, PD189/2/337.
51 Collyer, *Parents' and Guardians' Directory*, 194–95.
52 Chrisman Campbell, 'Face of Fashion', 160. For sewing schools in Scotland, see Lindy Moore, 'The Value of Feminine Culture: Community Involvement in the Provision of Schooling for Girls in Eighteenth-Century Scotland', in *Women in Eighteenth-Century Scotland*, ed. Barclay and Simonton, 97–114.
53 Amanda Vickery, *The Gentleman's Daughter: Women's Lives in Georgian England* (New Haven: Yale University Press, 1998), 27–28.
54 She was Lucia Hannah Reeve, though her name appears as Reeves from time to time. See also Shani D'Cruze, ed., *Colchester People, The John Bensusan Butt Biographical Dictionary of Eighteenth-Century Colchester*, 2nd ed. (private publication, 2010), v. 2, 141–42.
55 *Aberdeen Journal*, 22 June 1767; Elizabeth C. Sanderson, *Women and Work in Eighteenth-Century Edinburgh* (London: Macmillan, 1996), 184–94.
56 Phillips, *Women in Business*, 32–3, 54, 107–8.
57 Sanderson, *Women and Work*; AMLR, HH 18: *Tableau des Maîtres Tailleurs.*
58 Ann Buchanan to Dr Murray at Polmaise, 10 February 1758, 22 March 1757, SCA, Murray of Polmaise Collection, PD189/2/340.
59 *Ipswich Journal*, 30 May 1767, quoted in D'Cruze, *Colchester People*, II, 88.
60 AMLR, HH 18: *Tableau des Maîtres Tailleurs.*
61 D'Cruze, *Colchester People*, I, 285–56, 352–54; II, 142, 3.
62 Smout, *History of the Scottish People*, 339–40.
63 Garsault, *Art du tailleur*, 54.
64 Chrisman Campbell, 'Face of Fashion', 160.

3 Gender and Luxury in Eighteenth-Century Grenoble

From Legal Exchanges to Shadow Economy[1]

Anne Montenach

The period between the 1720s and the Revolution is well known as a time of strong economic expansion in France, when towns of all sizes, and especially commercial centres, experienced significant growth in population and wealth. At the same time, people's lifestyles changed gradually, but dramatically, as can be seen from probate inventories in which the contents of townspeople's homes demonstrate their appetite for consumer goods.[2] Studies of Paris's new luxury and fashion industries show that an increasing number of women were entering these rapidly developing and diversifying markets.[3] The objective here is to review how changes in commercialization and consumerism affected an urban community in a border province and gave men and women new and different opportunities for participating in both the legal and the illegal market.

With a growing population of some 23,000 inhabitants by the mid eighteenth century, Grenoble was the capital city of the Dauphiné, and as such was home to the local aristocracy and members of the provincial Parliament, a situation which created a dynamic market in luxury goods. Thanks to its geographical location and special customs status, the Dauphiné was a hub for a number of smuggling networks linking Geneva, the Piedmont, the Savoy and Lyon, especially during the ban on sales of calicos (1686–1759). This chapter examines the various roles played by men and women in the trades relating to luxury goods and especially the garment sector. In addition to a review of attitudes within male-dominated guilds, it will explore not only the situation of women working legally in specific activities such as mercers and milliners and their business strategies in the town, but also the involvement of both men and women in alternative distribution networks and the black market for luxury goods.

These alternative retail circuits played an important role in the supply of luxury or semi-luxury goods, two complex and shifting notions that this chapter will re-interrogate. Because of the lack of sources, it is difficult to identify producers and consumers, and for this reason the study will concentrate on the distribution process. Information on production centres and techniques and on the quality of raw materials is also very scarce and renders the task of categorising the goods discussed here particularly tricky: Jewellery, perfumes, combs, razors, mirrors, silk stockings, ribbons and lace, umbrellas and sunshades are but a few examples of this 'world of goods' so eagerly sought after by various social groups, especially from the mid eighteenth century onwards, given the wide range of quality and prices. Most goods probably did not meet the stringent criteria that would ensure their inclusion in the category of 'aristocratic luxuries' (characterized as rare, expensive and ostentatious). However, Maxine Berg's research into eighteenth-century England suggests that they could be identified as 'new luxuries' or 'commodities', categories that could also be of interest for other countries, including France.[4] It is extremely difficult to define these goods *a priori* as luxury or semi-luxury goods, however, by taking a case-by-case approach, we can examine how they became part of the prevailing lifestyle. Historians have sought to analyse these two categories, together with Cissie Fairchilds's contested suggestion of 'populuxe' goods.[5] Calicos offer a specific, and particularly emblematic, example of this new form of segmentation in the market since they appealed to a wide range of consumers and, despite the wide differences in quality and price, demand increased rapidly throughout eighteenth-century France.

In order to shed light on the opportunities offered to multiple economic actors by these new markets and to reconstruct the various retail circuits for luxury goods in towns, this chapter will review not only traditional source materials for the urban economy—guilds' archives, applications for business licences, advertisements in the local newspaper (*Les Affiches du Dauphiné*)—but also specific documentation on market practices, such as police ordinances and court proceedings. It will demonstrate how, during the eighteenth century, a new culture of luxury developed in a provincial town in France's border provinces and how this led to the creation of new forms of trade that had a profound impact on the role of both men and women in the town's economic activities. It will also allow us to analyse these sources from the gender perspective in order to obtain a more precise idea of their relationship with the urban environment.

EMERGENCE OF NEW FASHION TRADES IN THE EIGHTEENTH CENTURY

Although eighteenth-century Dauphiné was not a particularly urbanized province, the population of its capital, Grenoble, increased substantially in line with demographic trends in most French towns at the time: The number of inhabitants grew from 20,000 around 1690 to 24,000 by 1790. Moreover, with the presence of the Dauphiné Parliament, the Chamber of Accounts and the Finance Office, Grenoble was the province's administrative, judicial and financial capital. Many noble families in the Dauphiné lived at least part of the year in the town: some 200 noble families at the beginning of the century, rising to 300 just prior to the Revolution, representing approximately

5 to 6 per cent of the city's population. Grenoble was also home to a large number of lawyers, prosecutors, notaries, merchants and shopkeepers, and it was *par excellence* a city of consumers, rather than of manufacturers. The strong presence of aristocrats, parliamentarians and officials contributed to the development of a market for specific crafts and trades in the construction, furniture and textile sectors (*métiers d'art*), including cabinetmaking, mirrors, tapestries, clothing, embroidery, stringed instruments, organs and pianos.[6] Lists of merchants and craftsmen drawn up in 1727 and 1784 also mention goldsmiths, 'tapestry-makers decorating furniture', 'glaziers working in earthenware', grocers, drapers, glovemakers and furriers, hatters, booksellers, clockmakers and 'mercers' (haberdashers).[7]

The mercers of Grenoble, who played a crucial role in the fashion and luxury markets, were concentrated at the very heart of the city in the Place aux Herbes—close to the Parliament House—and the Place Grenette, the market square. A royal decree issued on 16 April 1718 established regulations for Grenoble's arts and crafts, citing 44 professions, including the guild of 'mercers, canvas dealers, jewellers and ironmongers', which had about 20 members. Not surprisingly, women were under-represented in most guilds, as can be seen in various statements and lists drawn up during the eighteenth century. These sources rarely mention women, and then mostly as widows or single women. For example, the repayment schedule drawn up by the hatters' guild in 1727 lists eleven members; of these three were widows (referred to as '*Demoiselle*') and a fourth reference to '*Demoiselle* Gavet and her son' (presumably also a widow). The glovemakers' list for the same year includes two widows among its twenty-four masters.[8] However, other sources give a more nuanced picture: Poll tax registers (*capitation*) and mercers' inventories (after death or bankruptcy) show that women, whether married or single, played a significant role in this trade.

The 1739 *capitation* names twenty-four mercers, including 'Widow Blanc', 'Dusert *mercière*' and '*les demoiselles Perret marchandes mercières*'—most probably sisters, or mother and daughter(s).[9] Some mercers' widows continued their husband's business with their son or daughter, such as Elisabeth Bois, who in 1733 shared a small shop on Place Grenette with her daughter—a hosier—and her son-in-law, who was 'a candle-maker and a perfumer'.[10] More surprisingly, given her husband's profession, there is a reference in 1751 to Jeanne Moget, a glovemaker's widow, who ran a mercer's shop in Rue Perollerie where she sold mostly lace, ribbons, various kinds of fabrics and several silk 'bonnets' for adults or children at eight *livres* each.[11] Marianne Rivail, separated from her husband, had a similar business in Rue Très Cloîtres a few years later, but nothing in her shop was worth more than a few *sols*.[12] These examples not only demonstrate that '*mercerie*' was seen in some cases as a niche market for independent women, but also that the 'luxury' trade covered a wide variety of goods sold and wealth distribution, as confirmed by poll tax registers. In 1781, Widow Tournu and her son stocked a wide range of fashionable and luxury items worth more than 30,000 *livres*, and they acted as suppliers to various shopkeepers and pedlars in the town.[13] Some mercers seemed to specialize in selling fabrics or pieces of cloth, whereas others offered clothing accessories (buttons, ties, belts, handkerchiefs and so on), toiletries (combs, razors, mirrors), or toys, books and groceries.[14] Like their Parisian counterparts, they were allowed to sell, design, adapt and transform all types of objects, but were prohibited from manufacturing them.[15]

The number of mercers halved between the beginning and end of the eighteenth century. According to poll tax registers, there were eleven mercers in Grenoble in 1789, compared to twenty-one in 1716. Apparently, mercers were progressively replaced by more specialized shopkeepers, such as milliners, jewellers, grocers and booksellers.[16] The registers also mention twenty-three '*marchandes de modes*' (milliners) in Grenoble in 1789, working in a profession that did not exist in 1716.[17] According to Jennifer Jones, milliners, who embellished the female *toilette* by selling and arranging fancy wares and accessories, represented 'the new commercial culture as fashion merchants *par excellence* and the prototype of modern urban women' in the second half of the eighteenth century.[18] They were at the very heart of the urban fashion economy and were able to benefit from the presence of a wide variety of artisans and suppliers. Anne Durand, a milliner operating in Grenoble between 1758 and 1774, left a large collection of personal papers, letters and accounts showing that she sold lace and silk stockings, fans and fine fabrics, and that her network of clients and suppliers spread as far as Lyon, Paris, Le Puy, Geneva and Neuchâtel.[19] Further analysis of milliners' account books and correspondences will allow us to map their clientele in the town itself, both geographically and socially, as well as throughout the province.[20] In addition, police records provide some interesting cases. Towards the very end of the Old Regime, three fashion merchants, a widow and two sisters, made complaints against clients who had not paid on time: One client was *Demoiselle* Carpentier, a concert singer, and another an actress at the *Comédie, Demoiselle* Mezieres.[21] Though apparently anecdotal, these two cases subsume three major aspects of gender and luxury trades in eighteenth-century towns. First, they illustrate the universal recourse to offering credit to clients in the garment trades, an option that was not limited to aristocratic customers.[22] Moreover, these two clients and their female suppliers were all professional women working in the world of artifice and explicit sexual connotations—and as such were seen, by their detractors, as having close connections with prostitution. As milliners had developed a talent for decorating women's costumes, they could also provide articles of clothing such as shawls, capes, even dresses, and develop new lines of business activities. They thus would cross into the territory of other fashion professionals and, in particular, of seamstresses and dressmakers who specialized in bespoke clothes for women.[23] While Parisian fashion merchants did not have an independent guild until August 1776, Grenoble's milliners were already members of the large corporation of mercers, jewellers, canvas dealers, makers of mirrors, and ironmongers mentioned earlier.[24] Though predominantly a female occupation, men were not excluded from the millinery trade and, at least until the 1760s, there was no real distinction between mercers and milliners: On July 1767, François Moléon, a '*marchand de mode* in lace, ribbons and stockings of all sorts', solicited and obtained admission to the mercers' guild on the grounds that he had lived and worked in Grenoble for three years.[25]

Apart from the specific case of milliners, and in particular female milliners, who managed to carve out a market in the town, the development of the fashion sector opened up many opportunities for women in the production of clothing throughout the eighteenth century. This situation inevitably created competition and conflicts not only amongst the women themselves, but also with men and those working in other spheres of commercial activity. Looking more closely at the situation in eighteenth-century Grenoble, we can see that dressmaking and sewing were ranked second after the glovemaking industry, which had expanded dramatically during this period (see below) as employers of women in the garment trade: The Tailors' Guild listed twenty-three 'mistress tailors' ('*mestresses tailleuses*') and forty-eight 'master tailors' in its repayment schedule for 1727. Grenoble offers an interesting contrast with other French towns, such as Aix or Caen, where seamstresses strongly outnumbered tailors during the first decades of the early eighteenth century.[26] However, the traditional male monopoly in the clothing industry was, as elsewhere, progressively losing ground.

According to the statutes for the Tailors' Guild, drawn up in October 1741, 'mistress seamstresses' (Art. IV) were authorized to hire female apprentices, thus ensuring that they could transmit their professional skills to girl apprentices using the same notarized contracts as those used by guild masters for hiring boy apprentices. There is also evidence that families were transferring skills from one generation to another: A reference to '*Mademoiselle* Gouvernet aunt' and '*Mademoiselle* Gouvernet niece' seems to suggest a family tradition in this profession. However, it is still unclear whether Grenoble master tailors were allowed to hire female apprentices and vice versa, a practice that was strictly forbidden in Lyon in the same period. Apprenticeship was far from being a gender-neutral process and therefore contributed to the construction of masculinity and femininity.[27] Unlike their colleagues in Paris, Le Havre or Rouen, Grenoble's seamstresses did not succeed in establishing an independent and exclusively female guild and, as in Aix-en-Provence, they joined the tailors' guild as subordinate members exclusively involved in producing women's and children's clothing.[28] In 1776, when Turgot's reforms were challenging the way the guilds operated and were structured, Grenoble's guilds issued a general statement, which mentioned not only 'female tailors for women's clothing' (*tailleuses pour habits de femmes*) but also 'female tailors for bodices' (*tailleuses pour corps*).[29] As in other cities, the reasons for this sexual division of labour between tailors and seamstresses were probably twofold: economic, in order to combat female involvement in illegal production, and moral, on the understanding that only women should dress women and that sewing was a virtuous profession for them.[30]

Nevertheless, although women represented one-third of master tailors in 1727, men did not easily tolerate their presence. As in Paris, according to research by Daniel Roche, Clare H. Crowston and Jennifer Jones, there was considerable rivalry between men and women working in the clothing industry, particularly since, as in Grenoble, women were not keen to limit themselves to cutting and sewing female garments.[31] In 1772, two women resisted attempts to exclude them from the male monopoly in men's clothes: The first described herself as a 'female tailor making men's clothes' (*ouvrière tailleuse pour hommes*) and the second described herself as a 'mistress trouser-maker' (*maîtresse culottière*). Both challenged traditional guild practices in terms of the division of labour by taking advantage of increased demand from clients to extend their activities in competition with master tailors.[32] Unfortunately, because of the lack of sources, we have very little information on whether or how the latter reacted to their new rivals.

INCREASING MARKET SHARE: GENDER, APPLICATIONS AND ADVERTISEMENTS

In Grenoble, where guild archives are extremely scarce, police records and local newspapers give insights into new trades and alternative distributive circuits. Police lieutenants were expected to handle disputes between 'foreign' merchants who wanted to settle in Grenoble and local shopkeepers who protested against what they saw as unfair competition. By studying applications to the police lieutenant for licences to sell goods in Grenoble, whether for short periods or permanent residence, it is possible to obtain a better understanding of the development of this new luxury market during the period 1731–1789. *Les Affiches, annonces et avis divers du Dauphiné*, a weekly newspaper published between 1774 and 1792, provides insights into marketing practices developed by artisans and shopkeepers to increase the number of their clients, while 'lost-and-found' notices give details on new goods on the market. Thus this newspaper is a rich source of information on the wide range of goods marketed in Grenoble, various distribution circuits and the evolution of male and female advertising strategies.

Most applications for licences were submitted to the police lieutenant after 1750, indicating that trade in goods and novelties increased in the second half of the century, and that Grenoble was attracting a large number of merchants from other areas of France and even from abroad.[33] All applicants were men, probably because large-scale mobility was more difficult for single women merchants in eighteenth-century Europe and because business networks—even when they involved women—relied mostly on male travellers.[34] Approximately 50 per cent of requests to open stores in Grenoble were submitted by foreigners, mostly Swiss and Italian. In November 1774, two Italians, Celestin Carvarola and Jean Dorigo, were awarded a licence to make and sell 'barometers, thermometers, glasses, compasses, and other objects in glass and crystal'. Twelve years later, the Piedmont blazon-maker Paul Charmet settled in the city and was authorized to 'print and hand out brochures advertising his trade to the public'. During the same period, three Swiss confectioners opened shops in the town after presenting their passports and baptism certificates.[35] Applications were also received from a perfumer from Champagne, an embroiderer in gold and silver thread, born in Saint-Pierre-de-Chartreuse (near Grenoble) but now a merchant in Lyon, and a merchant from Verney d'Oz in Oisans (in the Dauphiné) who sold 'canvas, muslins, handkerchiefs, silk stockings and other similar goods'.[36] For some merchants, Grenoble might represent the final phase in a long itinerant life. For instance, Leonard Caën, a converted Jew born in the German-speaking area of Lorraine, described himself to the police lieutenant in 1787 as 'having lived for a long time in Limoges, where he had his business, and then working as a pedlar in various provinces of the realm, he decided to maintain his business and take up this same activity in the Dauphiné with his wife and children'.[37] In each case, the success of an application for opening a shop seemed to depend on whether the newcomer's trade and products were going to compete with the city's established merchants and craftsmen or whether there was no one else carrying out the trade in Grenoble.

Given significant changes in consumer tastes, particularly in the retail trade, and a new trend towards commercial promotion in European towns, newspaper advertisements provide information on both the wide range of new goods and services offered to the consumers and the selling strategies pursued by male and female retailers.[38] The provincial press, including *Les Affiches du Dauphiné*, played a key role in France's fashion and luxury market in the second half of the eighteenth century. Newspapers offered a vast array of commercial information targeting a market-orientated readership—from which women were not excluded.[39] Both local shopkeepers and foreign merchants used them, whether they made only a short stay or were recently established in Grenoble. Many used advertisements to announce a change of address, partnership arrangements, or a business closure and sales of its stock. Commercial messages were both informative—giving the retailer's name, location and goods for sale—and seductive, emphasising the variety ('*toutes sortes*', '*de toute espèce*', '*en différents genres*') and 'modishness' of particular objects: 'In the latest taste' was the expression most frequently used in advertisements. Often the advertisers would refer to their connections with Paris, Europe's fashion capital at the time—even though Anglomania and the taste for dresses '*à l'anglaise*' and exotic fabrics were gaining ground in the 1780s.[40] A few years before the Revolution, *Dame* Boquet, who lived on Place Grenette in Grenoble's town centre, placed an advertisement describing the quality and 'modishness' of her supply of Parisian and English gauze, aprons, scarves and ribbons as being 'of a much higher quality than those made in Lyon'.[41] Paris was clearly the most important source of luxury and fashion items, and by emphasising their connections with the capital, provincial shopkeepers could attract their aristocratic and female clientele with the latest Parisian *folies*. Although it is hard to say whether the advertisements were actually written by those selling the products and services in question, they rarely targeted one sex rather than another. Moreover, as noted by Hannah Barker in her research on Northern England towns, '[W]omen advertisers did not appear more shy of promoting their businesses than men'.[42] On the contrary, female hairdressers, embroiderers and milliners insisted on their perfect technical skills and *savoir-faire* ('she flatters herself of perfectly executing . . .', 'she has the secret of . . .') and occasionally referred to the 'satisfaction' of potential users. Where prices were mentioned, both men and women advertisers offered various rates—indicating a wide range of clients—and referred to their modest prices (with a vague '*à juste prix*'). Rarely did the advertisements provide specific prices, but in 1784 Widow Mercier claimed that she 'whitens and renovates all sorts of calicos, giving them lustre and colour as if they were just from the factory': Her advertisement provided a detailed list of prices for each item, such as dresses and aprons.[43] This type of advertisement appeared more and more frequently during the last decade of the Old Regime and was more often written by male itinerant merchants or by women living in Grenoble who might be trying to earn a living by 'renovating' fabrics or furniture. Far from appealing to the aristocrats' taste for luxury, they reflect growing consumer interest in more 'ordinary' goods that were becoming socially indispensable—tapestries, paintings, lace, silk or cotton fabrics and so on—and which had to be made to last.

ALTERNATIVE DISTRIBUTION NETWORKS: NEW COMMERCIAL OPPORTUNITIES

While police records and advertisements help us to know more about the new economics of taste in eighteenth-century towns, they also shed light on alternative distribution networks for luxury goods, from legal trade to parallel markets. Itinerant merchants and pedlars appeared to play a crucial role in the sale of new luxury items and were frequently allowed to offer goods in the town for a specified period, usually a few days. Applications for renewal of their permits, which increased substantially during the last decades of the Old Regime, provide valuable information on the growing variety of objects on sale in Grenoble: umbrellas and silk parasols mainly from Auvergne, German carpets, lace and ribbons from Switzerland and from Velay and Forez in the Massif Central, jewellery, buckles, snuffboxes and accessories for hats and headdresses.[44] In most cases, itinerant merchants were restricted to wholesale trade in order to protect local merchants from possible competition, and pedlars were allowed to supply local shopkeepers and act as intermediaries between shopkeepers and manufacturers.[45] As shown by Laurence Fontaine's seminal work, most pedlars were members of extensive family networks, usually emigrants who had succeeded in opening up a shop in the city. However, it is difficult to find traces of women involved in these networks in the town and, in particular, contributing to the rapidly growing market for luxury goods and novelties. To date, the records contain only a few cases of applications submitted by a travelling merchant and his wife: One such couple came from Tours and asked for a temporary licence to sell 'little sugar sweets'.[46]

In the town, 'the boutique and peddling world interpenetrated at all levels'.[47] On the one hand, mercers and drapers, together with second-hand clothes dealers (*fripiers*) who had formed a corporation, regularly complained about 'foreign' pedlars and Jewish merchants, accusing them of reselling stolen or lower quality goods without paying fees to the guilds. These pedlars were largely tolerated by the police authorities and, above all, by the Dauphiné Parliament, a strong advocate of economic liberalism rather than regulated trade.[48] On the other hand, local shopkeepers—who frequently came from the ranks of itinerant merchants—used male and female pedlars and subcontractors to distribute their goods throughout the town, which confirms the lucrative nature of this market and illustrates the complex ways in which luxury goods circulated.[49]

The glovemaking industry in France, which expanded dramatically during the eighteenth century, offers a particularly interesting example of female involvement in the second-hand market. Controlled by the glovemakers' guild, this was in fact a strongly feminized trade, involving masters' wives, women from the local poorhouse and repentant prostitutes (*filles repenties*) working in convent-supervised workshops. This sector also employed many thousands of rural and urban women predominantly for sewing and embroidering, two tasks that were considered to be specifically feminine and therefore paid at half the rate for men. In 1775, this workforce produced about 100,000 dozen pairs of gloves for customers in Lyon and Paris, as well as for the international market in the rest of Europe, Russia and North America. Made principally of lambskin, a highly prized leather, often dyed in fashionable colours and decorated with ribbons or gold and silver embroideries, they could be sold for a small fortune—probably well above the average price of 13 *livres* per dozen mentioned in 1787 by the Inspector of Factories for Dauphiné (*Inspecteur des manufactures*). Grenoble's glovemakers deliberately targeted a growing market for these luxury items among high-ranking women keen to obtain perfumed long gloves and fans to match their dresses and men whose military and ceremonial uniforms included gloves. As in the Lyon silk industry, women in the glovemaking sector were known to spirit away or buy back second-rate pieces at lower prices in order to resell them through pedlars and dealers in the second-hand clothes trade. They were also suspected of working clandestinely for 'foreign' glovemakers, a practice strictly forbidden by the local guild.[50]

As indicated by the wide range of advertisements published in *Les Affiches*, this lively second-hand market went hand in hand with a booming market in lost-and-found and stolen goods. Both were at the heart of a grey economy that contributed to the social redistribution of luxury goods and to the promotion of new appearances.[51] Umbrellas, snuffboxes, jewellery, watches and buckles were among the objects most frequently advertised in the lost-or-stolen columns: Among other items of interest stolen from the *Demoiselles* Codé's millinery shop in Grand Rue on the night of 18 September 1781 was a vast array of lace, ribbons and pieces of fabrics.[52] Finally, *Les Affiches* also published announcements of auctions and lotteries used by merchants to reduce their stock of luxury goods. In April 1732 Sieur François Larivière, a Parisian jeweller who had been peddling in the province over the previous six months, was granted permission to arrange a dice lottery 'in order to facilitate the sale of his goods' which consisted of paintings, mirrors, clocks, swords, knifes, coffee mills, silverware and 'other interesting and very fashionable items'.[53] In February 1739, *Demoiselle* Rose Allioud, 'female merchant in Grenoble', sold 948 lottery tickets (at 12 sous each) for 12 prizes described as handkerchiefs, ivory fans, embroidered cuffs, silk scarves, lace and artificial bouquets of flowers.[54]

Even in a provincial town like Grenoble, the growing luxury market created new business prospects for many men and women, whether fixed or itinerant merchants, operating at all levels in the fashion cycle.[55] It also opened up opportunities for small-scale criminal activities by women, especially at a time when they had few chances of entering the official market through membership of the guilds. Not surprisingly, reports by police commissioners mention many cases of women working illegally as seamstresses, as wigmakers and hairdressers or, less frequently, as breeders of silkworms.[56]

A GENDERED BLACK MARKET FOR LUXURY GOODS?

Probably less well known are the various roles that women played in the highly gendered black market for calicos, which was expanding in the Dauphiné during the first half of the eighteenth century. The arrival of Asian goods, and more specifically cotton textiles, and their impact on the European fashion market during the seventeenth and eighteenth centuries has been widely investigated by historians.[57] In France, calicos became very fashionable during the last decades of the seventeenth century, as we can see in Molière's play *Le Bourgeois gentilhomme* (1670). The spectacular interest in cotton textiles brought to France by the French East India Company quickly encouraged French manufacturers of silk, linen and woollen cloth to call for an embargo on imported Indian cottons. Opponents of calico importers described Indian textiles as a threat to the national industry and claimed that they caused excessive cash outflows and widespread unemployment among male weavers. In October 1686, Louis XIV accepted the merchants' arguments in favour of prohibition and issued a royal decree—the first in a long series—banning the import, production and use of painted or printed calicos. But demand for cotton textiles was already well established in French society, and a black market in calicos flourished in many provinces until the embargo was lifted in 1759 following a long debate on free trade, known as the *querelle des toiles peintes* (dispute over painted cloth).[58]

The introduction of the ban on imports of white cotton in 1709 led to the emergence of networks of smugglers and illegal fabric-printing workshops supplying the black market. Given its geographical and administrative situation as a border province, the Dauphiné lay at the crossroads for numerous illicit trafficking activities. The largest of these networks was probably centred on Geneva and several other Swiss towns (Lausanne, Neuchâtel and Basel) where French calico printers had taken refuge after 1686.[59] The main sources of information on the black market are statements of confiscations drawn up by the Intendant's Office between 1736 and 1759.[60] These documents mention two main types of offences: wearing cotton clothes, punishable by a fine, and importing, receiving and selling black market calicos, severely penalized by fines up to 3,000 pounds, sentences to the galleys for men and exile for women.

The first conclusion is that women were more likely to be convicted for wearing printed cotton fabrics outside of their homes: Of the forty-one confiscations between October 1736 and July 1739, thirty-eight involved women. The offending articles were mainly colourful handkerchiefs, aprons, and dresses, but also included blouses, petticoats and bonnets. People in all social categories, from high-ranking women to servants, were interested in wearing calicos—from authentic Indian painted cotton textiles to popular imitations—which the wide range of prices and quality made possible. In 1729, the Inspector for Industry in the Dauphiné, Boutillier, reported that in Grenoble 'calicos were worn in public by both upper-class women and simple *bourgeoises*' and that 'even servants wore cotton aprons'.[61] In French provinces, just as in Paris or England at the same period, fashion was not limited to upper-class women.[62] Middle- and lower-class buyers were also good customers for contraband calicos. In many cases, women arrested in the Dauphiné were married to craftsmen and shopkeepers: bakers, grocers, carpenters, tailors, shoemakers, etc. In their defence, others spoke of their 'extreme poverty' and were therefore exempted from fines, suggesting that there might have been a market in second-hand cotton clothes for poor customers; on the other hand, it appears that confiscated clothing was only described as 'new' in two cases. Moreover, records of confiscations in small and medium-sized towns such as Gap and Embrun in the southern part of the province and even in market towns such as Veynes or Tallard show that the market for calicos was far from limited to the provincial capital.[63]

Historians of the fashion and luxury markets have raised three questions about the importance of calicos. First, are calicos 'luxury goods' when they were worn by people in all social classes? Maxine Berg's analysis of the concept of semi-luxury goods allows us to qualify these novelty consumer goods as exotic in style but 'produced and traded at a level which made them available not just to traditional elites, but to the rapidly expanding middling and urban populations of Europe'.[64] In this sense, calicos can be associated with goods that Jan de Vries calls 'new luxuries', as opposed to 'old luxuries' acquired by aristocrats to reinforce their social superiority.[65] Second, the desire for calicos, as shown in the records of confiscations, cannot simply be dismissed as emulation, which is, according to McKendrick, the driving force of fashion, although his analysis has been strongly contested.[66] Smith's suggestion that the fashion for calicos as *substitute status commodities* was linked to a growing interest in gentility is also not very satisfactory in this case.[67] More prosaic explanations for the growing black market in calicos can be suggested: They were lightweight and colourful (two qualities seen as very tasteful during the eighteenth century, according to Roche), about 20 per cent cheaper than equivalent fabrics, easier to wash, and therefore long lasting, economical and convenient. Third, the central role of women in the textile and fashion market, clearly evidenced in contemporary writings and in historical studies, is confirmed here.[68] Increasing demand for cotton offered women opportunities for entering the market, not only as active and influential customers but also as participants in the distribution and production of printed calicos.

Taking a broader perspective, contraband calico was brought in by large bands of smugglers, either acting for themselves (such as the famous bandit Mandrin) or for established merchants or members of Grenoble's Parliament.[69] Unsurprisingly, given the restrictions on their legal status and their right to engage in economic activities, women seldom appear in this group of major traders in contraband. Very few women were condemned by Valence's famous Commission, which was established in 1733 specifically to hear cases against smugglers and had a reputation for severity.[70] However, in border towns such as Le Pont-de-Beauvoisin on the frontier between Dauphiné and Savoy, which were obviously a hub for smuggling networks, and also in Grenoble and other towns, women were frequently hired at the end of the chain as intermediaries in handling and dealing in contraband goods.[71] In 1757, Jacques Pont and his wife, who were suspected of selling calicos in Grenoble on a large scale, were accused of hiring Thérèse Caillat, a female pedlar, to hawk 15 *aunes* of cotton fabrics.[72]

Among the women found guilty of handling or reselling calicos on the black market (a third of cases), many were widows or spinsters: For instance, Widow Dimanche was found guilty of handling 73 *aunes* of cotton fabrics in Grenoble in September 1758. Did she intend to resell the fabrics in smaller quantities or to make up pieces of calico and handkerchiefs for the black market? In the latter instance, prohibition made it possible for poor women to earn a little money by entering the market and exercising a traditional feminine craft to meet growing demand for cotton clothing. Smuggling of cotton was sometimes linked to other contraband goods such as tobacco or, more interestingly, implements used for dying and painting fabrics. They show that women could set up clandestine workshops for manufacturing calicos in their homes, possibly managing a small cottage industry that would have served to employ other women or men. In September 1752, 21 rolls of painted canvas, 38 stencils with various designs, 21 paintbrushes and three platters filled with ground colours were found in Widow Vaillet's house in Grenoble.[73] Several arrests were made of widows or women who appear to have been spinsters, sometimes living in the same house as a way to pool their resources, as can be observed in other contexts.[74] Smuggling and reselling contraband calicos and printing or dying banned cotton fabrics were probably, for most women participating in the black market, part of a range of makeshift and pluri-active strategies involving both legal and illegal activities in order to survive poverty. However, these female clandestine businesses were small compared to those run by men. The largest seizure was carried out in the home of Antoine Gilibert: 150 wooden moulds 'in various shapes and designs for use in painting canvas and 12 *aunes* of the said canvas which the said Gilibert had made'.[75] The underground market for calicos thus appears to have been profoundly gendered, involving very few women at the macro level, while their presence in the micro-spaces within and around the towns was dramatically more significant.

CONCLUDING REMARKS

The growing luxury and semi-luxury markets created in Grenoble, as in most European towns at the same time, a wide range of business opportunities for many men and women, on both the legal and the informal or illegal side of the urban economy that were not completely cut off from the legal trade and deserve to be more systematically scrutinized. Demand for luxury goods was probably in itself a powerful incentive for fraud, especially within the capital of a border province at a time of prohibition. From that perspective, one cannot simply define luxury or semi-luxury goods according to how they circulated or the places where they were sold, since fixed and itinerant, licit and illicit retail circuits were frequently imbricated: Expensive handmade Indian calicos could be illegally introduced into the kingdom and silverware offered for raffles, whereas buttons and combs were legally sold by mercers who had themselves strong and sometimes conflictual relations with the world of peddlers.

In a town with strong administrative offices, the presence of a large number of *bourgeois* and noble consumers encouraged the development of specific crafts and trades—most of them mostly male—while the growing glovemaking and fashion industry provided new opportunities for female employment. However, gender played an important part in structuring women's work both in the licit and the illicit economy, condemning many women to act at the tail end of the chain, whereas men's labour seemed to have be more affected by their social status. While women held real buying power and agency as consumers of fashion, they encountered contrasting reactions to their employment in the luxury trades and often had to fight to be accepted in a male-dominated corporate world, as shown in the case of the seamstresses. In the last decades of the Old Regime, however, the existence of well-established *marchandes de modes* with shops on the principal streets and squares of the city centre, as well as the numerous advertisements published by female merchants in *Les Affiches du Dauphiné*, demonstrate that, far from being systematically condemned to second-hand or clandestine activities, some women could become really successful within the fashion and luxury market by using the same new business strategies as men and, over time, enjoy the same visibility on the urban stage. From this perspective, the spread of fashion as both an urban and a feminine concern contributed, by empowering some female economic actors, to the shift of gender constraints and ideologies.

NOTES

1 UMR 7303 TELEMME (CNRS-Aix Marseille Université) paid for the translation into English of this chapter, while Caroline Mackenzie put all her linguistic talents in this work.

2 John Brewer and Roy Porter, eds, *Consumption and the World of Goods* (London: Routledge, 1993); Daniel Roche, *The Culture of Clothing. Dress and Fashion in the Ancien Régime* (Cambridge: Cambridge University Press, 1994); Annick Pardailhé-Galabrun, *The Birth of Intimacy: Privacy and Domestic Life in Early Modern Paris* (Philadelphia: University of Pennsylvania Press, 1991).

3 For a recent overview, see Natacha Coquery, *Tenir boutique à Paris au XVIIIe siècle. Luxe et demi-luxe* (Paris: CTHS, 2011).

4 Maxine Berg, 'New Commodities, Luxuries and their Consumers in Eighteenth-Century England', in *Consumers and Luxury: Consumer Culture in Europe 1650–1850*, ed. Maxine Berg and Helen Clifford (Manchester: Manchester University Press, 1999), 63–85.

5 Jean-Claude Daumas and Marc de Ferrière le Vayer, 'Les métamorphoses du luxe vues d'Europe', *Entreprises et Histoire* 46 (2007): 6–16; Patrick Verley, 'Essor et déclin des industries du luxe et du demi-luxe au XIXe siècle', in *Le luxe en France du siècle des 'Lumières' à nos jours*, ed. Jacques Marseille (Paris: ADHE, 1999), 107–23; Cissie Fairchilds, 'The Production and Marketing of Populuxe Goods in Eighteenth-Century Paris', in *Consumption*, ed. Brewer and Porter, 228–48.

6 René Favier, *Les villes du Dauphiné aux XVIIe et XVIIIe siècles* (Grenoble: Presses universitaires de Grenoble, 1993), 285–86.

7 Archives municipales de Grenoble (AMG), HH 42 (22 April 1727, May 1784).

8 Known as *rôles de repartition*, these identified members' contributions to the payment of taxes. AMG, HH 42 (16 April 1718, 22 April 1727, May 1784).

9 Archives départementales de l'Isère (ADI), 2 C 510 (1739).

10 ADI, 13 B 537 (31 March 1733).
11 ADI, 13 B 572 (18 February 1751).
12 ADI, 13 B 594 (31 December 1759).
13 Bibliothèque municipale de Grenoble (BMG), Fonds ancien dauphinois, Q 957 (26 March 1781).
14 René Favier, '"Faiseurs de rien, vendeurs de tout". Les merciers de Grenoble au XVIIIe siècle', in *La boutique et la ville. Commerces, commerçants, espaces et clientèles XVIe–XXe siècle*, ed. Natacha Coquery (Tours: Publications de l'Université François Rabelais, 2000), 99–112.
15 Carolyne Sargentson, 'The Manufacture and Marketing of Luxury Goods: The Marchands Merciers of Late Seventeenth- and Eighteenth-Century Paris', in *Luxury Trades and Consumerism in Ancien Régime Paris. Studies in the History of Skilled Workforce*, ed. Robert Fox and Anthony Turner (Aldershot: Ashgate, 1998), 99–137.
16 Favier, *Les villes du Dauphiné*, 369, 380–82.
17 Favier, '"Faiseurs de rien"', 100.
18 Jennifer M. Jones, *Sexing la Mode: Gender, Fashion and Commercial Culture in Old Regime France* (Oxford: Berg, 2004), 5. For a deeper investigation of milliners and mantuamakers, who were at 'the top end of the needle trades', see Simonton's chapter in this book.
19 ADI, archives de l'Hôpital de Grenoble, H 690–692 (1758–1773).
20 These source materials are currently under examination in Lyon and Grenoble.
21 AMG, FF 66 (26 April 1786, 30 January 1788).
22 Laurence Fontaine, *L'économie morale. Pauvreté, crédit et confiance dans l'Europe préindustrielle* (Paris: Gallimard, 2008), chapter 3; Natacha Coquery, *L'hôtel aristocratique: le marché du luxe à Paris au XVIIIe siècle* (Paris: Publications de la Sorbonne, 1998), 163; Clare H. Crowston, *Fabricating Women: The Seamstresses of Old Regime France, 1675–1791* (Durham: Duke University Press, 2001), 164–68.
23 Crowston, *Fabricating Women*, 68; Coquery, *L'hôtel aristocratique*, 58.
24 ADI, 2 C 88 (10 August 1776). Unfortunately, no more information has been found about the destiny of milliners' guild in Grenoble after Turgot's disgrace in August 1776.
25 AMG, FF 56 (18 July 1767).
26 Crowston, *Fabricating Women*, 339.
27 AMG, HH 42 (1727); FF 44 (15–20 October 1741). Archives municipales de Lyon, 1 C 305 267; Crowston, *Fabricating Women*, 341–42. See also, Deborah Simonton, 'Apprenticeship: Training and Gender in Eighteenth-Century England', in *Markets and Manufactures in Early Industrial Europe*, ed. Maxine Berg (London: Routledge, 1991; reissued in Routledge Revivals, 2013), 227–58.
28 Crowston, *Fabricating Women*, 197.
29 ADI, 2 C 87 (1776).
30 Daniel Roche, 'Between a "Moral Economy" and a "Consumer Economy": Clothes and Their Function in the Seventeenth and Eighteenth Centuries', in *Luxury Trades*, ed. Fox and Turner, 219–29, here 226. See also Simonton's chapter in this book.
31 Crowston, *Fabricating Women*; Jones, *Sexing la Mode*; Roche, *Culture of Clothing*, 303–4.
32 AMG, FF 56 (15 April and 23 July 1772). See also FF 52 (25 November 1775).
33 Berg and Clifford, eds, *Consumers and Luxury*; Sara Maza, *The Myth of the French Bourgeoisie: An Essay on the Social Imaginary 1750–1850* (Cambridge, MA: Harvard University Press, 2003), 44–52.

34 Laurence Fontaine, *History of Pedlars in Europe* (Cambridge: Cambridge University Press, 1996). But see Carol Gold, 'On the Streets and in the Markets: Independent Copenhagen Saleswomen,' in *Female Agency in the Urban Economy, Gender in European Towns, 1640–1830*, ed. Deborah Simonton and Anne Montenach (New York: Routledge, 2013), 35–55.
35 AMG, FF 52 (28 November 1774); FF 53 (9 April 1779); FF 54 (31 August 1785); FF 55 (20 December 1786).
36 AMG, FF 46 (22 May 1753); FF 47 (11 May 1758); FF 51 (1 December 1773).
37 AMG, FF 55 (2 August 1787).
38 Maxine Berg and Helen Clifford, 'Selling Consumption in the Eighteenth Century. Advertising and the Trade Card in Britain and France', *Cultural and Social History* 4 (2007): 145–70; Dries Lyna and Ilja Van Damme, 'A Strategy of Seduction? The Role of Commercial Advertisements in the Eighteenth-Century Retailing Business of Antwerp', *Business History* 51 (2009): 100–21; Clemens Wischermann and Elliott Shore, eds, *Advertising and the European City: Historical Perspectives* (Aldershot: Ashgate, 2000).
39 René Favier, 'Les *Affiches* et la diffusion de l'innovation en Dauphiné à la fin du XVIIIe siècle (1774–1788)', *Annales du Midi* 97 (1985): 159–67; Gilles Feyel, 'Négoce et presse provinciale en France au XVIIIe siècle: méthodes et perspectives de recherche', in *Cultures et formations négociantes dans l'Europe moderne*, ed. Franco Angiolini and Daniel Roche (Paris: Editions de l'EHESS, 1995), 439–511; Colin Jones, 'The Great Chain of Buying: Medical Advertisement, the Bourgeois Public Sphere, and the Origins of the French Revolution', *American Historical Review* 101 (1996): 13–40.
40 Coquery, *L'hôtel aristocratique*, 102–10; Crowston, *Fabricating Women*, 43; Maxine Berg, *Luxury and Pleasure in Eighteenth-Century Britain* (Oxford: Oxford University Press, 2005), 197, 248.
41 *Affiches, annonces et avis divers du Dauphiné* (20 January 1786).
42 Hannah Barker, *The Business of Women. Female Enterprise and Urban Development in Northern England 1760–1830* (Oxford: Oxford University Press, 2006), 83; Manfred Görlach, 'A Linguistic History of Advertising, 1700–1890', in *Sounds, Words, Texts and Change*, ed. Teresa Fanego, Belén Méndez-Naya and Elena Seoane (Amsterdam: John Benjamins Publishing Co., 2002), 83–104, here 92.
43 *Affiches* (22 October 1784).
44 AMG, FF 50 (24 March 1766, 22 June 1769); FF 51 (30 April 1771, 8 May 1772); FF 52 (7, 9, 11, 12, 18, 19 and 23 July 1774, 9 January 1776). See also the *Affiches*.
45 Fontaine, *History of Pedlars*; Laurence Fontaine, 'The Circulation of Luxury Goods in Eighteenth-Century Paris: Social Redistribution and an Alternative Currency', in *Luxury in the Eighteenth Century: Debates, Desires and Delectable Goods*, ed. Maxine Berg and Elizabeth Eger (Basingstoke: Palgrave, 2003), 89–102.
46 AMG, FF 52 (9 August 1774).
47 Fontaine, 'The Circulation', 91.
48 Favier, '"Faiseurs de rien"', 106–8. AMG, FF 45 (6 November 1747); FF 49 (18 February 1763); FF 54 (9 November 1784).
49 AMG, 13 B 594 (31 December 1759), 13 B 616 (3 January 1769). BMG, Q 957 (26 March 1781).
50 AMG, FF 52 (29 August 1775). ADI, B 2479 (21 May and 9 June 1727). BMG, Fonds dauphinois, 27738: *Règlement et statut pour le corps des maîtres gantiers de la ville de Grenoble* (Grenoble: J. Cuchet, 1749); Xavier Roux, *La corporation des gantiers de Grenoble avant et après la Révolution*

(Grenoble: G. Dupont, 1887); Daryl M. Hafter, *Women at Work in Preindustrial France* (University Park: The Pennsylvania State University Press, 2007), 135–42.

51 Roche, 'Between a "Moral Economy" ', 226.

52 *Affiches* (21 September 1781).

53 AMG, FF 43 (16 April 1732).

54 AMG, FF 43 (12 February 1739). See also *Affiches* (10 March 1780; 17 August 1781; 1 February, 17 May and 21 June 1782).

55 Laurence Fontaine, 'The Exchange of Second-Hand Goods between Survival Strategies and "Business" in Eighteenth-Century Paris', in *Alternative Exchanges. Second-Hand Circulations from the Sixteenth Century to the Present*, ed. Laurence Fontaine (New York: Berghahn Books, 2008), 97–114.

56 AMG, FF 52 (1 August 1776); FF 57 (11 June 1733); FF 64 (17 November 1781); FF 65 (11 June 1783).

57 For a recent bibliography, see Giorgio Riello, *Cotton: The Fabric that Made the Modern World* (Cambridge: Cambridge University Press, 2013) and Beverly Lemire, *Cotton* (Oxford: Berg, 2011), especially Chapter 3, which explores socio-political issues relating to the gendered wearing of calico in eighteenth century England at a time when the emergence of popular fashion reshaped the country's economy and society.

58 Serge Chassagne, *La manufacture de toiles imprimées de Tournemine-lès-Angers (1752–1820)* (Paris: Klincksieck, 1971), 35–69; Edgar Depitre, *La toile peinte en France aux XVIIe et XVIIIe siècles: industrie, commerce, prohibitions* (Paris: M. Rivière, 1912).

59 Many were Calvinists who escaped from France after the Revocation of the Edict of Nantes in October 1685.

60 AD Isère, 2 C 101 (1736–1780). The king was represented by an intendant in each French province.

61 ADI, 2 C 100 (1729).

62 Philippe Haudrère, 'La contrebande des toiles *indiennes* à Paris au XVIIIe siècle', in *Tisser l'histoire. L'industrie et ses patrons XVIe–XXe siècle. Mélanges offerts à Serge Chassagne*, ed. René Favier, Gérard Gayout, Jean-François Klein, Didier Terrier and Denis Woronoff. (Valenciennes: Presses universitaires de Valenciennes, 2009), 169–82; Chloe Wigston Smith, ' "Callico Madams": Servants, Consumption, and the Calico Crisis', *Eighteenth-Century Life* 31 (2007): 29–55. In the English pro-wool pamphlets analysed by Smith, calico was attacked specifically because it undermined social differences and taste.

63 ADI, 2 C 100 (1729).

64 Berg, *Luxury and Pleasure*, 83.

65 Jan de Vries, *The Industrious Revolution: Consumer Behaviour and Household Economy, 1650 to the Present* (Cambridge: Cambridge University Press, 2008), 40–58.

66 Neil McKendrick, 'The Commercialization of Fashion', in *The Birth of a Consumer Society: The Commercialization of Eighteenth-Century England*, ed. Neil McKendrick, John Brewer and J. H. Plumb (London: Hutchinson & Co., 1983), 1–8; Lemire, *Cotton*, 43.

67 Woodruff D. Smith, *Consumption and the Making of Respectability 1600–1800* (New York: Routledge, 2002), 52.

68 Serge Chassagne, *Le coton et ses patrons. France, 1760–1840* (Paris: Ed. de l'EHESS, 1991), 22. Crowston, *Fabricating Women*; Jones, *Sexing la Mode*; Roche, *The Culture of Clothing*. Among contemporaries, see for instance Charles Louis de Secondat, baron de La Brède et de Montesquieu, *Lettres persanes* (Amsterdam: P. Brunel, 1721), and Louis-Sébastien Mercier, *Le Tableau de Paris*, 1781–1788 (Hamburg: Virchaux & Compagnie, Libraires).

69 See Anne Montenach, '"Uncontrolled Crossings": Gender and Illicit Economic Territories in Eighteenth-Century French Towns', in *Gendering Spaces in European Towns, 1600–1914*, ed. Elaine Chalus and Marjo Kaartinen (London: Routledge, 2015), forthcoming.
70 Archives départementales de la Drôme, B 1304 (1733–1771).
71 ADI, 2 C 101 (22 and 31 May 1739).
72 ADI, 2 C 101 (18 April 1757). An *aune* is about 1.5 meter.
73 ADI, 2 C 101 (29 September 1752).
74 ADI, 2 C 101 (18 September 1758, 20 March 1754, 19 January 1751).
75 ADI, 2 C 101 (11 June 1739).

4 Women in the Late Eighteenth-Century-Copenhagen Luxury Trades

Carol Gold

In 1784, the young Danish crown prince Frederik (later to be Frederik VI) took over personal control of the government in a palace coup against his father, King Christian VII, who was certifiably insane. This moment marked the beginning of a new 'reform era', filled with liberal reforms which were successful in midwifing Denmark's new capitalist economy. Danish historiography has tended to focus on the impact of these reforms on the agricultural sector, since this was the overwhelming basis of the Danish economy at the time. Equally important, one might argue, was the impact on the urban economy, which brought in the outside capital that helped to fuel these changes. Front and centre of this process was the royal residence and capital city of Copenhagen. With a total population of 100,000, about ten per cent of Denmark's population lived there, and mostly lived well.

These were boom times in Copenhagen. The city flourished on monies that came from the vibrant overseas trade, as well as the thriving agricultural sector. The port of Copenhagen was home not only to the Danish navy, but also to a large merchant marine. The Danish name of the capital city, *København*, literally means 'trade harbour'. Wealthy Copenhageners of the time engaged in bouts of conspicuous consumption, building lavish townhouses around the king's 'new square' [*Kongens Nytorv*]. Erich Erichsen, a merchant and shipowner, built one such house to live in with his wife, Johanne Wadum Black, after the fire in 1795 destroyed much of the city (see Figure 4.1). It is now the main headquarters of *Den Danske Bank*, one of the largest banks in Denmark.

Since Copenhagen was the royal residence and housed both an army and a navy base, the city had slightly more men than women, but women were interwoven throughout the city's economic activities. Women, although they could not be formal guild members, nonetheless often ran their own businesses and thus contributed to the good life of Copenhagen's 'golden age', and 'palmy days'.[1] This chapter focuses on women who were engaged in the luxury trade, that is, in providing the luxuries that enabled the 'golden' living. Since some of these women, such as Johanne Wadum Black, were at the top of the economic structure, they cannot be viewed as representative

Figure 4.1 Erichsen's Townhouse on Kongens Nytorv, Museum of Copenhagen.

of all women, but they can be seen as reflective of the *possible*. This is what women *could do*.

These women also reflect the intersection of the four elements of this chapter: town, luxury, gender and the economy. The issue is one of how they interacted. This chapter argues that 'luxury' was an important part of Denmark's transition to a modern capitalist economy by bringing goods and capital into the economy. Since these goods mainly arrived through the capital city of Copenhagen, they had a dramatic impact on the urban economy as well as on the face of the city. The Copenhagen economy, in turn, played a major role in this economic shift—and women played a significant part in this trade.

There are several sides to the 'luxury trade': production, distribution and consumption. This chapter deals with production and distribution. Although most consumers of luxury came from upper or wealthier classes, distributors and producers did not necessarily share in that wealth. Many of the women who produced fine clothes or gold jewellery bought by the upper classes barely made ends meet themselves. Despite dealing with a capital-intensive production (silk and gold cost money), they had little spare cash to spend on luxuries for themselves. Seamstresses, for example, hardly lived the good life of their customers, but were nonetheless important links in the transmission of luxury goods. They produced the luxury goods that others bought.[2]

LUXURY

Luxury is a social and historical construct, the specifics of which change over time and space. In the Danish case, Christian V's Danish Law of 1683 detailed items of absolute necessity at that time.

> It should be so arranged, that each for a reasonable value may purchase those goods, which the country's inhabitants have need of and which ought to be offered for sale in the towns . . . fresh beef, salted and dry fish, Danish beer and bread; similarly, to put a cheap charge on wine, salt and other items, nothing excepting, which merchants and artisans and others for their wares and work must have;[3]

Thus it is very clear that all Danes were entitled to the bare necessities, defined in 1683 as fresh beef, salt and dry fish, Danish beer (not imported) and bread, at a reasonable price. And they were entitled to the opportunity to buy these necessities. Wine, salt 'and other items, nothing excepting' were added, but additional charges were allowed on these. One may then start with the assumption that these were the necessities; anything else was a luxury.

Although Danes had an extensive debate on 'economic issues' at the end of the eighteenth century, the discussion about luxury (*overdaadighed*) was neither as extensive nor as liberal. The discussion on the economy dealt with the impact of possible agricultural reforms. Overwhelmingly this discourse, supported by the crown prince's reform government, favoured liberal reforms, which would sever the bonds between peasant and landlord and allow peasants title to their own land. This, writers asserted, would encourage the new farmer-owners ('self-owners', in direct translation of the Danish, *selvejere*) to improve their own property, which in turn would benefit the state's economy.

However, early treatises on luxury, those that appeared prior to the crown prince's coup in 1784, favoured the mercantilist idea that luxury was overindulgent, immoral, and bad for the country and should be regulated. Christian Sommerfeldt, a geographer and Danish civil servant (*Kammerraad*), for example, wrote in 1772: 'Can there be any doubt, that luxury . . . wastes industry and funds and additionally hinders people's happiness? Is it not therefore determined that the more a country overindulges, the less happy is its condition?'[4] Authors agreed that importing foreign goods was a bad idea. It sent money out of the domestic economy and encouraged unnecessary extravagance. Gold, silver, silk, wine, too many courses at mealtimes, fancy carriages—all were seen as unnecessary indulgences, which weakened the state and individuals.

The Guldberg government passed a sumptuary law in January 1783; this was the year before the crown prince's coup, so it is doubtful it was ever enforced.[5] But its provisions provide a guideline of what was considered luxury at the time. Basically, it aimed to promote domestic production, stop foreign imports and preserve the distinctions of rank. Gold, silver and silk were banned for an extensive series of uses—clothing, furniture, wagons, curtains, buttons. Imported furs and embroidery, foreign beer, wines and liqueurs, Italian and other flowers, foreign glass, porcelain and mirrors were prohibited. Dinners (noon meal) to which guests were invited might consist of no more than eight dishes plus two dessert dishes, although there could be unlimited domestic salads and fruits. At weddings, two additional dishes might be added and during a second day dancing was allowed, albeit with no food.[6]

An interesting gendering rears its head here as well. Several authors commented that 'luxury' made people 'soft and womanly', or 'cowardly and womanly'.[7] Hans Marinus Hemmeleff, a poet and playwright, started off by complaining that people were spending too much money just as the Napoleonic wars started and that they should really be thinking about saving money, since wars are expensive.

> That a country's monetary situation always gets worse with a war is obvious; but what can one say when it seems as though the *entire fair sex* has conspired with an exaggerated extravagance to destroy that part of the country's economy, which could undoubtedly have been saved with frugality [emphasis added].[8]

Twenty-two pages later he has convinced himself that not only is this waste all the fault of women, but that it leads to the immorality of prostitution, as young girls are lured into spending more than they have and so resort to prostitution to earn money. The way to stop this is to punish the women. 'No punishment is too harsh. To be flogged, branded and imprisoned for life, they deserve this'.[9] Hemmeleff makes crystal clear the contrast between stoic, frugal militaristic masculinity and soft, indulgent, unpatriotic femininity or luxury, to which others allude.

METHOD AND BACKGROUND

Given the somewhat fluid nature of luxury, women in the following fields will be discussed: merchants who imported overseas goods; women who worked with other imported goods, such as silk and cotton, tea and coffee; and, finally, those who used precious metals, such as goldsmiths, jewellers and watchmakers. One could, perhaps, also add wine, but since some wine from France was not considered to be a luxury, the distinction is difficult to research. This is, admittedly, a rather arbitrary list and somewhat dependent on available sources. But all of these trades dealt with materials upon which there was agreement that they were luxuries. There may be others as well (such as tobacco and non-French wine), but the trades mentioned certainly provide a beginning basis.

At least 3,000 women in Copenhagen engaged in some sort of independent business, in their own names, between 1740 and 1830. Their names show up in official records—tax records, censuses, guild records, city records, applications for licenses and permits.[10] This does not include women who worked for someone else, such as a husband, father, landlord or other employer, nor does it include women who did not need licenses, such as laundresses and people taking in boarders. It also does not include illegal, black or grey work.[11] The process will be to go back and forth between discussions of individuals and the groups of which they were a part.

In late eighteenth-century Denmark, married women were technically *femmes couvertes* who needed their husbands' permission to engage in business. However, the assumption at the time was that any woman who engaged in business had her husband's permission; otherwise it was up to him to object.[12] Widows were allowed to continue in the family property, both real estate and businesses, un-probated after their husbands' deaths (*at sidde i uskiftet bo*—literally, 'to sit in un-transferred possession'). The law allowed them to retain control of the property, and permission was almost always granted from guild or government authorities to carry on with husbands' businesses or to exchange it for another livelihood. Single women needed to apply for permission to act on their own, and usually got it, as did the handful of women who were divorced. What this meant is that it was legally possible and permissible for most women to act on their own. Many took advantage of this possibility, and probably at least ten per cent of Copenhagen's legal, registered economic activity was carried on by women.[13]

WOMEN IMPORTING LUXURY GOODS

The 'palmy days' of the late eighteenth century were completely dependent on overseas trade. In 1800, there were 327 merchant ships operating out of Copenhagen, with a total carrying capacity of 25,792 *kommercelæster*.[14] The Danish merchant marine was the fourth largest in Europe, and Ole Feldbæk estimates that 'Copenhagen, during its palmy period, was actually the city in Europe that had the largest per capita shipping and trade'.[15] Danish shipping interests spanned the world with overseas colonies or outposts in the West Indies (the US Virgin Islands), on the coast of Guinea and on the Indian subcontinent. In sum, Jens Vibæk concluded that 'overseas trade was the main pillar in the economic structure of the 18th century. . . . It was wholesale merchant trade and shipping which brought us our wealth'.[16]

Trade and shipping were closely intertwined. Indeed, part of the definition of being a 'merchant' (*grosserer*) was that one owned a ship or had a share in a ship. When the Merchants Society (*Grosserer-Societet*—GS) was founded in 1742, it included only 'registered merchants'. To be 'registered' one had to have 'citizenship' (*borgerskab*) as a merchant *and* own at least some share in a ship. In 1790, when GS formalized its structure and hired an executive director, there were sixty-eight registered merchants in the city of Copenhagen, of whom thirty-nine signed the Society's reorganization plan. By 1800, the numbers had grown to eighty merchants, forty-nine of whom were now members of GS.[17] There is a membership list from 1772 in the Society's minute book. Of the forty-nine members, three were women, all widows—Widow Cicilia Jørgensen & Company, Franz Hinr. Kreutzfeld's Widow and J.P. Schellenbeck's Widow (see Figure 4.2). Although these names never appear again and none of these women signed any of the documents, including meeting minutes, they were listed here along with the men, with no apparent distinctions.[18]

In 1771, three women paid taxes as merchants—Catarina Gustmeyer (or Gustmejer, of whom more later), Cicilia Jørgensen and Mrs Severin (?)

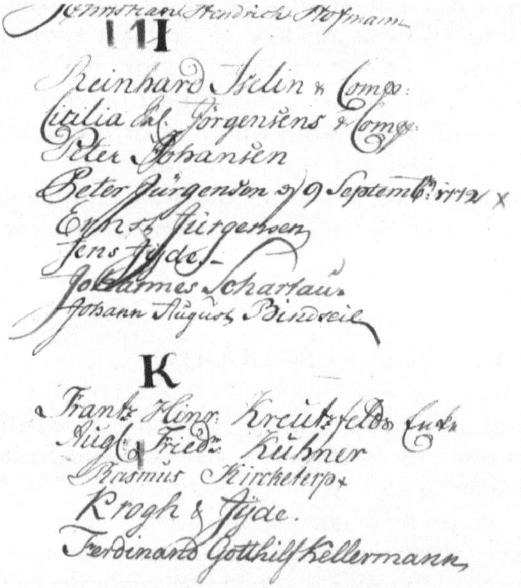
Johan Hendrich Hofmann
I
Reinhard Iselin & Comp:
Cicilia Sal. Jörgensens & Comp.
Peter Johansen
Peter Jürgensen 29 Septemb. 1772 x
Ernst Jürgensen
Jens Tyde
Johannes Schartau
Johann August Bindseil
K
Frantz Hinr. Kreutzfelds Enke
Aug. Friedr. Kühner
Rasmus Kircheterp
Krogh & Tyde.
Ferdinand Gotthilf Kellermann

Figure 4.2 Page from Grosserer-Societet *Forhandlingprotokol*, listing Cicilia Sal. Jörgensens & Comp. (second line under 'I') and Frantz Hinr. Krutzfelts Enke (first line under 'K'), 1772.

Kreusfelt (or Kreutzfeldt). All three were widows whose husbands had been members of the Merchants Society. Thirty years later, in 1801, tax records list eighty-nine people paying taxes as merchants, including two women—Charlotte Sophie Falck, a forty-three-year-old widow who was in business with her son and paid two portions in tax, and Margretha Elisabeth Perch, the forty-six-year-old widow of Jens Perch. Jens Perch, a tea merchant whose firm still exists, was an active member of GS; his widow continued the firm. This list does not include C.S. Black's Widow and Co., a company that owned three warehouses on Christianshavn and that was definitely in the wholesale merchant business as well. The Widow Black (Johanne Wadum Black) was no longer alive in 1801, since she had died the previous year, but her second husband, Erich Erichsen, continued the firm, still using her first husband's name.

Since luxury goods were often identified as anything coming into Denmark from overseas, foreign goods would, by definition, be luxury goods. Advertisements placed by 'C.S. Black's Widow and Company', show up frequently in *Adresseavisen*, a Copenhagen newspaper, which came out four times weekly. The paper was an eclectic mix of official notices, ship traffic, theatre notices and advertisements for just about everything.[19] 'C.S. Black's Widow and Company' advertised overseas goods for sale. On 9 January 1801, cotton goods were offered for sale from the ship *Marianne*, as well as advertising space on ships sailing both to and from the Danish West Indies.[20] They apparently also acted as agents, since in 1791 they advertised for anyone having business with the son of Isaac Benners, a planter who died on St. Croix.[21]

The widow C.S. Black is also listed in the 1801 tax records as owning three warehouses on Christianshavn and paying three and one-half portions self-employment tax, a very considerable amount, but she is not listed as living on Christianshavn, and in fact the 1801 census has no record of any Black (or Blach). However, Christen Schaarup Blach (or Black) was well known in the *Grosserer-Societet*. His father, Oluf Blach, was one of the founders of the Society in 1742. His son, Christen Schaarup (C.S.), was a member of *Grosserer-Societet*'s three-man executive body from 1776 until his death in 1781. He was also a director in *Asiatisk Compagni* and a member of the board of The Royal Islandic-Finmark Trade Society. At some point, C.S. married Johanne Wadum, who, when C.S. died in 1781, then became 'C.S. Black's widow'. Eighteen months after C.S.'s death, Erich Erichsen, an employee in C.S.'s company, married his boss's widow, Johanne, and took over the firm—an import-export/shipping company, now operated under the name of 'C.S. Black's Widow and Company'.[22] The firm was highly successful. Erichsen built a large house on Kongens Nytorv in Copenhagen, and by 1797 owned the third largest private shipping company in Denmark, with 13 ships and a total carrying capacity of 1,422 *kommercelæster*.[23] Although the shipping business ran into hard times during the Napoleonic Wars, Erichsen was able to transfer his primary business into money lending, where he was, again, highly successful, the Danish state being one of his main creditors. Meanwhile, Johanne died in 1800, but Erichsen continued to run the firm under the name of 'C.S. Black's Widow and Co'.[24]

It is difficult to sort out the business relationship between Johanne and her husband Erich. An earlier historian, Albert Fabritius, is convinced that Johanne Wadum Black Erichsen had nothing to do with running the company and claims Erichsen handled it alone. But his only evidence is implicit and circumstantial. If Erichsen had such a flourishing company after the death of his wife, Fabritius assumes that Erichsen must have been involved with the company before Johanne died as well.[25] But the firm continued with *Johanne's* name. Continuing the firm under the name of 'Black and Company' would make good business sense. The Blacks were well known in merchant and shipping circles and one would want to continue with the good will of the earlier company. But the name change to 'C.S. Black's Widow' would seem to imply that at some point between the death of her first husband and her remarriage Johanne was actually managing the company herself. And, if this were the case, why automatically assume she relinquished all control when she remarried? Maybe there was a partnership between the spouses.[26]

There is equal circumstantial evidence for a different possible scenario, one that has Johanne in change of the company under own her name. Johanne Wadum was born in Ålborg; her father was a grocer (*købmand*). It is not clear if the family moved to Copenhagen or if Johanne moved on her own, but she did come from a middle-class background. Middle-class girls often received an education commensurate with that of their brothers, as fathers expected them to be helpmeets for future husbands.[27] So, Johanne was probably *capable* of carrying on the family business, although that does not prove that she did. Marrying into the Black family would have been a step up socially.

It is clear that when C.S. Black died, *someone*, presumably Johanne, changed the company name to 'C.S. Black's Widow and Company'. It is also probable that Erichsen, in an early example of product branding, decided to continue the firm with the well-known name of 'Black', although that still does not explain why the term 'Widow' continued to be used after their marriage in 1784 and even after Johanne's death in 1800. And it is a reversal of the more common pattern of a widow disappearing into the name of her second husband or son—as, for example, Mrs. Kreutzfeldt did, who disappeared as Franz Hinrich's widow when she married Marius Gotthard Holm, also a member of GS.[28] Similarly, when her husband Laurentius Nicolas Cramer died in 1796, the widow Cramer announced to her associates that the firm would continue in her sons' names, as 'Cramer and Sons'. She signed the document, 'H.M. sal. [widow] Cramer'.[29] It would, of course, be equally interesting to know to what degree these women had been or continued to be involved in their husbands' businesses, but we know even less about them than about the Wadum-Erichsen connection.

Furthermore, in 1784, after Wadum and Erichsen had married, the signatures of both appear in GS's minute book, as 'pr.pr. C.S. Blacks Enke [Widow]' and 'E. Erichsen' (see Figure 4.3). This is the only time when both names appear. After this, 'C.S. Black's Widow and Co.' is signed when it is on behalf of the company, and 'E. Erichsen' when Erichsen signed as an individual, chair or member of the board. (Both formulations appear to be in Erichsen's hand.) However at this one point, when they were newly married, both names appeared, perhaps indicating a partnership.[30]

The Blacks, Wadums and Erichsens owned a lot of property in Copenhagen and were active in wealthy merchant and social circles. Their shipping and import business brought many luxury goods and much capital into the city. For at least some of the time, the business was owned outright by Johanne Wadum, the widow Black, and was most likely managed by her as well. It is also highly probable that after her second marriage she continued as a partner in the business with her name.

Madame Catarina Gustmeyer (or Gustmejer), *née* Sprich, (1710–1773) was a merchant and shipowner who specialized in supplying the Danish navy with timber. She inherited the firm on the death of her husband, Carl Hieronimus Gustmeyer, in 1756.[31] For several years, until successfully challenged in 1762 by Andreas Bodenhoff, the Gustmeyer firm held a monopoly on timber deliveries.[32] In 1771, nine years after the loss of the timber monopoly, the firm was still highly successful, and Madame Gustmeyer paid three portions self-employment tax as a wholesaler and timber merchant. The company, Gustmeyer and Bargum (Catarina's son-in-law) also owned a warehouse on Christianshavn, but paid no taxes on it.[33] In 1772, Gustmeyer sent a ship to the Virgin Islands with provisions to help the islands which had been devastated by a hurricane; the implication is that this was a charitable donation, which would attest to the wealth of the owner.[34]

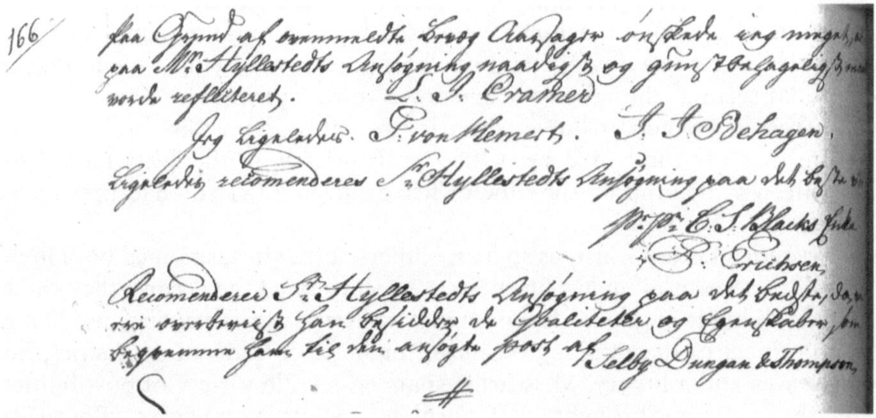

Figure 4.3 Signatures of 'C.S. Blacks Widow' and 'E. Erichsen'; Grosserer-Societet, *Forhandlingsprotokol, 1774–1790*, 1784, 166.

Gustmeyer was also one of the founders, with her son-in-law Bargum, of the Danish Guinea Company, a classic triangle trade operation. Ships were supposed to sail from Denmark to the coast of Guinea in Africa and buy gold, ivory and slaves, which would then be transported across the Atlantic to the Danish West Indies, where they would be exchanged for raw sugar to sail back to Denmark. The firm invested in a sugar refinery in Copenhagen as well as in three ships. For whatever reason, Catarina pulled out of the operation shortly after it started, although Bargum continued, albeit not very successfully. In 1775, he was forced to flee the country to avoid his creditors and died around 1800, perhaps in France.[35]

The firm of Gustmeyer and Bargum is a good example of the diversity that can hide under the category of 'merchant' or 'wholesaler'. While timber is easily categorized as a necessity, hardly a luxury, gold and ivory could definitely be considered luxuries. Sugar is more ambiguous. At some point it crossed from a luxury to a necessity, although probably not until the nineteenth century. According to Ole Hyldtoft, 'the use of sugar in Denmark in 1835 was still small', and so could still be considered a luxury.[36] As for slaves, difficult as it is to view human beings as commodities, they were seen as a necessity as labourers on West Indian plantations, but the products of their labour were luxuries—primarily sugar and tobacco.

Although not a widow, and with a title listed simply as '*Frøken*' (Miss), Frederica Louise Ernst (1714–1781) was also involved in overseas shipping and importing. In 1765 she petitioned the royal Commerce Department for permission to establish a manufactory in Denmark for cleaning and combing flax and hemp. The Commerce Department responded that she was 'a sensible and diligent woman' who had already received permission to control her own funds. At that time she owned a part interest in a warehouse, ships and a sugar plantation on St. Croix, all of which were involved in the slave trade. The Commerce Department granted Ernst permission for her factory, which employed nine cleaners, one sorter and one 'master'. Thirty-seven hand-operated machines were used for cleaning the hemp. In 1771, Ernst is listed as paying one and one-half portions self-employment tax, so it would seem as though her business was rather profitable. The next year, however, in financial trouble, she tried to call in her loans. In 1778, she wrote that her funds had been 'tied up fruitlessly in the West Indies' for seventeen years, and by the time of her death in 1781 she had apparently lost most of her money.[37]

Frederica Louise Ernst, as so many others at the time, spanned both luxuries and 'necessities' in her businesses. As ships plied the oceans, they transported all kinds of goods, depending on what was available. Flax and hemp, both critical to the shipping business, might be considered necessities, but sugar was still a luxury. Miss Ernst spanned a wide variety of possibilities, and the money she brought into Copenhagen while her businesses flourished undoubtedly helped the economy. However, like Erichsen and Bargum, her experiences proved overseas trade could be a risky business.

What these women—widowed, married or single—all have in common is that they were engaged in a capital-intensive, highly risky and, potentially, extremely lucrative trade, focusing mainly, although not exclusively, on luxuries. Theirs was the distributive part of the process; their firms imported goods, which were then sold to others (including many other women), who then either worked the goods or sold them in smaller portions to others. This was a trade that brought investment capital into the city, enabling it to flourish and develop into the principal urban space in northern Europe. Merchants also developed entire sections of the city, such as the warehouse district of Christianshavn, and built luxurious townhouses in downtown Copenhagen. This money literally helped to change the face of the city.

SMALL-SCALE DISTRIBUTORS OF IMPORTED GOODS

People who bought goods from wholesale merchants either broke them into smaller portions for retail sale as part of a long distribution chain, or acted as producers who changed goods in some fashion prior to resale, such as seamstresses who sold finished dresses or dyers who printed imported white cotton fabric. However, the line between distribution and production could become blurred when one included those who dispensed individual cups of coffee or tea in the new beverage shops.

The shortest distribution line was probably that of women who had licenses specifically to deal in imported goods, usually stipulated as 'foreign', 'east Indian', 'west Indian', 'Asian' or 'Chinese' goods, although sometimes specified as silk or cotton. These women did not have permission to transform goods in any way. They bought their wares from importers, probably from the stalls in the Stock Exchange Building, broke them into smaller portions and peddled them on the streets, in doorways or from their own homes. Husbands, insofar as there is any information on them, all worked or had worked independently of their wives. They included such professions as a customs inspector, a journeyman silk weaver, a dyer, a skipper and a distiller.[38] Although dealing in luxury goods and making them available to the city's clientele, these women probably were never able to use these goods themselves.

But eighteenth-century Copenhagen was also a centre of textile production. Silk weaving, which had reached a peak in the 1760s with 303 looms, was on its way out by the end of the century. It was being replaced by factories that dyed imported Indian cotton fabric, of which there were 16 in 1798, employing 598 people.[39] The widow Jensen, for example, paid taxes in 1771 on a 'silk factory', which she presumably inherited from her husband. Maria Margret Bentley received permission in 1795 to import silk for dying. She was exempted from having to pay customs on her imports, because, as her license said, there were no Danish products of an equal quality. The implication is that imported goods were superior to those manufactured locally.

Bentley paid a self-employment tax in 1801 of one-quarter portion. This was the smallest amount possible, but certainly more than those who paid no taxes. Anna Dorothea Grosman received permission in 1803 to continue her husband's profession of cotton printer after his death. She paid no taxes, so although cotton was an exotic, imported fabric, tax collectors apparently did not consider it significant enough to tax.[40]

Two women also received licenses in 1801 to trade in imported porcelain, along with imported tea. Although the Royal Danish Porcelain Factory had been producing quality china since the early eighteenth century, the imported variety had a certain cachet, absent from the domestic one. This was a classic example of a product that those who opposed 'luxury' thought should not be imported, but which was imported anyway. Tea and coffee were classic imported colonial goods, so much so that the current Danish word *kolonialvare*, which literally translates as 'colonial goods', today refers to groceries or dry goods. In 1801 seventy people paid taxes as dealers in tea and coffee; the same individuals almost always sold both. Additionally, twenty-seven people paid taxes as 'pourers' of tea and coffee, presumably tea and coffee shops for on-site consumption. Of these roughly one hundred taxpaying purveyors of colonial drinks, only five were women. But a much greater number of women were given licenses to trade in tea and coffee, although they did not pay taxes on this employment. Despite the fact that Dr Henrich Callisen, writing in 1807, claimed that 'no drinks are more common in Copenhagen than coffee and tea', he was not a fan of these new drinks and may have overestimated their use.[41] Mikkel Venborg Pedersen, in a recent book, *Luksus,* states that most recollections place the popular breakthrough sometime later, in the 1830s or 1840s.[42] In the early nineteenth century, coffee and teas were still exotic imported wares, which had not yet made it into private kitchens and dining rooms.

The women who were given permission for these shops were overwhelmingly widows. They returned the licenses their husbands had used for other businesses and in exchange received licenses for tea and coffee shops. This was true for the widows of a merchant, printer, coppersmith and ropemaker, for example. The licenses clearly stated that the widows could continue to distribute tea and coffee only so long as they remained unmarried, making it quite clear that authorities saw this as a means of support for them as widows. If they remarried, their new husbands were expected to support them. That may have been the theory; the reality was often different, in that two incomes were frequently required in order to keep up the desired lifestyle. The extent to which remarried women might have actually turned in these licenses is unknown.

Several of the licenses also stipulated that no dancing was to be allowed on the premises. Elsewhere—in England, for example—coffee houses were seen as an antithesis to local taverns or pubs. Coffee was the 'great soberer', and coffee houses were places of communication, where serious discussions took place, often of a political nature.[43] Disallowing dancing would help to solidify the difference between places of consumption of these new exotic beverages and older establishments where alcohol was served. Although coffee houses were quintessentially male space, women were nonetheless often present as owners and servers. As coffee houses sprang up across the Copenhagen landscape, they changed the nature of the city's geography, its social context and political content.

WOMEN WORKING WITH PRECIOUS METALS

People dealing in precious metals such as gold included goldsmiths, jewellers and watchmakers. In 1806, there were eighty-three master craftsmen in the goldsmith guild, of whom sixty-one paid self-employment taxes in 1801. There were thirty-eight full members of the watchmakers guild, but forty-six watchmakers paid taxes.[44] There was no separate guild for jewellers, but seven men paid taxes as jewellers in 1801. These were all men, since by definition women could not be guild members. However, three widows paid taxes as goldsmiths in 1771 and two in 1801, and two as watchmakers, one each in 1771 and 1801 (one married, one widowed). No women paid taxes as jewellers. So, although there were not many women in these fields, there were some, overwhelmingly widows who received permission to carry on their husbands' businesses and often to retain journeymen as well.

One example is Anne Marie Ruder, who in 1801 applied to the city of Copenhagen for permission to carry on her husband's watch business with the use of an apprentice. She wrote that she had accompanied her husband to auctions and that there was remaining stock which had not yet been sold, but for which she was now in debt. She appeared to be making the case that she was already a partner in the business. Her request was forwarded to the Watchmaker's Guild, which responded that it did not understand how keeping an apprentice would help get her out of debt, and returned the request to the city. The city responded that since she had previously acted as a second-hand junk dealer, albeit illegally, she should continue with that as a means to sell her stock. Finally, however, they issued her a license allowing her to continue her husband's business. It is uncertain what happened to the apprentice, although theoretically it would have been possible for him to continue in her employ. It should also be noted that her husband was a free master and not actually a guild member.[45] This seems at first blush like a case of everyone passing the buck, but the end result makes it clear that the city was, in the final analysis, more interested in allowing Ruder to be able to support herself and so willing to turn a blind eye to previous illegal activity and to circumvent guild authority.

One very important point to make in the case of all of these women is the fact that municipal authorities firmly believed that it was possible for unattached women to support themselves legally. The city acted wherever possible to encourage these women to engage in economic activity and thus not become recipients of municipal charity.

CONCLUDING THOUGHTS

The Crown Prince's liberal reform government introduced a series of laws which had the result of moving the Danish economy into a modern capitalist phase. These new laws included the abolition of *stavnsbaandet* (the requirement tying male peasants to their place of birth), financial help for both peasants and landlords in shifting title of agricultural land to the peasants who worked it and redistribution of the old strip farming into compact, geographically contiguous plots. New laws also encompassed citizenship for Jews, the abolition of the slave trade, the introduction of compulsory education (for both girls and boys) and an improved criminal code, as well as the elimination of the old mercantilist trade laws and the introduction of new laws that introduced something akin to free trade. The impact of these government actions was a new economy, which successfully weathered the 'bad times' and bankruptcy brought on by the Napoleonic Wars.

Women were engaged in many aspects of the luxury trade in late eighteenth- and early nineteenth-century Copenhagen. The initial expense required to get into business was not a hindrance—probably because they were mostly widows carrying on a family business and often borrowed money from family or social networks. Nonetheless, these were expensive, capital-intensive businesses, and there is no indication that these women had any difficulty or hindrance in administering or borrowing the funds necessary to compete successfully. Luxury trades brought money and goods into the Copenhagen economy. This availability helped to support a prosperous lifestyle and to create a new face to the city. Women played a role in this transformation.

Looked at from the woman's perspective, the possibilities inherent in the system were manifold. The fact that estates were *presumed* to transfer undivided to surviving widows reflects an implicit acceptance of the idea that not only was this possible, but actually probable. When a businessman died, his business was neither ended, broken up nor transferred automatically to the nearest male relative. It continued to be the property of his surviving widow. This reflects an acceptance of the idea that women could and would run businesses on their own. Women like Johanne Wadum, Catarina Sprich and Frederica Louise Ernst grew up knowing that they had the possibility and presumed ability to run businesses on their own. Even if, like Ernst, they never married, there was a societal acceptance of women's entrepreneurship. Women in business were so common that there was little if any discussion of it. When Hemmeleff attacked women and luxury, it was directed at women as consumers. He never commented on the idea that women might be involved in the luxury trades as producers or distributors. But women were there. They were to be found interwoven throughout the entire urban economy of preindustrial Copenhagen. In their roles as producers and distributors, as well as consumers, women helped to change the largest urban community in northern Europe.

NOTES

1 'Palmy days' was a term used at the time; 'golden age' is a term from literary and art history reflecting on the outpouring of creative activity at the time.
2 See the chapter by Deborah Simonton in this volume.
3 *Christian V Dansk Lov*, par. 3.4.8, 1683.
4 Christian Sommerfeldt, 'Tanker om Overdaadighed og dens Virkninger', (Sorøe: Jonas Lindgrens Enke, 1772), 7.
5 The Danish king Christian VII was incapable of ruling himself, and his reign was characterized by a succession of others controlling the government. From 1770–1772, Johan Friedrich Struensee ran the government and issued a series of liberal laws, including freedom of the press. Struensee was arrested and executed by a coalition led by Hereditary Prince Frederik, the Dowager Queen Julianne Marie and Ove Høegh Guldberg. Guldberg was a religious and economic conservative, believing in the redemptive value of religion and in mercantilism. This is the government that the crown prince overthrew in 1784, bringing in new social and economic ideas.
6 Jacob Henric Schou, ed., *Chronologisk Register over de Kongelige Forordninger og Aabne Breve*, vol. 8 (Copenhagen: L.C. Simmelkiær, 1784), 470–77.
7 Sommerfeldt, 'Tanker om Overdaadighed', 18; Ezechiel Gallatin, *Herr Ezechiel Gallatin's franske Prædiken om Overdaadighed*, trans. Frederik Lütken (Copenhagen: Nicolaus Møller, 1778), 15.
8 H. M. Hammeleff, *Om den overdrevne Luxus i Hovedstaden og de bedste Midler til at hemme den* (Copenhagen: Bogbinder Brænnings Forlag, 1818), 6.
9 Ibid., 20–21. See also the discussion in the introduction to this volume.
10 The city of Copenhagen paid the Danish government a specified amount every six months in *lieu* of quartering soldiers in private homes. The money to cover this was collected through a levy on individuals who were self-employed. It has not proved possible to discover how the tax was calculated, but it seems obvious that tax amounts corresponded roughly to perceived income levels.
11 See chapter by Anne Montenach in this volume for a discussion of women in illegal trades.
12 Inger Dübeck, *Købekoner og konkurrence* (Copenhagen: Juristforbundets Forlag, 1978), 218.
13 Seven per cent of those who paid self-employment taxes in Copenhagen in 1801 were women. Since women tended to be concentrated at the very lower end of the economic scale, among those who made too little to have to pay this tax, the percentage has been rounded up to ten.
14 One *kommercelæst* = 150 cubic feet or 2,600 kilograms.
15 Ole Feldbæk, *Danmarks Økonomiske Historie, 1500–1840* (Herning: Systime, 1993), 140, 147.
16 Jens Vibæk, 'Komiteens Oprettelese', in *Grosserer-Societet 1742–1942*, ed. Vilh. Lorenzen (Copenhagen: Gyldendal, 1942), 65.
17 Ibid., 68.
18 Grosserer-Societet, 'Forhandlingsprotokol' (Aarhus: Erhvervsarkivet, 1774–90), 19–23.

19 A riotous send-up of *Adressavisen* can be found in [anonymous], 'Skilderie af vore Tider', in *Et original Ugeblad* (Copenhagen: 1790–91), nr. 14 (April 1, 1791). Note the date: It is an April Fool's joke.
20 Hanberg, 'Kiøbenhavns Kongelig Adress-Contoirs Efterretninger', (Copenhagen: Morthorskee Enke & Comp. (?), 1801), Jan. 9, 1801, nr. 11.
21 Ibid., 1791, nr. 8.
22 They seem to have had no children. At least, there are none listed in the 1787 census, by which time Johanne was forty, so it seems unlikely, although theoretically possible. In 1787 Erich was thirty-six (*Folketælling*, Copenhagen, 1787). Erichsen brought first his brother and then his nephews into the company, further supporting the idea that he had no sons of his own. The nephews apparently ran the company into the ground and Erichsen went into bankruptcy in 1833. Harald Jørgensen, 'Erich Erichsen', in *Dansk Biografisk Leksikon*, ed. Sv. Cedergreen Bech (Copenhagen: Gyldenal, 1980), 205.
23 One *kommercelæst* equals 2,600 kg, so Erichsen's ships could carry 3.7 million kg.
24 Lorenzen, *Grosserer-Societet*, 138–39, 165, 147–48; Johannes Werner, *Christian Wilhelm Duntzfelt, En dansk Storkøbmand fra den glimrende Handelsperiode, Skildringer* (Copenhagen, 1927), 41; Jørgensen, '*Dansk Biografisk Leksikon*'.
25 Lorenzen, *Grosserer-Societet*. Daniel Rabuzzi repeats the assertion, stating that Wadum 'clearly played a subordinate role despite lending her name to the enterprise'. But his only sources are earlier historians. Daniel A. Rabuzzi, 'Fading Images, Fading Realities? Female Merchants in Scandinavia and the Baltic', *Social History/Histoire Sociale* 34 (2001): 359.
26 One is tempted to construct an entire novel around this couple. Johanne's first husband, C.S., was twelve years older than she was. Did she want to get married? Or was this a marriage of convenience between two successful middle-class families? Was Johanne encouraged by her parents to 'marry up'? Erichsen, on the other hand, was three years younger than Johanne—a modern man who signed his name with confidence and no unnecessary flourishes and allowed himself to be portrayed without a wig. Maybe the two fell in love while he was working for her first husband?
27 Carol Gold, *Educating Middle-Class Daughters* (Copenhagen: Museum Tusculanum Press, 1996).
28 The 1787 census lists a Severine Holm married to merchant Marius Gotthard Holm. This is probably Franz Hinr. Kreutzfeld's widow since there are two children, Johan Severin Kreutzfeld and Hinriette Jacobine Kreutzfeldt, both listed as children of the wife's first marriage. The ages are possible and it would not have been uncommon for Severine to marry someone from the same background.
29 Grosserer-Societet, 'Journalsager', (Aarhus: Erhvervsarkivet, 1795–7).
30 Ibid., 1781–90, 1792–4.
31 Harald Jørgensen, 'Carl Hieronimus Gustmeyer', in *Dansk Biografisk Leksikon*, 396. Most secondary accounts clearly credit Catarina Gustmeyer with being in charge of the firm. See also, Rabuzzi, 'Fading Images'.
32 Maria Ekberger, 'Andreas Bodenhoff: Leverandør til Søetaten i det 18. århundrede', *Maritim Kontakt* 13 (1989): 36–37.
33 København, 'Indkvarteringsmandtal', (Copenhagen: Stadsarkivet, 1771).
34 Jul. Schovelin, *Fra den danske Handels Empire—Forhold og Personer i det 18. Aarhundredes sidste Halvdel*, 2 vols. (Copenhagen: Det Nordiske Forlag, 1899–1900), 151.
35 Rabuzzi, 'Fading Images', 359–60; Eiler Nystrøm, 'Henning Frederik Bargum', in *Dansk Biografisk Leksikon*, 455.

36 Ole Hyldtoft, *Mad, drikke og tobak 1800–35* (Copenhagen: Museum Tusculanums Forlag, 2012), 136.
37 Kaj Foltmar, 'Frøken Frederica Louise Ernst, fabrikant og negotiant i Københavns florissante handelstid', *Historiske Meddelelser om København* (København: GAD, 1966), 81–135; København, 'Indkvarteringsmandtal'.
38 Carol Gold, 'On the Streets and in the Markets: Independent Copenhagen Saleswomen', in *Female Agency in the Urban Economy, Gender in European Towns, 1640–1830*, ed. Deborah Simonton and Anne Montenach (New York and London: Routledge, 2013), 35–55.
39 Feldbæk, *Danmarks Økonomiske Historie, 1500–1840*, 138.
40 Or cotton was a new enough import that government bureaucracy had not yet cottoned on to it (pun intended). See Montenach's chapter in this book discussing the impact of cotton, specifically textiles as a new 'luxury' commodity.
41 Henrich Callisen, *Physisk Medizinske Betragtninger over Kiöbenhavn*, vol. 1 (Copenhagen: Frederik Brummers Forlag, 1807), 468.
42 Mikkel Venborg Pedersen, *Luksus–Forbrug og kolonier i Danmark i det 18. århundrede* (Copenhagen: Museum Tusculanums Forlag, 2013), 213.
43 Wolfgang Schivelbusch, *Tastes of Paradise: A Social History of Spices, Stimulants, and Intoxicants*. (New York: Pantheon Books, 1992), 34, 52.
44 The discrepancy may be due to the existence of 'free masters', craftsmen who had training as journeymen and royal permission to establish themselves in business, but who were not formal guild members.
45 2. Hovedfag Københavns Magistrat. *Journalsager*. Copenhagen, filed 1801–1805. case nos. 249 & 331/1801.

5 Feminisation and the Luxury of Visual Art in London's West End, 1860–1890

Kemille Moore

In May of 1891, art critics and journalists Alice Meynell and Florence Fenwick Miller could have visited the Egyptian Hall at Piccadilly to view paintings by Louise Jopling at the annual exhibit of the Society of Lady Artists (Figure 5.1) and then walked north along New Bond Street to stop in and see watercolours by Helen Allingham at the Fine Art Society at 148 New Bond Street (Figure 5.2).[1] After possibly stopping for tea at one of the recently opened tearooms, they could continue northward, stopping at the Hanover Gallery at 47 New Bond Street to see recent work by the highly regarded French artist Rosa Bonheur on display along with works by Camille Corot and Constant Troyon.[2] It is also possible, though not specifically verifiable, that they may have been members of one of the newly opened ladies clubs in the area, such as the University Club for Ladies. While scenarios such as the one just described were no doubt commonplace in London's West End in the 1880s and 1890s, such outings were not only impossible, but in many respects unimaginable, just a few decades earlier.

The significant research done by Deborah Cherry, Lynne Walker and Erika Rappaport documents many important aspects of this change. Their investigations help to illuminate the complex picture of women shoppers, activists and artists moving through London's West End in the second half of the nineteenth century. The role of women in Victorian London as artists, students, collectors and 'matrons' has been carefully explored by Cherry in her 1993 monograph, *Painting Women, Beyond the Frame: Feminism and Visual Culture Britain 1850–1900*, and more recently in her 2003 article 'Going Places: Women Artists in Central London in the Mid-Century'.[3] Walker writes on women, space and architecture in Great Britain, primarily focusing on the nineteenth century, and Rappaport carefully explores and documents the role of women shoppers in London's West End in the nineteenth century.[4] Other scholars such as Lynda Nead, Colleen Denney and Susan Casteras have published on specific topics within this arena, such as London's physical transformation or the Grosvenor Gallery.[5] Additionally, two online research projects have recently helped to fill in many details of the art exhibition world during this era. The *London Gallery Project* by Pamela Fletcher and David Israel explores the dynamic world of the

Figure 5.1 Louise Jopling (1843–1933), *Phyllis*, oil on canvas, 1883, 52.0 cm × 44.0 cm. Russell-Cotes Art Gallery and Museum, Bournemouth.

Figure 5.2 Helen Allingham (1848–1926), *Cowdry Cottage*, watercolour, n.d., 34.5 cm × 38.8. The British Museum.

commercial gallery, and the *Exhibition Culture Project*, under the leadership of Patricia de Montfort, chronicles individual artists and their participation in commercial exhibitions during this period.[6] The *London Gallery Project* makes available critical information regarding the individual histories and practices of the West End's commercial galleries in both a textual and interactive geospatial format, allowing the user to not only understand a chronology of development, but also to see the geographical proximity of many firms. The *Exhibition Culture Project* provides a searchable database of artists' exhibition participation in these commercial galleries during the same period.

Taken together, the work of these scholars has given us a language and a framework for the complex exploration of how these women interacted with each other, art institutions and dealers, and with the urban environment of London in the nineteenth century. This body of work provides a solid foundation for understanding the changing status of women artists, the nature of shopping and the space of art in this unique neighbourhood. This knowledge can be deepened when one considers how changes in the production and consumption of luxury goods, especially art, along with the feminisation of the West End, contributed to a wide array of cultural transformations. The West End acted as a nexus for women artists to be both consumers and producers of objects of luxury in the unique urban neighbourhood of London's West End. Chief among the objects of luxury which these women produced and consumed were works of fine art, especially watercolour paintings. These women artists also participated in another type of luxury, the luxury of space itself. London's West End was increasingly being fashioned into an area where women could surround themselves with spaces dedicated to providing pleasing sensory experiences. The West End was not generally considered a place for a hasty shopping trip, but instead an area full of welcoming tea shops, elegant department stores and diverse art galleries where one was encouraged to linger. The West End offered an inviting environment full of fashion, beauty and elegance—a space of luxury.

As women became more important players in the domain of fine art, they became increasingly involved in a domain that—whether considered from the viewpoint of production or product—was diverse and full of luxury. Artists employ a variety of techniques while working in a variety of media to create a huge range of works of art—all of which might fairly be viewed as objects of luxury. Two-dimensional products such as paintings, prints and drawings, non-utilitarian sculptural works, utilitarian three-dimensional works such as fine porcelains, textiles and laces—all of these and more can meet any reasonable definition of luxury. Works in all of these media, for example, are likely to go well beyond the minimum standard of meeting some basic human need. Works of fine art are often rare or at least uncommon, either universally or, in the case of certain exotic works, because an object, although common in a distant land, has been imported in a limited quantity. Objects of art are often expensive or otherwise difficult to obtain.

At the same time, artistic works are generally put on display and thus can serve as symbols of status. Finally, creations of visual art are intended to please or otherwise stimulate the senses. The visual arts gives us items that are rare if not unique, special, coveted, precious, sensual—in short, luxurious. Although artistic expressions produced in many media have equal claim to the title of object of luxury, the focus of this chapter will be limited to the two-dimensional artistic expressions of oil paintings, watercolours, drawings and original prints (as opposed to reproductions), because these are the works of art that were exhibited in the galleries and institutions of fine art in London in the latter half of the nineteenth century.

The transformation of London's West End in the latter half of the nineteenth century not only is an important component in the story of women's changing role in the art world of Europe at the time, but also provides a compelling case study of how multifaceted complex changes in the structure of an urban neighbourhood can create an environment that opens opportunities for previously disenfranchised groups, in this case women artists, to become significant players in the consumption and production of luxury in an urban setting. This chapter examines how the West End of London became a unique urban experience for female artists and consumers of art as they experienced and participated in the intricacies of the producing, exhibiting, selling and buying of a time-honoured item of status and luxury—fine art.

THE CHANGING URBAN ENVIRONMENT: LONDON'S WEST END C. 1860–1900

In the decades between 1860 and 1910, the city of London underwent significant transformation in public works, transportation, consumer behaviour, gender definitions and the ways in which the visual arts were taught, exhibited, marketed and consumed. The role of gender, specifically the role of women as consumers and producers of art, provided new opportunities for women to participate in the art community and the larger network of the urban environment in which it was embedded. While the whole of London was a dynamically changing urban experience, the art and retail world—the locus of many aspects of the luxury trade—was focused in London's West End. Though the region referred to as 'West End' has no official boundaries, the descriptor is generally used to identify the fashionable area of central London west and north of Charing Cross and ending at Regent's Park in the north, with Hyde Park defining its western border. The West End encompasses many prominent neighbourhoods, such as Soho, Mayfair and Bloomsbury. This discussion focuses on the galleries, shops and other institutions within the south central portion of the West End around Piccadilly Circus, Oxford Street and New Bond Street. This area is shown in Figure 5.3: *Detail of London's West End*, which also identifies some of the key locations discussed below.

Detail of London's West End

Key locations discussed below are identified here by title and year of their establishment.

1. **Egyptian Hall 1858.**
2. **Fine Art Society 1876**
3. **Hanover Gallery 1880**
4. **The University Club for Ladies 1891**
5. **Debenham and Freebody**
(became Debenham and Freebody in 1851)
6. **Marshall and Snelgrove**
(became Marshall and Snelgrove in 1871)
7. **Royal Academy of Arts**
(moved to Piccadilly in 1868)
8. **Alexandra Club for Ladies 1891**

Figure 5.3 Detail of London's West End.

Source: *Watkins Commercial & General London Directory Map* (J. Cross and Son's Engravers, 18 Holborn (Opposite Furnival's Inn) London, 1852); additional map assistance by Edward Irvine.

During the second half of nineteenth century, this area was the most fashionable retail centre in London, and it became the home of the largest number of commercial art galleries in the city, as well as traditional exhibition spaces. It was but a brief stroll from an exhibition at the Fine Art Society on New Bond Street to the luxurious salesrooms of Debenham and Freebody at 44 Wigmore Street, just off Oxford Street, or the elegant establishment of Marshall and Snelgrove just across Oxford Street at Vere Street.

THE CHANGING URBAN ENVIRONMENT: INFRASTRUCTURE

In the 1860s the West End specifically, and greater London in general, was an urban centre under construction and experiencing dynamic change. With a population of nearly 3 million in 1860, which was an increase from about 1 million in 1800, London was the largest city in the world. By 1900, Greater London had 6.5 million residents. As the capital city of an expanding empire, at mid century it was often perceived as the most exciting and influential urban environment in Europe, rivalled only by Paris. Both London and Paris underwent significant modernisation in the latter half of the nineteenth century. The transformation of Paris was largely the result of the work of Baron Eugene Haussmann, who was appointed by Napoleon III in 1853 to make Paris a more modern city. Haussmann's grand scheme of boulevards and traffic flow created a new Paris, which boasted wider streets, trains and gas lamps. However, it was also a city that had displaced thousands and created a sense of disorder and confusion. London's modernisation was not as systematic as Haussmann's transformation of Paris, but it has been called more democratic and deeply enmeshed in the infrastructure of the city. As Lynda Nead explains,

> In the last years of the 1860s contemporaries were increasingly willing to compare London to Paris. Although the processes of modernisation and improvements were less rapid in London, they were more solid and lasting; they were the achievements of a democratic government, rather than a vainglorious despot. London certainly had a different approach to improvement. Whereas urban space in Paris was treated as a totality, in London modernity took the form of a collection of partial and unrelated projects for street building and land reclamation.[7]

The establishment of London's Metropolitan Board of Works in 1855 was an indication of the sense London had of moving itself forward as a modern city.[8] The Metropolitan Board of Works not only oversaw the design and construction of the massive London Sewer project. It was also responsible for such accomplishments as the creation of the Thames Embankment and the Holborn Viaduct. The Thames Embankment was a multistage project carried on throughout the 1860s and early 1870s, with the final section from

Chelsea to Battersea opening in 1874. In addition, numerous thoroughfares were widened at this time, and four major railway stations, Victoria, Cannon Street, Charing Cross and St Pancras, were built between 1860 and 1866. The first Underground Railway opened in 1863, taking passengers six kilometres from Paddington to Farringdon Street. These projects created new avenues of movement and new connections, such as the Holborn Viaduct connecting the financial centre of the city to the more fashionable and retail-dominated West End.

The development of a large retail district along Regent and Oxford Streets, the coming of public transport to the area and the terminus of the Holborn Viaduct provided easier access to the West End. Electric lighting also expanded the hours in which shops might be patronised. The Grosvenor Gallery, a luxurious commercial gallery that operated on New Bond Street from 1877 to 1890 was among the first private buildings in the area to have electric lighting, creating even more hours and occasions for the viewing and consumption of its luxury wares and enjoying the luxury of dining in its restaurant.[9] These improvements in infrastructure led to increases in the time women spent, whether for work or leisure, in the West End, which in turn led to a feminisation of the area, as discussed below. The impact of the shifts associated with the improved infrastructure were greatly magnified by concurrent cultural changes in London, including the expansion of fine arts in the area, growth of retail establishments frequented by women and changes in women's roles within society.

THE CHANGING URBAN ENVIRONMENT: SHOPPING, DINING AND LADIES CLUBS

Though the West End remained largely a place dominated by male power and influence, through the last decades of the nineteenth century it became increasingly welcome to and supportive of the activities of the Victorian woman. As had been the case in earlier decades of the Victorian era, in the 1860s it was customary for a middle-class woman to be chaperoned if she was out and about in London.[10] As women's employment in the West End increased, retail establishments offering goods of particular appeal to women became more numerous along Regent Street and Oxford Street; clubs especially designed for women became more common and restaurants and tearooms for women became available. The sight of unaccompanied women or women travelling in groups became much more common in the West End. An excursion to the West End could be an elaborate outing, filled with stops and simply viewing the goods in the area, an earlier version of today's 'window shopping'. It was also a place to meet friends and renew acquaintances. Charles Pascoe's London guidebooks for American travellers, which are full of elaborate lists and comments on all the places to visit, dine, shop and take rest in London, states this succinctly in his 1885 edition:

> Among the leading so-called linen-drapers of the metropolis are Marshall and Snelgrove, Debenham and Freebody, Howell and James, Redmayne, and Lewis and Allenby. The first would seem to have two distinct classes of customers: those that pass in by the Oxford Street entrance and pay over the counter and those who patronize the Vere Street side and are on the books of the firm. The right side, in an afternoon in the Season, is a place where fashionable ladies meet half their acquaintances.[11]

Such an outing to the West End, which could consume most of the day, often involved refreshment and rest, which, prior to the late 1880s, could be found only at a limited number of restaurants where it was appropriate for a lady to dine. He explained,

> As a rule, Ladies will find themselves restricted to a choice of half-a-dozen London restaurants or confectioner's shops, in which they may lunch or dine with comfort. The chief of these are Verrey's Café Restaurant, the Bristol, the Burlington in Regent Street, St. James, before mentioned, the Grosvenor Gallery Restaurant, ... The principal confectioners patronized by ladies are Charbonnel and Walkers, 173 New Bond Street, who stand supreme; . . . Simpson's 247, Oxford Street, Duclos', near the Princess Theatre (178, Oxford Street); Buszard's 197, in the same street (south side).[12]

By the end of the 1880s there were more restaurant options for ladies. One important example was Dorothy's, a restaurant for women run by women, first established in 1888 on Mortimer Street by Isabel Cooper-Oakley. A second branch was opened in 1889 at 446 Oxford Street.[13] Dorothy's was a women-only restaurant aimed at serving meals for women who worked, studied, shopped or simply visited in the West End. Because a complete meal could be purchased for the modest sum of eight pennies, even a shop assistant could enjoy the luxury of having a meal out in a welcoming environment.[14] In the section 'Luncheon Places and Tea-Rooms for Ladies' from his 1890 edition, Pascoe bemoans the poor quality of the food at Dorothy's and other ladies' restaurants, expressing a desire for a ladies restaurant where the quality is more keeping with the finer establishments.[15] This review suggests that, while the dining options for unescorted women were on the increase, equity with men in terms of the top-end luxury dining options had not yet been achieved.

Even if Pascoe is critical of the fare at the restaurants, he is more complimentary of the growing number of tearooms in the 1880s.[16] The establishment of tearooms in London, particularly in the West End, parallels the increasing popularity of that area for afternoon excursions to shop, look at art and meet acquaintances. By 1902, it is reported that there were at least five tearooms in Bond Street alone.[17] These tearooms provided light refreshment as well as clean lavatories, a critical need during long afternoon outings. A delightful illustration of the pleasures of shopping and meeting friends can be found in a *Queen* issue from June 1893. The central portion of the full-page image shows four well-dressed men and women enjoying tea, while the caption next to it reads, 'Perhaps the pleasantest part of shopping. Meeting one's brother and a friend and dropping into a confectioners for tea.'[18] Taking time to enjoy the luxury and experience of having a social tea was clearly a valued part of the shopping excursion.

One more category of gathering places that was critical to the female nexus of the West End was the founding of ladies clubs, particularly in the late 1880s and 1890s (see Figure 5.3). In *Shopping for Pleasure*, Rappaport chronicles the formation of women's clubs from the founding of the Berner's Club by Barbara Bodichon and others involved in women's suffrage, to the vast array of club choices enjoyed by Edwardian women.[19] These clubs, similar in function to the famed gentlemen's clubs of Pall Mall, provided numerous informal gathering places for women shopping, dining or working in the neighbourhood. Clubs, which allowed both male and female members, had existed since mid century and helped normalise the idea of women in club society. These 'Cock and Hen Clubs', according to artist Louise Jopling, provided 'entire freedom from worry'.[20] The clubs exclusively for women not only offered a worry-free environment designed to be a space of luxury and leisure, they provided a space for women to meet, socialise and develop friendships, some of which might be very strategic in their professional pursuits. Among the earliest of these women's clubs was the Alexandra Club established at 12 Grosvenor Street in 1884, and which was reported to have nearly six hundred members by 1888.[21] The Alexandra was definitely an upper-class ladies club, with the membership restricted to women who would not 'be precluded from attending Her Majesty's Drawing Rooms'.[22] Other prominent ladies clubs date from 1891 and include The Victoria Club in Cavendish Square, the Somerville Club at 231 Oxford Street and the still-surviving University Club for Ladies, which was first located at 31 New Bond Street. Ladies clubs grew quickly in popularity and membership. In fact, 'Tens of thousands of women had joined the clubs since the 1880s. Edwardian women could choose among nearly forty different clubs, most of which were situated in the very heart of the West End shopping district'.[23] These clubs provided opportunities for women, much as they had for men for decades, to connect with each other—to network.

> How many a valuable acquaintance has been improved, how many an important introduction obtained in that convenient neutral territory of 'club-land.' . . . But it is to professional women when all is said, that the club offers the most substantial advantages. What woman engaged in art, in literature, in science has not felt the drawbacks of her isolated position?[24]

THE CHANGING URBAN ENVIRONMENT: FEMINISATION

Importantly, it was not just the increasing number of establishments available to women that was responsible for the changing patterns of the use of space, but also the complex weaving of changing commercial establishments with rapidly changing cultural attitudes, including the rise of feminism within London, particularly in the West End. It is the intersection of the feminist movement and other changes in cultural attitudes with the efforts made by female artists to gain a stronger foothold in a heavily gendered culture that birthed a new environment for women to produce and consume luxury in the West End. For example, the family home of Barbara Bodichon, a well-known painter and leading figure in the suffrage movement, was near the West End on Gower Street. Her home served as a hub of activity for many involved in the 'votes for women' campaign. In addition, during the 1860s the *Englishwoman's Journal* was published out of 19 Langham Place, just off Oxford and Regent Street. The same address housed the Ladies Institute, the Society for Promoting the Employment of Women (SPEW) from 1858 to 1875 and the Ladies Sanitary Association.[25] The participation of women in art education increased significantly during this period. The Female School of Art maintained premises in Queen's Square in adjacent Bloomsbury after 1861, and the Royal Academy consistently admitted women as students in 1863.[26]

As Cherry points out, the linkage of art and activism played a key role in feminist politics of the age.

> From the 1840s onwards feminist politics was an important strand in the professional practice of art by women, and artists were among the independent women whose networks formed the movement's strong alliances. . . . By the later 1840s a group of young women including Barbara Bodichon, Anna Mary Howitt, Eliza Fox and Bessie Rayner Parkes had established ties of friendship linked by emotional bonds, professional commitment to cultural productions and political commitment to equal rights for women.[27]

Among the changing cultural norms was a reacceptance of the practice of women walking unaccompanied in the West End, whether it was for a leisure excursion or going to and from their place of employment. Certainly as early as the sixteenth century, women would take social walks about London as part of the season, visiting such notable sights as Westminster Abbey, attending concerts in the parks or visiting friends.[28] However, even though social walking was prevalent among women in the seventeenth and eighteenth centuries, it ceased to be an appropriate activity for many in the increasingly industrial and urban London of the first three decades of the Victorian era. Contemporary sources argue both for and against women walking unaccompanied in London in the 1860s.[29] By the 1880s there seems to be a much wider expectation that to see a woman walking solo along New Bond Street to visit a gallery, go shopping or stop for tea would be considered commonplace.

Because the West End was becoming more feminised during the 1880s and 1890s and because it was more acceptable for women to walk unescorted than it had been in the previous few decades, women, including artists, could navigate the nexus more strategically, with fewer implied limitations on their movements and interactions.[30] Thus the creation of a leisure space filled with luxury offerings supported the production of luxury objects of fine arts, particularly by women artists. This is not to imply that the production and marketing of art was not still highly gendered, but the playing field, while not level, was less precipitous.

WOMEN AND ART IN THE WEST END

A key transformation in the second half of the nineteenth century was that the visual arts, both in terms of their production and consumption, became inextricably woven into the culture of luxury in the West End. This period saw the relocation of the Royal Academy to Burlington House in Piccadilly in 1869, the opening of several art societies and exhibition spaces in the 1860s–1880s, and a burgeoning commercial art gallery trade, commencing in the 1860s and reaching thirty galleries in operation by the end of the century. This number of galleries does not take into account those that opened and closed during this time frame, such as the Grosvenor Gallery, which opened in 1877 and closed in 1890. The *Exhibition Culture Project*, used alongside the aforementioned *London Gallery Project*, shows a pattern of increased representation of female artists in commercial galleries through the last two decades of the nineteenth century. Figure 5.4 shows a screen shot from the *London Gallery Project* for 1880. The dots, which are different colours on the interactive website, show retail establishments and commercial galleries active in 1880.[31]

The Royal Academy's move to its new premises at Burlington House provided more room, not only for exhibits but also for teaching the Academy's pupils. As Anne Helmreich points out,

> Moreover, the academy functioned as a quasi-economic center; artists' colourmen as well as commercial dealers clustered around the site of the academy, particularly after it located to Burlington House in 1869 in close proximity to the luxury trade located on Bond Street.[32]

The mapping work of Fletcher and Israel, Walker and Cherry reveals a West End in the second half of the century that was increasingly home to dozens of commercial galleries, art-teaching institutions and artist's homes in addition to many social clubs and restaurants—for men and women. The West

Figure 5.4 Retail establishments and commercial art galleries in the West End in 1891. Pamela Fletcher and David Israel, *London Gallery Project*, Bowdoin College, Maine, 2007.

End was expanding and changing to provide an array of places to study, purchase or view art—as an artist, buyer or pedestrian who chose to wander the area as a consumer of the space of luxury.

Commercial galleries increased in number through the decades, particularly along New Bond Street. *The London Gallery Project* shows that in 1860s there were five commercial galleries in Bloomsbury and the West End; by 1900 there were thirty-two, primarily clustered along New Bond Street and between St James Square and Trafalgar Square.[33] One such gallery was the Fine Art Society, founded in 1876 and still operating today at 148 New Bond Street. The Society focused on British art and exhibited works by James Whistler and John Everett Millais, as well as hosted frequent spring watercolour exhibits of Helen Allingham's works.[34] By the last decades of the century, an enormous number of commercial galleries clustered in the West End and turned Bond Street into 'one elongated picture gallery tempered by tea shops!' in the words of a reviewer from *Truth*.[35] Viewing art thus became a year-long spectacle, integrated with shopping or window shopping for other luxury goods.

Among the commercial galleries that came to prominence in the second half of the century was the Grosvenor Gallery, the most elegant and prestigious establishment in the area, until it closed in 1890. The Grosvenor was owned and operated by Sir Coutts Lindsey and his wife Blanche, Lady Lindsey. While Sir Coutts was technically the proprietor of the Grosvenor, it was largely started with Lady Lindsay's money, and she remained a dominant force in the direction of the gallery in its early years. Lady Lindsey's support of and participation in the Grosvenor ceased in 1882, when she and Sir Coutts separated. Sir Coutts continued to run the gallery until 1890, when he closed it due to financial troubles.[36]

One established artist of the era, Louise Jopling, writing in her autobiography about the initial exhibit of the Grosvenor in 1877, stated that,

> Many were the reputations made at the Opening. Artists saw, for the first time, justice done to the creations of their brain. . . . I exhibited a picture called, 'It Might have Been.' Its subject was a young girl, seated beside a Japanese cabinet. . . . It was sold for two hundred pounds to Mr. Ben Lockwood of Huddersfield.'[37]

The Grosvenor operated primarily for the purpose of showing artists who essentially remained outside of the official recognition of the Royal Academy. In its annual summer exhibitions, it tended to show contemporary British artists, such as Lawrence Alma-Tadema, John Everett Millais, William Blake Richmond and George Watts. In a review of the 1878 exhibition in the *Examiner* it is clear that the range of artists is quite broad.

> If this year's exhibition has any special feature beyond being a representative collection of all existing schools of English, as well as some

> Foreign art, . . . it may be said to lie in the amount of space conceded to our younger painters, Mr. Cecil Lawson, Mr. Gregory, Mr. John Collier, Mr. Herkomer, Mr. Macbeth, Mrs. Jopling, Mr. Frank Dicey, Mr. Pellegrini, and the prominence assumed by the works that they exhibit. But, indeed, the catholicity of the present collection is its most remarkable feature. The visitor who cannot find many things to his sympathy must indeed be hard to please.[38]

The Grosvenor was welcoming to women artists, including Maria Spartali Stillman, Anna Lee Merritt, Clara Montalba, Helen Allingham, Louise Jopling and many others. The presence of Blanche, Lady Lindsay, who was a woman of considerable wealth and also a painter, clearly strengthened the gallery's interest in showing works by women. The Grosvenor became a prestigious and highly visible venue for women artists, and the Lindsays 'reserved the watercolour room for their contributions'.[39] While Louise Jopling was a very close friend of Lady Lindsay's, Blanche ended the friendship after Jopling refused to cut off all ties with Sir Coutts and the gallery following the couple's separation in 1882.[40]

While the Grosvenor was known for the range of artists it exhibited, it was not the only commercial gallery that frequently included works by women artists in their exhibitions. For example, as mentioned above, the watercolourist Helen Allingham exhibited regularly at the Fine Art Society. Henrietta Rae Normand exhibited regularly at the Dudley Gallery and the Royal Academy, and also contributed black and white work to nearby Mendoza Gallery in St James, all in the early 1880s.[41]

In addition to the increasing number of commercial galleries in the area, The Royal Academy continued to be a powerful force for art in the area. With its annual exhibition of thousands of works, which was attended by tens of thousands of visitors every June, the Academy remained the principal means of achieving recognition and establishing a professional career as an artist. However, while women could submit works for consideration for the annual exhibition, they were not allowed to become members of the Academy until 1936, even though two of the forty founding members in 1768, Angelica Kauffmann and Mary Moser, were women. Furthermore, even though women could submit works for consideration, works by female artists accounted for only a small percentage of compositions shown at the Royal Academy in the nineteenth century, varying from a low of 5.5 per cent in 1810 to a peak of 20.6 per cent in 1895.[42] Throughout the century, the highest percentage of works by women was to be found in the watercolour section, which could be as high as 43.3 per cent in 1900.[43] Less restrictive, but still limiting, women could only become associate members of the Royal Society of Painters in Watercolour until 1890.[44]

A significant resource utilised by women for presenting their art was the Society of Female Artists, founded in 1856. The organisation was renamed the Society of Lady Artists in 1872 when membership rules changed to allow only professional artists to become members, and the name was changed again in 1899 to the Society of Women Artists.[45] This organisation, which never really had a permanent exhibition location, mounted their exhibitions at a variety of venues, including the Egyptian Galleries in Piccadilly and the Architectural Union in Conduit Street. The actual importance of the Society of Female Artists in advancing the goals of professionalism and reputation of women artists is a subject of much scholarly discussion.[46] While it clearly provided increased opportunities for women to exhibit in the West End and for works by women to be viewed by the public and the press, its exhibitions were uneven in quality, and some women chose not to join and thus be categorised as a 'woman artist' rather than 'an artist'.[47] In 1900 the painter Anna Lee Merritt wrote in '*A Letter to Artists: Especially Women Artists*',

> Recent attempts to make separate the exhibitions of women's work were in opposition to the views of the artists concerned, who knew that it would lower their standard and risk the place they already occupied. What we so strongly desire is a place in the large field; the kind ladies who wish to distinguish us as women unthinkingly do us harm.[48]

Even though the Society of Female Artists was established in the 1850s, Merritt makes clear the concerns about categorising women artists as apart from the general population of artists was still troubling at the end of the century.

ARTISTS UTILISING THE CHANGING WEST END

The artists Helen Allingham (1848–1926), Louise Jopling (1843–1933) and Henrietta Rae (1859–1928) provide informative examples of the diverse ways women artists utilised the resources of the West End and contributed to the feminisation of the neighbourhood. The exhibition histories and careers of these three are representative of many of the stories of professional women artists who were teaching, painting and exhibiting in London's West End during the second half of the nineteenth century. Many professional women artists no doubt were actively involved in the vibrant district of the West End, where shops, galleries, restaurants, ladies clubs and tearooms flourished together, creating a space of opportunity and luxury.

Allingham provides an example of a woman artist who painted within well-established cultural expectations—the execution of landscape watercolours of rural England—and who achieved significant success and recognition by tapping into specific resources available in the West End. Jopling represents women artists whose *oeuvre* included more diverse media and subject matter and female artists who were more prominent and active in the West End. Finally, in Rae, the youngest of these three artists, we see an example of a woman artist who utilised a very broad set of resources within the West End to achieve wide recognition, including unprecedented success among Victorian woman artists in the genre of mythological nude figure painting—an area where woman artists had previously consistently fallen short in the eyes of critics and male artists.

While Helen Allingham exhibited in multiple venues, she owed much of her success to her connection with the Fine Art Society. She was one of the few women artists who regularly exhibited at the Fine Art Society, and the Fine Art Society appears to have championed her as an artist. In addition to including her works in group exhibits, the Society displayed her paintings in several small solo shows in the 1880s, 1890s and the early years of the twentieth century.[49] Additionally, Marcus Huish, a primary dealer for the Fine Art Society, authored a loving chronicle of her work, *The Happy England of Helen Allingham* in 1903. The book carefully identifies and describes many of the landscapes she painted, and comments on her popularity and favourable reviews by the press.[50] An examination of the book shows that Allingham's *oeuvre* was within the arena where woman artists had long been accepted—watercolour painting, including rural landscapes. Thus, she represents neither an artist who utilised the West End broadly nor one who stepped out of traditional media and subject matter. She did, however, utilise selected resources within the West End, specifically the Fine Art Society, to effectively advance her career.

Allingham was distinguished as one of the few women selected to be an associate member of the Royal Watercolour Society. While her frequent participation in exhibitions at the Fine Art Society were instrumental to her success, she also exhibited at McLean's Gallery in 1879, at the Royal Academy, and regularly with the Royal Society of Painters in Watercolours.[51] Allingham, who was largely self-taught, is referred to in contemporary reviews as one of the finest watercolourists of the age.

> Mrs. Allingham deservedly ranks with the best water-colour painters of to-day through her appreciation of the simplest beauties of nature, and her persevering endeavours to delineate truthfully all that is picturesque in the fields and hedgerows, the cottages and lanes, the meadows and woodlands, and the daily toils and pleasures of humble dwellers in some of the most charming rural distracts of England. The results of her labours have, for more than a decade of years, been numbered amongst the successes at the gallery of the Old Water Colour Society in Pall Mall. It is there she has become known, and there that we may hope to see her drawings for many years to come.[52]

Louise Jopling was among the best-known and most highly regarded women artists of the Victorian age. Two sources of information that are particularly helpful in understanding Jopling's role are Patricia de Montfort's extensive web-based research project on Jopling, and Jopling's autobiography, *Twenty Years of My life 1867–1887*.[53] Jopling's autobiography is largely a social and family diary, but it does provide nuggets of information about her sales and attendance at, and participation in, exhibitions, especially the Grosvenor and Royal Academy, which clearly indicate that her presence in the West End was a critical component of her success. These sources show us that Jopling was a successful painter, teacher and author who was very active in the West End.

Jopling exhibited at the Royal Academy and the Paris Salon as early as the 1860s. She frequently exhibited works at the Grosvenor Gallery, and in 1878 she exhibited works at the Grosvenor as well as in exhibitions of the Society of Lady Artists, and participated in two exhibitions at the Dudley.[54] She was an associate member of the Royal Watercolour Society, a member of the Royal Society of Portrait Painters, a member of the Society of Women Artists and also, in 1901, among the first women to be elected to the Royal Society of British Artists.[55] She was also friends with some of the most highly recognised artists of the day, including James McNeill Whistler.[56] In addition to watercolours, Jopling exhibited oil paintings and drawings. As noted above, she was a recognised portraitist and executed numerous genre scenes.[57] Thus, her recognised accomplishments, in contrast to Allingham's, extended beyond the media and subject matter traditionally associated with women artists. Her utilisation of West End resources was also much broader than Allingham's.

Jopling showed extensively at the Grosvenor Gallery. She had a friendship with the proprietors of the Grosvenor, Sir Coutts and Lady Lindsay. Given Jopling's well-established reputation, it is not surprising that the Grosvenor showed her works to their mutual advantage, including exhibiting Jopling's work in the first Grosvenor exhibition. A comment in a review of a Dudley Gallery show demonstrates the careful attention the press was paying to Jopling's exhibited works. The writer knew at least one of her earlier exhibited works well enough to recognise it as related to one in the Dudley exhibition and critically compare the two: 'Mrs. Jopling sends a small replica (72) of her picture in the Grosvenor Gallery. It has the Strength but not the finish of the original.'[58]

Henrietta Rae, also referred to as Henrietta Rae Normand, utilised the resources of the West End broadly to move even further beyond the traditional confines of woman artists. Younger than Jopling and Allingham, Rae became successful later, in the 1880s, and undoubtedly owes some of her success to the persistent efforts and precedents established by woman artists such as Allingham and Jopling. Rae was the first female student at Heatherley's School of Art, located on Newman Street, just North of Oxford Street.[59] Heatherley's was, and still is, a London art school that focused on portrait painting and painting from the figure. Rae's *œuvre* includes many mythological scenes with nude figures at rest or at play. Her painting *Ariadne* was exhibited at the Royal Academy in 1886, where a Mr. Pochin purchased it and the Berlin Photographic Company secured the copyright.[60] She exhibited at the Royal Academy, the Society of Lady Artists, the Institute of

Painters in Oil (an organisation formed in 1891) and the Gallery of Modern Art, formerly the Doré Gallery (1895). This final exhibition was a small joint exhibition including Henrietta's works as well as those of her husband Ernest Normand. The previous proprietor of the Doré Gallery, George Lord Beeforth, who had commissioned Rae to paint his portrait, offered the space of the Doré Gallery for this joint exhibition. This exhibition was seen as an important event in her career by her biographer, Arthur Fish: 'The exhibition remained open for nine months, and materially assisted to familarise the public with Mrs. Normand's work. It afforded an opportunity of judging her work and its development in a manner which had not before been possible.'[61]

The exhibition histories of Louise Jopling, Helen Allingham and Henrietta Rae provide tangible insight into how the West End provided a critical environment for women artists. It was a district that had become increasingly feminised, allowing women artists to move freely and independently to exhibitions, clubs and teaching venues. From the number of female artists' residences, training locations and exhibition opportunities in this area, it can be concluded that female artists were not only producing objects of luxury in the West End, but they were also navigating the sidewalks, frequenting tearooms and shopping in stores catering to female customers.

CONCLUSION

It was within this complex setting, which had undergone significant changes in infrastructure, retail and social establishments and feminisation, that the Victorian woman, including artists, could produce and consume luxury, whether it involved paintings or simply consuming the space of luxury in an afternoon outing—visiting exhibitions, shops and stopping for tea. The West End became a nexus where a woman artist could be welcomed and successful in furthering her training or commercial endeavours; this West End culture became an urban place that was uniquely suited to the production and consumption of the luxury of visual art.

In the 1890s, women artists moved through and operated within the West End as producers and consumers of luxury in a way unimaginable to both women and men of the 1860s. While the growing feminist movement, other attitudinal shifts and developments within the physical constructs of the city have much to do with these alterations, the dynamics of the changes in the West End community itself are certainly an important contributor to the cultural transformation. It is clear that many of the changes built upon one another synergistically. The West End had long been an area with high-end retailers, but prior to the mid nineteenth century these were relatively small shops catering to an established clientele. The development of such large retail establishments such as Debenham and Freebody, which sold a vast array of items, brought in a much broader range of shoppers, primarily women. The relocation of the Royal Academy and its art-related businesses helped place the visual arts at the centre of the neighbourhood. As the concept of commercial galleries took hold, it was clear that being located near the Royal Academy and the luxury retail centre of the West End would be a smart business decision. In the last two decades of the nineteenth century, restaurants, clubs and tearooms that were designed for, or made an effort to be welcoming to, women became common in this mix of commercial luxury and art. Among the women who capitalised upon the opportunities and resources provided by this new urban environment were assertive women involved in the arts, including many painters, art journalists and art instructors. Their art, activism and influence have become part of the fabric of London's West End, which continues to be a very vibrant centre for shopping, browsing and partaking of the visual arts.

NOTES

1 The Fine Art Society Ltd, *One Hundred Years of Exhibitions at The Fine Art Society Ltd* (London: Fine Art Society Ltd, 1976), 1891.
2 'Society of Lady Artists', *Times* [London, England] 5 May 1891: 1.
3 Deborah Cherry, *Painting Women: Victorian Women Artists* (London: Routledge, 1993); Deborah Cherry, 'Women Artists and the Politics of Feminism 1850–1900', in *Women in the Victorian Art World*, ed. Clarissa Campbell Orr (Manchester: Manchester University Press, 1995), 49–69; Deborah Cherry, *Beyond the Frame Feminism and Visual Culture, Britain 1850–1900* (London: Routledge, 2000); Deborah Cherry, 'Going Places: Women Artists in Central London in the Nineteenth Century', *The London Journal* 28 (2003): 73–96.
4 Lynne Walker, 'Vistas of Pleasure: Women Consumers of Urban Space in the West End of London 1850–1900', in *Women in the Victorian Art World*, ed Orr, 70–85; Lynne Walker, 'Home and Away: The Feminist Mapping of Public and Private Space in Victorian London', in *The Unknown City: Contesting Architecture and Social Space; A Strangely Familiar Project*, ed. Iain Borden, Joe Kerr, Jane Rendell, with Alicia Pivaro (Cambridge, MA: MIT Press, 2001), 296–310; Erika Rappaport, *Shopping for Pleasure: Women in the Making of London's West End* (Princeton: Princeton University Press, 2000).
5 Lynda Nead, *Victorian Babylon: People Streets and Images in Nineteenth-Century London* (New Haven: Yale University Press, 2000); Susan Casteras and Colleen Denney, *The Grosvenor Gallery: A Palace of Art in Victorian England* (New Haven: Yale University Press, 1996); Susan Casteras and Linda Peterson, *A Struggle for Fame, Victorian Women Artists and Authors* (New Haven: Yale Center for British Art, 1994).
6 Pamela Fletcher and David Israel, *London Gallery Project*, Bowdoin College 2007, accessed 26 Oct. 2013. Revised Sept. 2012, http://learn.bowdoin.edu/fletcher/london-gallery/; *Exhibition Culture in London 1878–1908* database, University of Glasgow, 2006 www.exhibitionculture.arts.gla.ac.uk/.
7 Nead, *Victorian Babylon*, 56–57.
8 Ibid.
9 Christopher Newall, *The Grosvenor Gallery Exhibitions* (Cambridge: Cambridge University Press, 1995), 12.
10 Walker, 'Vistas', 75.

11 Charles Eyre Pascoe, *London of To-Day An Illustrated Handbook for the Season* (Boston: Roberts Brothers, 1885), 323.
12 Ibid., 51.
13 Rappaport, *Shopping*, 102, 256, n.146.
14 Rappaport, *Shopping*, 102, and Franny Moyle, *Constance: The Tragic and Scandalous Life of Mrs. Oscar Wilde* (New York: Pegasus Books, 2012), 164–65.
15 Pascoe, *London of To-Day* (1885 ed.), 77.
16 Pascoe, *London of To-Day* (1890 ed.), 78–79.
17 Rappaport, *Shopping*, 256, n. 142.
18 Reproduced in Rappaport, *Shopping*, 104.
19 Walker, 'Vistas', 72–73. Walker includes a map of the West End identifying the founding year and location of many of the women's clubs.
20 Louise Jopling, *Twenty Years of My Life 1867–1887* (London: John Lane, 1925), 120.
21 Amy Levy, 'Women and Club Life', in *The Complete Novels and Selected Writings of Amy Levy*, ed. Melvyn New (Gainesville: University Press of Florida, 1993), 534.
22 Ibid., 533–34.
23 Rappaport, *Shopping*, 74.
24 Levy, 'Club Life', 533–36.
25 Cherry, 'Going Places', 74.
26 Cherry, *Painting Women*, 57; Stephanie Brown and Sara Dodd, 'The Society of Female Artists and the Song of Sisterhood', in *Governing Cultures: Art Institutions in Victorian London*, ed. Paul Barlow and Colin Trodd (Aldershot: Ashgate, 2000), 87.
27 Cherry, *Painting Women*, 47–48.
28 Marjo Kaartinen, 'Women's Metropolis—Elite Women in Early Modern London', *Women's History Magazine* 53 (2006): 4–12.
29 Nead, *Victorian Babylon*, 62–67. An exchange of letters to the editor of the *Times* in 1862 illuminates this topic when a '*pater familias*' from the provinces expresses concern over the way his daughter is being treated when she walks in London. *The Times* [London, England], Jan 1862: 7. *The Times* [London, England], Jan 1862: 10.
30 Walker, 'Vistas', 72–76; Rappaport, *Shopping*, 2–15.
31 Fletcher and Israel, *Gallery Project*, accessed 26 October 2013. http://19thc-artworldwide.org/fletcher/london-gallery/map/
32 Anne Helmreich, *Victorian Exhibition Culture: The Market Then and the Museum Today*, RaVoN (Romanticism and Victorianism on the Net), 55, 2009, www.erudit.org/revue/ravon/2009/v/n55/039556ar.html.
33 Fletcher and Israel, *Gallery Project*, accessed 26 October 2013. http://nineteenthc-artworldwide.org/fletcher/london-gallery/map/.
34 Fine Art Society, *One Hundred Years*, under years 1886, 1887, 1889, 1891, 1894, 1898, 1901 and 1904.
35 Pamela Fletcher, 'Shopping for Art: The Rise of the Commercial Art Gallery, 1850s–90s', in *The Rise of the Modern Art Market in London, 1850–1939*, ed. Pamela Fletcher and Anne Helmreich (Manchester and New York: Manchester University Press, 2011), 51.
36 Colleen Denny, 'The Grosvenor Gallery as a Palace of Art', in Casteras and Denny, *Grosvenor Gallery*, 35.
37 Jopling, *Twenty Years*, 115.
38 'The Grosvenor Gallery', *The Examiner*, 4 May 1878, 569.
39 Colleen Denny, 'Introduction', in Casteras and Denny, *Grosvenor Gallery*, 5.

40 Jopling, *Twenty Years*, 195.
41 Arthur Fish, *Henrietta Rae (Mrs. Ernest Normand)* (London: Cassell and Company, 1905), 31.
42 Charlotte Yeldham, *Women Artists in Nineteenth-Century England and France* (New York: Garland, 1984), 199.
43 Ibid.
44 Cherry, *Painting Women*, 66.
45 Brown and Dodd, 'The Society of Female Artists', 87.
46 Cherry, *Painting Women*, 66.
47 Ibid., 67–68.
48 Anna Lee Merritt, 'A Letter to Artists: Especially Women Artists', *Lippincott's Monthly Magazine, LXV* (1900): 467.
49 Fine Art Society, *One Hundred Years* (see note 34 for specific years).
50 Marcus Huish, *The Happy England of Helen Allingham* (London: Adam & Charles Black, 1903).
51 'Winter Exhibitions', *Times* [London, England] 14 November 1879: 3, *The Times Digital Archive.* Web. 2 Sept. 2013.
52 Laura Dyer, 'Mrs. Allingham', *Art Journal* (1888): 198–201.
53 Patricia de Montfort, *Louise Jopling 1843–1933: A Research Project*, accessed 26 Oct. 2013. http://www.louisejopling.arts.gla.ac.uk/; Jopling, *Twenty Years.*
54 'Water-Colour Exhibitions', *Times* [London, England] 6 Mar. 1878: 4, *The Times Digital Archive.* Web. 20 Jan. 2014. 'The Dudley Gallery', *Times* [London, England] 28 Nov. 1878: 4, *The Times Digital Archive.* Web. 20 Jan. 2014.
55 de Montfort, *Louise Jopling*, accessed 26 Oct. 2013 http://www.louisejopling.arts.gla.ac.uk/life/.
56 Jopling, *Twenty Years.* Jopling refers frequently to her friendship with Whistler, particularly in the years around 1880.
57 de Montfort, *Louise Jopling*, accessed 26 Oct. 2013, http://www.louisejopling.arts.gla.ac.uk/life/.
58 'Exhibit of Water-Colour Drawings, Dudley Gallery', *Athenaeum*, 9 March 1878, 322.
59 Fish, *Henrietta Rae*, 22.
60 Ibid., 36.
61 Ibid., 87.

Part II

Metropole and Province

6 Men, Women and the Supply of Luxury Goods in Eighteenth-Century England

The Purchasing Patterns of Edward and Mary Leigh

Jon Stobart and Mark Rothery

The pursuit of luxury has long been seen as a key element in the consumption practices of the elite: It marked their status and distinguished them from lower social groups. Such concerns have, in the past, been viewed as part of a male domain concerned with dynastic spending that defined status. Men were the builders of country houses, the discerning Grand Tourists, the collectors of art and antiquities and the inheritors of estates.[1] The consumption of landowners is thus seen as essentially male: It embodied masculine virtues of self-control, taste and pride in family.[2] Of course, women also bought a wide range of luxury goods. Indeed, for Sombart, it was female addiction to luxury that underpinned spending and was ultimately responsible for the emergence of capitalism—an argument that is rehearsed by McKendrick and others when emphasising the key role played by women in a fashion-led consumer revolution.[3] Yet only recently have historians begun to scratch the veneer of male dynastic spending, to discover men relying on their wives to determine and carry out decorative schemes, implicitly if not explicitly acknowledging their refined taste.[4] At the same time, there is a growing body of research on the consumption practices of elite women which emphasises their key role in exercising restraint and care, rather than succumbing to the decadent pleasures of luxury and seducing their men to do the same.[5]

Perhaps unsurprisingly, distinctly masculine forms of consumption have received rather less attention (but see the chapters by Ijäs and Ilmakunnas in this volume): They are often the un-variegated 'other' against which the subtleties of female consumption are highlighted. Recent studies have begun to question some of the stereotypes of ostentatious display, connoisseurship and overt manliness, highlighting instead the importance of character, life cycle and status.[6] Yet the focus is often on bachelors, not least because this is the surest way of knowing that it is male rather than family consumption being assessed. Attempts at drawing together male and female consumption are generally done within the confines of marriage, the contrast being made most clearly by Vickery in her analysis of the account books of elite husbands and wives. She shows men indulging their tastes and passions, buying coaches and saddlery, wine and fine clothes. Their wives, meanwhile, were responsible for managing the household budget and supplying the everyday needs of their husband and children. Moreover, men enjoyed a close, even chummy relationship with suppliers, whilst women interacted with tradesmen in a more functional and transactional manner.[7]

From such analysis, we know a growing amount about the ways in which male and female consumption was interrelated within the nuptial home. However, there is a danger that we conflate male and female with husband and wife: Gender becomes confused with marital relationships. By looking instead at the consumption practices of a brother and sister, we try to bring a different perspective on the relationship between gender and consumption, one that challenges some of the stereotypes of dynastic husband and domestic wife. This chapter offers an analysis of the consumption practices of Edward, fifth Lord Leigh (1743–1786) and the Honourable Mary Leigh (1736–1806)—successive owners of Stoneleigh Abbey in Warwickshire. Their father, Thomas fourth Lord Leigh, had died when they were still in their minority, and they were brought up under the care of relatives. Neither Edward nor Mary married. He appears to have been troubled by mental problems from the age of about twenty-five and was declared insane in 1774, the administration of the estate passing to the hands of a Commission comprising a cousin, William Craven and Mary.[8] Mary had considerable independent wealth and spent much of her time in London, yet never appears to have attracted suitors. Together, they form an interesting case against which to test some of our assumptions about gender and luxury consumption. Drawing on a large collection of receipted bills and related correspondence, we begin by mapping out the overall spending patterns of Edward and Mary, and assess the importance of gender in relation to status, life-course and the character of the individual. Building on this, we examine the nature of their relationship with suppliers and thus with the urban economy. Unsurprisingly, most supplies came from towns, but examining how the pattern and geography of supply varied with status, gender and life stage allows us to explore the dynamic relationship between town and country, and challenge any simple dichotomy of urban supply and rural consumption. Overall, our analysis challenges conventional stereotypes of gender-based consumption by highlighting the complexities of consumption practices and the layered nature of gender identities.

SPENDING, GENDER AND LIFE-COURSE

We know little about Edward's early life. He was educated at Westminster School in London and probably spent some of his time during the 1750s at the Warwickshire estate of his guardian, William Craven, before matriculating to Oriel College, Oxford, in 1761. As a consumer, Edward sparkled brilliantly but briefly in the mid 1760s. When a young man at university in

Oxford, his spending comprised mostly the costs he incurred within college, although there were outlays for buying, mending and cleaning clothes, for books and for some luxury items such as a watch and chain bought at Woodstock.[9] Most of his discretionary spending took place between his inheritance in 1763 and the onset of his mental illness, which appears to have occurred sometime in 1768, although he was only officially declared insane six years later.

Edward's major areas of spending show a concern with his estate and financial obligations, as would be expected of a substantial landowner. His spending on the estate included the renewal of leases on land, and the purchase of additional land and shares in the South Sea Company to the tune of £20,546, although the latter do not feature in the receipted bills.[10] What we do find there is investment in the estate, including costs associated with enclosure, although some of this took place during the period after he was declared insane and while a committee of trustees was running the estate. This suggests that such spending was integral to the running of a successful estate. Edward's discretionary consumption was marked more particularly by his spending on Stoneleigh Abbey itself. Building, decorating and furnishing an impressive residence was, of course, an important aspect of elite male spending. It served to define men's status within society, the elite and the family.[11] Edward certainly made an important impact in this area and patronised a wide range of artists and craftsmen.[12] However, his ultimate ambitions were unfulfilled. In addition to several sketched designs in his own hand, he commissioned plans for a new north front, a large and impressive library, a new set of service buildings, including a large brew house and laundry, and a huge new north wing—no doubt with an eye to complementing and perhaps upstaging his grandfather's monumental west wing.[13] That few of these plans came to fruition because of his insanity and early death might be seen as curtailing Edward's masculinity in terms of his dynastic impact. Yet this reflects a much broader tendency for the ambitions of even elite consumers to run ahead of their ability to realise them. Building may have been the ultimate expression of gentlemanly virtue, but it could easily be frustrated by demographic or economic misfortune. Moreover, we might argue that a failure to follow through lavish building programmes in fact demonstrates appropriate manly restraint—an argument in line with French's and Rothery's analysis of elite masculinity. Control and management of the self was believed to be the basis of the projection of power and authority over others, whether family members or the lower orders, and the control of finances was considered to be a particularly important component of elite masculinities throughout the early modern and modern periods.[14]

Edward's income was considerable, but he spent within his means—even during the period of highest expenditure immediately following his inheritance when major interior work put the house 'in greater confusion than ever'. The decorative work undertaken in the west wing included two impressive fireplaces for the hall, papering most of the upper-storey rooms, and painting much of the house, which together cost £667 14s.[15] Edward also commissioned impressive plasterwork for the hall, staircase and chapel, for which few bills have survived but which must have cost several hundred pounds. Analysis by the architectural historian Andor Gomme confirms that these interiors were not just rich and ornate, but executed to a very high standard.[16] However, they were far from being ruinously expensive. The same was true of the large quantities of furniture purchased to fill the many rooms left under-furnished by his grandfather and father. Most of this came in two huge orders placed with London cabinet makers William Gomm & Co. and Thomas and Gilbert Burnett, suppliers who were perhaps a notch or two down from the best and most expensive.[17] He eschewed men like Adam and Chippendale, engaged by some of his Warwickshire neighbours, yet still acquired a number of very fine pieces, including a large mahogany music table for the library and a splendid communion table.

The apparent restraint shown by Edward was, in part at least, down to his guardian, William Craven, who must have played an important part in shaping the character of his ward. Training in the control of finances began when young gentry men first left home for boarding school and continued through to university education, the Grand Tour and into adulthood.[18] It is significant, then, that Craven continued to look after the young man as he planned his new home, corresponding with the steward at Stoneleigh Abbey about the need to manage outgoings in order to avoid financial embarrassment.[19] There was a huge spike in Edward's spending as bills for decorating and furnishing flooded in, the peak coming in 1765 when the bills record total spending of nearly £5,000. It appears that cash flow, rather than shortage of capital, was the main concern, and we must recall that this amounted to well under half the income derived from the estate. Edward's general restraint in spending might be said to reflect his successful absorption of masculine values probably learnt under Craven's guidance. At the same time, Craven's correspondence reflects the tension in masculine consumption between the imperatives of restraint and display.

Edward also spent handsome sums on books. This formed another typical area of elite male spending—communicating taste, discernment and learning—yet it is surprisingly missing from Vickery's sample of gentry families.[20] Some book owners aimed at an assembling impressive collection, characterised by the quality, rarity and completeness of its contents; others sought to build a library that would be useful and used. Edward appears to have tended towards the former, but also bought many 'useful' volumes. His books were visually impressive, and he was clearly concerned with their physical appearance. Perhaps even more striking was the pace at which he assembled his impressive collection, laying out around £1,500 in just six years.[21] This speed might be seen as displaying a lack of self-control, but again the spending was far from ruinous and it is clear that his library reflected a genuine interest in the arts and especially sciences. At Oxford, he was praised for his diligence and his 'literary qualifications', and was later appointed High Steward of the University and made a Doctor of Civil Law.[22] He appears to have had a particular interest in science and maths, amassing a collection of scientific instruments that went beyond what was typical of the aristocratic man of leisure. He had the usual globes and barometers, but also bought an air pump, syringes, receivers, cylinder glasses and so on from Edward Nairne, a famous scientific instrument maker of Cornhill in London who patented several electrical machines.[23] Edward's decision to bequeath both his library and his scientific instruments to his alma mater might be seen as further evidence that he wanted these things to be used—a point underlined by his gift of £1,000 to the Vice Chancellor of Oxford University and the Provost of Oriel College to purchase scientific equipment to illustrate lectures.[24]

Edward thus engaged in typical elite male practices of collecting but was seemingly exceptional in his erudition and intellectual abilities. This same paradox was also seen in his plans for remodelling the west front of Stoneleigh Abbey: they reflect a wider tradition of the gentleman architect, but reveal an individual with extraordinary vision and either a playful or eccentric willingness to experiment with different styles. These characteristics also tie into his masculine identity as a virtuous scholar. This was a different kind of masculinity from that outlined by Vickery: horses, clothes and wine were purchased, but they did not define his spending or his identity as a consumer. Indeed, Edward appears to have been relatively uninterested in conforming to the stereotype of the polite gentleman, with its concern for display, sociability and manners.[25]

Mary lived much longer than her brother and her life included more complex and complete transformations of status. Like Edward, little is known of her childhood, spent in the care of Elizabeth Verney.[26] She emerges in the Stoneleigh Abbey bills in the early 1750s, living in the vicinity of Hanover Square, London. Here she remained through much of the 1760s, although she also had a room at Stoneleigh Abbey. When her brother was declared insane in 1774, her life moved into a different phase as she took on joint responsibility for the estate. It shifted to a third phase when she inherited twelve years later. Unsurprisingly, these changes brought about considerable shifts in Mary's spending as revealed through the receipted bills. Overall, this was characterised by large sums laid out on clothing and consumables, but to dismiss her as interested only in frocks and food would be to miss the complexities of her life and consumption habits.

As a young woman, Mary's spending centred on millinery, drapery and dressmaking. Through the 1750s and 1760s, these accounted for an average of about £50 per annum—a relatively modest sum that suggests moderation on the part of a very wealthy young woman. At the same time, there were also bills for music and language lessons;[27] entertainments, such as trips to the opera and Ranelagh Gardens; tableware, tea and mineral water; hiring and buying coaches and charitable contributions. By the 1760s she was renewing the furnishings in her London rooms, acquiring a new chair, repairing other pieces and having curtains refashioned. In all, this was fairly typical expenditure for a wealthy woman without family responsibilities. Mary spent freely, but not to excess. Dress embodied gender identities, and Mary's focus on this area of spending reinforced her identity as a woman, especially when augmented by her purchases of jewellery. It also underlined her status: a woman, but the sister of a peer of the realm and in possession of a substantial private fortune.

The little we know of Mary's spending during the period of the Commission suggests that she continued to live in London and that her overall pattern of spending remained broadly stable, although the substantial sums laid out on the hire of horses and coaches suggests a significant amount of travel, perhaps to and from the Warwickshire estate. On becoming owner of Stoneleigh Abbey in 1786, her spending took on a very different character: established female patterns were now overlain with much larger sums relating to those of a wealthy landowner and a minor player in London society. As a landowner, there were costs incurred in running the estate. These form a continuation of the patterns established by her brother and were interrupted during the time Mary and William Craven ran the estate during Edward's insanity, with spending on enclosure, ditching and fencing, maintenance of farm buildings and so on. Like the aristocratic women studied by Lewis, Mary was also engaged in impressing her own character in the house, albeit in ways that might appear modest against the building programme of her grandfather or the major refurbishment undertaken by her brother.[28] In the ten years following her inheritance of Stoneleigh Abbey, Mary spent about £460 on furniture and upholstery, to which we should add a further £299 for repainting the interior of the house.[29]

The amounts of furniture were, perhaps, quite modest, but the amount of work being undertaken was clearly considerable, as was its impact on Stoneleigh Abbey. This was perhaps clearest in the 'new rooms' and print room created by Mary, apparently in the late 1780s. It is likely that some of the work undertaken by the upholsterer, David Frost—probably a Warwick craftsman—involved furnishing and decorating these rooms. In a 1790 letter written to her friend and solicitor, Joseph Hill, Mary described these as being 'pretty', but the 1806 inventory suggests that they were relatively plainly furnished with a range of mahogany and japanned furniture.[30] If these were, indeed, rooms seen as particularly personal to Mary, they were markedly different from her bedroom, which in 1764 had been lined with pea green wallpaper and decorated with two large and eight small Chinese landscapes.[31] This feels a far more feminine space than that apparently created by Mary herself. Of course, it is possible that Mary was describing to Hill her more general improvements to the house. Like those of Lady Irwin at Temple Newsam and Lady Boringden at Saltram, these produced comfortable and sociable spaces in which to entertain her friends, including a print room furnished with fashionable satinwood furniture.[32] But there was hardly a room in the house left untouched. As well as introducing new items and refreshing the soft furnishing, she moved many items between rooms. In the principal entertaining rooms—the Breakfast Room and Dining Parlour—the turnover was considerable, furniture being brought in to create a more informal atmosphere and serve a range of recreational uses. The result probably resembled Humphrey Repton's 'Modern Living Room', which he juxtaposed with the stuffy and old-fashioned formality of the 'Old Cedar Parlour'.[33]

Mary's attitude to paintings is especially interesting. She moved many of these between rooms, augmenting the display in the Breakfast Room and Dining Parlour with additional landscapes and conversation pieces. These were hung alongside fifteen family portraits left in place whilst these rooms were reworked, a practice which was repeated across the whole house—portraits being left largely where they were. There was no apparent attempt to produce the kind of pictorial family tree created by Henrietta Cavendish at Welbeck.[34] Yet Mary was clearly conscious of her family's lineage, carefully marking all her silverware as well as her coach with the arms, supporters and coronet that signalled her rank and dignity—a practice she had begun in the 1750s when still a young woman in London.[35] That said, Mary did more than simply preserve and present the marks of lineage that she inherited. She was willing to replace heirloom items such as silverware, imprinting her own taste on the family collection. Purchasing £1,031 of silver from William Makepeace, Mary received £534 for unspecified but clearly unwanted items that she sold back to the silversmith.[36] In this way she augmented her gendered status as a woman with her social status as a titled and landed gentlewoman.

Mary's claim on her family's inheritance and her place within this lineage served to cement her social status (an aspect of landed women's activities that historians have recently begun to note).[37] However, Mary also struck an importantly independent note, acquiring a house in Kensington Gore from which she could comfortably retain her connections and social life in London. This occupied much of her attention in the early 1790s, a series of bills being paid to builders, carpenters, plumbers, painters, glaziers and plasterers.[38] This work helped to make Grove House a comfortable and pleasant place in which Mary spent her winter months. Moreover, it is clear that this presence in London was important to her public reputation as well as being a convenient base for her social activities. This is most evident from her purchases of livery—an important marker of rank and status. Mary's servants at Stoneleigh and Kensington appear to have received new livery each year through the 1790s.[39] The average outlay per servant at Stoneleigh was about £7 5s—a considerable sum, but one that was significantly outweighed by the provision that Mary made for her London servants, each of whom received four suits costing a total of about £25 per head.[40] This public display of status was clearly a matter of some importance to Mary—indeed, the surviving bills show that she spent far more on these than had her brother, who seems to have been in London for only limited periods of time.

This was spending linked to status more than gender, but Mary also crossed into a world more closely associated with specifically male identity. Whilst she acquired her first coach in the 1760s, most of her transport needs during this period were met through hiring rather than buying. By the 1790s, she was still hiring coaches, horses, coachmen and postilions in London, but was also paying for horse feed and repairs to her own carriage. Moreover, there were regular bills for a bewildering variety of harnesses, whips, combs, etc.—what Vickery refers to as 'an utterly masculine, dark brown territory of goods'.[41] There is no evidence that Mary herself went to the coach makers to finger or commission these things, but then it is not always clear that elite gentlemen immersed themselves in such worlds—they had servants who could readily bespeak these goods. What is clear is that Mary prioritised them as part of her material culture, incurring a total of thirty-two separate bills for coach repairs and saddlery. This behaviour might be seen as making Mary a masculine consumer—something perhaps seen more clearly in the fascination that such goods appear to have held for Anne Lister.[42] More likely it reflects Mary's desire for a public display of status and dignity, which was not defined by gender in a straightforward sense.

Just like the family portraits and silverware in Stoneleigh Abbey, servants' livery and the coaches emblazoned with the family arms were a means of maximising the status that Mary could achieve, whether in London or in the country: the status of a wealthy gentlewoman, part of a long line of honourable landowners. Yet Mary, like her brother, spent well within her means, the improvements being relatively modest and the bills trifling in comparison with her considerable wealth. The repairs to Grove House, for example, amounted to around £350 in total. We might see this self-control as characteristically masculine consumption but, again, it is perhaps better understood as part of the expectation placed upon any landowner: that they should foster and manage resources to augment rather than dissipate the family estate.[43] Certainly, we can see the skills of good financial management in other elite women; Alice le Strange, for instance, managed resources so that her husband was free to invest in and improve the building and estate. Mary thus conformed to certain norms of the respectable (male) landowner, showing self-control, pride in family and lineage and economy at a scale beyond the domestic.[44]

TRADESMEN AND TOWNS: THE RELATIONSHIPS OF SUPPLY

Edward and Mary both dealt with hundreds of retailers and craftsmen, of which about one-third can be definitively located in space. Overall, London dominated their supply systems, with the towns and villages around Stoneleigh accounting for most of the other purchases recorded in the bills.[45] However, life course changes and particularly the responsibility of estate ownership made important differences to the geography of supply.

Edward's pattern of spending was relatively straightforward. As a young man, his purchases were largely restricted to Oxford and its environs. In addition to his college bills, the bills record purchases of stockings and shoes and the cost of cleaning and repairing clothes.[46] Once he came of age and took ownership of the estate, the geography of his spending refocused onto London and, to a lesser extent, the towns and villages around Stoneleigh Abbey (Table 6.1). The metropolis dominated in terms of total spending, in part because of the large bills for furniture presented by Gomm & Co. and Burnett, but Edward also settled substantial bills for books, architectural plasterwork, paintings, wallpapering, silverware, household linen, wines, chinaware and a carriage, as well as tailoring for himself and livery for his servants. London was clearly central to his refurbishment of Stoneleigh Abbey. At the same time, Edward turned to tradesmen and women in Coventry and Warwick for groceries, china and earthenware, coopery and hardwares, but also for house painting and building work. He undoubtedly employed many craftsmen and labourers from the surrounding villages as well, but these are more difficult to attribute to a specific location. That said, men like Michael Clarke, who undertook masonry work, Richard Gardener, who supplied ironmongery and periodically repaired the pump, and Richard Cheshire, who was paid for labouring, probably lived in one of the villages around Stoneleigh Abbey.

During her long life, Mary patronised over 500 suppliers, of which 241 can be definitively located in space. In the 1750s and 1760s, London dominated both in terms of the number of suppliers and the total value of goods and services provided. This reliance on London suppliers is remarkable, but unsurprising since Mary appears to have spent little time outside the capital during these years. The occasional purchases made in the Warwickshire towns of Coventry and Warwick were for small amounts of cloth, haberdashery and gloves, often from retailers who also supplied other family members. In short, Mary shopped locally. In the later period, when she had inherited the Stoneleigh estate, the geography of supply was more complex. London accounted for fewer than half of the suppliers and around two-thirds of goods by value; Coventry and Warwick were now more important points of supply, as was the village of Stoneleigh and Kenilworth, a small town situated just two miles to the west of the estate. From these places came groceries, haberdashery, upholstery, stationery, medicines, earthenware and livery, plus painters, braziers and farriers. More striking, perhaps, is the emergence of Kensington tradesmen supplying meat, bread, coal, fish and candles, amongst other things. Again, these shifts are readily explained by Mary's new role as a Warwickshire landowner and her winter residence in Kensington. Much shopping was still being done locally, but this now meant a number of different spaces, so that flows of goods ran not simply from town to country, but from London to suburb and province, and sometimes from countryside to town as game from the estate was sent up to Grove House.[47]

Table 6.1 The distribution of retailers supplying Edward Leigh, 1763–1786, and Mary Leigh, 1750–1806.

	Edward Leigh				Mary Leigh							
					1750–1769				1786–1806			
					Suppliers		Total value		Suppliers		Total value	
	No.	%	£ s d	%	No.	%	£ s d	%	No.	%	£ s d	%
Bedworth	1	1.1	71-5-0	0.7	1							
Birmingham	–	–	–	–	–	–	–	–	1	0	25-17-0	0.0
Coventry	16	17.2	408-13-9	4.1	7	7.1	35-11-0	1.9	28	19.6	824-11-5	7.9
Kenilworth	1	1.1	27-2-0	0.3	0	0	0	0	2	1.4	419-1-2	4.0
Kensington	–	–	–	–	0	0	0	0	18	12.6	1217-14-5	11.7
London	65	70.0	9035-14-6	91.0	88	89.8	1819-9-2	95.9	69	48.3	6880-15-1	66.1
Other	3	3.2	2-0-0	0.0	1	1.0	14-6-11	0.8	–	–	–	–
Stoneleigh*	1	1.1	138-11-11	1.4	0	0	0	0	13	9.1	229-18-4	2.2
Warwick	6	6.5	233-15-9	2.3	2	2.0	27-4-4	1.4	12	8.4	812-14-4	7.8

Source: SCLA, Stoneleigh Abbey bills, series DR18/5

Note: Figures for Stoneleigh exclude servants' wages, which are only rarely recorded in the bills.

There was a certain logic to the patterns of supply servicing both Edward and Mary. A hierarchy of goods was written onto the urban hierarchy, so that luxury and other high-end products (silverware, furniture, books, artwork, etc.) came from London, whilst everyday goods and services (provisions, ironmongery, ditching, plumbing, etc.) were drawn from local suppliers. There were exceptions, of course: Warwick provided highly skilled craftsmen and designers, including Williams Hiorns and Timothy Lightholer, who played a vital part in completing the interiors at Stoneleigh Abbey;[48] and the Coventry china dealer William Allen supplied chinaware, cutlery and a tea chest and tea board.[49] Conversely, large quantities of everyday goods were bought in London. In part, this is attributable to Mary's residence in London and later Kensington, which meant that provisions were drawn not from the environs of Stoneleigh, but from the metropolis and its suburbs. Such life cycle or seasonal shifts in residence serve to complicate the relationship between urban and supply hierarchies.

Convenience and the necessity to acquire fresh food on a regular basis encouraged local shopping. For Mary, this meant patronising Kensington retailers such as the butcher Roger Buckmaster, the poulterer Henry Davies and the fishmonger John Loader,[50] but she also sent into London for a wide range of groceries and household goods, as well as clothing, silverware and so on. For her, London was readily accessible, although if goods were ordered by correspondence and delivered by the carrier, the distance between shop and residence mattered little. Bills rarely make it clear whether Edward or Mary visited shops in person to bespeak the goods they required. We know that Edward frequented London bookshops, and it is likely that many of Mary's purchases of cloth and clothing in the 1750s involved going into shops. Most purchases, however, were probably made remotely. The friction of distance was effectively lubricated by the Leigh's ability to pay for the packaging and carriage of goods—just as it was for many other wealthy consumers. With a trusted supplier or an agent acting upon their behalf, provincial elites could thus bypass local towns and send to London for a wide range of goods: not just luxuries but everyday items such as groceries. We see this in the distribution of grocers supplying Mary in the period 1786–1806, when a large proportion of goods came from retailers in the city of London—some distance from her Kensington home and, of course, around one hundred miles from Stoneleigh. It is made clearer still in the correspondence of Elizabeth Purefoy, who ordered groceries from a number of London grocers in the 1730s and 1740s. These letters also illuminate some of the mechanisms whereby trust was established between retailer and customer. Elizabeth Purefoy was always very clear in her requests, leaving little room for error, and was quick to complain if she felt poorly served in terms of price or quality.[51] Perhaps most important, though, she remained loyal to her preferred suppliers, patronising Mr Cossins of St Pauls Churchyard in the 1730s and continuing to do so when the business passed to Wilson and Thornhill in the 1740s.

Such loyalty built trust and was central to shopping practices of the elite and others in the eighteenth century, since it encouraged good service and reduced the transaction costs of shopping.[52] Indeed, Berry argues that Judith Baker, gentlewoman from Durham, bought from a small set of suppliers on her trips to London. Her choice was 'predicated upon a system of patronage, personal acquaintance and credit'.[53] Such priorities can be seen in the behaviour of Edward and Mary Leigh, both of whom returned to known suppliers over a number of years. Given Edward's rather truncated period of active purchasing, it is unsurprising that only a handful of tradesmen supplied him for more than five or six years. Amongst these, local craftsmen were most common: Thomas Howlett of Stoneleigh, who undertook blacksmithing between 1764 and 1780, Arthur Roome, who did bricklaying work from 1764 to 1774, and Thomas Harman, who presented bills for carpentry and painting between 1768 and 1776. Continuity, then, came primarily in terms of servicing the estate—a process that continued through Edward's mental illness. Those supplying goods were generally patronised for shorter periods, but were often used intensively during that time: the London tailor, William Fell, presented six bills totalling over £224 between 1763 and 1767, and Thomas Payne, also of London, billed Edward on twelve occasions in four years, as did the Coventry grocer Hugh Jones.[54]

Once established, relationships between elite provincial consumers and urban, often metropolitan, retailers could be strong and long lasting. Yet the question arises as to how choices of retailer were made in the first place. Here, attention usually focuses on consumers' assessment of quality and price, and on the ability of retailers to construct and project a good reputation.[55] The former could be judged in person, most readily by visiting the shop, but also by having samples sent to one's home.[56] The latter drew on links to previous proprietors, the prestige of certain streets and cachet of patronage by nobility or royalty.[57] It was then communicated and augmented through networks of family and friends. Of particular interest, therefore, are the suppliers which Edward and Mary had in common, since they can reveal something of the mechanisms through which knowledge, trust and reputation were transmitted.

There are many instances where Mary used tradesmen initially patronised by her brother. At one level, we see William Butler twice supplying livery to Edward before Mary began using him in 1787.[58] More telling, perhaps, is when, undertaking some small changes to the furnishings of her rooms in London in 1768, Mary turned to Thomas and Gilbert Burnett, the upholsterers who had played such a large part in the refurbishment of Stoneleigh Abbey three years earlier. That they were willing to execute such a modest order may reflect the importance of her brother's patronage.[59] Much the same appears true of Mary's purchases of coaches: She followed Edward's lead in going to the same coach maker, John Hatchett of Long Acre, that he had used in 1771, first to purchase a new coach (1794) and later to have it repaired (1799).[60] As we have seen, Edward spent a lot of money on books in his quest to amass a library befitting a gentleman. Mary was far less of a bibliophile, but again followed Edward's judgement on booksellers, making a small purchase from James Robson—an important bookseller who supplied over £400 worth of books to Edward between 1766 and 1768.[61] In some ways, these introductions are unsurprising, especially as the dynastic nature of many of these goods meant that men most often purchased them. Edward's familiarity with these areas of spending put him in a position to provide a personal link to reliable and trustworthy tradesmen.

On other occasions, Mary took the lead, especially when it came to buying textiles and clothing. We have already seen that she patronised a great variety of London drapers, haberdashers and milliners. Several of her favoured suppliers were later patronised by her brother. For example, Edward made two purchases of material from the drapers Carr, Ibetson and Bigge in 1763 and 1768—a supplier that Mary had begun using in 1754 and to whom she remained loyal through to the early 1770s.[62] Similarly, he made four purchases from Budd and Devall, milliners in Bruton Street, London, following Mary's initial purchase of ribbons and muslin in 1760.[63] In the 1760s they both used Jordan H. Biggar, drapers in Leadenhall Street, London. Again, Mary had made the first contact in 1762 when she was billed for linen to the value of £1 1s 8d. Quite likely on her recommendation, Edward looked to these suppliers when placing a much larger order (worth over £128) for a variety of table and furnishing linens the following year.[64] The lines of communication in operation here resemble those described by Walsh and others, who have demonstrated how provincial elites frequently drew on knowledgeable friends in convenient locations (often London or Paris) to provide information about goods and suppliers and sometimes to acquire specific items.[65] In this light, we can see Edward drawing on Mary's experience as an experienced metropolitan shopper with first-hand knowledge of retailers and goods.

Some suppliers held a different and perhaps even stronger relationship with the family. Thomas Gilpin, a London silversmith and engraver, first supplied the Leigh family back in 1737 when Edward, third Lord Leigh, paid a bill for some engraving work.[66] His grandson, Edward, fifth Lord Leigh, bought jewellery and silver as a young boy in 1751 and, when in charge of the estate, made more substantial purchases, as well as selling around £700 of unwanted silver to Gilpin in 1765.[67] Over a similar period, Gilpin also supplied Mary with silverware and jewellery on three occasions, in 1751, 1753 and 1765.[68] Similarly, Edward and Mary's father, Thomas, fourth Lord Leigh, made five purchases of clothing and material from Robert Hughes of Coventry during the 1740s.[69] Edward, or more probably his guardians, then went to Hughes for livery in 1753, as did Mary in 1753 and 1756.[70] In both cases there appears to be a shared culture of consumption that both Edward and Mary inherited from earlier generations. Since both of them were very young when their father died we can assume that this information on reliable suppliers of quality must have been transferred through their guardians, who were both related to the Leighs, or through the stewards of the house, which adds another possible layer to the relationship of the family with their suppliers. In some cases the consumer choices of Edward and Mary continued across several generations of the suppliers' families—continuity being provided by the customer rather than the tradesman. Two generations of the Fell family, of St Martin's Lane, London, supplied drapery and livery for Edward and Mary from the 1760s through to the early nineteenth century. These common suppliers confirm that Edward and Mary shared information, probably both in terms of quality and reliability, and thus defined *together* the relationships of the Leigh family with their suppliers. Such choices were personal and individual, and to some extent gendered along conventional lines, but they were also embedded in family relationships.

CONCLUSION

Edward and Mary spent their money in very different ways: They bought different things for different reasons, reflecting and constructing their gender identity through their choices. But these gender identities were tempered by aristocratic status, which brought with it a set of common responsibilities, not least in servicing a substantial country house and a leisured lifestyle underpinned by luxury consumption. To some extent, the geography of Edward's and Mary's spending—and therefore their relationship with towns—flowed from the goods they purchased, both in terms of value and type, but they were also defined by their lifestyles and different courses their lives took. Mary's London residence and sociability was reflected in her purchases of fine clothing and food from metropolitan suppliers. Edward's love of books and architecture were similarly reflected in his engagement with the luxury market in London, partly transferred through his sister and her knowledge of that complex city. Their upbringing was, of course, defined in part by gender: Edward, with his natural assumption of the role of a country landowner after a young life formally educated in the classics, and Mary, with her life of a sociable young lady amid the social circles of London. But they shared and inherited information on suppliers and showed considerable loyalty to favoured tradesmen and women. Gendered and personal preferences were thus tempered by family as well as by status.

All of this illustrates the close and complex ways in which gender and social status interacted and how such identities could shift across the lifecourse. Edward's consumption choices may not have been 'utterly masculine', to use Vickery's phrase, but they were masculine nonetheless: they showed self-control, taste, learning and pride in family/pedigree.[71] Mary's concerns may have strayed beyond the enduring female concerns centred on the private domestic sphere, but as the owner of almost twenty-thousand acres, one of a long line of wealthy powerful landowners, it was inevitable that her purchases became more 'masculine' than we might anticipate. Of course, the classic patriarchal relationship of a married couple with its attendant systems of power and subjugation is not represented here. To some extent Edward and Mary were unusual in that they both died unmarried and experienced a more subtle form of gender relationship as brother and sister. These findings do, however, inform our understandings of gender, status and consumption precisely because of the way in which they isolate elite consumption practices from those more rigid familial and domestic spheres.

NOTES

1 See, for example, Richard Wilson and Alan Mackley, *The Building of the English Country House* (London: Hambledon Continuum, 2000); Christopher Christie, *The British Country House in the Eighteenth Century* (Manchester: Manchester University Press, 2000). With the middling sort, this translated into a male predominance in shaping the household economy—see Karen Harvey, *The Little Republic: Masculinity and Domestic Authority in Eighteenth-Century Britain* (Oxford: Oxford University Press, 2012), 65–67, 80–86.
2 Colin Campbell, 'Understanding Traditional and Modern Patterns of Consumption in Eighteenth-Century England: a Character-Action Approach', in *Consumption and the World of Goods*, ed. John Brewer and Roy Porter (London: Routledge, 1993), 40–58; Henry French and Mark Rothery, *Man's Estate: Landed Gentry Masculinities, 1660–1900* (Oxford: Oxford University Press, 2012).
3 Werner Sombart, *Luxury and Capitalism* (Michigan: University of Michigan Press, 1967); Neil McKendrick, 'The Consumer Revolution of Eighteenth-Century England', in *The Birth of a Consumer Society*, ed. Neil McKendrick, John Brewer and J. H. Plumb (London: Methuen, 1982), 9–33.
4 Jane Whittle and Elizabeth Griffiths, *Consumption and Gender in the Early-Seventeenth-Century Household: The World of Alice Le Strange* (Oxford: Oxford University Press, 2012), 55–64, 117–55; Hannah Greig, 'Leading the Fashion: The Material Culture of London's *Beau Monde*', in *Gender, Taste and Material Culture in Britain and North America*, ed. John Styles and Amanda Vickery (New Haven: Yale University Press, 2006), 293–313; Judith Lewis, 'When a House is Not a Home: Elite English Women and the Eighteenth-Century Country House', *Journal of British Studies* 48 (2009): 336–63; Amanda Vickery, *The Gentleman's Daughter: Women's Lives in Georgian England* (New Haven: Yale University Press, 1998); Amanda Vickery, *Behind Closed Doors: At Home in Georgian England* (New Haven: Yale University Press, 2008), 106–28, 184–207.
5 Vickery, *Gentleman's Daughter*, esp. 183–94; Vickery, *Behind Closed Doors*, 106–28, 184–207; Helen Berry, 'Prudent Luxury: The Metropolitan Tastes of Judith Baker, Durham Gentlewoman', in *Out of Town: Women and Urban Life in Eighteenth-Century Britain*, ed. Penelope Lane and Roey Sweet (Aldershot: Ashgate, 2005), 130–54; Maxine Berg, *Luxury and Pleasure in Eighteenth-Century Britain* (Oxford: Oxford University Press, 2005), 234–43.
6 See, for example, Margot Finn, 'Men's Things: Masculine Possession in the Consumer Revolution', *Social History* 25 (2000): 133–55; Vickery, *Behind Closed Doors*, 49–82; David Hussey, 'Guns, Horses and Stylish Waistcoats?

Male Consumer Activity and Domestic Shopping in Late-Eighteenth and Early-Nineteenth-Century England', in *Buying for the Home: Shopping for the Domestic from the Seventeenth Century to the Present*, ed. David Hussey and Margaret Ponsonby (Aldershot: Ashgate, 2008), 47–72; David Hussey and Margaret Ponsonby, *The Single Homemaker and Material Culture in the Long Eighteenth Century* (Farnham: Ashgate, 2012), esp. 117–23.

7 Vickery, *Behind Closed Doors*, 114. This pattern is confirmed for the middling sort by Harvey, *Little Republic*, 82–86.

8 For details, see Mark Rothery and Jon Stobart, 'Inheritance Events and Spending Patterns in the English Country House: The Leigh Family of Stoneleigh Abbey, 1738–1806', *Continuity and Change* 27 (2012): 379–407.

9 Shakespeare Center Library & Archive (hereafter SCLA), DR18/5/4017. This type of spending was fairly typical of young men at Oxford although, as mentioned earlier, young men were expected to control their finances whilst at university. See the several examples of parental advice on this matter in French and Rothery, *Man's Estate*, 85–137.

10 SCLA, DR18/31/456 Auditors account, Nov. 1763–May 1774.

11 See Campbell, 'Understanding Traditional Consumption'. Women played a key role when it came to interior decoration, a point discussed in detail by Vickery, *Behind Closed Doors*, 129–65.

12 There are bills for chimney pieces, plasterwork, wallpapering and painting—see, for example, SCLA DR18/5/4203, DR18/5/4395, DR18/5/4402.

13 SCLA, DR671/33 Designs for Stoneleigh Abbey by Edward Leigh and Timothy Lightholer, N.D.; DR18/5/4291 Architectural designs by Giovanibatista Cipriani, 1 April 1765.

14 French and Rothery, *Man's Estate*. For studies of other social groups see Alexandra Sheperd, 'Manhood, Credit and Patriarchy in Early-Modern England c.1580–1640', *Past and Present* 167 (2000): 75–106; Anthony Fletcher, 'Manhood, the Male Body, Courtship and Household in Early-Modern England', *History* 84 (1999): 419–36; Helen Berry, 'Soul, Purse and Family: Middling and Lower-Class Masculinity in Eighteenth-Century Manchester', *Social History* 33 (2008): 12–35.

15 SCLA DR18/5/4203, DR18/5/4395, DR18/5/4402.

16 Andor Gomme, 'Abbey into Palace: A Lesser Wilton?', in *Stoneleigh Abbey: The House, Its Owners, Its Lands*, ed. Robert Bearman (Stratford-upon-Avon: Shakespeare Birthplace Trust, 2004), 82–115.

17 SCLA, DR18/5/4408, DR18/3/47/52/15.

18 French and Rothery, *Man's Estate*, 85–184.

19 SCLA, DR18/17/27/97, Letter from Samuel Butler (Estate Steward) to William Craven re: costs of house and garden alterations, 11 Feb. 1764.

20 Vickery, *Behind Closed Doors*, 106–29; Campbell, 'Understanding Traditional Consumption'.

21 Vickery, *Behind Closed Doors*; Jon Stobart, 'Gentlemen and Shopkeepers: Supplying the Country House in Eighteenth-Century England', *Economic History Review* 64 (2011): 885–904.

22 SCLA, DR18/17/27/52; M. Purcell, "'A lunatic of unsound mind': Edward Lord Leigh (1742–86) and the refounding of Oriel College library", *Bodleian Library Record*, 17 (2001): 249.

23 SCLA, DR18/5/4515, DR18/5/4385.

24 SCLA, DR18/13/7/13–4, Will of Edward Lord Leigh, proved 22 July 1786.

25 See Campbell, 'Understanding Traditional Consumption'; French and Rothery, *Man's Estate*, passim.

26 Mairi MacDonald, '"Not Unmarked by Some Eccentricities": The Leigh Family of Stoneleigh Abbey', in *Stoneleigh Abbey*, 148, 153–55.

27 See, for example, SCLA, DR18/5/3593, DR18/5/4308.
28 Lewis, 'When a House is Not a Home'.
29 SCLA, DR18/5/5864, DR18/5/5822, DR18/5/5905, DR18/5/5703.
30 SCLA, DR671, 22 August 1790; DR18/4/59, Inventory, 1806.
31 SCLA, DR18/5/4402. For a fuller discussion of wallpaper and colour, see Vickery, *Behind Closed Doors*, 166–83.
32 SCLA, DR18/4/43.
33 Humphrey Repton, *Fragments on the Theory and Practice of Landscape Gardening* (London: T. Bensley and Son, 1816).
34 Kate Retford, 'Patrilineal Portraiture? Gender and Genealogy in the Eighteenth-Century English Country House', in *Gender, Taste and Material Culture*, 337–38; Adrian Tinniswood, *The Polite Tourist: Four Centuries of Country House Visiting* (London: National Trust, 1999), 108.
35 SCLA, DR18/5/3194.
36 SCLA, DR18/5/5809.
37 For example, see Peter Mandler, '"From Almack to Willis": Aristocratic Women and Politics, 1815–1867', in *Women, Privilege and Power: British Politics 1750 to the Present*, ed. Amanda Vickery (Stanford: Stanford University Press, 2005), 152–67; Retford, 'Patrilineal Portraiture?'.
38 See, for example, SCLA, DR18/5/6122–6130.
39 SCLA, DR18/5/6051, DR18/5/6099.
40 SCLA, DR18/5/6098.
41 Vickery, *Behind Closed Doors*, 124.
42 Helena Whitbread, ed., *I Know My Own Heart: The Diaries of Anne Lister, 1791–1840* (London: Virago, 1988), esp. 249–50.
43 On masculine self-control, see French and Rothery, *Man's Estate*, 61–66, 78–80, 169–71.
44 Whittle and Griffiths, *Consumption and Gender*, 203–8; Harvey, *Little Republic*, 24–35, 65–76.
45 Stobart, 'Gentlemen and Shopkeepers'; Jon Stobart and Mark Rothery, 'Geographies of Supply: Stoneleigh Abbey and Arbury Hall in the Eighteenth Century', in *Consuming the Country House*, ed. Jon Stobart and Andrew Hann (London: English Heritage, forthcoming).
46 See, for example, SCLA, DR18/5/3925, DR18/5/3982, DR18/5/3980.
47 Stobart, 'Gentlemen and Shopkeepers'.
48 Gomme, 'Abbey into Palace', 87, 95, 97–99, 101–5. The hierarchy of supply is discussed in more detail in Stobart and Rothery, 'Geographies of Supply'.
49 SCLA, DR18/5/4192, DR18/5/4031, DR18/5/4078, DR18/5/4171.
50 See, for example, SCLA, DR18/5/6351, DR18/5/6172, DR18/5/6434.
51 G. Eland, ed., *Purefoy Letters*, 1735–1753, 2 vols. (London: Sidgwick & Jackson, Ltd., 1931) nos. 103, 104, 105, 106, 111. See also Jon Stobart, *Sugar and Spice: Grocers and Groceries in Provincial England, 1650–1830* (Oxford: Oxford University Press, 2013), 203–13.
52 Bruno Blondé and Ilja Van Damme, 'Retail Growth and Consumer Changes in a Declining Urban Economy: Antwerp 1650–1750', *Economic History Review* 32 (2010): 638–63; Stobart, *Sugar and Spice*, 134–35, 144–45, 156–67.
53 Berry, 'Prudent Luxury', 146.
54 For examples, see SCLA DR18/5/4133 (Jones), 4195 (Howlett) and 4389 (Payne).
55 See Blondé and Van Damme, 'Retail Growth'.
56 Claire Walsh, 'Shops, Shopping and the Art of Decision Making in Eighteenth-Century England', in *Gender, Taste and Material*, 151–77; Stobart, *Sugar and Spice*, 147.

57 Jon Stobart, 'Selling (Through) Politeness: Advertising Provincial Shops in Eighteenth-Century England', *Cultural and Social History* 5 (2008): 309–328.
58 SCLA, DR18/5/4657, DR18/5/5062.
59 SCLA, DR18/5/4620; DR18/3/47/52/15.
60 SCLA, DR18/5/6054, DR18/5/6446.
61 SCLA, DR18/5/5000 (Mary's purchase). For examples of Edward's purchases from Robson, see DR18/5/4529.
62 SCLA, DR18/5/4035, DR18/5/4661.
63 SCLA, DR18/5/3970, DR18/5/4126, DR18/5/4139, DR18/5/4511.
64 SCLA, DR18/5/3960, DR18/5/4028.
65 Walsh, 'Shops, Shopping'. See also Vickery, *Gentleman's Daughter*, 168–69.
66 SCLA, DR18/5/1989.
67 SCLA, DR18/5/3121, DR18/5/4574, DR18/5/3121.
68 SCLA, DR18/5/3136, 3194 and 4333.
69 For example, see SCLA, DR18/5/2129.
70 SCLA, DR18/5/3331 (Edward), and DR18/5/3349, DR18/5/3638 (Mary)
71 Vickery, *Behind Closed Doors*, 124; Campbell, 'Understanding Traditional Consumption'; French and Rothery, *Man's Estate*, 61–66, 78–80, 169–71.

7 The Luxury Shopping Experience of the Swedish Aristocracy in Eighteenth-Century Paris[1]

Johanna Ilmakunnas

During the eighteenth century, relations between Sweden and France were good. Close diplomatic contacts helped political and cultural influences circulate in a variety of forms, including political alliances, philosophical ideas, objects of art and luxury goods.[2] Swedish aristocrats acquired French silk and velvet dresses, snuffboxes, ribbons, laces, hats, fans, shoe buckles, silverware, furniture, books and paintings, all those objects historians have called luxuries and semi-luxuries in research on the production, distribution and consumption of eighteenth-century luxury goods.[3] French culture and French luxury were both desired and detested in Sweden. Furthermore, the attitudes towards luxury were ambiguous and the concepts of luxury, necessity and extravagance were constantly defined and redefined in eighteenth-century Sweden.[4] The Swedish aristocracy was politically powerful, cosmopolitan, francophone, well educated and familiar with aristocratic circles in other European states. Their contacts with France, especially Paris, opened the markets of luxury goods to them.

This chapter discusses the luxury shopping experience of the Swedish aristocracy in Paris, as well as the meanings and representations of luxury for this aristocracy. The concept of experience is here understood in terms of experiencing an act and describing it in epistolary form. It also shows how a considerable number of the imported French luxury goods were introduced and distributed to Sweden by the diplomatic corps. It analyses subjective choices in urban shopping and decision-making and explores the role of gender in individual cases. Through case studies from the 1740s to the 1780s, it demonstrates how the Swedish nobility made purchases in Paris either for themselves or as commissioners for others. The chapter also presents the variety of goods the Swedish aristocracy bought in Paris. Choices of luxury objects and shopping experiences are studied with examples from the highest ranks of the Swedish nobility: diplomats and aristocratic travellers who socialised at European royal and imperial courts and in the highest circles of Paris, Stockholm and other cities. Many Swedes—diplomats, officers, tradesmen, artists, architects and craftsmen—sojourned shorter or longer periods, even years, in France. Charlotta Wolff argues that from the early eighteenth century, Paris became a second hometown for the Swedish cosmopolitan aristocracy, and France its other fatherland.[5]

Private letters written by Swedish aristocrats to the members of their families and diplomatic correspondence between Swedish envoys in Paris and the sovereign form the key source material. Goods, fashion, buying, choosing, paying and credit were topics often discussed in correspondence. News about the latest fashion articles and luxury goods circulated rapidly from France to Sweden in letters, journals, almanacs, fashion plates and magazines and fabric samples. To find the pleasures of shopping, the best source is letters between equals. Correspondence between siblings or friends reveals more often the pleasurable part of shopping or acquisition than correspondence between subordinates does. Rarely would a son write to his father about how he enjoyed shopping. The difficult relationship with money and economic dependence on parents shaped how children described purchases to their parents to whom they had to legitimise their shopping. Their correspondence with siblings or friends was influenced rather differently.

SWEDISH ARISTOCRACY, LUXURY AND SHOPPING IN THE EIGHTEENTH CENTURY

In eighteenth-century Sweden, sumptuary laws forbade most foreign luxury goods. The economic policies of the crown aimed at protecting Swedish production by taxing or banning foreign—most often French—luxury. In addition to protecting domestic production, sumptuary laws intended to maintain social order and retain differences between the privileged and non-privileged.[6] Despite the intentions of the legislature, however, sumptuary laws did not manage to restrain luxury consumption.[7] On the other hand, in *ancien régime* societies, where outer appearance and the lifestyle of high society required splendour and display, luxury was a necessity. Thus Swedish aristocrats were incessantly faced with choices between the good of their country, the necessities of their status and rank and their personal desires and wants.[8] For the Swedish aristocracy, French goods represented both positive and negative sides of ever-drifting connotations of the concept of luxury, since the aristocrats were well aware of the requirements of their rank, of the economic welfare of their country and of contemporary debates on luxury. Luxury was necessary for an aristocratic lifestyle, but opulence and excess provoked criticism. These different sides of the issue competed with each other both on a national and on a personal level, often causing individual consumer choices to collide with the political and economic policy of Sweden as a state. The confrontation could be relatively tangible to the aristocracy holding political power in Sweden since they also decided on national economic issues, such as sumptuary laws or tolls on the import of foreign luxury goods.

Despite satirical writings and caricatures of spendthrift nobility, aristocratic luxury was not the principal issue of the luxury debates in Sweden. Scholars have stressed the relative and contingent nature of luxury and reminded us that the very definition of luxury is shifting and fluctuating throughout history. Moreover, one of the key questions of the eighteenth-century debates on luxury was the relativity of luxury both morally and economically.[9] The luxury debates often connected shopping to feminine, unreasonable and extravagant behaviour. It was regarded throughout Europe as an effeminate and negative act typical of women who could not control their purchasing lust.[10] Both contemporaries and researchers have thus given significant space to the discussion about women's luxury consumption. However, recently researchers have argued that both male and female agency is equally significant in everyday life and consumption, as Stobart and Rothery argue in this volume.[11] Karin Hassan Jansson argues that in Sweden, as in other countries the luxury debates focused on luxury consumption of the middling sorts, criticising both male and female consumption of luxuries as effeminate. The key arguments were that luxury disrupted the social order and drove honest, hard-working Swedes to poverty.[12]

From the seventeenth century onwards Paris was the capital of fashion and luxury for the Swedish aristocracy.[13] The diversity and myriad of shops in Paris offered them manifold shopping possibilities and experiences compared to those in Swedish cities. For aristocrats throughout Europe, Paris was an iconic city for shopping. Its metropolitan shopping opportunities created an aura of elegance, exclusivity and taste no other city could claim before the second half of the twentieth century. Shopkeepers, merchants and guidebooks actively advertised Paris as a luxury venue, thus adding to its lure.[14] Aristocrats wished to go shopping in Paris, the most important foreign city for Swedes during the era, and experience a variety of shops, a world apart from the modest shopping possibilities in Swedish towns. The nobility craved fashionable luxurious goods that were not available in Stockholm or that were regarded as more desirable and of better quality in Paris than in Stockholm. Since the aristocracy sojourned in Stockholm from autumn to spring, living in their town houses and participating in political and social life, they had time and means to experience the shopping possibilities Stockholm offered in full, not only during visits of shorter or longer periods. For Swedish aristocrats, luxury shopping in Paris or luxury goods commissioned from Paris were signs of distinction, taste and the quality of a person.

There is little research on shops and shopping in eighteenth-century Sweden against the growing quantity of international research on the topic.[15] Luxury shopping in eighteenth-century Stockholm remains to be explored despite a wide amount research on Swedish merchant houses, important distributors of luxury goods at the time.[16] In this chapter, however, the shopping patterns and experiences of Swedish aristocracy in eighteenth-century Paris offer us an image of the most luxurious shopping amongst an elite that also shopped in Stockholm.

SHOPPING FOR PLEASURE, SHOPPING FOR NECESSITY

Eighteenth-century consumers were actors who actively made choices and decisions and took delight in their consumer experience.[17] In Paris, Swedish aristocrats bought luxury and semi-luxury goods for pleasure, but also as a necessity that grew from the demands of an aristocratic lifestyle and the vitality of distinction in the court society.[18] Swedish aristocrats socialised in the salons of Paris high society and at the royal court of Versailles, and for their shopping they relied on the taste and advice of French aristocrats and royals.[19] The demands of fashionable outer appearance were especially powerful in Paris, where all aristocrats had in principle immeasurable possibilities for shopping. The pleasure of shopping, walking through arcades and stepping into shops, seeing and touching a variety of products, making decisions and finding a way to pay for the purchases made up the elements of the Swedish aristocracy's shopping experience in Paris. The city itself and its opulent luxury markets were pivotal for the experience of shopping and selecting. However, individual economic prospects and subjective attitudes to luxury restricted consumption, as the following examples illustrate.

Count Carl Gustaf Tessin, diplomat, statesman and collector, enjoyed beautiful, tasteful, luxurious objects, artwork and shopping. During his time as the Swedish ambassador in Paris (1739–1742) he described his purchases of art as follies. In February 1740, for instance, he bought a snuffbox on which a portrait of his niece Charlotta Sparre was painted by Jean-Baptiste Massé, and a portrait of his dachshund, Pehr, was painted by Jean-Baptiste Oudry. Tessin also bought paintings from François Boucher, Jean-Siméon Chardin and Carle van Loo. In addition, he bought several drawings from Edmé Bouchardon and Nicolas Lancret. He wrote to his friend, architect Baron Carl Hårleman: 'Let's close the curtain over other [products], I see you are looking at me with pity'.[20] Tessin does not write where or how he acquired the paintings, but most probably from one of the most famous art dealers in eighteenth-century Paris: Edme Gersaint, whose shop on Pont Notre-Dame Tessin frequented.[21]

In eighteenth-century towns, shopping became a past-time, enjoyable and social leisure.[22] The art dealers' shops and artists' ateliers were spaces for sociability, to see and to be seen, as Antoine Watteau's famous painting on Gersaint's shop depicts.[23] In Paris, shopping was part of Tessin's social and professional life. He bought paintings, drawings, books and luxury goods because he enjoyed their beauty and because he could not help himself, as he acknowledged in his letters.[24] Through his purchases of French luxury goods, Tessin consolidated his masculinity and status as a cosmopolitan collector, connoisseur of contemporary art and as a man of taste, despite facing financial problems because of his acquisitions.

Though Count Tessin hinted that his shopping was uncontrolled, at the time capricious shopping was more often linked to women and femininity. In 1745, Countess Brita De la Gardie took carriages in order to avoid anybody knowing where she went, visited friends and the opera, and 'she calls on different artisans and merchants she finds on her route and buys, not what she would like to buy but [goods] they want to sell her'.[25] For Brita De la Gardie, shopping seems to have been an act of which she was not entirely in control. Perhaps shopping became her way to deal with the personal distress caused by her terminally ill mother and the religious turmoil that later led to her conversion to Catholicism.[26] Presumably the competence of Parisian merchants in marketing their products had an impact on the countess's shopping. In eighteenth-century Paris, merchants skilfully and actively promoted their goods and created new needs for eager consumers.[27] The countess could not resist their marketing strategies, verifying the contemporary image of unrestrained feminine shopping, even if hers was not entirely typical.

A year later, in 1746, shopping acted as a remedy for Brita De la Gardie's then thirteen-year-old sister Hedvig De la Gardie, who was alone in Paris after their mother's death and her sister's conversion. The Swedish envoy Baron Carl Fredrik Scheffer was responsible for her and let her go shopping to cheer herself up a bit. Going shopping was Hedvig De la Gardie's own desire, and Scheffer did not want to refuse her wish because of her dire situation.[28] Shopping was an efficient method to channel the young girl's thoughts away from family sorrow and toward more mundane occupations. Another reason for finding something else to think about was probably Scheffer's fear that the young countess would follow her sister and convert to Catholicism, a constant dismay for Lutheran Swedes in Catholic France.[29]

Hedvig De la Gardie bought several dresses, laces, ribbons and undefined other ornaments for over 1,200 *livres*. For her, it was the first time she could choose by herself what and where to buy. According to Scheffer, Hedvig De la Gardie used her freedom of shopping extravagantly and bought much more than was proper. He did not express his views explicitly in his letter to his predecessor as envoy, Hedvig's guardian and brother-in-law Count Clas Ekeblad, but his opinion and attitudes towards luxury and feminine shopping are clear.[30] Unfortunately, we don't know how Hedvig De la Gardie herself experienced her shopping in Parisian boutiques since there are no surviving letters from her on the topic. Nevertheless, the letter from Scheffer to Ekeblad reveals how he perceived the countess's behaviour and his perplexity over of the excess of her shopping behaviour. The demand for French luxury in Sweden was to the extent that Scheffer referred to luxury goods as drugs and noted that it would have been easy to sell those items Hedvig De la Gardie did not necessarily need.[31] Scheffer's strong antipathy against shopping arises presumably from his person, his Lutheran moralist attitudes and the situation where he, as the Swedish envoy and unmarried nobleman, was responsible for the De la Gardie sisters after their mother's death. It has to be taken into account, though, that Scheffer does not seem to condemn all luxury, only the excessive and ostentatious luxury consumption he saw as morally disintegrating.[32]

Envoy Scheffer was not alone with his critical views on luxury consumption and the effect shopping had on a person's morals. Influential Swedish politicians demanded that the nobility should act as an example for the rest of the society in its consuming choices. Aristocracy had a moral responsibility to consume in accordance with its rank and status, but excessive flamboyance was considered neither noble nor elegant.[33] Critical voices towards luxury arose remarkably often among fathers who were paying the bills their sons incurred in Paris. Almost without exception, the fathers had lived in Paris and were familiar with the shopping prospects of the city. In the 1770s, Count Clas Ekeblad wrote to his son Clas Julius Ekeblad that he was angry about his son's shopping in Paris. He concluded that he had wasted his father's money by buying a velvet coat in spring, shortly before the summer heat, when a velvet coat was a most impractical piece of clothing. Count Ekeblad also argued that the coat would be out of fashion in autumn when it would again be suitable for the season.[34] Disputes about money in between generations were discussed in numerous letters. Correspondence between fathers and sons brings to light how young noblemen were economically dependent on their parents if they did not have sufficient income from an office or inherited wealth of their own. Sons had to legitimise their purchases and consumption to fathers who held the purse strings and decided how much sons could consume and on what. Ekeblad's attitude towards his son's purchases shows also the importance and rapid change of fashion at the time. A coat bought in the spring would be old-fashioned in six months, and would be ridiculous in the aristocratic circles of Parisian society and at court in Versailles. Perhaps Ekeblad stressed the importance of fashion in order to make his argument stronger.

Count Clas Julius Ekeblad's cousin, Count Hans Axel von Fersen, was likewise financially dependent on his father, despite Fersen's successful military career in French service. Fersen's salary was not adequate for his lifestyle, and his father Count Axel von Fersen helped him financially, though often involuntarily. In spring 1778, son and father corresponded, among other issues, on the subject of a carriage that the son wanted to buy. However justified the son's request, Axel von Fersen did not give his permission for the purchase, and the son was left disappointed because he could not afford the carriage himself.[35]

The relative nature of luxury and necessity is clearly exposed by contrasting the monthly expenses in Paris by Clas Julius Ekeblad, Hans Axel von Fersen and Curt von Stedingk in the 1770s and the 1780s. In 1767, Ekeblad lived on 159 *livres* per month; in 1770, Stedingk lived on 100 *livres* per month; and in 1780, Fersen lived on 1,100 *livres* per month.[36] They all belonged to the same aristocratic circles and socialised at the French court and in Parisian high society. Fersen's and Stedingk's military careers in French service were to develop equally successfully. Although Ekeblad's and Stedingk's expenditures are from a period when they stayed with their regiments in garrison towns and had lower expenses than in Paris, the difference between their and Fersen's expenditure is considerable. It shows clearly how attitudes towards luxury and necessity could be different among individuals with equal social backgrounds and similar connections. For Fersen, a certain level of luxury and quality of products was more important than for his friends and kin. His father could also afford his son's lifestyle, whereas Stedingk and his father had insufficient economic resources for equally luxurious life.

The example of another Swedish officer in French service, Gustav Adolf von Siegroth, narrates the shopping experiences of Swedish aristocrats in Paris, bringing to light luxury consumption of a more modest nobleman. In 1751, Siegroth travelled to Paris and immediately bought a black suit, which was more suitable in Paris than his uniform. This was his only expense on clothes during his stay in town from December 1751 to February 1752. Siegroth's financial situation was, like many young gentlemen's finances, rather modest, which made him economise in Paris. He tried to gain powerful protectors, the Swedish envoy Baron Scheffer, the French war minister Count d'Argenson and other aristocrats, in order to get a promotion to colonel; however, he did not succeed. Siegroth enjoyed the Parisian sights, entertainments and cultural life in his leisure time. He bought a map of Paris, books and drawings. At the Saint-Germain fair, one of the yearly fairs in Paris that was most often linked to luxury goods, Siegroth bought several semi-luxuries such as small boxes and ivory gaming chips from a stand with a pretty shop girl.[37] Jennifer M. Jones argues that during the eighteenth century a pleasant masculine shopping experience was considerably fostered by *grisettes*, shop girls who were linked both to the business of fashion and titillating immorality.[38] Siegroth particularly mentioned the pretty girl in his diary, suggesting a sensual nuance in his shopping experience. Shopping was social interaction that temporarily could lower the barriers between social groups.

SHOPPING BY PROXY—FAMILY AND FRIENDS

An excellent account of the complex networks of credit and trust, kinship and friendship necessary for proxy shopping are the purchases of Baroness Charlotta Fredrika Sparre between 1742 and 1743. She had been in Paris between 1739 and 1741 with her relatives, the Swedish ambassador Count Carl Gustaf Tessin and his wife Countess Ulla Sparre, experiencing the shopping possibilities of the metropolis and enjoying the attention she attracted in high society and at court. Thus, Charlotta Sparre had vivid memories of how luxury markets operated and how an aristocrat should negotiate her space when shopping either in shops or when merchants and *marchandes de modes* visited aristocratic town houses selling their goods.

In spring 1742, Charlotta Sparre wrote to Tessin asking him to send her a pair of the finest handiwork scissors for cutting thin muslins and silks.

Sparre gave detailed instructions about the size and sharpness of the scissors and wrote that she regretted not having bought the scissors herself when in Paris.[39] Scissors were considered of better quality in Paris than those available in Stockholm at the time.[40] Since elegant needlework and handicrafts were part of eighteenth-century sociability, genteel ladies commissioned and bought materials and objects needed for their work. Aristocratic needlework was expensive and time consuming. Materials such as silks, laces, sequin and ribbons were luxury items that were not only bought in Stockholm but also occasionally commissioned from Paris. It was more common to commission luxury artefacts that were used in the making of embroideries. The scissors Charlotta Sparre ordered are one example; others are shuttles in Sèvres porcelain or gold and silver thimbles. Thus shopping, while on one hand considered frivolous, could lead on the other hand to female industriousness through scissors, thimbles, fabrics, threads and other objects needed in producing handicrafts.

In 1743, she commissioned more luxury goods from Paris. Again the envoy—now Count Clas Ekeblad, Tessin's successor in the Swedish embassy—took care of her instructions. Sparre wrote individual letters to different artisans and suppliers commissioning stockings, shoes, gloves, jewellery and cosmetics. She wanted only the finest quality, using the language the merchants themselves used when marketing their goods in written form in almanacs or bill headings.[41] Sparre advised Ekeblad to ask for help in shopping from Marquise de Broglie, because 'she is a person who [has] good taste, and who likes to help foreigners . . . '. Charlotta Sparre personally knew Madame de Broglie and could thus indirectly ask her for a favour. She wanted someone with good taste and connections to take care of her commissions. Perhaps she hoped it would be easier to Ekeblad to find the goods if he had someone to help him. However, it is interesting to notice that Sparre asked Ekeblad not mention her name to *Madame la marquise*. She wrote openly that she did not want to be obliged to write to thank Madame de Broglie.[42]

To a merchant named Alibert, Charlotta Sparre proudly wrote: 'Monsieur Alibert remembers without a doubt Mademoiselle Sparre who he kitted out last year when she was in Paris with Madame la Comtesse Tessin'.[43] Charlotta Sparre's choice of words hinted to the merchant that she was an important client with powerful connections. Naming Countess Tessin, who was a personal friend of the Queen Marie Leszczyńska and French aristocrats, immediately showed Alibert that the commission came from the highest aristocracy. In Paris, aristocrats did not entirely choose freely which shops they went to or on which suppliers and merchants they relied. In Parisian luxury markets, the most famous merchants, *marchands de modes*, milliners and shopkeepers could choose their clientele. To become accepted, the clientele required good connections, name and wealth, as Natacha Coquery has shown.[44] From Alibert, Charlotta Sparre ordered stockings, mentioning the price of white silk stockings, twelve *livres* per pair, and demonstrating her knowledge of the suitable price level. In her letter, she also gave detailed instructions about the size and embroideries on the stockings.[45] The Swedish sumptuary laws prohibited the import of silk stockings, but aristocrats did not consider it necessary to conform to the rules, demonstrating how ineffective the laws were.[46]

From another merchant, Guereaut, Sparre ordered four pairs of finest fashionable silk mules. She again mentioned being an old customer and part of the merchant's clientele, as well as giving an exact description of the shoes, their size, shape and colour. Furthermore, she indicated that Count Ekeblad would collect the shoes from Guereaut's shop.[47] The sumptuary laws also prohibited the import of shoes, but again the embargo was not an issue. In Stockholm, foreign diplomats, such as the French envoy, were frequently organised to receive the goods, ensuring the free import of luxury goods because of their diplomatic immunity.[48] Sparre ordered a pair of earrings and a pearl necklace from jeweller Pierre Jaquin, to whom she again mentioned both Countess Tessin's and Count Ekeblad's names. The baroness sketched the jewels in the commission letter in order to have exactly what she wanted.[49] In her fourth commission, which was to the perfumer Lluet, Sparre mentioned Countess Tessin's name when ordering a dozen white and a dozen grey gloves as well as cosmetics, pomade and perfume.[50]

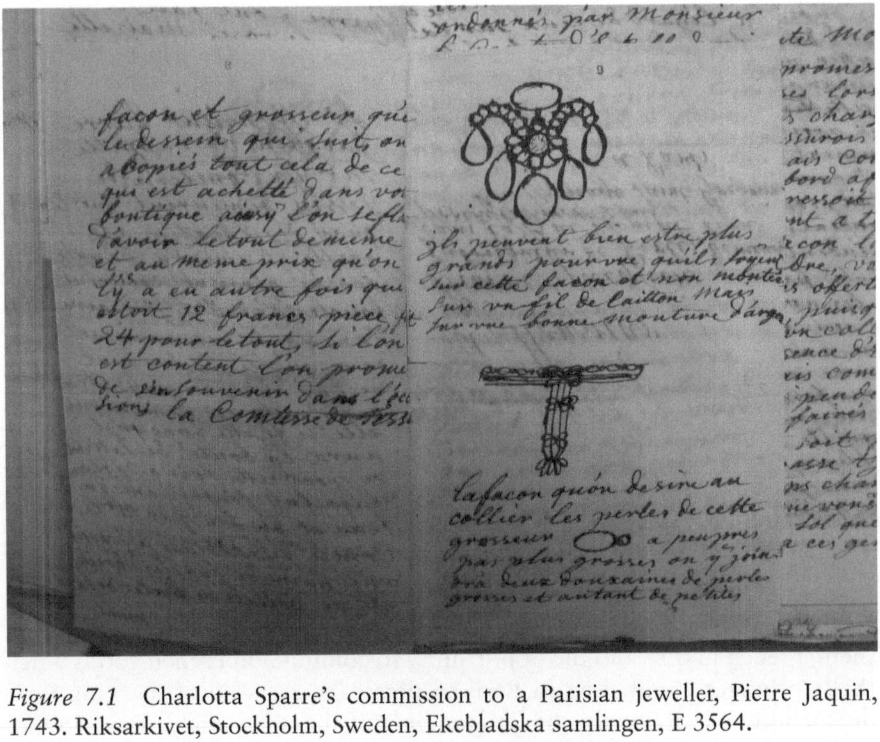
ordonnés par Monsieur

facon et grosseur qui
le dessein qui suit, on
a copiés tout cela de ce
qui est achetté dans vo
boutique ainsy l'on se fl
d'avoir le tout de meme
et au meme prix qu'on
l'y a eu autre fois qui
etoit 12 francs piece et
24 pour le tout, si l'on
est content l'on prome
de s'en souvenir dans l'e
tions la Comtesse de Tessi

ils peuvent bien estre plus
grands pourvue quils soyent
sur cette facon et non montés
sur un fil de Caillou mais
sur une bonne monture d'argent

la facon quon desire au
collier les perles de cette
grosseur a peu pres
pas plus grosses on y joindra
deux douxaines de perles
grosses et autant de petites

Figure 7.1 Charlotta Sparre's commission to a Parisian jeweller, Pierre Jaquin, 1743. Riksarkivet, Stockholm, Sweden, Ekebladska samlingen, E 3564.

The sources do not reveal more about Charlotta Sparre's commissions. We do not know how long it took before she got the goods she ordered or if they were as she had pictured them when her commission arrived. We also do not know how she paid for her commissions. In many cases of aristocratic purchases, money never changed hands. The aristocratic consumption of French luxury goods was based on a network of trust, credit and credibility as well as family connections and friendship. Often the goods were regarded as gifts and were paid for by return presents or services.[51] This was of course the case when the commissions were not spectacularly valuable. The diplomats did not pay for the commissions generated by royal households themselves, for example. But it was a fact that purchasers often lingered a long time before goods eventually were paid for. Charlotta Sparre assured Ekeblad that she would pay for everything she commissioned, asking Ekeblad not to mention her requisitions to Count Tessin, who then would pay for everything himself: Tessin was a 'generous mind, who always makes gifts of the commissions one makes from him'.[52]

Charlotta Sparre is a good example of a consuming lady in the eighteenth century. She represents a cosmopolitan Swedish aristocracy who moved in European societies and courts with ease because of the common cultural codes. She had spent a few years in Paris where she was admired because of her beauty, charm and manners. Certainly this gave her the self-confidence that followed her through her life. She was an active consuming subject, whose desires, needs and knowledge of quality guided her choices and behaviour as a consumer. For her, French luxury represented exclusive objects with which she fashioned herself in Stockholm society and at court.

In 1778 and 1779 Count Hans Axel von Fersen sent his mother, Countess Hedvig De la Gardie, ribbons, laces and rouge from Paris. Swedish sumptuary laws prohibited the import of foreign laces, but Fersen did not write a word about it in his letters. He was more worried about how to pay the lace merchant's enormous bill of 1,453 *livres*. Apparently Fersen had not thought about paying at the time or even at all, but the merchant himself came to collect his debt after waiting for some months, and Fersen wrote to his father in order to ask for advice. Almost without exception, the merchants gave long credit for aristocrats, but perhaps Fersen's credit amongst the Parisian merchants was not solid enough that he could allow bills to accumulate without paying. Amongst the nobility, not paying artisans or merchants' bills was common.[53] An aristocrat could always take his or her shopping to another shop or order the goods from another stockist if the debts grew too heavy at the first ones. However, in the end, Hans Axel von Fersen paid the debt to the lace merchant with his father's money.[54]

Charlotta Sparre and Hedvig De la Gardie had experienced luxury shopping as unmarried young women in Paris, the capital of luxury. For both of them, French luxury and the opportunity to commission French goods when they no longer could shop in Paris in person was a way of marking their distinction as individuals and as members of the aristocracy. Their luxury shopping was enabled by personal connections to members of Swedish aristocracy in Paris. For Charlotta Sparre, the proxy was the Swedish envoy, and for Hedvig De la Gardie, her son, who had to deal also with questions about credibility and paying the bills amassed because of his mother's expensive purchases. In eighteenth-century Sweden, French culture and French luxury were part of the everyday life of the highest echelons of the nobility. It was through French manners, language and luxury that Charlotta Sparre and Hedvig De la Gardie manifested their rank and gender.

COMMISSIONS FROM THE ROYAL HOUSEHOLD

Commissions from the Swedish royal family in Stockholm to Swedish diplomats in Paris were numerous during the eighteenth century. Luxury played a seminal role in the manifestation of royal power in early-modern Europe. Since the diplomatic and cultural relations between France and Sweden were close, and French artists' and artisans' skills often surpassed those of Swedish artisans, France was a natural source for royal luxury. Moreover, the diplomatic contacts between the two countries could be consolidated through the Swedish crown's commissions of French goods. The role of diplomats in shopping and distributing French luxury goods to Sweden was considerable; it was their work and duty as servants of their sovereign and country. An ambassador's good taste and contacts with the French aristocracy were a guarantee of the quality of the goods and art works commissioned. Charlotta Wolff calls the eighteenth-century Swedish diplomats 'luxury commissioners', and underlines the significance of luxury, splendour and ceremony in court society.[55] While previous research has frequently associated consumption and shopping with leisure, the examples of diplomatic purchases suggest that luxury shopping also could be explored as a part of the work of early-modern diplomats.

In the early 1740s, Swedish ambassador Count Carl Gustaf Tessin was to buy paintings and furniture for the royal palace in Stockholm. Since Tessin held the office of chief intendant, it was part of his mission in France to report back to Sweden on contemporary French art and architecture. In the 1730s and the 1740s, the royal palace in Stockholm was renovated after a fire in the 1690s, and the architect in charge, Baron Carl Hårleman, asked Tessin to acquire paintings and furniture for it. For Tessin, it was a pleasant task since he was interested in both older and contemporary arts, knew personally many French artists and appreciated being trusted on his good taste. Tessin's letters to Hårleman record his knowledge of art and the art market in Paris.[56] Furthermore, they explain how Tessin enjoyed selecting and commissioning paintings, furniture and decorations. Commissions for the royal palace gave Tessin a possibility to luxuriate in buying art and use his knowledge of art, even though he could not always afford to buy for his own collections.

In June 1766, the then new Swedish envoy, later ambassador, in Paris, Count Gustav Philip Creutz, received a commission from Crown Prince Gustaf, future King Gustav III of Sweden. The prince wished to have a fashionable suit *à la française* with accessories for his wedding to the Danish princess Sofia Magdalena. He also wished to have a dressing gown, nightcap and slippers all based on the fashion the late French Dauphin had had in his weddings in 1745 and 1746. The list continued with fabric for three suits that would be made up in Stockholm, laces and shoe buckles decorated with strass (rhinestones) after the latest fashion. The prince's letter of commission was detailed in the materials and explicitly indicated the prices that should not be exceeded.[57]

Creutz, who was to become well known in Paris for his taste and elegance, set about finding and commissioning the most elegant garments for the crown prince, even though there was not much time because the prince's letters had lingered on their way from Stockholm to Paris. A sartorial problem was that the crown prince had not sent his measurements to Creutz with his commission. Creutz resolved it by using the measurements of a 'slim, young man'. Despite the prince's detailed instructions, Creutz did not hesitate to diverge from his commands to obtain a more elegant and fashionable choice of fabric, embroideries and patterns. He wrote to the prince that cascades of silver and gold would offer elegant, graceful attire suitable for every season. Count Creutz also suggested substituting lace from Alençon, though the prince had wished for lace from Argentan, because it was, according to Creutz, 'more beautiful, artistic and fashionable'.[58]

In August 1766, Creutz informed the crown prince that his costumes had been shipped by extraordinary post. The envoy wrote that the prince's wedding suit was perhaps the most beautiful ever made, and assured him that the suit was of latest fashion and most elegant. Parisian suppliers Le Roux and La Salle delivered the silver moiré fabric and embroideries for the suits that cost more than 12,000 *livres*, considerably more than the prince had estimated in his commissioning letter. However, Creutz assured him that the price was modest compared to the quality and the fact that forty people had worked day and night to finish the suit in time. He wrote that the King of Denmark's clothes were less elegant and more expensive.[59] At the same time, Christian VII of Denmark, brother of Crown Prince Gustaf's fiancée, Princess Sofia Magdalena, who also was to be married in November 1766, commissioned a wedding suit similar to Prince Gustaf's from Paris.[60]

In early modern society and the world of royal and imperial courts, clothing and appearance were interpreted as part of the power relations. Bernard Hours stresses that clothing was an essential part of politeness and polite society, and thus of immense importance that distinguished an aristocrat courtier from lesser nobility and sovereigns from their subjects.[61] In the mid-eighteenth century, the luxury of men's clothes surpassed that of women's, according to Daniel Roche, who emphasises the importance of the French royal court in setting fashion during the seventeenth and eighteenth centuries.[62] The significance of French fashion and fashionable attire is explicit in Creutz's letters to Price Gustaf. Creutz took considerable trouble in finding out how the French Dauphin was dressed in his nuptials two decades before.[63] Because fashion changes did not affect ceremonious dresses very rapidly, the late Dauphin's wedding attire from 1745 and 1746 was still a significant model for Swedish royal nuptials twenty years later in 1766. However, Count Creutz emphasised that the dresses for Prince Gustaf were of latest fashion.

In court society, the wedding suit of Crown Prince Gustaf symbolised and represented his personal qualities and, even more importantly, the qualities of Sweden as a modern European state. Rich embroideries on the vest and coat depicted rays of sun behind shifting clouds, symbolising both the power of Sweden and the crown prince himself, the future king.[64] The elegance of the prince's wedding suit and its symbolical embroideries displayed to spectators the importance of Sweden not only in Sweden during the wedding ceremony, but also in Paris, where members of society, including influential ministers like the Duke of Choiseul, called the Swedish envoy in order to see the suit which had become famous in Parisian society.[65]

CONCLUSION

The examples of the shopping experience of Swedish aristocrats in eighteenth-century Paris bring to light a nexus of connections and commissions, credit and trust as well as individual desires and preferences that shaped luxury acquisition between Stockholm and Paris. In spite of a multitude of shopping experiences, attitudes towards luxury were ambiguous. The impact of economic thought on aristocratic luxury consumption was perhaps more moral and theoretical than practical. Regardless of the law and economic thinking, French luxury and semi-luxury goods were a seminal part of aristocratic lifestyle. They acted as positive status symbols to a certain point, after which necessary luxury turned to unnecessary and immoral ostentation. This boundary was constantly under redefinition. For the aristocracy, luxury was a question of subjective urban experience and individual taste as well as sociability between sexes and across social groups. Swedish aristocrats were nevertheless aware of the impact of their consuming choices for their country, its industry and welfare. Excessive shopping for French luxury and semi-luxury goods was criticised as unpatriotic, effeminate and unsuitable for the nobility.

Luxury was very much a personal experience of elegant and fashionable goods and quality. In eighteenth-century towns, individuals positioned themselves in urban sociability by their consuming choices. It was vital to express status, gender and rank through shopping and luxury consumption in urban and court society. Aristocrats were victims of luxury, constantly seeking novelties and enjoyable experiences. For the Swedish aristocracy,

French luxury and shopping in Paris, the emblematic metropolis of luxury, represented a possibility for distinction as individuals and as a social group. Since all aristocrats did not have equal taste, interests or economic prospects, the aristocratic luxury shopping experience was subjective, whether experienced in person or through intermediates.

Swedish diplomats had a key role in presenting the Parisian luxury markets to Swedish aristocrats and distributing luxury goods to Sweden. The highest-ranking aristocrats were related to the envoys either through family and kinship or through friendship and connections. In court society, the outer appearance of an individual represented his or her status, rank and inner qualities, and the individuals represented their country when abroad. Luxury consumption was thus vital for men's career development and for women's marriage prospects. Despite being an enjoyable and urban aristocratic leisure, shopping created industry in the form of women's handiwork, made by luxurious materials and with luxurious tools women bought in Paris or commissioned from there. For the envoys, the Swedish court commissions for French luxury goods were a part of their official role and profession as ambassadors of their country, whereas the commissions from Swedish aristocrats belonged to a complex network of trust, credit, duty and recreation. Hence shopping for Parisian luxury was a necessity, pleasure and obligation for Swedish aristocrats, regardless of their sex, economic status or opportunities for luxury shopping in Stockholm or other Swedish cities.

NOTES

1 This chapter has been written with the support of the project 'Diligent Aristocracy: Nobility, Service and Work in Sweden, from the Great Northern War to the Napoleonic Wars' (266059), funded by the Academy of Finland.
2 Charlotta Wolff, 'Voyageurs et Diplomates Scandinaves, Acteur de Circulations Culturelles Internationales 1680–1780', in *Les Circulations internationales en Europe, années 1680–années 1780*, ed. Pierre-Yves Beaurepaire and Pierrick Pourchasse (Rennes: Presses Universitaires de Rennes, 2010), 373–84.
3 Maxine Berg, *Luxury and Pleasure in Eighteenth-Century Britain* (Oxford: Oxford University Press, 2005); Maxine Berg and Helen Clifford, eds, *Consumers and Luxury: Consumer Culture in Europe 1650–1850* (Manchester: Manchester University Press, 1999); Natacha Coquery, 'The Language of Success: Marketing and Distributing Semi-Luxury Goods in Eighteenth-Century Paris', *Journal of Design History* 17 (2004): 71–89; Natacha Coquery, *Tenir boutique à Paris au XVIIIe siècle: Luxe et demi-luxe* (Paris: Éditions du Comité des travaux historiques et scientifiques, 2011); Cissie Fairchilds, 'The Production and Marketing of Populuxe Goods in Eighteenth-Century Paris', in *Consumption and the World of Goods*, ed. John Brewer and Roy Porter (London and New York: Routledge, 1993), 228–48.
4 Leif Runefelt, *Dygden som välståndets grund: Dygd, nytta och egennytta i frihetstidens ekonomiska tänkande* (Stockholm: Stockholms universitet, 2005), 101–23; On the definition of luxury in the eighteenth century, see, e.g., Dominique Margairaz, 'Luxe,' in *Dictionnaire européen des Lumières*, ed. Michel Delon (Paris: Quaridge/PUF, 2007), 762–65.

5 Charlotta Wolff, *Vänskap och makt: Den svenska politiska eliten och upplysningstidens Frankrike* (Helsingfors and Stockholm: Svenska Litteratursällskapet i Finland and Atlantis, 2005).

6 Marjatta Rahikainen and Kirsi Vainio-Korhonen, 'Manlig och kvinnlig lyx: Överflödsförordningar och modeartiklar', in *Det svenska begäret: Sekler av lyxkonsumtion*, ed. Klas Nyberg and Paula von Wachenfeldt, (Stockholm: Carlsson Bokförlag, forthcoming); see also Alan Hunt, *Governance of the Consuming Passions: A History of Sumptuary Law* (London: Macmillan Press, 1996).

7 Hunt, *Governance of the Consuming Passions*, 120–29, 216–20; Johanna Ilmakunnas, *Ett ståndsmässigt liv: Familjen von Fersens livsstil på 1700-talet* (Helsingfors and Stockholm: Svenska Litteratursällskapet i Finland and Atlantis, 2012), 140, 155–56, 217; Daniel Roche, *La culture des apparences: une histoire du vêtement XVIIe–XVIIIe siècle* (Paris: Fayard, 1989), 54–56; Rahikainen and Vainio-Korhonen, 'Manlig och kvinnlig lyx'.

8 Ilmakunnas, *Ett ståndsmässigt liv*, passim.

9 Fernand Braudel, *Civilisation matérielle, économie et capitalisme (XVe–XVIIIe siècle)* (Paris: Librarie Armand Collin, 1967), 135; see also 'Introduction' in this book; Maxine Berg and Elisabeth Eger, eds, *Luxury in the Eighteenth Century: Debates, Desires and Delectable Goods* (Basingstoke and New York: Palgrave MacMillan, 2003); Christopher J. Berry, *The Idea of Luxury: A Conceptual and Historical Investigation* (Cambridge: Cambridge University Press, 1994); Philippe Perrot, *Le luxe: Une richesse entre faste et confort XVIIIe et XIXe siècle* (Paris: Seuil, 1995); Leif Runefelt, 'Nytta och ära—Frihetstidens ekonomiska debatt', in *Jordpäron: Svensk ekonomihistorisk läsebok*, ed. Anders Björnsson and Lars Magnusson (Stockholm: Atlantis, 2011), 201–2; Werner Sombart, *Luxus und Kapitalismus* (Munchen and Leipzig: Verlag von Duncker & Humblot, 1912).

10 Berg, *Luxury and Pleasure*, 234–43; Jennifer M. Jones, *Sexing La Mode: Gender, Fashion and Commercial Culture in Old Regime France* (Oxford and New York: Berg, 2004), 146–50 and passim.; Claire Walsh, 'Shops, Shopping, and the Art of Decision Making in Eighteenth-Century England', in *Gender, Taste, and Material Culture in Britain and North America, 1700–1830*, ed. John Styles and Amanda Vickery (New Haven and London: Yale University Press, 2006), 162–68.

11 Gudrun Andersson, *Stadens dignitärer: Den lokala elitens status- och maktmanifestation i Arboga 1650–1770* (Stockholm: Atlantis, 2009); Margot Finn, 'Men's Things: Masculine Possessions in the Consumer Revolution', *Social History* 25 (2000): 133–55; Hannah Greig, *The Beau Monde: Fashionable Society in Georgian London* (Oxford: Oxford University Press, 2013); Karin Hassan Jansson, 'When Sweden Harboured Idlers: Gender and Luxury in Public Debates, c. 1760–1830', in *Sweden in the Eighteenth-Century World: Provincial Cosmopolitans*, ed. Göran Rydén (Farnham: Ashgate, 2013); Jones, *Sexing La Mode*; Amanda Vickery, *Behind Closed Doors: At Home in Georgian England* (New Haven and London: Yale University Press, 2009). See Ilmakunnas, *Ett ståndsmässigt liv*, 129–249, 401–8.

12 Hassan Jansson, 'When Sweden Harboured Idlers', 264–71.

13 Kekke Stadin, *Maktens män bär rött: Historiska studier av manlighet, manligt framträdande och kläder* (Stockholm: Carlssons, 2010), 71–93.

14 Coquery, *Tenir boutique à Paris*; Coquery, 'The Language of Success'.

15 See, for example, Martin Wottle, *Det lilla ägandet: Korporativ formering och sociala relationer inom Stockholms minuthandel 1720–1810* (Stockholm: Stads- och kommunhistoriska institutet, 2000); Klas Nyberg, ed., *Till salu:*

Stockholms textila handel och manufakturer 1722–1846, (Stockholm: Stads- och kommunhistoriska institutet, 2010).
16 Leos Müller, *The Merchant Houses of Stockholm, c. 1640–1800: A Comparative Study of Early Modern Entrepreneurial Behaviour* (Uppsala: Uppsala universitet, 1998); Klas Nyberg, ed., *Kopparkungen: Handelshuset Björkman i Stockholm 1782–1824* (Stockholm: Stockholmia förlag, 2006); Kurt Samuelsson, *De stora köpmanshusen i Stockholm 1730–1815: En studie i den svenska handelskpitalismens historia* (Stockholm: Ekonomisk-historiska institutet, 1951); Karin Ågren, *Köpmannen i Stockholm: Grosshandlares ekonomiska och sociala strategier under 1700-talet* (Uppsala: Uppsala universitet, 2007).
17 Berg, *Luxury and Pleasure*, 20–21; see also Natacha Coquery, *L'hôtel aristocratique: le marché du luxe à Paris au XVIII*[e] *siècle* (Paris: Publications de la Sorbonne, 1998).
18 Coquery, 'The Language of Success', 76.
19 Ilmakunnas, *Ett ståndsmässigt liv*, 204–9.
20 Carl Gustaf Tessin to Carl Hårleman, 1/12 February 1740, in *Tableaux de Paris et de la cour de France 1739–1742: Lettres inédites de Carl Gustaf, comte de Tessin*, ed. Gunnar von Proschwitz (Göteborg and Paris: Acta Universitatis Gothoburgensis and Jean Touzot, 1983), 70–71.
21 Ibid., 54n12.
22 Coquery, 'The Language of Success,' 77–80; Coquery, *Tenir boutique à Paris*; Jon Stobart, Andrew Hann and Victoria Morgan, *Spaces of Consumption: Leisure and Shopping in the English Town, c. 1680–1830* (Abingdon: Routledge, 2006); Walsh, 'Shops, Shopping, and the Art of Decision Making'.
23 Antoine Watteau, *Gersaint's Shopsign*, 1721. Stiftung Preussische Schlösser und Gärten Berlin-Brandenburg, Potsdam. See Kemille Moore's chapter in this volume, which discusses the art market, gender and luxury more widely, but in the London context.
24 See Carl Gustaf Tessin's letters to Ulla Sparre and Carl Hårleman, *Tableaux de Paris*.
25 Carl Fredrik Scheffer to Carl Gustaf Tessin, 17 September 1745, in Carl Fredrik Scheffer, *Lettres particulières à Carl Gustaf Tessin 1744–1752*, ed. Jan Heidner (Stockholm: Kungl. Samfundet för utgivande av handskrifter rörande Skandinaviens historia, 1987), 96.
26 See Wolff, *Vänskap och makt*, 287–94.
27 Coquery, *Tenir boutique à Paris*; Coquery, 'The Language of Success', 76–7.
28 Carl Fredrik Scheffer to Clas Ekeblad, 4 March 1746, f. 222–23. E 3565 Ekebladska samlingen, Riksarkivet, Stockholm (henceforth RA).
29 Wolff, *Vänskap och makt*, 287–94.
30 Carl Fredrik Scheffer to Clas Ekeblad, 4 March 1746, f. 222–23. E 3565 Ekebladska samlingen, RA.
31 Ibid.
32 See Charlotta Wolff, 'Carl Fredrik Scheffers brevväxling med franska fysiokrater', *Historisk Tidskrift för Finland* 89 (2003): 185–201.
33 Ilmakunnas, *Ett ståndsmässigt liv*, 115–6, 140.
34 Clas Ekeblad to Clas Julius Ekeblad, 8 April 1767. Engeströmska samlingen, vol. C XVII 1.6. Kungliga biblioteket, Sweden.
35 Hans Axel von Fersen to Axel von Fersen, 24 May 1778. Axel von Fersen d.ä.:s arkiv, vol. 8. Stafsundsarkivet, RA.
36 Ilmakunnas, *Ett ståndsmässigt liv*, 101–2; Wolff, *Vänskap och makt*, 110.
37 F. U. Wrangel, *Resor och resenärer i Frankrike* (Stockholm: P. A. Nordstedt & Söners Förlag, 1928), 57–76.

38 Jones, *Sexing la Mode*, 145–69. See also Simonton's chapter in this volume, linking millinery and sexuality.
39 Charlotta Sparre to Carl Gustaf Tessin, 30 April 1742. Autografsamlingen vol. 196. Eriksbergsarkivet, RA.
40 See, e.g., Carl Fredrik Scheffer to Carl Gustaf Tessin, 17 September 1745, in *Lettres particulières*, 95.
41 See Coquery, 'The Language of Success'.
42 Charlotta Sparre to Clas Ekeblad, undated letter, f. 14–15. E 3564 Ekebladska samlingen, RA.
43 Charlotta Sparre to Alibert, f. 6–7. E 3564 Ekebladska samlingen, RA.
44 Coquery, *L'hôtel aristocratique*. See also Anne Montenach's and Aurélie Chatenet-Calyste's chapters in this volume.
45 Charlotta Sparre to Alibert, f. 6–7. E 3564 Ekebladska samlingen, RA.
46 Ilmakunnas, *Ett ståndsmässigt Liv*, 211.
47 Charlotta Sparre to Monsieur Guereaut, f. 10–11. E 3564 Ekebladska samlingen, RA.
48 Ilmakunnas, *Ett ståndsmässigt liv*, 211–12.
49 Charlotta Sparre to Pierre Jaquin, f. 8–9. E 3564 Ekebladska samlingen, RA.
50 Charlotta Sparre to Monsieur Lluet, f. 12–13. E 3564 Ekebladska samlingen, RA.
51 François Bluche, *La noblesse française au XVIIIe siècle* (Paris: Hachette, 1995), 25; Ilmakunnas, *Ett ståndsmässigt liv*, 208–9, 370–71, 385–86.
52 Charlotta Sparre to Clas Ekeblad, undated letter, f. 14–15. E 3564 Ekebladska samlingen, RA.
53 See Coquery, *Tenir boutique à Paris*, 211–60.
54 Hans Axel von Fersen to Axel von Fersen, 26 August 1778, 21 June 1779. Axel von Fersen d.ä.:s arkiv. Stafsundarkivet, RA.
55 Wolff, *Vänskap och makt*, 129–44, 208–17; Charlotta Wolff, 'Sveriges representation i Paris: Sändebuden och besickningen under frihetstiden och den gustavianska tiden,' *Historisk Tidskrift för Finland* 86 (2001), 174.
56 von Proschwitz, *Tableaux de Paris*.
57 Lena Rangström, *Kläder för tid och evighet: Gustaf III sedd genom sina dräkter* (Stockholm: Livrustkammaren, 1997), 65–75.
58 Gustav Philip Creutz to Crown Prince Gustaf, 14 July 1766, in *Le Comte de Creutz, Lettres inédites de Paris, 1766–1770*, ed. Marianne Molander (Göteborg: Acta Universitatis Gothoburgensis, 1987), 36–38.
59 Gustav Philip Creutz to Crown Prince Gustaf, 19 August 1766, 7 September 1766, *Lettres inédites de Paris,* 38–40, 42–45.
60 Rangström, *Kläder för tid och evighet*, 73, 75.
61 Bernard Hours, *Louis XV et sa Cour: Le roi, l'étiquette et le courtisan* (Paris: Presses Universitaires de France, 2002), 39–40.
62 Roche, *La culture des apparences*, 98–99, 134–40, 177–93.
63 Gustav Philip Creutz to Crown Prince Gustaf, 7 September 1766, *Lettres inédites de Paris*, 42–5.
64 Rangström, *Kläder för tid och evighet*, 68–69.
65 Gustav Philip Creutz to Crown Prince Gustaf, 19 August 1766, *Lettres inédites de Paris*, 38–40.

8 Gender and Luxury in Eighteenth-Century Catalonia: Town and Countryside[1]

Belén Moreno Claverías

The eighteenth century was one of expansion of luxury and fashion in Spanish towns as elsewhere. Evidence of this is the vast literature generated by the debates surrounding this process, which was said to be upsetting the 'natural order of things' in the economic, social and political domains. A number of theories emerged at the end of the eighteenth century to explain the attraction that women supposedly felt towards inessential novelties, which made them potential consumers of these objects to a greater extent than men. This chapter examines whether it is possible to verify this female attraction for luxury and fashion in the documentary sources of the time, and whether gender really was a determining factor shaping consumption patterns. Probate inventories show in detail the type of objects with which women and men of the Old Regime surrounded themselves. However, the analysis of these documents for different geographical areas—rural and urban—suggests different patterns for the impact of luxury and fashion among its male and female inhabitants. For example, the lack of luxury in rural homes was the norm except for specific cases, in contrast to the urban experience.

This chapter takes into account two variables, gender and place of residence, to study the impact that new items had among the population, by paying particular attention to the patterns of consumption of women in the city of Barcelona during the eighteenth century, as opposed to the women of nearby rural areas. In order to do so, several notarial sources, as well as texts written by witnesses of the social and economic transformations of that time, are used. The literature of luxury and fashion expansion provides a valuable indication of the magnitude of changes in the patterns of consumption that were occurring.

GENDER AND LUXURY IN THE EIGHTEENTH CENTURY

In the eighteenth century, luxury, as 'any extravagance that goes beyond the necessary',[2] was still limited by the parameters of the social group to which an individual belonged. At the time, Spanish society was halfway between a stratified and traditional society and a fully developed market society, which affected patterns of consumption. It was a period of transition in which the market economy was gradually imposing itself, first in the cities, and eventually, after some delay, in the countryside. For this reason, it could be said that two worlds coexisted during this period: a 'traditional' one, in which the distinguishing signs depended on birth and rank, and a 'modern' one, in which money played an important role in consumption patterns. The conservative nobility, decidedly opposed to the spread of luxury, insistently demanded that the authorities vigorously apply the sumptuary laws. One of the many Spanish exponents of this argument was Don Melchor de Macanaz, who in 1724 urged Felipe V, 'to decree that each individual dress according to his class, so that his clothes indicate his profession, and so that neither nobles are confused with commoners, nor high-ranking persons with the middle ranks'.[3]

There seems to be a unanimous agreement that this ever-increasing tendency to consume luxury and fashionable goods was situated within the context of large cities and the development of urban life. From the theoretical point of view, Thorstein Veblen emphasised the connection between both variables, consumption of luxury goods and level of urbanization: '[C]onsumption is a more important element in city life than in country life'.[4] Fashions spread most rapidly in national capitals, not only because of the physical proximity of people, which greatly facilitated emulation, but also because the city was the place where the new means of promoting products, such as newspapers, prints and gazettes, were first introduced, and where shop windows began to be used to display fashionable products to the public.[5] Another factor could also explain the extent of the changes in consumption habits according to the level of urbanization: The usefulness of luxury in cities is accentuated by anonymity. In a large population centre, individuals need to denote their social position by consuming *visible* goods, because otherwise hardly anybody would be able to recognise their status. In a small community, on the other hand, everybody knows each other, and so it is easy to know who is who. Therefore, in small communities the *visible* consumption of luxury goods has less importance when it comes to establishing the social status of individuals and families than in urban areas. What is the point of acquiring new and refined products when there is nothing to prove? The analysis of Catalan homes' probate inventories shows, for example, that luxury amongst country people consisted primarily in the accumulation of bed linen and other home textiles.[6] In the eighteenth century, peasants preferred to invest their money in land, barrels, wine presses, ploughs and anything that could increase production. This coincides with what Werner Sombart observed much later: 'In small agrarian towns, family wealth could be shown by means of the accumulation of cattle or traditional objects'.[7]

The development of foreign trade in modern Europe facilitated changes in demand in many population centres, especially if they, as Barcelona, had a nearby port. Francisco de Zamora wrote at the end of the century that, while the 'fabrics that rural people wear are from the country, in Barcelona many from abroad are used.'[8] According to the same author, the citizens of Barcelona (a city of 120,000 to 130,000 inhabitants at the end of the eighteenth century) are 'increasingly adulterated with luxury, greater dealings, foreign fashions, the progress of trade, the love of comfort and liberty, and the neglect of time-honoured seclusion and seriousness'.[9] Rafael d'Amat, Baron of Maldá, an impoverished nobleman living in Barcelona, wrote in his engagement book:

> nowadays, luxury and fashion, most of which comes from French actresses, has altered in many men and women the good order of the purity of customs and class distinction as far as clothing is concerned. Luxury has driven many men and women mad, as it seeks to put craftsmen on an equal footing with merchants, and the latter on a par with honest citizens [gentlemen].[10]

The growing demand for luxury or fashionable goods and services coincided with the increase in supply and the consequent proliferation of shops and businesses capable of satisfying and intensifying these new needs. The same Baron pointed that, in the Barcelona of the end of the eighteenth century,

> there are some watchmaker's shops that are constantly expanding because nearly everyone carries a pocket watch; there are ironmonger's, cap maker's, dressmaker's, hairdresser's and chocolate maker's shops that are growing every day . . . ; due to the great consumption of chocolate, there is now a chocolate maker's guild.[11]

What part did gender play in this process of expansion of luxury and fashion? The Baron often wrote that this process affected both men and women. His comments show that there were two more important variables than gender in the creation of new consumption patterns: the place of residence and age. In his opinion, those who were transforming traditions of dress and social habits were thirty- to forty-year-old male and female city dwellers. However, for some contemporary authors like Daniel Roche, women were the indisputable protagonists of the new predilection for accumulating ostentatious objects that took Paris by storm in the eighteenth century. In all social categories, women were responsible for spreading the new objects and the new values of superfluous consumption: '[L]eaders in sensibility, they were already the shop windows of men'.[12] Some theories about the attraction of women for frivolities and novelties had already emerged by the end of eighteenth century, propounding women as potential consumers of these objects to a greater extent than men. For example, Jean-Jacques Rousseau emphasised women's capacity to rapidly absorb the visual world around them. Women excelled in anything that required the senses, whereas men shone in activities that require intellect. Female sensory capacities made women highly susceptible to pleasant and frivolous objects and, therefore, more likely to consume these objects than men.[13] However, it is important to bear in mind that most of the theorists who detected this 'eminently female' manner of consuming based their theories on the observation of a small group of women: those belonging to the upper classes in important cities such as Paris and London.[14]

Notary and literary sources from the eighteenth century for Catalan and Spanish cases suggest that the attraction of new and luxurious objects affected both men and women of the middle and upper urban classes. This process led to the emergence of new personages like *petimetre* and *petimetra*. *Petimetres* were individuals 'crazed' for fashion who utilised much of their time and money to look after their external appearance. Many comedies of the time ridiculed them because of their craving to adorn their bodies, which symbolically threatened the traditional order with respect to ornaments, dressing codes and distinguishing signs.

The Baron of Maldá used the concept *currutaco*—equivalent to *petimetre* or *pisaverde*—to refer to men from Barcelona influenced by French fashion. An important defender of traditional customs, the Baron perceived the so-called *currutacos* or *petimetres* as impolite, 'alienated to Catalan education' and with a tendency toward aggressive and unsocial behaviour.[15] Regarding women, he clarified that *petimetra* was the name given to 'first rank' women, meaning nobility. In his 1796 diary, he claimed that 'the *currutaca* fashion' was complicating aristocratic marriages, since *petimetras* were very expensive to maintain because of their taste for fashion and attraction to luxury. Quoting the Baron: '*Currutacas* wore big rings on all their fingers except the thumb, and some foolish ones would have them on all of them'. This French-style fashion standardised the physical appearance of its followers to the point of 'not knowing who was Catalan and who was Spanish'. The Baron particularly hated men's 'horn hats' and women's jewellery and shapeless dresses that made single ladies 'look like they were pregnant women and dressed worse than actresses'. In 1798, he complained that French fashion spread 'all over among first rank people and those between the age of 30 and 40'. On top of such attire, *currutacos* and *currutacas* were known for elaborated dances, like *contredanse*, for introducing French words into their conversation, and for being up-to-date about French theatre and music.

According to Rebecca Haidt, the *petimetras* were resistant to the rules of thrift, diligence and modesty which society expected from the female. At the beginning of the century, the image was aristocratic, but as the century progressed, theatrical plays often depicted *petimetras* as servants and labourers' wives. Haidt argues that the *petimetra*, whether upper or lower class, was much more than a vain female:

> the problem represented by *petimetra* in eighteenth century Spanish texts is that of the female consumer whose primping and spending (that

> is, whose purchases and coordination of shoes, frills, fans) amount to unlicensed decisions about the use of resources and thereby threaten the stability and structure of families, communities and nation.[16]

To visit stores, to choose and buy textiles, to have the clothing made up and try it on several times, finally to combine the different clothing pieces and to adorn them with the appropriate accessories, occupied a large part of their days. For this reason, detractors of luxury and fashion in the eighteenth century used to classify *petimetras* or *currutacas* as idle people, especially urban upper-class women: 'In their uncurbed desires for luxury, privileged urban women spend more time thinking about their appearance and shopping than about working for the good of the nation through marriage and childrearing'.[17]

Actually, in urban environments these characteristics were a fact, but in contrast, in rural areas none of examples above could be found. It can be shown through study of post-mortem inventories that in the countryside, sumptuous and fashion products were only an exception. In addition, most women had very little leisure time and their incomes were very low, despite their multiple economical activities, such as animal and orchard care and putting-out system tasks, among others. To them, *petimetras* were unknown figures. Only the wives of doctors, judges and the most successful merchants living in rural villages could afford certain luxuries. As we shall see, the relationship of women with luxury and fashion depended not only on their social standing, but also on the place of their residence. It seems that in the eighteenth century, in order to be able 'to go crazy' about luxury and fashion it was necessary to live in a big city.

THE INFLUENCE OF LUXURY AND FASHION ON URBAN AND RURAL WOMEN'S APPEARANCE

Other studies have demonstrated the influence of luxury and fashion on male and female consumption patterns in rural Catalonia, showing that the impact was much weaker than in urban areas.[18] In addition to probate inventories, there are several testimonies of the time that demonstrate this. Francisco de Zamora, who claimed that the citizens of Barcelona were being 'adulterated' by luxury and foreign fashion, also pointed out that 'customs in the villages and homes of peasant are innocent, simple and natural'.[19] In other words, he not only clearly differentiated between rural consumption and its urban counterpart, but also introduced a moral evaluation of both types of behaviour as far as consumption was concerned.

Catalan post-mortem inventories, both urban and rural, show considerable differences in the material culture of women depending on the status of their fathers and husbands. However, the differences between women's living conditions seem to stem more from the different prevailing consumption strategies in their family or their social group, rather than from the greater or lesser extent to which they were allowed to manage important sources of income.[20] Antoinette Fauve-Chamoux has observed that the widows of the wealthiest families in pre-industrial France were not wealthier than those of poor families.[21] However, they did consume more than other women. In the Catalan case, an analysis of the inventories of some widows of liberal professionals, rich merchants or noblemen confirms this phenomenon. These women consumed more than peasant women or craftswomen, but less than their husbands, as a comparison of the goods listed in the inventories of both spouses shows.[22] For example, Orosia Ravella Nin, wife of a Doctor in Law deceased in 1773, had 24 shirts, 44 silver objects, 8 jewels, 16 sheets, 19 placemats, 58 napkins and 250 books fewer than her husband. Also, he had more cutlery, glassware and crockery than his wife. Orosia only had more objects of devotion: 43, while her husband owned 31.[23]

On the other hand, there was also a difference in feminine consumption patterns depending on their marital status. The Catalan juridical regime entailed that women lived their whole life under male tutelage: The father (for single women), the brother (when the father was deceased) or the husband. Their lives were restricted to men's homes.[24] Whilst notarial documents classified men depending on their profession and honorific titles, women were classified only as single, married, widows or nuns.[25] With marriage, the social prestige of women grew independently of her husband's social status. The fact itself of living with a male with whom they had established a marriage contract was a source of respect, and it meant a step up in the female social hierarchy.[26] Marriage was, after all, the goal, the natural state women had to reach.[27] Nuns were the only women who could remain single without risking social exclusion; after all, they were already married to God.

This increase in the status of married women by comparison to single ones had to be translated into a substantial improvement of their appearance. It is not that they became more sensitive to conspicuous consumption, but it was a consequence of the role they had to perform from then on. During their single women stage, women had to maximise their saving skills, to elaborate their trousseau and to show a 'modest' and 'discreet' appearance. A condition required of all marriageable women, especially among peasants, was that they would be thrifty, austere and not given to superfluous spending.[28] In contrast, after marriage, they could not only display their jealously kept objects, but they also had the obligation to become the living proof of their husband's social and economical status. Their primary route was through jewellery.[29]

In 1789, Manuel Barba described the population of Penedés, an agrarian region south of Barcelona: '[T]here isn't a distinguishing trait between single and married [men]', while differences between women were clear. 'Married women wear better gold and silver earrings than single women and they also dress better. Widows generally wear black'.[30] This variance between married and single women also existed in the cities. Francisco De Zamora, describing Barcelona women, claimed that for 'women it's easier to tell if they are married or single by their earrings and other ornaments, and by the quality of their dresses'.[31] Some of Baron of Maldá's texts from the end of the eighteenth century suggest the same. For example, he described the appearance of Barcelona women married to muleteers and peasants, saying that they wore velvet doublets and adorned their bodies with big golden or precious stones earrings, golden or silver buttons and golden rings and necklaces for their parties. Nevertheless, their single daughters did not wear 'a married distinguishing sign', they dressed in a simple way, for example, dark doublets made with cheap fabrics during winter, and sleeveless doublets and loose shirts during summer, and they embellished their bodies only with silver or brass buttons, buckles and rings.[32]

What is evident is that, in contrast to rural women, urban women had better and more access to the new products that were flooding the markets and shops. Table 8.1 below indicates the distinguishing traits specified by Francisco de Zamora regarding rural and urban women's dressing style at the end of the eighteenth century.[33]

Post-mortem inventories confirm these distinguishing traits of purchasing patterns between rural and urban women. Table 8.2 compares characteristic female clothing registered in the post-mortem inventories of Vilafranca del Penedés (a small village of barely 4,000 inhabitants) and those from Barcelona's inventories between 1770 and 1790.

In addition to having more clothing and all kinds of accessories, women from the capital embellished themselves with far more jewellery than those from rural areas, especially those from the upper classes. In the eighteenth century, the golden watch became—along with the engagement ring—the distinguishing trait of the Barcelona aristocratic women who had become

Table 8.1 A comparison of women's clothing between country and town.

Women's clothing	Rural areas	Urban areas
Head	White hood, net or kerchief	White or black shawl, big hairnet
Neck/Chest	Tie of kerchief	Tie or kerchief
Torso	*Jubón* (doublet),[a] *basquiña*[b] of *bayeta* (loose wool cloth).	*Cotilla* (corset)[c] or doublet, silk skirts (*basquiñas*).
Legs	Blue tights or naked legs	Tights
Feet	Espadrilles or shoes	Shoes with silver buckles.

a. '*Jubón*' (doublet): Clothing that covered from shoulder to waist, tight and adjusted to the body.
b. '*Basquiña*': Skirt used by women on their clothes when they had to leave their houses.
c. 'Cotilla' (corset): Fitter used by women, made of linen, silk and whale.

Table 8.2 Characteristics of clothing presented in post-mortem inventories of Vilafranca del Penedés and Barcelona (1770–1790).

	Vilafranca	Barcelona
Average number of items of clothing[a]	27	40
Underwear	Not registered	Underskirts
Presence of silk tights	16% of the cases	47% of the cases
Presence of kerchiefs	26% of the cases	62% of the cases
Colour of the clothing	Predominance of varieties of blue and bright colours	Predominance of brown, grey and black.

a. Skirts, mantles, underskirts, doublets, hoods, raincoats, aprons, corsets, tights, ties, kerchiefs, gloves, girdles and shoe wears are included.

engaged. On 12 February 1792, the Baron of Maldá wrote in his diary that Mrs Felipa de Dusai left her home wearing the 'engagement traits: fine gold watch and equally fine engagement ring'.[34]

In the rural areas, in contrast, a watch was a rare object, exclusively used by men. Middle- and lower-class women rarely used watches. Most were satisfied with traditional objects, like rings, earrings and bracelets, often decorated with fake materials that led to a 'popular luxury'.[35] Among the possessions of Barcelona women we frequently encounter the so-called 'fake stones' that ornamented earrings and golden rings, and 'fake pearls', with which necklaces and bracelets were made. For instance, in 1783 Margarida Morera, widow of a Barcelona craftsman, had two pairs of silver buttons adorned 'with fake stones', a ring 'of ormolu with three fake stones', a necklace of 'fake stones' and a set of 'fake garnets', among other gold pieces and gemstones.[36] These adornments, repeatedly banned by sumptuary laws, were strictly ornamental. They had little economic value, and for this reason they could not be used as a source of credit in a moment of need, as was the case with quality jewellery. However, women from rural areas could not even afford this cheap 'luxury'. No imitation jewellery pieces appeared among their possessions. Similarly, Barcelona craftswomen frequently used 'Montserrat's silver rings' and silver needles for the topknot—two uncommon artefacts in the Penedés area of the same years.

LUXURY AND FASHION IN FURNITURE AND DECORATIVE OBJECTS

Fashion and luxury affected not only dress codes, but also the furniture and decorative objects of homes. For example, while rural women kept their objects in boxes or trunks, urban women used chests of drawers (*calaixeres*), while the wealthiest used closets. Drawers became the substitute for the trunk and an important piece of the urban bride's dowry—and later for rural brides. For this reason, it is not strange to find notes in the Barcelonan inventories like the following one dating from 1781: 'A chest of drawers owned by Geltrudis, designed herself as part of her dowry brought to her deceased husband and in it, the clothing of her usage and wearing'.[37] Chests were present in fifty-eight per cent of the Barcelona inventories, but in only sixteen per cent of the ones from Vilafranca del Penedés over the same period. A good bureau, made of rich materials and artistically sculpted, was equivalent to a jewel, and it was common to place a family image for invocation and the chandeliers or the home's most valuable objects on top of it.[38] Normally, it was ordered from a carpenter and made and adapted to each family's economy. Each bourgeois woman had at least two chests of drawers in her bedroom. However, the number increased as weddings were celebrated and presents were received, until their homes became a showcase of chests of all styles and periods.[39]

The same was true of *boudoirs* (furniture with drawers and a mirror): While their presence was infrequent in rural inventories, they appear in a third of Barcelona registers, especially in the homes of merchants and independent professionals. In the middle of the eighteenth century, boudoirs named 'Pompadour' began to be very valuable. Ornamented with tulle curtains, doily and light colour bands, these noble boudoirs had the advantage of being adaptable to the poorest homes by substituting laces, percale and crochet for the tulle and the expensive doilies.[40] Another new element was the *escaparate* (cabinet), which urban women particularly desired. It was a glass cabinet in which families placed an adored image or an object of great value. Many women hung their best jewellery on the clothing of the family's saint. Religious objects such as medals, reliquaries, crosses and souvenirs brought from Rome were kept in *escaparates*. As a Barcelona inventory of 1785 described: 'a cabinet of three glasses, and in it an image of the Virgin of Carmen wearing silk with a golden braid on the scapular and on the underdress, a silver necklace with white pearl and a little silver jewel'.[41] These glass cabinets began to be more common in Barcelona inventories during the last decades of the eighteenth century, while in rural areas they only appeared later.

The multiplication of furniture items and ornaments in urban houses was a general phenomenon in eighteenth-century Europe, intensifying in its last decades. Likewise, Cissie Fairchilds points out that in Paris around 1785, as in London:

> inventories show that bookcases, chests of drawers, secretaries, writing tables, tea tables, gaming tables and the like, joined the standard bed, table and cane-seated chairs to brighten even modest apartments, and the invention of lighter, cheaper textiles allowed even the lower classes

> to add cloaks, shirts, caps, muffs, fichus, underwear and nightclothes to their wardrobes.[42]

The growing tendency to adorn the person extended to the interior of the homes, fundamental centres for socialising. The more refined ornaments and objects a house had, the more enthusiastic the owners were to display it on any pretext: a local party, a wedding, an anniversary, etc. In fact, in Catalonia at that time, a practice called '*seguir la casa*' (to follow the house) emerged, a practice of showing the interior of the house, room by room, to guests. Women were the main stars of this social activity, and went in groups to visit them. The Baron of Maldá, in his diary of 1777, narrates how he showed his house to a few acquaintances who were passing Barcelona in the autumn of that year:

> They followed most of the house, and I showed them my upstairs bedroom and other annexes. Afterwards, they went downstairs and saw the salon and the *estrados*, which they liked very much, especially the striped taffeta hanging curtains, the sanctuary and the boudoir. Afterwards, I showed them the downstairs offices and they were dazzled by the paintings.[43]

Sometimes they even opened closet doors and drawers to show the 'treasures' kept inside, especially textile items. This was most frequent at the homes of the newly married, and of those who had many objects to display. For example, two days after the wedding of Marquis of Castellbell in 1771,

> came to the house a group of women, little women and children, men as well, to follow the house, salon, *estrados*, boudoirs, drawers and I don't know what else . . . One friend was invited by the owners to follow the house and five or six more were added . . . to walk by and adore.[44]

Bourgeois and noble homes had spaces reserved exclusively for social events. For instance, seventeen per cent of urban houses had a *recibidor* (hall) that substituted for the *entrada* (entrance) of most of rural and urban homes. This room was austere but had some quality furniture; owners placed benches or chairs where the visitors could comfortably wait. Another area of the house, typically bourgeois, was the *estrado* (twenty-two per cent of urban houses), the space where ladies received their visitors.[45] Luxurious furniture, such as game tables, daybeds, mirrors, armchairs and numerous ornaments, like carpets, crystal lamps, draperies, paintings and sculptures, usually adorned this room. Gatherings such as the *visitones*, the *refrescos* and the *saraos*—fashionable ways of socialising among the urban upper classes—took place in the *estrado* and the *sala principal* (main room), similarly embellished. The *visitón* was the equivalent of the French *grande soirée*, and the abundant and exquisite refreshments offered at the party were called *agasajo*. The greatest attraction points of *visitón* were the *sarao* (the dance), the *refresco* (chocolate, *horchata*, coffee, meringue, sweets) and games (cards, the goose game, the *poule*), and sometimes concerts were added to brighten the party. The preparation for these assemblies was complex, and the salon had to show its maximum splendour through lighting the crystal lamps, the candlesticks, the cornucopias and creating the best possible table setting.[46] Regular attendance at these social events had become a symbol of social distinction, and women, as guests and hosts, played an important part.[47]

The extent to which men or women were the authors of the decoration of these rooms and the organisers of these social events is subject to debate. According to some authors, the progressive separation of the public/private spheres and gender-defined roles placed the responsibilities for family consumption on women. As Victoria De Grazia and Ellen Furlough argue, with the development of bourgeois consumption based on a 'feminised' home world, women were in charge of acquiring, keeping up and transmitting the new middle-class identity. In order to create a bourgeois home, the *maîtresses de maison* had to spend their money strategically on food, clothing and furniture, and had to organise the family's socialising. Their main objective was to demonstrate the social position of the family, expressing their styles and tastes to other *bourgeoisies*, and to differentiate their social class from the working and aristocratic classes.[48] Surprisingly however, the majority of purchasers of goods sold in auctions held in Vilafranca between 1770 and 1790 were men. They bought eighty-eight per cent of the most expensive objects (more than five pounds). Men, typically learned gentlemen and businessmen of the local middle-class, purchased the majority of luxury goods, most of which came from priests' homes. They bought the majority of window curtains, bed draperies, mirrors, bureaus, rugs, display cabinets, easy chairs and other quality pieces of furniture, as well as books and silver and gold objects.[49] The evidence suggests that eighteenth-century Catalan women of all social groups had very little autonomy in spending the family income. In fact, women needed the husband's expressed authorization for any significant financial transaction.

Veblen said that the ladies of the leisure class existed to consume and to display what men produced. Women were the best testimony of the wealth and social status of their husbands, and the clothing they wore was tangible proof of their purchasing power.[50] Nevertheless, according to Sombart, women not only reflected their husband's wealth, but also were very active consuming agents, and dominant when it came to family comfort. The tendency to 'interiorise', or in other words, the conversion of luxury into something private in the modern age, was the result of women's taking on this responsibility for their homes. At the same time, luxury went from being something periodic to something stable. Sombart attributed the unusual increase of luxury in the eighteenth century to the courtesans and aristocratic women of the big cities. In this process, men appear as passive subjects whose basic function was to pay for feminine whims.[51] Nevertheless, the Catalan documents cannot confirm this passivity of men in the changes that were occurring during the eighteenth century. Men, especially important merchants, liberal professionals, rich craftsmen and priests, were active purchasers of new goods.

Along the same lines as Sombart, Amanda Vickery highlights that women in their role as house guardians gave private and familiar meanings to these belongings. The connections between the expansion of the world of objects and the change of the role of women in the eighteenth century could have been vital in this respect. The new accent placed on the domestic sphere and the emotional intensification of the nuclear family would lead, partially, to the growth of opportunities for the care and the comfort of the house, where women played an important part.[52] The fact that women found themselves banned from owning properties of importance and from exercising professions consequently meant that they focused on 'personal and household artefacts to create a world of meanings and ultimately to transmit their history'.[53] Vickery arrives at these conclusions through the analysis of the diaries of a 'gentlewoman' of Lancashire between 1762 and 1781, and states that post-mortem inventories are useless to perceive these sorts of things.

Catalan sources however, suggest that in the eighteenth century public and private spheres were not separate. The vast majority of women not only worked, but their incomes were essential for household maintenance. The work of women was more versatile and lower paid than men's, since women at different times in their lives could spin, sell, assist in craft workshops, wash clothes, work the land, carry water, be a wet nurse or a domestic.[54] Usually, they carried out several of these activities simultaneously. Few women could fully devote themselves to looking after family comfort, which in any case was largely unknown to most of urban and rural people. Fortunately, the Catalan probate inventories permit the analysis of the living conditions of all social groups, so it is possible to state that in this period 'separate spheres' only operated in bourgeois and noble houses.

Despite the limitations of probate inventories, Lorna Weatherill analysed the consumption patterns of English women from 1660 to 1740, comparing those of women with men's. While men had more books and personal watches than women, the latter had more gold and silver objects (especially widows), linens and household textiles, glassware, mirrors and paintings. However, Weatherill concludes that the gender contrasts were too subtle to suggest the existence of a distinct feminine sub-culture: '[A]mong the popular classes, the influence of status, wealth and occupation were more important than gender'.[55] The results from analysing several hundred Catalan post-mortem inventories match those of Weatherill. It was mainly among urban upper-class women that the consumption of 'frivolities' is detected—'frivolities' which supposedly, according to some authors, characterised the 'female consumer'. Most poor women living in rural areas had to do without many superfluous objects and they tended to have fewer objects for personal use, including clothing, than the men living with them.[56] If gender was a determinant of consumption patterns, it is fair to say that eighteenth-century Catalan men were more prominent consumers than women. In general, they had more clothing, wigs, watches, books and rings, etc., than female members of the family.

THE PINNACLE OF FEMALE CONSUMPTION: BARCELONA ELITE WOMEN

To find true demonstrations of luxury among Catalan women, one has to investigate Barcelona women from the upper class. In 1784, the Baron of Maldá described their appearance according to their 'rank'. 'First class' or 'first rank' women were the wives or daughters of nobles, knights, soldiers and judges. To go to church, a place of public display of excellence, they wore shirts with expensive and fine lacing, black skirts, of *moiré* in the summer and velvet in the winter, and a cloak or shawl of the same colour, a recent fashion which the Baron considered as 'decent'. Other women of this class wore white shawls and 'the most *petimetras*', that is, the most smug and modern, wore shawls 'too transparent, not appropriate to attend the sacred temples of God'.[57] All adorned themselves with gold and/or diamond watches hanging from gold or steel chains on their skirts, and with many rings on their fingers. The ornaments multiplied at the *visitones*, the social parties such as weddings or important receptions. According to the Baron, these had specific 'requirements' in terms of ornaments, such as diamonds, emeralds, rubies and other precious stones in earrings, bracelets and rings worn on several fingers. Jewels were the quintessential sign of distinction. Shoes had to be of the same colour as the 'cut dresses' or *basquiñas* they wore, and with shiny buckles made of gold or silver. Hair was adorned with *picohas*, flower-shaped jewels with or without rhinestones, and *tembleques*, feathers to highlight the hairstyle. They had bottles of *samparelle* or lavender water 'to smell' in their pockets.[58]

The Baron described second-ranking women, i.e., wives and daughters of merchants, notaries, attorneys and lawyers, as dressed almost as well as noble ladies, although they had no footman or servant but 'a mere student to accompany them to mass, to visit or to walk'. They had no carriage, but in everything else they 'almost equalled noble ladies'. Similarly, 'the husbands of all of them dress nearly as well as the noblemen, the main reason for this being the luxury which is being introduced every day more and more'.[59] Imitation of those of the first rank by members of the second rank was a fact.

The post-mortem inventories of women of first and second rank include these objects that the Baron described. The inventory, drawn up in 1799, of Mrs Maria Francisca de Blanas Centelles Marimon, widow Countess of Centelles, from a family of Catalan nobility is full of objects quite foreign to the vast majority of Catalan women of the time.[60] The most valuable items, jewellery, clothing and house documents, were in dressers and closets placed in the room in which the Countess died. Most of her shirts—over thirty—were made of 'Holland cloth'. There was plenty of lace for collars and cuffs, silk gloves, 'combs' of various types, 'ties of Cambray', sleeping caps and hair nets and an object not found in any other inventory: 'six face-cleaners'. Toiletries were still rare, even among the upper classes. Among her numerous jewels was 'a replay gold watch', a box containing numerous emeralds and diamonds and a big diamond ring. That ring was famous because the Baron of Maldá noted in his diary that 'this noble lady has given to Our Lord (God) the best ring, of diamonds very fine and large'.[61] The Baron described the bequests of the Countess of Centelles in his diary. On 5 January 1799, three days after her death, he wrote that she had left orders for all her clothes—'that's a lot, not having used it'—to be divided in two parts: one for Mariana, 'her favourite maid', to whom she also bequeathed seventy-five pounds yearly for life, and the other half to the other servants, each of whom received fifteen pounds. The Baron wrote that the clothes she left 'were of great value, for the multitude of fine English laces and other costly fabrics'.[62] Clearly, these maids were lucky to be able to dress like ladies, distinguished from the vast majority of urban women.

CONCLUSIONS

Place of residence and social class were more decisive factors than gender in shaping consumption patterns in eighteenth-century Spain. The documents relating to the consumption of Catalan women show that luxury was limited to upper-class women, mainly urban and, to a lesser extent, rural, and novelties, thanks to cheap imitations, were within the reach of a growing number of women, especially in urban areas. The same can be said for men. However, uniformity of taste and the democratization of fashion were still far from established. The appearance of a woman of that time was a clear indicator of her location on the social ladder, her place of residence, her level of income, and referenced the profession of her father or husband. The descriptions of contemporary observers on the outward appearance of women confirm these differences, making it difficult to generically characterise a 'female consumption'. In fact, a predilection for superfluous and fashionable objects was more a feature of 'bourgeois' consumption than of 'feminine' consumption. So much so that, what contemporaries called 'frivolities', like mirrors, silk products, perfumes, watches, wigs, etc., were equally abundant—or even more so—in the inventories of bourgeois men than in those of bourgeois women. However, things were beginning to change. There were as many 'female consumptions' as social categories, but at the same time, a trend of consumption among common urban women coveting more and newer things was taking place.

The most daring people—and those with the means to do so, like the *petimetras*—began to break with established standards regarding appearance. Women of the urban gentry took advantage of the cracks that were emerging in the traditional social order, opening these fissures even more. Indeed, social boundaries were becoming diluted, signs of identity ceased to be exclusive of certain social groups because of emulation, appearances were transformed and money, rather than birth, had a determining role in this. This process occurred earlier and with greater intensity in cities compared to rural areas. Barcelona women of the upper bourgeoisie and followers of foreign fashion played a decisive role. In their effort to look like noble women, they became barely distinguishable from them. The other middle classes would want to emulate, in turn, the high bourgeoisie. Emulation was increasing for women and men who could afford it.

NOTES

1 This work is linked to the research project: '*Ciudades, gentes e intercambios en la Monarquía Hispánica: política económica, cambio institucional y desarrollo de los mercados*' ('Cities, gentry and interchanges in the Hispanic monarchy: economic policy, institutional change and development of the markets'), Ministerio de Educación y Ciencia (Ref: HAR2012–39034-C03–02.)
2 Werner Sombart, *Lujo y Capitalismo* (Madrid: Alianza Editorial, 1979).
3 In Juan Sempere Guarinos, *Historia del Lujo y de las Leyes Suntuarias en España*, vol. 2 (Madrid, 1788), 160–64.
4 Thorstein Veblen, *Teoría de la Clase Ociosa* (Barcelona: Orbis, 1988), 90.
5 Daniel Roche, *La culture des Apparences: Une Histoire Du Vêtement, XVIIe–XVIIIe siècles* (Paris: Fayard, 1989), 481–82.
6 Belén Moreno Claverías, 'Révolution de la Consommation Paysanne? Modes de Consommation et Différentiation Sociale de la Paysannerie Catalane, 1670–1790', *Histoire et Mesure* 21 (2006): 141–83. On luxury in the countryside, see Paolo Malanima, *Il Lusso dei Contadini: Consumi e industrie nelle campagne toscane dei sei e settecento* (Bologna: Il Mulino, 1990).
7 Sombart, *Lujo y Capitalismo*, 63–64.
8 Francisco De Zamora, *Diario de los Viajes Hechos a Cataluña, 1788–1789* (Barcelona: Curial, 1973), 461.
9 *Ibid.*, 463–464
10 Rafael d'Amat, Baró de Maldà, *Viles i Ciutats de Catalunya. 1784* (Barcelona: Barcino, 1994). 86.
11 *Ibid.*, 87.
12 Roche, *La culture des Apparences*, 480. See also the discussion in the introductory chapter to this volume.
13 Jennifer Jones,'*Coquettes* and *Grisettes*: Women Buying and Selling in Ancien Régime Paris', in *The Sex of Things: Gender and Consumption in Historical Perspective*, ed. Vittoria De Grazia and Ellen Furlough (Berkeley: University of California Press, 1996), 35–36. See also Paul Hoffmann, *La femme dans la pensée des Lumières* (Paris: Ophrys, 1977); G. J. Barker-Benfield, *The Culture of Sensibility. Sex and Society in Eighteenth-Century Britain* (Chicago: Chicago University Press, 1992); John Styles and Amanda Vickery (eds), *Gender, Taste, and Material Culture in Britain and North America, 1700–1830* (New

Haven: Yale University Press, 2006); Elizabeth Kowaleski-Walace, *Consuming Subjects: Women, Shopping, and Business in the Eighteenth Century* (New York: Columbia University Press, 1997).

14 Belén Moreno Claverías, 'Luxury, Fashion and Peasantry: The Introduction of New Commodities in Rural Catalan Areas, 1670–1790', in *The Force of Fashion in Politics and Society: Global Perspectives from Early Modern to Contemporary Times*, ed. Beverly Lemire (Burlington, VT and Farnham, Surrey, UK: Ashgate, 2010), 67–96.

15 This and other references of the Baron of Maldá about *petimetres* and *currutacos* in Vicent Pascual, *El Baró de Maldà: Materials per a una Biografia* (Barcelona: Publicacions de l'Abadia de Montserrat, 2003), 105–8.

16 Rebecca Haidt, 'Luxury, Consumption and Desire: Theorizing the Petimetra', *Arizona Journal of Hispanic Cultural Studies* 3 (1999): 33–50, 34.

17 Ibid., 37.

18 Moreno Claverías, 'Révolution de la Consommation Paysanne?' and 'Luxury, Fashion and Peasantry'.

19 De Zamora, *Diario de los Viajes*, 463.

20 In this respect, Victoria De Grazia argues that 'the gendered study of consumption brings class back through the front door. The changing meaning of consumption habits in successive form of social stratification highlights very different roles for women and men, over time and from class to class' (*The Sex of Things*, 8).

21 Antoinette Fauve-Chamoux, 'Vedove di Città e Vedove di Campagna nella Francia Preindustriale: Aggregato Domestico, Trasmissione e Strategie Familiari di Sopravvivenza', *Quaderni Storici* 98 (1998): 301–32, 324.

22 Moreno Claverías, 'Luxury, Fashion and Peasantry', 89.

23 Arxiu Històric Comarcal de Vilafranca del Penedès (AHCVP), Arxiu de Protocols Notarials (APN), Joan Rovira, P-XVIII-64–1, f. 12.

24 See Isabel Pérez Molina, 'Las Mujeres y el Matrimonio en el Derecho Catalán Moderno', in *Las Mujeres en el Antiguo Régimen: Imagen y Realidad. S.XVI–XVIII* (Barcelona: Icaria, 1994), 24–25.

25 Louise A. Tilly and Joan W. Scott point out that 'anthropological investigations have established the important differences each of these life-cycle stages have for the work, status, and power of women . . . Social-sexual references—single, married, mother, widow—then, as well as occupational designations, are important for any historical understanding of women's experience. The absence of even the simple distinction between married and single women has confused many an interpretation of the impact of industrialization on women'. In *Women, Work and Family* (New York: Holt, 1978), 4–5.

26 Several popular sayings reflect this fact: '*La dona casada on vol ella és respectada*' ('The married lady is respected where she wants to be'). Joan Amades, *Folklore de Catalunya: Cançoner. Cançons, Refranys, Endevinalles* (Barcelona: Selecta, 1982), 57.

27 '*La dona desgraciada, cent anys fadrina, cents anys vídua i un any casada*' ('The unfortunate lady, a hundred years single, a hundred years widowed and only one married'). Ibid., 58.

28 See the eighteenth-century diary of Catalan peasant Sebastià Casanovas i Canut, who does not tire of repeating that austerity and simplicity of dressing were essential virtues of the countryside woman. Sebastià Casanovas i Canut, *El Manuscrit de Palau-Saverdera: Memòries d'un pagès Empordanès del segle XVIII*, ed. J. Geli and M. A. Anglada (Figueres: Carles Vallès editor, 1986).

29 Belén Moreno Claverías, 'Mito y Realidad de la Feminización del Consumo en la Europa Moderna: las Pautas de Consumo de las Mujeres en la Cataluña Preindustrial', *Arenal. Revista de Historia de las Mujeres* 1 (2004): 119–54.

30 Manuel Barba i Roca, *El Corregiment i Partit de Vilafranca del Penedès a L'últim Terç del segle XVIII* (Vilafranca del Penedés: Museu de Vilafranca, 1991), 82.
31 De Zamora, *Diario de los Viajes*, 464.
32 D'Amat, *Viles i Ciutats*, 260.
33 De Zamora, *Diario de los Viajes*, 464–69.
34 D'Amat, *Viles i Ciutats*, 10.
35 Cissie Fairchilds uses the word 'populuxe' to refer to cheap imitations of luxury products in eighteenth-century France. For example, the watches worn by a small proportion of the lower classes were always made of silver, as opposed to gold in the case of the middle classes and the urban aristocracy. The dress coats, traditionally upper- and middle-class items of clothing, were made of cheaper and lower-quality fabrics. Cissie Fairchilds, 'Determinants of Consumption Patterns in Eighteenth-Century France', in *Material Culture: Consumption, Life-style, Standard of Living 1500–1900*, ed. Anton J. Schuurman and Lorena S. Walsh (Milan: Bocconi, 1994), 50–70. See also Laurence Fontaine, *Histoire du Colportage en Europe XVe–XIXe siècle* (Paris: Albin Michel, 1993).
36 Ormolu ('*similor*'): Alloy made by melting zinc with three or four parts of copper, which results in a metal of similar brightness to gold. Arxiu Històric de Protocols de Barcelona (AHPB), B. Oliveras de Plana, *Inventaris*, (1780–85), f. 70.
37 AHPB, R. Font Alier, *Inventaris* 1762–1785, f. 388.
38 Josep Mainar and Francesc Català, *El Moble Català* (Barcelona: Destino, 1976), 127.
39 Francesc Curet, *Visions Barcelonines 1760–1860: La Vida a la Llar* (Barcelona: Dalmau, 1952), 75–77.
40 Ibid., 109.
41 AHPB, R. Font Alier, *Inventaris* (1762–1785), f. 349.
42 Fairchilds, 'Determinants of Consumption Patterns', 229. For the English case, see Lorna Weatherill, *Consumer Behaviour and Material Culture in Britain 1660–1760* (London: Routledge, 1988), and Carole Shammas, *The Pre-Industrial Consumer in England and America* (Oxford: Clarendon Press, 1990).
43 Rafael d'Amat, Baró de Maldà, *Calaix de sastre I, 1760–1791* (Barcelona: Curial, 1988), 63.
44 Ibid., 55.
45 According to the RAE dictionary of 2001, the '*estrado*' was 'the set of furniture used to garnish the place or room where ladies received their visitors, and was composed by carpet, pillows, stools or chairs' or 'the place where women sat and received their visitors'.
46 Curet, *Visions Barcelonines*, 300–20.
47 Jesús Cruz, 'Elites, Comerciantes y Consumo en Madrid a Finales del Antiguo Régimen', *VI Simposio de Historia Económica* (Bellaterra-Terrasa, 1992), 2: 283–88, 284.
48 De Grazia and Furlough, *The Sex of Things*, 18–19.
49 Moreno Claverías, 'Luxury, Fashion and Peasantry'.
50 Veblen, *Teoría de la Clase Ociosa*, 58.
51 'Who drove men to acquire as many splendours? It does not require much thought. The room, where the distinguished society of the old regime lived, is the nest that the female carefully and with caution constructs to keep the male under control . . . The woman invents other ways to make the house comfortable and retain the man inside; she perfumes the rooms, decorates them with flowers'. Sombart, *Lujo y Capitalismo*, 103.

52 John Brewer and Roy Porter, eds, 'Introduction', in *Consumption and the World of Goods* (London: Routledge, 1993), 5.
53 Amanda Vickery, 'Women and the World of Goods: A Lancashire Consumer and Her Possessions', in *Consumption and the World of Goods*, 274–301, 294.
54 Montserrat Carbonell, *Sobreviure a Barcelona: Dones, Pobresa i Assistència al segle XVIII* (Vic: Eumo, 1997), 123.
55 Lorna Weatherill, 'A Possession of One's Own: Women and Consumer Behaviour in England, 1660–1740', *Journal of British Studies* 25 (1986): 131–56, 151.
56 Moreno Claverías, 'Mito y Realidad' and 'Luxury, Fashion and Peasantry'.
57 D'Amat, *Viles i Ciutats*, 256.
58 Ibid., 257.
59 Ibid., 257–8.
60 AHPB, Josep Ribes i Granés, *Inventaris i Encants 1798–1803*, 1046/84, f. 16.
61 Rafael d'Amat, Baró de Maldà, *Calaix de Sastre IV–1798–1799* (Barcelona: Curial, 1990), 144–45.
62 Ibid., 145.

9 Gender, Craftwork and the Exotic in International Exhibitions c. 1880–1910

Stana Nenadic

International exhibitions were urban showcases in which luxury goods were displayed to articulate a gendered dynamic that linked an ephemeral event to such permanent sites of consumption and spectacle as department stores and museums. Though they were phenomena of the later nineteenth and early twentieth centuries, international exhibitions built on developments of the century before, seen particularly in the idea of luxury and consumption as a manifestation of modern 'romantic' conditions of unrealisable fantasy and longing.[1] Continuities were also apparent in the relationship between gender, exotic luxury goods imported into Europe from the East and urban contexts for exhibition or display. In eighteenth-century France, for example, the city of Paris, with its capitalist businesses embedded in *ancien régime* structures, acted as a stage for the exhibition of fine textiles, imported and also made at home in provincial cities like Lyon.[2] In London and Amsterdam, the engagement with luxury was seen strikingly through the activities of the British and Dutch East India Companies. The latter was focused on the import of spices to Europe along with luxury foods such as sugar and tea and certain manufactured goods, particularly porcelain.[3] The former traded in many similar wares and also in fine Indian textiles and shawls, which were displayed in quayside warehouses and in their central London premises.

East India House in London's Leadenhall Street, which began life as an aristocrat's mansion, was a monument to masculinity reflecting the focus on military conquest and trade that defined the East India Company. But the building also contained a museum, open to the public free of charge from 1801, which had a more subtly gendered ambience. A tourist guide to London, *The Leisure Hour* (1858), having enumerated the museum's displays of lacquer and glassware, raw materials, metals and arms, provides the following description.

> Re-crossing the lobby and entering the chamber to the left, we find ourselves in a department in which, to confess the truth, we are not very much at home. This chamber contains a dazzling exhibition of female garniture and dresses, of gold-embroidered cloaks and head-dresses, of

> muslins bearing patterns printed in gold instead of colours, of chintzes, of shawls of Cashmere, of silk handkerchiefs and gown-pieces, of net-work as fine as gossamer, of delicate embroideries, of kincobs or massive textures ponderous with golden lace-work, of embroidery on velvets, of lace muslins, the lace wrought with threads of gold and minute devices of flat gold laminse—and more of the sort, at which the ladies present are in convulsive raptures, but which poor we want the wit to appreciate or describe. We can appreciate, however, the furniture of the room, which is of the most luxurious and costly kind, all full of that elaboration already hinted at; and we can appreciate the Nawab Schurff of Lucknow, in his niche at the end of the gallery. There he sits, as large as life, and just as natural, smoking his hookah under his awning of crimson velvet, with his legs crossed beneath him on the mat, and surrounded with all the elements of wealth and splendour becoming his condition.[4]

This account, describing goods displayed with particular appeal for women—'the ladies present are in convulsive raptures'—alongside a lifelike wax model of an Indian ruler in all his finery, was part of a convention that was evident in all exhibitions of eastern wares. But it was also increasingly apparent, as discussed below in other types of exhibitions of manufactured goods made in Europe and exported to Empire, as well as in exhibitions of luxury craft goods made in Europe, particularly by women of 'peasant' traditions for consumption at home. This formed a potent mix of fantasy, spectacle, curiosity, luxury, exoticism and longing that was international in scope, though commonly used to articulate a national and urban ideal, and which found its highest expression in the late nineteenth-century international exhibition movement.

EXHIBITIONS AS IDENTITY AND ASPIRATION

International exhibitions were competitive articulations of national and urban identity and aspirations. They were a city-focused form of state and regional 'boosterism', mostly devoted to industry and new technologies, particularly electricity. The latter was first displayed in Paris in 1881 and thereafter in the industry stands at all exhibitions, as well as in the travel infrastructure for reaching exhibition sites and in fairground entertainments. On one level, international exhibitions represented a culture that was masculine and aggressive, as famously represented by the advertising poster for Berlin 1896, showing a fist holding a hammer.[5] Yet there were also distinctively feminine and feminising themes consistent with modern consumerism, as seen in another exhibition poster, this time for Glasgow 1901, which represented the four corners of the earth in attractive female form.[6] Most exhibition-guide images were of fashionably dressed young women, as for the Turin exhibition of 1911, which was designed to highlight the local clothing industry and to challenge the regional dominance of Milan, whilst also celebrating the anniversary of Italian unification. There were many advertisements for motorcars, while publicity included aerial views taken from planes, but the advertising of goods, made by women for consumption by women, was also much in evidence.[7] An example, which also appeared in many popular women's magazines, was the whole-page advertisement for the book *La Donna Medico Di Casa*, an Italian translation of an international best seller of 1901 by a German 'maternal feminist' and family doctor.[8]

International exhibitions usually took place on greenfield sites bordering cities and comprised temporary buildings and thoroughfares, which were later mostly demolished. This ambiguous 'urban' character was further conditioned by the fact that many events, while attached to individual cities, sought to represent an idea of the nation, even in manifestly provincial cities, such as Glasgow or Turin, where themes of national representation were often articulated in direct competition with rival cities such as Edinburgh or Milan. The urban identity of individual exhibitions was rendered further complex by the presence of prominent displays representing the cities of other countries, sometimes as a proxy for the nations concerned. So, the Amsterdam Colonial Exposition of 1883 had a large display area given over to the city of Paris, which for many was a distillation of 'Frenchness' exemplified in its goods and services.[9] A less glamorous but decidedly ambitious Glasgow, at the height of its reputation for industry and the arts and crafts movement, provided a series of Glasgow-celebrating exhibition stands at early twentieth-century European events, such as Budapest and Turin, both in 1902, where displays from the 1901 Glasgow exhibition were recreated.[10]

As sites of luxuries for purchase, international exhibitions were different from the usual places for urban consumption in city-centre shopping streets and department stores. The latter cultivated a social tone to attract moneyed customers and excluded others, and while discount department stores with a broader clientele existed, there was still a sense that certain streets belonged to certain social classes, and that leisured women were the primary customer groups.[11] The ephemeral character of most international exhibitions as physical space meant that they did not possess an established social tone or those policing devices, such as a uniformed doorman, that were seen at the entrances to high-class stores. They were inevitably, therefore, more democratic than department stores, with democracy further promoted when the consumerism that many exhibitions endorsed was designed to evoke pre-modern, open, 'market' styles of retail experience.

International exhibitions were complex economic phenomena—some highly successful as financial ventures, though many were not. The organisers made money by charging exhibitors for space, and exhibitors, who also bore the costs of mounting and staffing their displays, expected to profit by selling goods, though this was often strictly controlled by taking orders for future supply, by advertising and by winning prizes which were subsequently used in advertising. Commercial ventures which in their ordinary existence were devoted to gendered forms of luxury and spectacle—such as department stores—also took stands in the international exhibitions and created elaborate displays, as with Pettigrew and Stephens of Glasgow with their glamorous 'Moorish' temple in Glasgow 1901.[12] In a further exchange between the department store and exhibitions, many of the consumer goods that were sold off at the end of events were purchased by retail entrepreneurs, who then recreated some of the exhibition displays in their shop premises, such as another Glasgow store, the Royal Polytechnic Warehouse, which in 1875 advertised, 'a great sale of Indian, Chinese and Japanese exhibition goods . . . the greater part purchased from the Commissioners of the London and Vienna international exhibitions'.[13] The mass appeal of international exhibitions was crucial to profitability, and mass appeal inevitably meant attracting the working and lower-middle classes, in particular those young men and women, mostly single, who had flocked to big industrial and commercial European cities for work in factories, or as clerks or shop girls. People went to exhibitions to engage in a promenade of youthful demotic fashionability and leisure, as well as to seek entertainment and education. One of the American commentators on the Vienna Universal Exhibition of 1873 gave a succinct description when he said, in a report to the US Centennial Commission as they prepared to host an event to mark the revolution of 1776: 'People gravitate to exhibitions not only to see the objects displayed, but to see each other—to see the crowd and to be in it.'[14]

Although big industry and modern technology were conspicuously displayed at international exhibitions, these were not what the masses came to see. Rather they were seeking entertainment, spectacle and pleasure. Industrialists understood this well and included features in their stands, such as working machinery or novelty displays that attracted a broad audience. Many exhibits were staffed by attractive young women, who were doubtless cheaper to employ than men, but who also garnered attention. They were there as shop girls in the department store sections and the working machine stands, which were often devoted to the production of goods that could be purchased on site, included numerous attractive young female operatives engaged in such things as sweet making and pastry and biscuit making, which were the new mass consumption industries of the age. Young women commonly dominated displays of living individuals making handcrafted 'things' for purchase as exhibited 'objects' alongside the goods they were making. At the Manchester exhibition of 1887, the first of the big British provincial events, a newspaper report, having passed over with little comment the vast but uniform displays of cotton manufactures of 'undoubted excellence', described:

> The space to the north and south at the foot of the nave is occupied with the most heterogeneous exhibits, which go a long way towards lending

> variety to the Exhibition. Here, too, is the section devoted to handicrafts and here accordingly one may find girls at work making artificial flowers and leather goods, others sticking pins by machinery, and still another lot making dolls.[15]

In Glasgow 1901, a display stand for the Glasgow School of Art, which was designed by Charles Rennie Mackintosh and provoked much comment, comprised 'a sort of cage in which to confine a pair of lady bookbinders'.[16] So large were the numbers of single female attendants, many drawn from far away, and estimated to be over 500 at the Glasgow 1901 exhibition, that special Ladies' Committees were established to safeguard their welfare.[17] Newspaper reports of international exhibitions aimed at female readers further highlighted the feminine tone. An article of June 1900 in 'Our Ladies' Column by 'One of Themselves', which was a regular feature of the *Wrexham Advertiser*, described 'the Paris Exhibition from a personal point of view', with details of the lady visitor's journey via rail and steam ship and lengthy accounts of the art, furniture, jewellery and clothing displays.[18]

Reflecting the importance of gendered consumption, international exhibitions were important sites for new developments in the catering industry. Famous firms such as Lyons pioneered their tearooms at exhibitions, first in Newcastle 1887, the following year in Glasgow and then in Europe, including Paris 1889, before taking over the catering at Olympia and Crystal Palace in the early 1890s and creating their first permanent London tea shop in 1894.[19] Women were attracted to these premises by brand identities that in some cases were created by women entrepreneurs such as Glasgow's Miss Cranston of tearoom fame, where waitresses served them tea and confectionery in feminised luxurious surroundings. Chocolate consumption, as a drink and as confectionery, was promoted through exhibitions. In Berlin in 1896, there was a pavilion in oriental style built by rising manufacturer Hoffmann & Tiede, makers of Sarotti chocolate, of which it was said, 'this sweet brand . . . works an unfathomable magic, particularly on the more tender part of the visitor.'[20] In Glasgow, in addition to Mrs Cranston's tearooms, there was the Van Houten's cocoa house, which in 1888 took the form of a seventeenth-century Dutch town house, was in modern style in 1901 and in 1911 was reinvented as an 'Old English' pavilion. Luxury foodstuffs such as tea, sugar and chocolate were gendered to appeal to women consumers in much the same way as a century before, though the market was now wider. But this commercial dynamic was not distinct to women consumers alone, because men were catered for by smoking pavilions, often with Turkish or otherwise exotic interior decoration, promoted as men-only retreats and places of relaxation. Another type of catering mainly directed at male consumers were curry houses at the British exhibitions (and in Europe too, since Indian displays were popular there in the 1880s) with Indian men in traditional dress as cooks and waiters.[21]

International exhibitions, though dedicated mainly to the celebration of new industries and leading-edge technology were also significant for backward-looking displays that reinforced a nationalist agenda or spirit. As with refreshment facilities, these popular features were commonly described as an escape from the noise and bustle of the industrial exhibits. The Edinburgh 1886 exhibition was notable for the first use in Scotland of a distinctive historical reconstruction, titled 'Old Edinburgh'.

> Glad, perhaps, to escape from the heat and noise [of the engineering section] we re-enter the central court and walk eastwards to pay a visit to Old Edinburgh, where we can enjoy a thorough change of scene . . . bringing into close juxtaposition with the inventions of modern life the edifices around which clustered the traditions of centuries ago.[22]

The display comprised a representation of the medieval High Street with its notable buildings, made in wood and plaster. There were shop booths within the Old Edinburgh court, such as the 'Heart O'Mid-Lothian Boothe', where Jeanie and Effie Deans, characters from Walter Scott's novel of the same name, in historical costume sold 'braw presents and bonnie keepsakes o' ye Exhibition at mast canny prices'. Sheet music, described as 'Old Edinburgh Waltzes', was also for sale among other heritage-themed consumables, food and sweets.[23] Most of the costumed figures were women. Like Edinburgh, some European exhibitions, including Berlin in 1896, chose to focus on their own city past to foster a sense of local pride.[24] In many, however, the historical displays took the form of idealised rural villages, where traditional costume and pastimes, such as dancing or singing, were displayed alongside craftwork. The Scandinavian Art and Industrial Art Exhibition, held in Stockholm in 1866, had displays of ethnographic photographs, which could also be purchased as postcard souvenirs, of different traditional groups in regional dress, some engaged in work.[25] The Stockholm exhibition of 1897 included a reconstruction of medieval Stockholm, but is best remembered for the founding of Skansen, the pioneering outdoor museum and recreation of traditional rural life.[26]

Tradition and the modern were always carefully juxtaposed. As a fast-developing technology, photography featured in international exhibitions, allowing new and often exotic subjects to be brought before a mass audience, though often in nostalgic or backward-looking ways. At the Vienna Exhibition of 1873, there was an exhibit featuring photographic portraits taken from the 'People of India' series compiled by the British India civil servant John Forbes Watson. It was focused on male subjects engaged in traditional craftwork in rural or village settings, with displays of decorative goods and tools arranged around the sitters. Several portraits illustrated the various stages of fine textile production; others concentrated on pottery making or woodcarving.[27] The goods being made were also exhibited. The photographs were carefully composed to evoke a complex narrative of high-quality decorative production in contexts of tradition and timelessness divorced from the pressures of the modern world. They reflected an increasingly nostalgic engagement with Europe's non-White colonies and subject peoples that was intended to maintain an economic *status quo* whilst valuing the exotic. The photographs mostly represented processes of production in a single image, from raw materials through to finished object—a device that also featured in many modern industrial exhibits. A typical catalogue entry for Vienna 1873 describes a photograph of Indian pantile makers:

> Potters' yard, on the bank of the Lyaree River, near Karachi, with potters at work. The man represented standing on the right of the picture is kneading the clay which has been previously prepared in the pit represented on the right. The centre figure is represented with a lump of unfinished clay on the wheel. The left hand figure shows a drain pipe on the centre of the wheel which, on being removed, is cut so as to bisect it longitudinally . . . and thus the pipe fashioned is easily formed into two pan-tiles.[28]

International exhibitions generated a mass interest in the exotic 'other' and their modes of living and working. This interest was satisfied initially through photographic exhibitions, or through life-sized wax model tableau, but was soon extended to include live exhibits.[29] Of course, the interest in exotic people had developed from earlier circus or fairground displays going back to the eighteenth century, and in the later nineteenth century was matched by other sorts of display extravaganza, such as touring 'wild west' shows which included animals and native American Indians as well as cowboys engaged feats of daring. However, exhibition displays were more complex, and when they were juxtaposed with live exhibits of working women and village communities from an idealised domestic past, they became distinctive sites of gendered luxury and escape. The first event to host living displays on a large scale was the Amsterdam Colonial Exposition of 1883, which was also one of the first to give prominence to trade and commerce rather than to industry and production. It included a Javanese village with native people and a pagoda and bamboo bridge, reflecting Dutch colonial interests in Indonesia. Subsequent exhibitions also had 'village' displays that reflected the colonial interests of the countries involved. An example is furnished by the Franco-British Exhibition in London in 1908, held to celebrate the signing of the Entente Cordiale, which had a popular French Senegalese Village with women and children alongside an equally visited Irish Village inhabited mainly by young Irish women (described as 'colleens') engaged in domestic manufacture.[30] Looking in detail at some of the 'traditional' goods that were manufactured and displayed in Scotland and Ireland alongside such living exhibits, and at the Irish Villages that were mounted in London, further highlights connections between gender and luxury, oriental and domestic, past and present.

LUXURY AND CRAFTWORK AT THE EDINBURGH AND GLASGOW EXHIBITIONS

The first international exhibition in Scotland, which was devoted to showcasing electricity, was held in Edinburgh in 1886, but it was overshadowed by the London Colonial and India exhibition of the same year. It was not until Glasgow hosted its first event two years later that Scotland made its mark on the international scene, with an exhibition that attracted almost six million visitors. Glasgow 1888 was ambitious from the outset, designed to overshadow Edinburgh and building on London and Manchester events of the previous two years. It included significant India themes, with many exhibits that had been seen in London in 1886 in displays that were designed to celebrate and encourage traditional Indian village handicrafts. One of the government officials who selected goods for exhibit was T. N. Mukharji, a Bengali civil servant who made collections for various India courts in the 1880s, including the 1883 Amsterdam Exhibition, the 1886 London exhibition and exhibitions in both Glasgow and Melbourne in 1888. Glasgow 1888 had Indian workmen as part of the displays, attracting much interest.

> The portion of the department which receives earliest attention from visitors is that reserved for the Indian artisans, a party of nine men engaged in various avocations. It lies to the west of the trio of courts and it has half a dozen stalls, such as are to be seen in an Oriental bazaar for the accommodation of the workmen. . . . Four of the spaces are used as workshops and another serves the purpose of a salesroom, while the remaining one is a retiring apartment, concealed with a curtain, the design of which arrests notice. . . . All [of the workmen] are natives of Bengal, with the exception of the two woodcarvers . . . and they appear in native costumes, which are at once becoming and comfortable. . . . The recess at the back of the Bengal screen is converted into a stall, where Messrs Ardeshir and Byramji, Bombay, have a great variety of Indian goods for sale.[31]

The Indian artisans comprised two woodcarvers, two potters, two jewellers and three confectioners making pastries and sweets, and the goods that they produced were for sale. Indian themes were also seen elsewhere. There was the Royal Bungalow for refreshments, operated by a local licensed contractor, which include the Lucknow and Delhi rooms and the General Gordon buffet, serving curries. There was also Howell's oriental-styled tobacco kiosk, plus India and Ceylon tea pavilions.[32] Textile manufacturers continued the India theme in their exhibitions of calico and Turkey red printed cottons for export. The display by Messrs F. Steiner & Co. of Manchester included several full-size wax mannequins of Indian women displaying fabrics against dark skins and jewellery.[33]

In addition to the India court itself, Glasgow 1888 included the extensive 'Indian Pavilion' display by Doulton & Co. of Lambeth in London's East End, and the commodities being produced in the pavilion by its craft potters (some of them women) and described in the press were striking. Demand for pottery and ceramics and their display at exhibitions exemplifies most of the complex and evolving class and gendered dynamics that characterise the modern consumption of luxury goods. Imported valuable porcelain from the east was a luxury that only the very rich could afford in the early eighteenth century, but by the 1750s British entrepreneurs such as Wedgwood were making high-quality mass-produced copies for a broader clientele and used modern marketing techniques such as newspaper advertising and shop-window displays to sell their wares.[34] By the second half of the nineteenth century, the market for pottery and ceramics had expanded to embrace the urban working classes, and international exhibitions became a great showcase in which the masses could scrutinise and appreciate such commodities new and old, home-produced and from overseas.

In mounting displays of contemporary craft manufacturers, it was usual for exhibitions to include parallel displays of valuable antiques on loan from local aristocratic collections and in many instances in Great Britain, on loan from the Royal Collection. These heirloom collections—which included ceramics and glassware, embroidery, lace and jewellery—were popular spectacles that also gave consumers a notion of high status fashionability that they could then emulate through their own consumption of similarly styled goods. The late nineteenth-century demand for Chinese wares such as embroidery, carved wood and jade or blue and white ceramics—which was supplied in London through specialist West End department stores, including Liberty, and formed numerous exhibition displays—was built on knowledge of the aristocratic consumption practices of the past, which had generated vast inherited family collections.[35] At the time of the 1851 Great Exhibition, Doulton & Co. were mainly manufacturers of utilitarian stoneware for pipes and bathroom fittings. But from the 1860s, having formed a connection with the Lambeth School of Art from where they employed many designers and skilled craftworkers, including women, Doulton & Co. moved into the production of art wares for domestic decoration. Much of their output built on antique designs and techniques including Renaissance-styled vases, which were popular in the 1880s, and in the 1890s they developed vivid red glaze effects of the type used by ancient Chinese master potters.[36] The company exhibited across the globe, including Vienna in 1873, Philadelphia in 1876, and both Amsterdam (the first of the 'colonial' exhibitions) and Calcutta in 1883. From Calcutta, the company developed an interest in Indian art manufacturers, reflected in their growing investment in the manufacture of terracotta wares. They then exhibited at the London Indian and Colonial Exhibition of 1886, followed by Manchester in 1887 and Glasgow in 1888, where they displayed their great Indian Pavilion, 'a handsome building of glazed terracotta' of which it was said, 'this is the first time that operations in connection with the kilns have ever been attempted at a public exhibition.'[37]

At both Manchester and Glasgow, Doulton & Co. included a number of craftworkers in their exhibit, engaged in various types of pottery manufacture.[38] Queen Victoria was a patron of the firm and attended the Indian Pavilion in Glasgow to witness the decoration of a salt-glazed stoneware vase handcrafted in an Indian style. The vase, which is now in Glasgow's Kelvingrove Art Gallery and Museum, records the event in an inscription on the base, which also incorporates the initials of the makers—EC for Edith M. Coleman and EW for Emily M. R. Welch, who were senior assistants and noted art potters at the Lambeth works.[39] Edith Coleman and Emily Welch worked alongside male craftworkers from India, including a potter, and the contrast between them and the implications for contemporary understanding of the progress of civilizations was striking to visitors and commentators alike. James Paton, Superintendent of the Glasgow Corporation Art Galleries, in an exhibition report for the *Glasgow Herald* on the subject of 'Pottery and Glass', provides a telling narrative for the urban consumers who attended the exhibition and for the newspaper readers who 'consumed' the event vicariously.

> Within this Oriental erection Messrs Doulton make an honest and successful effort to illustrate some of the more important processes connected with the manufacture of pottery. The making of pottery is one of the most ancient of arts, and in the hands of the rude manufacturer is also one of the simplest . . . To this day in certain parts of the Western Islands old women are found who are the literal representatives of the old potters of the district and who out of the clay obtained around their doors will fashion and finish vessel such as at no very remote time formed the ordinary pottery of the islanders. But between these primitive and unassuming productions and the fabriques of Minton, Doulton, Sevres or Dresden there yawns a wide gulf. . . . Yet the art in its most lovely manifestations and in its highest achievements is in most of its processes and manipulations the same.
>
> Here at the western extremity of the Indian Court may be seen the Indian potter at work with his simple and primitive implements and appliances, just as his ancestors before him in the village communities of India exercised their craft for a period of not less than two thousand years. His apparatus is of a rude and clumsy enough character, consisting of a heavy wheel or table, mounted on a pivot, to which he gives motion of rotation by jerking with his hand, and while it is spinning he moulds with his hand into the form of a vessel the mass of clay he places or throws on the centre of the potter's wheel. The potters employed by Messrs Doulton, and the apparatus at their disposal, show many improvements on the simple art of the Hindoo.[40]

Not far from Doulton's Indian Pavilion, and immediately opposite the Indian craftworkers, were the home-based artisans and their craftworks. This feature was first seen in Scotland in Edinburgh in 1886, where the

Artisan's Court with 400 distinct displays, often just single items with space given free of charge, was the largest in the exhibition as a whole and involved wood carving and wood inlay, brass and metal work, clocks and jewellery. The 'Women's Industries' section of this and similar exhibitions included fine antique textiles, embroidery and tapestries, lent by royal and aristocrat female patrons, and also middle-class women who were part of the 'arts and crafts' movement, often with art college training, and who were engaged in a range of craft production, with displays that looked remarkably similar to the India stands. Indeed, the famous proponent of the British arts and crafts movement, William Morris, was also a great supporter of the promotion of Indian 'art manufacture' as a moral good designed to protect the integrity of Indian culture.[41]

In addition to the middle-class craftswomen, there were the popular and widely photographed 'living history' displays of Shetland knitting girls and Fair Isle weavers in native costume against a background of goods and furniture indigenous to those distant parts of Scotland, including, in Edinburgh 1886, four giant whale jaw bones erected to form a structure to support a tent in which the knitting girls could sit (See Figure 9.1). Queen Victoria

Figure 9.1 Zetland and Fair Isle knitters. The Jaw Bone Stand, Edinburgh International Exhibition, 1886. Shetland Museum Photographic Archive.

visited the 'jaw-bone stand' and was presented with a fine Shetland wool lace shawl of a type traditionally made as bridal shawls, which are so delicate that the best can pass through a wedding ring. Such royal patronage increased the fashionable appeal of this luxury commodity.[42] Edinburgh 1886 was the first time that a working display of knitting girls had been mounted, but Shetland shawls had featured in international exhibitions since the first in London in 1851, when London retailers Standen & Co., who first introduced such goods to metropolitan markets, exhibited a white bridal veil with Turkey red borders.[43] The encouragement of this home-based industry was part of a movement to generate income for women in distant rural areas and to prevent island depopulation. This is the description given of the Glasgow displays in 1888:

> Mrs Muir, of Lerwick, has brought with her three workers, who may be seen carding, spinning and knitting Shetland wool at her stand. This lady shows also a quantity of work knitted in the Fair Isles which is entirely different to the ordinary Shetland work, being bright and gay in colouring, and some of it very intricate in pattern. . . . Not far from Mrs Muir's stand is that of the Harris weaver [a woman] who, upon a very primitive loom, occasionally illustrates the weaving of the now famous and fashionable Harris tweeds. This loom was sent by Lady Scott, who takes great interest in the 'homespun' industry of the Hebrides; and to the exertions of this lady and several others these textile industries owe their revival and recent development.[44]

The exhibiting of attractive women in traditional dress was also seen in another popular group who toured and 'performed' at the international exhibitions, the Newhaven fishwives from a fishing village near Edinburgh, with their striped 'kilted' petticoats, floral blouses, knitted shawls and fish baskets (or creels) on their backs. These colourful representatives of a bygone age, widely photographed and the subject of much antiquarian and tourist interest, formed choirs that sang at the London Fisheries Exhibition in 1881, the Edinburgh International Fisheries Exhibition of 1882 and also in some of the Scandinavian exhibitions later in the century, where there was a similar interest in traditional fishing village culture.[45] And female craftworkers from other European countries making luxury goods for a largely female market were also displayed in Scotland. They included a group of Belgian lacemakers in the Glasgow 1901 Pettigrew and Stephen's department store exhibit.[46] There were also the Irish lacemaking girls who, like many craft groups featured in the Irish villages that exhibited throughout Europe, though their location in Glasgow 1901 provoked amusement.

> The most striking of these [store displays] is a sort of Alhambresque Kiosk of Messrs. Pettigrew and Stephens. The relation of its architecture to the Irish peasant industries, or to damask weaving, carried on

within its walls is not very apparent: but it is an attractive and really original facade.[47]

IRISH EXHIBITIONS AND IRISH VILLAGES

The first of the big Irish international exhibitions, held in Dublin in 1865, like all that followed in the wake of Crystal Palace in 1851, included extensive India craftwork exhibits, mostly antiques on loan from the royal collection at Windsor Castle or the India Museum in London. There were arms, saddles, carpets, fine textiles and metal and pottery wares and also extensive displays of raw materials. There were no displays of working Indian craftsmen, or of any other 'living exhibits', but there was a category described as 'photographs of the people of India', intended to portray the different tribes and castes, but also showing traditional working activity in villages, much of it revolving around craft textile production. There was a 'Medieval Court' at the Dublin exhibition—a mixture of modern manufactures and antiques—and a small display of handmade lace, most of it English or European in origin.[48] It was these displays that formed the basis of later developments in Irish luxury craftwork, including lacemaking.

As with the Shetland Isles and elsewhere in highland Scotland, aristocratic female patronage was employed in rural Ireland to stimulate craft production by women in order to offset poverty and rural depopulation.[49] In the process of encouraging such skill and industry, effected through the founding of craft training schools for girls, the granting of prizes and commercial quality control and marketing by middle men, the moral integrity of the village as a site of traditional values and the production of lace, embroidery or homespun woollens as morally valuable activities suited to traditional village contexts also gained emphasis, much as in the Indian case. The Dublin Exhibition of 1907 brought most of these themes into focus through an extensive home-industries building, with a 'lace court' and 'embroidery court' at the centre and smaller displays and working exhibits roundabout. The home industries hall also had a separate 'Arts and Crafts' section mainly showing women's work. The link with rural life was made explicit in the area outside the building which was designed to represent a village green surrounded by a village hall, a village hospital and two model workmen's cottages. The intention of the exhibition complex as a whole was to 'convey to visitors the desire of the Committee to form a display creditable to Ireland, and useful to those engaged in the work of rehabilitating rural life, thereby bringing work and leisure properly together, and tending to stay the tide of emigration.'[50]

The Dublin exhibition, like many of the period, was accompanied by an extensive published volume that included a list of the exhibitors and plan of the site, with reflective and context-setting essays. There was a commentary on lace and crochet making in Ireland, authored by R. M. Martin, Managing Director of the Irish Lace Depot. The link between craftwork and Irish traditional dancing was extolled in another essay, and the volume gave considerable focus to devices for maintaining the vibrancy of village life, through the founding of village halls and local charity hospitals. There were descriptions too of home industries in other European countries. The volume gives a powerful contemporary account of the emotional resonance of craftwork, suggesting the complex messages that attended the viewing and wearing of homespun textiles. With its references to glamour, charm and fancy, such accounts echoed many similar descriptions of the value of Indian handcrafted, rural village goods.

> There is something distinctive about a piece of homespun which appeals strongly to one's fancy, and invests it with an individuality quite different from machine-made cloth. If this glamour of the homespun—which appears to specially cast its spell over those who delight in nature, and the charm of rural life—is analysed, it will be found that the association of ideas connected with the production of the homespun has much to do with this feeling. The breezy mountainside, with its sunshine and shadows chasing one another across the hills, here and there dotted with sheep, in the wool of which the sun produces the luminous effects so dear to artists, is the home of the homespun.[51]

In addition to exhibitions in the country of Ireland (then part of Great Britain), groups of Irish craftworkers were a popular spectacle at great exhibitions elsewhere. An Irish Village, occupied by over 150 'colleens', who were selected for their looks and charm, was a major feature of the Franco-British Exhibition in London in 1908 and remained *in situ* in White City to the west of the capital for the 1909 Imperial International Exhibition and the 1910 Japan-British Exhibition. Called Ballymaclinton in recognition of the main sponsor, Brown & McClinton Ltd of Donaghmore, who were soap manufacturers, the Irish Village is reputed to have attracted over three million visitors who paid a six-penny entry fee with profits from the enterprise going to an Irish medical charity. Praised for its 'ancient features that make such villages so interesting', according to the *Times* newspaper report, 'it transports the visitor at a step from the whirl of London to the heart of Ireland.'[52] The Village included exhibitions and displays of craftwork and craftworking; there were country entertainments in the Village Hall and a restaurant where visitors could buy bread and cakes baked over the peat fires of the cottages. But tradition was matched with the modern, in the form of a Post Office and Telegraph Office placed centrally in the Village, with a shop selling souvenirs and postcards showing views of the cottages and their almost exclusively female, young and attractive inhabitants.[53]

CONCLUSION

International exhibitions were complex events where industrial displays coexisted with luxury handcrafted rural goods production, often generated in village contexts, in which there was a sense of 'permanence' and authenticity that had appeal to urban consumers. What was striking is that so much of this production was from female hands and consumed by women, or that it was 'oriental' in style or production or both, and that the contexts in which women (or 'Orientals') produced and exhibited were not traditional at all but were mostly invented, and emerged out of situations where rapid change was taking place. This was new in many ways—as the tide of rural depopulation and industrial modernisation was new. But the idea of fantasy, escape, transcendence, longing and romantic emotionality linked to luxury and consumption, particularly for women in an urban setting, had long existed among the middle class and elite, though it was now operating among the ordinary working classes.

International exhibitions provided little luxuries for consumption by the masses. A day off work, leisure-directed travel, a meal in a restaurant or cafe and sometimes a night or two in a hotel were now part of the popular experience of visiting an exhibition. The typical visitor was a young working- or lower-middle-class adult with money to spend on having a good day out, which they often marked with the purchase of a souvenir from one of the craft stalls. People such as these were eager to involve their family and friends who could not attend with a small part of the same experience through the purchase of a present to take or send home. Exhibitions usually included portrait photographer's studios, so that one type of souvenir that the visitor could buy or gift was a *carte de visite* photograph of themselves. Another type of souvenir and little shared luxury that was significantly associated with international exhibitions was the photographic postcard, whose rapid development in the second half of the nineteenth century went hand in hand with new production technologies, the rise of literacy and cheap and efficient postal services.[54] Commercial photography more generally in the form of stereoscopic cards for home entertainment or tourist literature as well as postcards was important for mediating a changing experience of the nineteenth-century cityscape, and the exhibition postcard photograph was part of this bigger process.[55] Two types of postcard dominated—views of the exhibition site, with aerial views particularly popular, as well as views of individuals or buildings from the exotic and village sections. Many of these postcards still survive, and their short messages provide eloquent insights to popular experience and the distinctive processes of gendered urban consumption that exhibitions generated. Here are four sent from the Franco-British Exhibition of 1908 held in London's White City, which were collected to celebrate the centenary.[56]

28 May 1908. I thought I must send you a card from here. It is a most wonderful place and so full of foreigners I feel in another country.

3 September 1908. I hear you are collecting PCs of the exhibition, so am sending you one. We were there last night, had dinner and saw the whole place lit up—a most glorious sight.

15 October 1908. I am sending you just a card to let you see we are really here. The exhibition is very grand. Have any of you been up? Crowds of people here. London is a very busy place. Traffic deafening.

8 August 1908. The Irish colleens at the village are OK. Hold me back!

The choice of language in these pithy communications—'wonderful', 'glorious', the 'crowds', the 'foreigners', the noise and the light—exemplify an almost timeless response to the urban experience, reflecting one clear aspect of international exhibitions as mounted in a great metropolis like London. But the mention of 'another country' and 'Irish colleens at the village' also positioned this, as with similar events elsewhere, as a cultural phenomenon that negotiated relationships between metropolitan centres across the developed world, and also negotiated the interface between the urban and an increasingly sentimentalised, gendered and consumerist notion of rural life.

NOTES

1 Colin Campbell, *The Romantic Ethic and the Spirit of Modern Consumerism* (Oxford: Oxford University Press, 1987); Stana Nenadic, 'Romanticism and the Urge to Consume in the Early Nineteenth Century', in *Consumers and Luxury: Consumer Culture in Europe, 1650–1850*, ed. Maxine Berg and Helen Clifford (Manchester: Manchester University Press, 1999).

2 William H. Sewell Jr, 'The Empire of Fashion and the Rise of Capitalism in Eighteenth-Century France', *Past and Present* 206 (2010): 81–120.

3 Harold Cook, *Matters of Exchange: Commerce, Medicine and Science in the Dutch Golden Age* (Cambridge: Yale University Press, 2007).

4 *The Leisure Hour*, 1858, online. www.victorianlondon.org/entertainment/eastindiahouse.htm

5 Dorothy Rowe, 'Georg Simmel and the Berlin Trade Exhibition of 1896', *Urban History* 22 (1995): 216–28.

6 *International Exhibition of Industry, Science and Art: Pen & Pencil Exhibition Number* (Glasgow: 1901), Front cover.

7 *L'Esposizione Di Torino. Giornale Ufficale Illustrato Dell'Esposizione Internazionale Delle Industrie E Del Lavoro* (Torino: 1911) [Online at www.italyworldsfairs.org/exist/worldsfairs/pages/torino?targ=array].

8 See Paulette Meyer, 'Physiatrie and German Maternal Feminism: Dr Anna Fischer-Duckelmann Critiques Academic Medicine', *Canadian Bulletin of Medical History* 23 (2006): 145–82.

9 Holly Griffin, '1883 Colonial Exposition, Amsterdam', in *A Treasury of World's Fair Art and Architecture*, University of Maryland Digital Collections, online. http://hdl.handle.net/1903.1/34

10 Juliet Kinchin, 'Re-visioning Glasgow: The "New Art" Exhibited at Home and Abroad, 1901–3', *Réseau Art Nouveau Network*, online. www.artnouveau-net.eu/LinkClick.aspx?fileticket=tA6bxXkmvi0%3D&tabid=204
11 See, Geoffrey Crossick and Serge Jaumain, eds, *Cathedrals of Consumption: The European Department Store, 1850–1939* (Aldershot: Ashgate, 1999).
12 Lewis F. Day, 'Decorative and Industrial Art at the Glasgow Exhibition', *Art Journal*, 9 (1901): 273–77.
13 *Glasgow Herald*, 5 March, 1875, 1.
14 W. P. Blake and Henry Pettit, *Reports on the Vienna Universal Exhibition, 1873* (Philadelphia: US Centennial Commission, 1873), 23.
15 *Glasgow Herald*, 14 May, 1887, 9.
16 Day, 'Decorative and Industrial Art', 277.
17 Perilla Kinchin and Juliet Kinchin, *Glasgow's Great Exhibitions, 1888, 1901, 1911, 1938 and 1988* (Wendelbury: White Horse Press, 1988), 70.
18 *The Wrexham Advertiser and North Wales News*, 23 June, 1900, 2.
19 D. J. Richardson, 'Lyons, Sir Joseph Nathaniel (1847–1917), Caterer', *Oxford Dictionary of National Biography Online*. www.oxfordnb.com.proxy1-bib.sdu.dk:2048/view/article/37703?docPos-14
20 Quoted in David Ciarlo, *Advertising Empire: Race and Visual Culture in Imperial Germany* (Cambridge Mass: Harvard University Press, 2011), 51.
21 Kinchin and Kinchin, *Glasgow's Great Exhibitions*, 36, 46, 58, 90.
22 *Cameron's Guide Through the International Exhibition of Industry, Science and Art (and Old Edinburgh), Opened 6 May 1886* (Edinburgh: J&A Cameron, 1886), 55.
23 *Cameron's Guide*, 54.
24 Katza Zelljadt, 'Presenting and Consuming the Past. Old Berlin at the Industrial Exhibition of 1896', *Journal of Urban History* 31 (2005): 306–33.
25 *Liste des Costumes Nationaux de Suède, de Norvège et de Finlande dans la Grandeur de Carte de Visite et de Portrait de Cabinet* (Stockholm: W. Eurenius, n.d.).
26 Magdalena Hillstrom, 'Nordiska museet and Skansen: Displays of Fleeting Nationalities', *Great Narratives of the Past: Traditions and Revisions in National Museums*. Paper presented at the conference of European National Museums: Identity Politics, the Uses of the Past and the European Citizen. Paris, 29 June–1 July, 2011.
27 See, John Forbes Watson, *Vienna Universal Exhibition, 1873: A Classified and Descriptive Catalogue of the India Department* (London, 1873).
28 Watson, *Vienna Universal Exhibition*, 192.
29 On wax models, see, Vanessa R. Schwartz, *Spectacular Realities: Early Mass Culture in Fin-de-Siècle Paris* (Berkeley and Los Angeles: University of California Press, 1998).
30 Alexander Geppert, *Fleeting Cities: Imperial Expositions in Fin-de-Siècle Europe* (Basingstoke: Palgrave Macmillan, 2010).
31 *The Scotsman*, 28 June, 1888, 5.
32 Kinchin and Kinchin, *Glasgow's Great Exhibitions*, 46.
33 *Supplement to the North British Daily Mail*, 26 September, 1888, 6. See also, Stana Nenadic, 'Exhibiting India in Nineteenth-Century Scotland and the Impact of Industry, Commerce and Design', *Journal of Scottish Historical Studies* 34 no. 1 (2014): 67–89.
34 Neil McKendrick, 'Josiah Wedgwood: An Eighteenth-Century Entrepreneur in Salesmanship and Marketing Techniques', *Economic History Review* 12 (1960): 408–33.
35 See, Sarah Cheang, 'Selling China: Class, Gender and Orientalism at the Department Store', *Journal of Design History* 20 (2007): 1–16.

36 Katharine Ellis, 'Royal Doulton at International Exhibitions', *Gallery: The Royal Doulton Collectors Club Magazine*, Spring 1992.
37 *Glasgow Herald*, 14 May, 1887, 9.
38 *Supplement to the North British Daily Mail*, 24, 1888, 3; *Glasgow Herald*, 23 August, 1888, 9–10.
39 Kelvingrove Art Gallery and Museum. Accession No. E.1986.4.
40 *Glasgow Herald*, 31 May, 1888, 9.
41 Peter H. Hoffenberg, 'Promoting Traditional Indian Art at Home and Abroad. "The Journal of Indian Art and Industry", 1884–1917', *Victorian Periodicals Review* 37 (2004): 192–213.
42 Shetland Museum and Archives, Accession Number, NE04535.
43 Ibid., Photo Number, 01398.
44 *Glasgow Herald*, 10 November, 1888, 4. See also *Illustrated London News*, 1 September, 1888, 12.
45 City of Edinburgh Museums and Galleries Accession Number, SECF ELO 0408.000.
46 Kinchin and Kinchin, *Glasgow's Great Exhibitions*, 72.
47 Day, 'Decorative and Industrial Art, 275.
48 *Dublin International Exhibition of Arts and Manufactures, 1865: Official Catalogue* (Dublin: The Committee, 1865), 35–49.
49 See Janice Helland, *British and Irish Home Arts and Industries, 1880–1914: Marketing Craft, Making Fashion* (Dublin: Irish Academic Press, 2007).
50 *Irish Rural Life and Industry with Suggestions for the Future; Issued in Connection with the Home Industries Section of the Irish International Exhibition, 1907* (Dublin: The Committee, 1907), 309.
51 'Homespun Manufacture in the West of Ireland, Mayo and Kerry,' in ibid.
52 *The Times*, 14 May, 1908, 5.
53 George Ithell, 'Ballymaclinton and the Post Office', *Exhibition Study Group*, 1998, online.
54 In 1850 there were 13.2 items of mail per head of population sent in GB. By 1890 it was 70 and 117 by 1910. F. H. Williamson, *Post and Postal Services* (London: Post Office, 1972), 211.
55 See David Prochaska and Jordana Mendelson, eds, *Postcards: Ephemeral Histories of Modernity* (Pennsylvania: University Press, 2010); Justin Carville, 'Mr Lawrence's Great Photographic Bazaar', *Early Popular Visual Culture* 5 (2007): 263–83.
56 Debra Kelly and Tom Jackson, 'The Franco-British Exhibition of 1908: Legacies and Memories One Hundred Years on', *Synergies: Royaume-Uni et Irelande*, 2 (2009): 11–23.

Part III

Class and Status

10 A Feminine Luxury in Paris: Marie-Fortunée d'Este, Princesse de Conti (1731–1803)

Aurélie Chatenet-Calyste

On 10 July 1789, Marie-Fortunée d'Este, Princesse de Conti and cousin to King Louis XVI, left Paris and then France to escape the French Revolution. She never went back to France and died in Venice on 21 September 1803. In 1792, the government sequestered her Parisian mansion and all of her French goods. Her personal papers, comprising the household accounts and the bills of her suppliers became the property of the French State and currently rest in the National Archives in Paris.[1] Her voluminous accounts allow us to study the daily consumption of this princess, especially from 1776 to 1789. These records demonstrate her material, mental and cultural universe. By focusing on her ordinary and exceptional consumption, it is possible to appreciate her lifestyle, her singularity, her personal tastes and her place in Parisian and aristocratic society.[2] This chapter characterises a feminine luxury that was the result of a perpetual interaction between her uniqueness, the norms that depended on her rank and the specific context of increased consumption in Paris at the end of the eighteenth century.

Marie-Fortunée d'Este (1731–1803), the daughter of Francis III Duke of Modena, came to France in 1759 after her marriage to Louis-François-Joseph of Bourbon-Conti, Count of La Marche. Thus, she became part of this younger branch of the Bourbon family which comprised an elder branch who reigned and the lateral families of Bourbon-Orléans, Bourbon-Condé and Bourbon-Conti. Together they represented the princes of blood and enjoyed a special status and prerogatives at court. Following the royal pattern, the Princesse de Conti had to demonstrate her rank and her social superiority by specific consumption practices based on profligate spending. As Norbert Elias' work has underlined, spending was necessary for an aristocratic woman who belonged to court society, and numerous studies have concentrated on the particular behaviour of French elites in the eighteenth century.[3] As Philippe Perrot asserts:

> Being aristocratic meant adopting a certain appearance and this appearance defined who you were. Rank determined how much you were expected to spend. The amount of money spent indicated your rank and spending only made sense in relation to your rank.[4]

French historians such as Natacha Coquery have highlighted the relentless aristocratic quest for distinction, their taste for exoticism and the forces of fashion at the end of the eighteenth century.[5] This chapter takes a fresh look at French aristocratic consumption by focusing for the first time on the princes of blood's consumption in the eighteenth century.

The Duke of Croÿ's famous statement that 'households ruined most elite families' represented the conservative opposition to luxury that can also be read in La Bruyère's books or even in the *Encyclopédie*. But consumption had become far more legitimate since the seventeenth century because it was intrinsically linked to the increased circulation of money and the growth of trade. 'All this wealth consists only of consumption', wrote the French economist Boisguilbert in 1707.[6] Historians have demonstrated that even if numerous nobles were in debt, it did not necessarily mean that they were ruined. Moreover, luxury stimulated trade and fed the commercial growth of Paris. From the sixteenth century Paris had been a leading arbiter of taste and was distinguished by the growth of its luxury trade. The splendour of the royal court and the dense concentration of artists and craftsmen encouraged the luxury industries. In the eighteenth century, Paris's position in the world of European luxury was reinforced by its population growth and the accelerating increase in consumption. Paris was one of the great European centres of the luxury industries and became the capital of fashion, celebrated by foreigners or acclaimed by books and the fashion press. As Baroness of Oberkirch wrote in her *Memories*: 'If fashion did not come from Paris, where did it come from?'[7] The Faubourg Saint-Honoré and the Palais Royal were considered as the height of the luxury market at the end of the century.

However, the case of the Princesse de Conti furthermore invites us to consider luxury from a gender perspective. Whereas a traditional historical vision associated women with frivolity, historians have recently emphasised women's key role in household management.[8] These studies have mainly focused on couples and families, while we know much less about the purchasing practices of single women. Although widowed women have drawn historians' attention, David Hussey and Margaret Ponsonby have recently regretted that 'there has been little work published on their homemaking strategies', although more recent conferences organised around single people's consumption suggests a shift in historians' interests.[9]

The study of Marie-Fortunée d'Este's consumption suffers from a double historiographical vacuum. Even though French historians have begun to study the topic of separation of goods, historians have shown less interest in the acquisitive patterns of separated women.[10] Moreover, they have not studied the eighteenth-century French princesses of blood at all. In 1776 this princess of blood separated from her husband and then led an independent life, splitting her single and childless life between her Parisian hotel in Rue Saint-Dominique, in the noble Faubourg Saint-Germain, and her castle of Triel, close to Paris. With the separation of goods, she became financially independent from her husband. She had a double pension of 180,000 *livres* a year given by both her husband and the King.[11] The Princesse de Conti was so extremely wealthy that she belonged to the 250 noble French families who earned more than 50,000 *livres* a year.[12] In return, she was responsible for all her expenses and her domestic management. But if the princess still belonged to the richest families, she seemed to be one of the poorest members of the royal family. The Countess de Genlis wrote in her *Memoires*, 'The Princesse de Conti is the least rich among the princesses; we can say she is very poor according to the rank she has to maintain'.[13]

On her own, without children but heading a fifty-person household, she was in a rather uncomfortable position: She had to reconcile the expensive requirements of her rank with the confines of her finances. Thus, her accounts make it possible to study the different meanings luxury had for such a princess at different stages in her life. Although the accounts have mostly been preserved from the period of her separation after 1776, sufficient conservation of bills before 1776 enables us to identify to what extent her conspicuous consumption depended on her marital status and her life-course. The sources allow us to reconstruct her changing purchasing patterns, from her wedding to her new independence resulting from the marital break-up. By highlighting her choices of Parisians suppliers across time, we can see how Marie-Fortunée's luxury consumption was both shaped by her new autonomy and restricted by her reduced lifestyle after the marital separation. The marital split seems to be a very important break in her life. A foreigner and ill at ease in French aristocratic society, she appeared less and less frequently at court during the 1780s. Her increasing age and her retreat from the world affected her spending. This case study aims at demonstrating how luxury consumption contributed to building Marie-Fortunée's identity and to what extent it depended on her life-course.

THE ACCOUNTS: A SOURCE FOR ARISTOCRATIC AND PARISIAN LUXURY

When she arrived in France in 1759, Marie-Fortunée d'Este left the dormant Modenese court for a brilliant court and the capital of fashion. In the eighteenth century, the princes of blood no longer lived at the palace in Versailles, where they still had apartments, but in Paris, in their mansions or around the city in castles such as Chantilly, residence of the Prince de Condé.[14] From 1759 to 1789, the princess mostly lived in Paris, while several stays in Versailles and the various aristocratic residences around Paris punctuated her life. For thirty years she lived in the European capital of fashion and luxury at a time of increased consumption and commercial growth. As she became a member of the extended royal family, she had to live according to her royal rank and to match her consumption accordingly.

The signature of a separation covenant in November 1775 followed by a court order in 1776 and 1777 established the rules of the separation of goods between the prince and the princess. The princess's departure from the marital mansion also led to the drafting of independent accounts. Following the usual aristocratic practices, the princess did not keep the account books herself but delegated these tasks to her treasurer, Armand Brési, a Modenese chosen by the princess from among her father's household. The accounts are different from French aristocratic ones in their form and, for example, from the Conti family account books.[15] The princess's accounts are not in bound books but loose sheets, and notably the typical French aristocratic double entry accounts are also missing. If income and expenditure were clearly separated, spending was noted as bills received and were not divided into thematic categories. The organisation of the accounts reveals that the treasurer was more a man of letters than a man of numbers, but also demonstrates the small size of this female household, because this system would be very inconvenient for a larger one with more important and varied incomes and expenses. Altogether, the accounts comprise 3,000 pages of invoices and statements. The general expenses and receipts are only known for two years: 1788 and 1789. The most frequent documents are suppliers' bills and the monthly statements of her expenses. These reports concern all aspects of the princess's and her household's daily life. The managers of each household sector supplied a monthly expense report for food, the stable, health, etc. Not all the suppliers' bills have been preserved and some years—especially 1782 and 1783—are less well documented. Two categories of spending can be distinguished: the general expenses (food, stable, etc.) and the princess's personal expenses. For her '*cassette*', or privy purse, the princess had a monthly budget of 2,500 *livres*.[16] At the beginning of the month, the treasurer gave her cash, and during the period he advanced money for the princess and paid the suppliers. Thus, he recorded all the advanced sums and noted all the dressmaker's or perfumer's bills in order to get a refund from the princess at the end of the month. At the same time, the princess bought items in cash, so she spent a part of her '*cassette*' without leaving any traces. With her cash she bought various items: personal objects like clothes, make-up, gloves, books or drawing lessons, little objects—a thermometer, a frame—but also heterogeneous expenditures like alms, travelling expenses, etc. There was permeability between the general accounts—her '*caisse*'—and her personal expenses—her '*cassette*'—which can be another sign of the treasurer's inexperience. Nevertheless, the suppliers' bills are a very useful source to study the princely market.

THE PRINCELY MARKET: AN ASPECT OF THE GEOGRAPHY OF PARISIAN LUXURY

Court society encouraged its members to consume excessively and gave rise to perpetually generating new requirements and desires. Retailers hastened to respond to these demands and, as a result, often created new trends, increasing the number of luxury shops in Paris.[17] With their extravagance and capacity to appeal to numerous suppliers, aristocrats affirmed their social pre-eminence. This is even truer in the case of a princess of blood. In the eighteenth century, the princes of blood's position had been weakened because of the growth of the royal family.[18] Therefore they tried to distinguish themselves from the rest of the French aristocracy at court by their consumption. Luxury consumption allowed the princess to demonstrate her particular status, to differentiate her from other aristocrats and, in contrast, to assert her blood ties to the royal family by specific behaviours. As Norbert Elias asserted, '[A] duke's house has to be a duke's house and not one that could be mistaken for a mere count's'.[19] The princess's consumption had to be commensurate with her princess's rank: It was omnipresent, quotidian, varied and abundant.

The princely market can be distinguished by its extent and its increase. The accounts and bills are a good indicator of the number of retailers who were in the service of the princess from 1776 to 1789. Four hundred and fourteen suppliers appear in the accounts and 325 of them worked in Paris. This large number of suppliers corresponded to the princess's rank and was greater than that of Parisian aristocrats. For example, Princess Kinsky, widow of Empress Maria-Theresa's chamberlain, who lived alone in Paris at the same time, had 285 suppliers, and the Fitz-James family, studied by Natacha Coquery, had 525.[20] The bloated princely market resulted from the enormous daily needs of these households. For example, the princess had 116 suppliers for the renovation and decoration works, 87 for food, 79 for clothes, 47 for the stables, 44 for luxury goods such as books and jewellery and 41 for health and body care. The outrageousness of the princely market was also due to the specialisation of work. Some suppliers only worked for one type of occasion—a mourning, for instance—or for specific members of the household, such as the princess or the pages. For example, the successive alterations of the mansion meant hiring thirty-six craftsmen in 1776 and thirty-four in 1787–1788. The presence of thirty '*tapissiers*' or tapestry makers was also notable; they were not only in charge of furniture decoration but also responsible for the complete decoration of the domestic spaces. Not only were the suppliers numerous but they were also famous.

Marie-Fortunée d'Este had to employ famous retailers, that is, those who supplied the court and the royal family. Many of these traders exhibited images of luxury and refinement either through the choice of the name of their trade or with their newspaper advertisements. The shops deployed the vocabulary of wealth and distinction, as the recurrence of numerous shops referring to gold demonstrates. Those who wanted to underline the quality of their products exploited this luxurious image. For example, the wool merchant Cassin from the *Couronne d'or* (the golden crown) played on two remarkable wealthy and royal images in his shop's name. In their advertisements, the shopkeepers demonstrated that they furnished the elite. Beaulard from the *Nœud Galand* specified in her bill heading that she '*garnit les grands habits*' (trims the court dresses); she spoke to the court ladies. In the same vein, the florist Duftoy dealt with the '*décoration pour les desserts des plus grandes tables*' (the dessert decorations for the high tables).[21] As Figure 10.1 shows, the décor comprised a crown associated with three '*fleurs de lys*' (lilies, the symbol of French monarchy) evoking royal patronage. Being a supplier to noble society increased the retailer's reputation.

As a princess, therefore, Marie-Fortunée d'Este had to choose suppliers among those who catered for princely society. This was particularly obvious in her decoration and furniture. For example, she hired craftsmen who were working for the other princes. She ordered pieces of furniture from famous cabinetmakers and carpenters like Nicolas Delaisement, recorded in the accounts in 1788, and François Reizell—who also worked for the Prince of Condé—employed in 1776. Nicolas Grevenich worked for the princess in 1779 and 1786, and furnished the Parisian aristocracy and the *Garde-Meuble*, the institution in charge of supplying and looking after the King's and his family's furniture, until 1791.[22] Georges Jacob, who

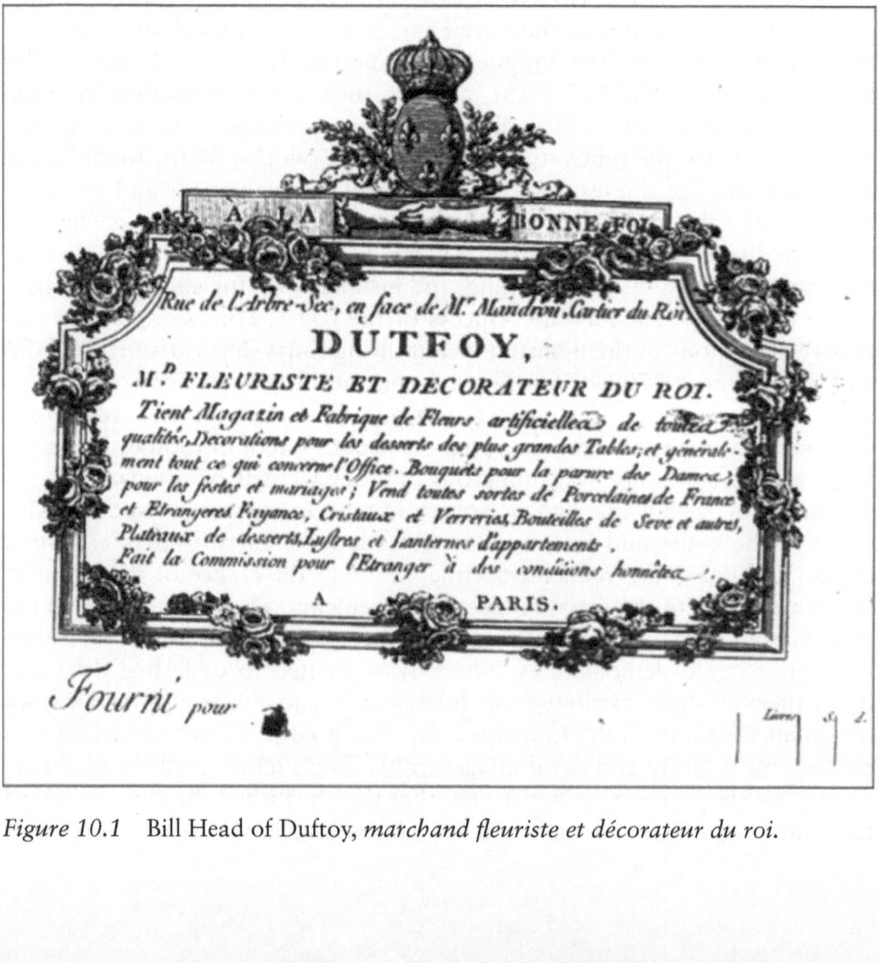

Figure 10.1 Bill Head of Duftoy, *marchand fleuriste et décorateur du roi.*

made a luxurious bed and some chairs for the princess in 1776, worked for the royal family, especially Marie-Antoinette.[23] The murals were made by well-known men, such as the sculptor François Duret, '*sculpteur ordinaire du comte de Provence*' (Earl of Provence's ordinary sculptor). Marie-Fortunée d'Este sought a 'shopkeeper aristocracy' that was located in the most fashionable quarters of Paris.

The princely market was characterised by its geographical extent, as the map of the princess's suppliers for decoration and renovation demonstrate. Retailers were chosen for their knowledge and their reputation, even if they worked at a distance from the princess's mansion. Marie-Fortunée d'Este commissioned suppliers from all quarters of Paris, and she did not hesitate to cross Paris to employ the best retailers and the most specialised or famous craftsmen. The geography of Parisian luxury appears in the princess's catchment area of shops (see Figure 10.2). The princess tried to follow a aristocratic pattern marked by recourse to numerous, famous retailers

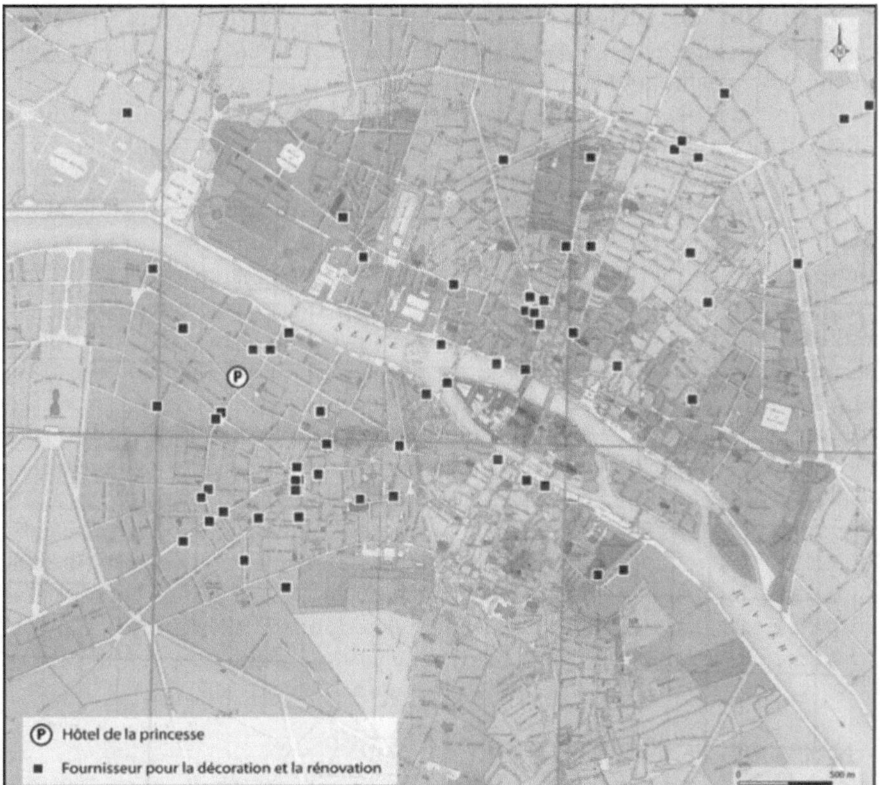

Figure 10.2 The Princesse de Conti's Parisian suppliers for decoration and furniture.

living in the most fashionable quarters in Paris, like the Palais Royal or Rue Saint-Honoré, on the right bank of the Seine. This contrast shows the geographical correspondence between aristocratic residential areas and the luxury trades.[24] Suppliers from the Faubourg Saint-Germain were the most numerous and represented about a third of her retailers. They had been attracted to the Faubourg by the presence of aristocratic residences. The princess chose suppliers from her neighbourhood because she could find numerous retailers with various skills located there. Every sort of consumption could be found in this area: necessities of life, but also saddlers and blacksmiths for her stables, clothes retailers and so forth. The area around the Palais-Royal had become the temple of fashion and largely dominated the fields of clothing and finery, and was also where the most famous perfumers such as Prévost or Dulac, who supplied the Princesse de Conti and the royal family, could be found. L'île de la Cité, the island in the centre of Paris, was marked by a very important concentration of goldsmiths, silversmiths and jewellers, which were long-established activities on the island. The high-traffic streets, the intersections and the bridges were also dynamic shopping centres. Finally, another commercial sector was situated on the right bank of the Seine between Rue Saint-Denis and Rue Saint-Martin, the two Parisian main North-South axes. It combined various businesses, including textile retailers and, further north, furniture makers.

There was also recourse to female suppliers: Fifty-one women appear in the princess's list of suppliers—that is to say, twelve per cent of the total number of suppliers. The female presence seems to be relatively high because women represented nine per cent of the retailers listed by the trading almanacs (which, however, omitted seamstresses).[25] The almanacs were a part of the trade literature that flourished throughout the eighteenth century. The stated aim of the trade almanac was to provide the public with a handy and useful description of shopkeepers in order to facilitate the easy location of shops.[26] The female presence was mainly visible among the clothing businesses (26.5 per cent of these suppliers) including seamstresses and laundresses, or in the health sector with home-nurses. Nonetheless, women also appeared in some professions considered *a priori* as male ones, which invites us to consider that female work not only turned towards textile professions, but also encompassed a wider range of trades.[27] Women could be furbishers, butchers, bakers, apothecaries or wood merchants. They were mostly widows who had taken over their husband's activities.[28] Although the princess seemed not to intentionally choose female suppliers, their presence in the accounts reveals the importance of female work in eighteenth-century Paris.

AN OMNIPRESENT AND DAILY LUXURY

For an aristocrat, needs and luxury merged. As Natacha Coquery has shown, every luxury met a need and every need was luxury.[29] Luxury was a means to social affirmation, as Max Weber has argued. The scale of needs and luxury can be found within the princess's spending. The sums discharged in every field of consumption contributed to distance the princess from others of the elite. Every kind of expense—food, stables and clothes—exceeded the simple response to vital, basic needs. The princess's consumption was luxurious because everything she bought was characterised by its variety, novelty, rarity and refinement. The expenses incurred by the princess, especially food, and her spending on decoration contributed to differentiate her from of the rest of the population and even most of the aristocrats.

Her food expenditures were very costly. For example, in 1788 these bills came to 27,055 *livres* and constituted 16 per cent of her total spending. Under normal circumstances, when she held receptions, the bills amounted to between 2,100 and 3,258 *livres* a month, or 90.5 *livres* a day. These sums were higher than those spent by the provincial female nobility; for example, a noblewoman from Bordeaux, Marie-Joséphine de Galatheau, spent about seven *livres* daily. They were even greater than those of the Parisian nobility; the Marchioness of Fleury, who also lived alone, spent forty-four *livres* daily from 1781 to 1783.[30] Under normal circumstances, the expenditures were enormous because of the numerical weight of her fifty-person household and the daily pomp imposed on the princess by her rank. Her refinement was shown both by the quantity and the quality of foodstuffs. The open table that daily offered numerous and various dishes served on plates of the highest quality and in a refined décor made the princess stand out.

Her mansion sat at the heart of her conspicuous consumption. It embodied her social status in bricks and mortar.[31] Her choice of neighbourhood reveals her membership in the second order of the kingdom. From 1759 to 1789, she stayed in the most famous quarter of Paris, in Saint-Germain-des-Prés Faubourg, on the left bank of the Seine. By the end of the eighteenth century, this Faubourg had become the main aristocratic quarter, and in 1789 more than ninety-five per cent of the noble people noted in the *Almanach royal* lived there.[32] From 1759 to 1776, the princess lived with her husband in Rue Grenelle at the Hotel de La Marche. In April 1776, she moved to one of the largest mansions in Rue Saint-Dominique, close to her former house. She rented and later bought the Hotel du Lude in 1787.[33] Built by Robert de Cotte, the premier architect of the King, the mansion followed the classical pattern and was erected between courtyard and garden, and it was known for its vast garden and the large scale of its buildings.[34] She adapted it to the princely way of life that required a number of rooms for receptions and for the housing a fifty-people household.

The mansion was a social marker, a symbol of power.[35] Its symbolic importance was reinforced by its cost, 400,000 *livres*, and its weight on the overall budget of the household. Buying a mansion in Paris, owning a castle near to Paris in usufruct and decorating her new apartments weighed down the princess's budget. Maintaining the buildings represented 39,883 *livres* and encompassed 24 per cent of her general expenditure in 1788–1789.

With these sums, she paid off her loans (thirteen per cent of the spending) and ordered renovation work (twelve per cent of the outlay). Not only did the princess own one of the biggest mansions in the Faubourg Saint Germain, but she also had to decorate it with splendour and according to fashion. In fact, she had to refurbish her apartment regularly, and from 1776 to 1789 she ordered renovations three times. The works were as long as they were costly: about 60,000 *livres* in 1777, 36,724 *livres* from May 1778 to March 1779 and 30,581 *livres* for the last works from 1787 to March 1789. The princess paid close attention to the renovations, and she kept an eye on the expenses. In 1776, renovating and refurbishing her mansion was a necessity because she had entered an empty house, which had to be adapted to the princely way of life and to her large household. She had to create an aristocratic interior and to follow the trends of the second half of the eighteenth century. Princely interiors were decorated according to aristocratic codes and colours: gold, white, red and green. The textiles, such as damask, were precious and costly. Her bedroom and the salon were markedly adorned with many seats whose hierarchy related to conventions in French etiquette. These rooms were furnished with expensive chairs, beds and tables made by court craftsmen. For instance, she ordered a Polish-style bed from Nicolas Delaisement for 600 *livres* and a console from Georges Jacob in 1776 for 380 *livres*. The embellishment of her reception rooms showed the public role of the princess who received many visitors in her salon and her bedroom.

Some aspects of the princess's luxury consumption were gendered. The first indication could be found in the frequent refurbishment of her interiors. Her decorative mania reveals her taste for renovation, which seems to be shared by the aristocracy, especially women, such as Princess Kinsky, whose taste for decoration and furnishing Natacha Coquery has highlighted. In Marie-Fortunée's mansion, the alteration works contributed to create a private apartment organised around her bedroom, her wardrobes and her boudoir. In these intimate rooms, the princess fashioned a refined and flowered setting. She organised secondary and intimate rooms that were clearly separated from the reception apartments. The walls and the chairs in the boudoir and cabinets were decorated with flowers, which can be seen as a female taste, and with exotic plants.[36] We can identify a feminine atmosphere with chairs adapted to women's dresses such as the '*bergères*' (wing chairs), sofas, armchairs '*en cabriolet*' and a '*cabaret*', a coffee and tea table. The furniture associated with feminine figures and the little objects for the powders, rouge and gloves reinforced this idea of a feminine intimacy. The second indication can be found in the importance of expenditure on the body. The spending on clothes represented her primary personal expenditure and was particularly costly because it encompassed 4,325 *livres* in 1784 and 6,183 in 1786, 43 per cent of her personal expenses. The manufacture of court dresses weighed heavily on her expenditure because of the cost of silk (between 45 and 108 *livres* for one '*aune*', about 1.143 metres) and the length of the fabric (about 22 *aunes*) used to make them. Cosmetics also represented a big expense. Royal rules forced court ladies to have powdered hair and a white and red face. The importance of the body expenditure can be seen as a feminine specificity at the end of eighteenth century because current historians have highlighted that during this period a sexual dimorphism in clothes and cosmetics spending in favour of women emerged.[37] Catherine Lanoë asserts that the use of cosmetics during the eighteenth century is marked by a very clear feminisation.[38]

A LACKLUSTRE LUXURY?

Luxury was an element of identity. This aspect became all the more important when Marie-Fortunée d'Este's position was weakened. She was the only non-born princess of blood in the French court at the end of the eighteenth century; in other words, it was only thanks to her marriage to the heir of the Bourbon-Conti family that she gained her particular status at court. Yet after 1776, she was no longer the Prince of Conti's wife but only his separated spouse. Consuming luxurious items was a way for her to continue to exist socially in Parisian high society. Unlike married women whose finances and households were subordinated to their husbands', the princess had to take on the cost of her household. Thus, her luxuriousness underlined her new status of a separated wife, an independent woman.

The accounts make it possible to study the princess's consumption particularly during the time of separation. Her marriage break-up was a very important change in Marie-Fortunée d'Este's life. During her marriage, the princess—as all French married women were—was placed under her husband's authority and financial supervision. Her suite was seen only as an annex of secondary importance in the prince's household. If she received a pension for her '*Menus Plaisirs*', her privy purse and her entertainment, she depended on her husband for big spending. Her financial conditions changed dramatically with the separation. Even though divorce did not exist in France, the separation of goods was relatively frequent within the elite Parisian nobility at the end of the century.[39] It dissolved joint ownership, and women obtained the complete administration of their incomes or their goods indicated in their marriage contract. Nonetheless, they were not liberated from their husband's authority. The separation covenant signed by the princess illustrates the ambivalence of the situation. With the separation, she had to assume her household's charges on her sole responsibility. Henceforth, her husband declared he was not responsible for her ex-wife's debts, even those taken out during the time of the marriage. Hereafter, the princess lived independently from her husband, and this new autonomy played a part in her luxurious consumption. However, luxurious princely consumption reveals a more nuanced independence and the princess's ambivalent situation.

Even if the princess lived separated from her husband, she kept a kind of financial and legal subordination. She needed masculine protection for big purchases like property acquisitions. For example, she required her husband's agreement to buy her castle in 1781.[40] In 1787, when she purchased her mansion, she called for a nominee to avoid her husband's authorisation.[41] As she could not afford paying for her residences in cash, she had to contract loans. As she did not want to ask for her husband's authorisation, she benefitted from her brother-in-law's protection when he offered a guarantee to buy her residences. The Duke of Penthièvre, widower of her elder sister Marie-Thérèse-Félicité d'Este (1726–1754), was the grandson of Louis XIV and Madame de Montespan and was very rich.[42] The duke helped her to find money and lenders through his network of relationships. To buy her mansion, she borrowed from seven lenders, among them four nobles and two women: An heiress, the Duchess of Lorges, and a widow, Louise-Anne Le Bernard de Chaumont, were the most important investors.[43] All of them belonged to the Duke of Penthièvre's network. In spite of her independence and the separation of goods, this woman remained under masculine protection.

Moreover, as she no longer belonged to the Conti family, she lost in consideration and in social importance. The marriage dissolution created new financial conditions and economic relationships with her Parisian retailers. With her financial independence, she lost credit and confidence. She no longer had the Conti's financial guarantee, and her suppliers no longer trusted her, which demonstrates how much credit was based on reputation. As the dictionary of the *Académie* said: '[C]redit is the reputation of being solvent and of paying well; which means that we find it easy to borrow'.[44] When she left her husband's mansion in April 1776 she was in debt to suppliers, because during her married period Marie-Fortunée d'Este had followed the aristocratic pattern characterised by big spending, important debts and the practice of deferred payments.[45] She had not cared about settling the perfumer's and the silk shopkeeper's bills. In 1776, she owed them 18,649 *livres*. However, her management changed radically after 1776, and with the marital break-up suppliers forced her to reimburse them. She had a year to pay, and by July 1777 she had settled all her debts. Then from 1776 to 1789, her daily expenses were paid regularly, without delay. Thus, the accounts showed a major alteration in the princess's practices in accordance with her new status and financial situation. The marital separation could be considered as a kind of social downgrading.

Indeed, if the princess remained fortunate, she became one of the poorest—or more precisely one of the least rich—among the princes of blood and the royal family. For instance, another princess of blood, Bathilde d'Orléans Duchess of Bourbon, daughter of the Duke of Orléans and daughter-in-law of the Prince de Condé, earned 278,045 *livres* a year in 1769 when she separated from her husband, but when she inherited from her father she received 1,000,000 *livres* a year.[46] Consequently, the Princesse de Conti had to suit her consumption to her new economic situation. Her luxurious consumption seemed less dazzling than that of the other aristocrats with whom she socialised. Her consumption had to be organised in a delicate balance: She had to keep a princely and aristocratic way of life and at the same time to take care not to spend too much. Thus her spending was limited, and so was the renewal and replacement of her goods.

First, the sums involved are curbed, which seems to reflect her reduced financial situation. For example, in 1776 Marie-Fortunée d'Este spent 60,000 *livres* to furnish and paint her new mansion, while the Duchess of Mazarin spent 70,000 *livres* for her big salon alone and the Earl of Artois, Louis XVI's brother, spent 30,000 *livres* just for his dining room.[47] In another area, when the Princesse de Conti spent about 4,000 *livres* at Lenormand's shop, a silk merchant, the Countess of Artois, sister-in-law of King Louis XVI, spent 19,870 *livres* at this shop alone—and she had other suppliers!

Secondly, the princess followed fashion, but with delays. She could not compete with the other ladies of the royal family. The study of her wardrobe indicates that she had little interest in exoticism and Anglomania. One of the most modish dresses at the end of the eighteenth century, the English dress, very fashionable under the reign of Louis XVI, and the Turkish dress, appeared in her wardrobe just once in 1784 and in 1787, and once again for each of them with a ten-year delay.[48] Thus, the princess did not respond to the extremely fast variations of fashion.

Finally, if the princess had to call for suppliers who were working for the royal family, she did not request the most sought-after. For example, in her mansion there was no furniture made by Joseph Baumhauer, Pierre Garnier and Jean-François Veben, the most popular craftsmen. Her consumption was characterised by several absences or lacks. She never bought items from the fashionable '*marchands merciers*' like Granchez from the *Petit Dunkerque,* where all the European high society shopped at this time. The art merchants Daguerre and Poirier, or the English '*marchand mercier*' from the Palais Royal, Sykes, did not appear in the accounts. The same approach can be seen in her clothing expenditure. Even if she ordered textiles from *Le Grand Turc*, one of the most famous silk merchants, she did not commission the most famous dressmaker, Rose Bertin, the 'minister of fashion' who designed many dresses for Queen Marie-Antoinette. In the same vein, there was no sign of other famous '*marchandes de modes*' such as Mrs Eloffe or Pompée who worked for the princesses of the royal family. The princess preferred to engage minor dressmakers who were less famous or almost unknown and who did not work in the heart of fashionable Paris, in the Palais Royal or in Rue Saint-Honoré, but in the neighbourhood of the princess's mansion, in the Faubourg Saint-Germain. While the Palais Royal became fashionable at the end of the century, the princess chose closer suppliers in the neighbourhood of her mansion, as Figure 10.3 shows.

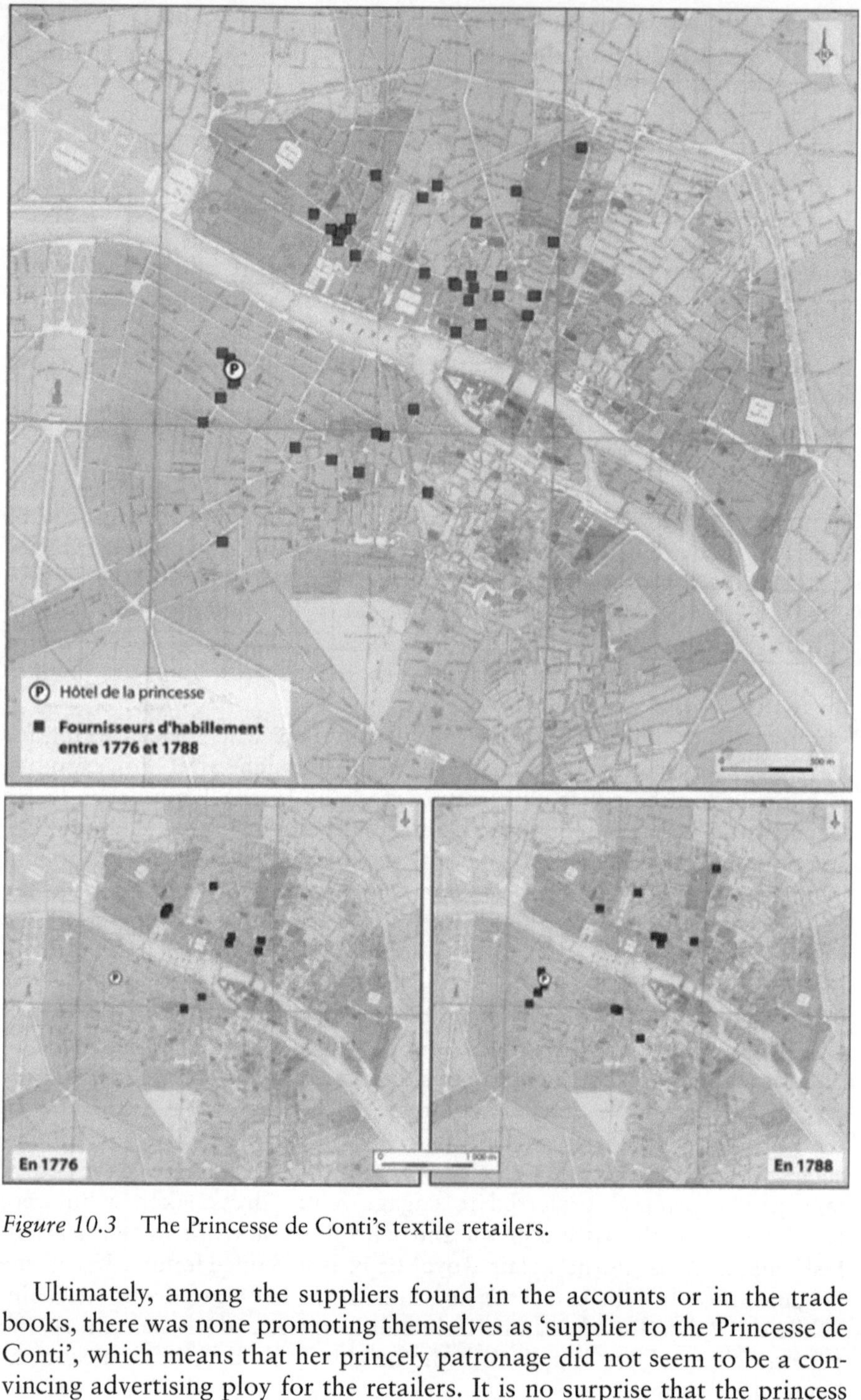

Figure 10.3 The Princesse de Conti's textile retailers.

Ultimately, among the suppliers found in the accounts or in the trade books, there was none promoting themselves as 'supplier to the Princesse de Conti', which means that her princely patronage did not seem to be a convincing advertising ploy for the retailers. It is no surprise that the princess did not play a leading role in fashion.

Moreover, her luxurious consumption changed according to the hazards of her existence. The marital separation obviously had important financial consequences but also influenced other aspects of her life. It contributed to her social withdrawal that played a role in her luxurious consumption. Her spending became less focused on luxury and social life and more on health and religion. In the 1780s, the increasingly elderly princess (she turned fifty in 1781) became sicker, and her spending on drugs replaced much of expenditure on clothes and cosmetics. The 1780s brought another change. She progressively left the princely and royal circles to live next to her brother-in-law, the Duke of Penthièvre. Her travel expenses were limited to her stays in her own residences or trips to take waters, such as in Bourbon-L'Archambault in 1787. Her life was now expressed by her religious practices and her alms. She left fashionable Paris with its shops and its social circles for her mansion or her castle and for religious Paris and its churches. Her religious spending increased with the costs of hiring chairs in churches or the alms. The princess's days were now organised by attendance at mass and visits to religious communities—far away from the traditional vision of aristocratic people ruining themselves on fancy goods and spending their time shopping in the most fashionable Parisian luxury boutiques. On the contrary, gifts and alms rose. Her alms represented 1,306 *livres* in 1780, 2,965 *livres* in 1784 and 3,718 in 1786. The princess surrounded herself with religious people, such as her new live-in companion, Marie de Courson, who became an intermediary between the princess and the recipients of her generosity and later canoness of the Order of Saint Antoine du Viennois.[49] The presence of this woman could be seen as a sign of a change in her circle and her way of life. The princess left aristocratic society.

More than a social marker, the luxurious expenditures were an identity element that showed the evolution of this woman between the times of the marriage, separation and withdrawal. If the luxurious spending were a necessity to materialise her status, the emergence of new expenses conveyed the change of her centres of interest.

CONCLUSION

The princess's case study recalls the social importance of conspicuous consumption based on luxury, novelties, fashion and pomp. This luxury consumption manifested itself in Parisian space by the choice of a mansion in the noble quarter of Paris, by the choice of suppliers living far away from her residence or in the most fashionable quarters of Paris. However, her consumption also depended on her identity and her life-course. As Stobart and Rothery demonstrate in the case of Edward and Mary Leigh, gender and social status were closely and complexly intertwined. The princess's life was regulated by four periods: first her youth in Modena, about which nothing or almost nothing is known, followed by her married life from 1759 to 1776, when Marie-Fortunée d'Este became wife to a prince of the blood.

This new status involved the adoption of a specific consumption pattern, including the practise of relying on credit from Parisian retailers. The princess received money for her personal expenses, for her '*Menus Plaisirs*', but big purchases needed her husband's agreement. Then after 1776 the time of separation began. Finally, 1789 and emigration represented the ultimate milestone. She left France at the beginning of the Revolution. With her escape and the accession of the Republic, she lost her pensions, her status and her way of life. She became an emigrant who had to live illegally with little means. When she died in Venice in 1803, she left unsettled debts and an insolvent estate.[50]

The case of this princess invites us to consider the unexamined situation of consumption by a separated wife. The marital break-up provided a financial and juridical independency, and a women gained the autonomy to manage her goods. Separated women recovered their dowry and their inheritance. They were considered as emancipated minors. The separation of goods was also a protection from a husband's debts and was used by couples as an economic strategy to save a woman's fortune and to protect a familial patrimony. The separation did not always mean the end of the couple. However, separated women did not have complete freedom. Their situation differed according to social customs and obviously according to their social status. Many women fell into familial dependence; only wealthy women recovered a real autonomy. Separation often meant impoverishment. These indications can be seen in the case of the Princesse de Conti. Her new independence was revealed through her maintenance of her own household and purchases of her own residences in the 1780s. However, the financial consequences of the marital break-up were important. She had to reconcile the requirements of her rank with her financial restraints. Marital separation weakened Marie-Fortunée's position and forced her to live a more reduced lifestyle. She could count on a familial solidarity from the Duke of Penthièvre, her brother-in-law, but as she was a foreigner in France, she could not benefit from strong family support.

This case of a separated wife's consumption has to be compared to other aristocratic consumption patterns in order to understand to what extent the separation caused a financial loss, induced a more reduced lifestyle and changed the relationship between separated women and suppliers. The retailers were often informed of the separation by a public display: Did the separation always mean a loss of confidence and credit? More broadly, the case of this princess invites further study of how marital status affected women's consumption. It would be illuminating to compare separated women's luxurious consumption with that of widows. Widowed women recovered a legal capacity, half of the community property and a dower. However, widows as well as separated women had a 'conditional freedom' that depended on provincial customaries and on their social status. Their way of life was shaped by numerous norms that highlighted the male concerns about single women's independence.

NOTES

1 Archives Nationales (from now on A.N.), Paris, R3, House of Conti, 172–184, personal spending of Marie-Fortunée d'Este. I am indebted to the editors for their crucial contribution to this chapter and am grateful to my sister Marjorie Le Hir who helped re-English the text.
2 Aurélie Chatenet Calyste, 'Une consommation aristocratique et féminine à la fin du XVIIIe siècle: Marie-Fortunée d'Este, princesse de Conti (1731–1803)'. PhD diss., University of Limoges, November 2010. Published version: *Une consommation aristocratique fin de siècle: Marie-Fortunée d'Este, princesse de Conti (1731–1803)* (Limoges: PULIM, 2013).
3 Norbert Elias, *La société de cour* (Paris: Flammarion, 1969, 1985).
4 Philippe Perrot, *Le luxe: une richesse entre faste et confort, XVIIIe–XIXe siècle* (Paris: Seuil, 1995), 51.
5 Natacha Coquery, *L'hôtel aristocratique: le marché du luxe à Paris au XVIIIe siècle* (Paris: Publications de la Sorbonne, 1998).
6 Pierre Le Pesant de Boisguilbert, *Factum de la France* (1707) in *Collection des Principaux Ecomistes*, v. 1, ed. M Eugène Daire, (1843 edition, reprinted, Osnabrück: Otto Zeller, 1966), 271.
7 Baronne d'Oberkirch, *Mémoires* (Paris: Editions Suzanne Burkard, 1862), 94–95.
8 Edmond and Jules de Goncourt, *La femme au XVIIIe siècle* (Paris: F. Didot, 1862); Thorstein Veblen, *The Theory of the Leisure Class: An Economic Study of Institutions* (New York: Macmillan, 1899); Amanda Vickery, *The Gentleman's Daughter. Women's Lives in Georgian England* (Yale: Yale University Press, 1998); Claire Walsh, 'Shops, Shopping, and the Art of Decision Making in Eighteenth-Century England', in *Gender, Taste, and Material Culture in Britain and North America, 1700–1830*, ed. John Styles and Amanda Vickery (New Haven: Yale University Press 2006),151–77.
9 David Hussey and Margaret Ponsonby, *The Single Homemaker and Material Culture in the Long Eighteenth Century* (Aldershot: Ashgate, 2012), conclusion. For example, the workshop 'Single People and the World of Goods' at the University of Wolverhampton, November 2013, examined the consumption, economic independence and material culture relating to spinsters, bachelors and the widowed between the seventeenth and nineteenth centuries.
10 Alain Lottin, *La désunion des couples sous l'Ancien Régime: L'exemple du Nord* (Paris: Editions universitaires, 1975); Marie Landelle, '"Les plaintes en séparation sont éternelles". La séparation de biens dans la haute société parisienne au milieu du XVIIIe siècle (1730–1761)' (thesis, Ecole des Chartes, March 2012). http://theses.enc.sorbonne.fr/2012/landelle
11 In *ancien régime* France, the currency was based on the *livre tournois*: One *livre* equals twenty *sols* or *sous* and one *sol* makes twelve *deniers*. For example, a mason who worked at her mansion was paid one *livre* a day.
12 Guy Chaussinand-Nogaret, *La noblesse au XVIIIe siècle: de la féodalité aux Lumières* (Bruxelles: Complexe, 1984), 77.
13 Comtesse de Genlis, *Mémoires inédits de Madame la comtesse de Genlis, sur le dix-huitième siècle et la Révolution française* (Paris: Ladvocat, 1825), 331.
14 William Ritchey Newton, *L'espace du roi, la cour de France au château de Versailles, 1682–1789* (Paris: Fayard, 2000).
15 Bibliothèque historique de la ville de Paris (BHVP), CP 4584 à 4599, Manscourt's accounts 1770–1786; CP 4600 à 4602, Dubosc's accounts, treasurer of the princes de Conti, 1737, 1740 and 1742.

16 In *ancien régime* France, the '*cassette*' meant a small safe. The '*cassette du roi*' was the money brought to the king by the guard of the Royal Treasury each month (*Dictionnaire de l'Académie française*, 4th ed. (1762), '*cassette*'). By extension, the word '*cassette*' meant the King's or the prince's privy income in contrast to general expenditure.
17 Natacha Coquery, *Tenir boutique à Paris au XVIIIe siècle* (Paris: CTHS, 2012).
18 Coquery, *L'hôtel aristocratique*, 279.
19 Elias, *La société de cour*.
20 Coquery, *L'hôtel aristocratique*, 275.
21 Mathurin Roze de Chantoiseau, *Tablettes royales de renommée* (Paris: Royez, 1788).
22 François De Salverte, *Les ébénistes du XVIIIe siècle, leurs œuvres et leurs marques* (Paris: F. de Nobele, 1985).
23 Michel Beurdeley, *Georges Jacob 1739–1814 et son temps* (Paris: M. Hayot, 2002).
24 Coquery, *L'hôtel aristocratique*, 48.
25 Coquery, *Tenir boutique à Paris*, 205.
26 Natacha Coquery, 'The Language of Success: Marketing and Distributing Semi-Luxury Goods in Eighteenth-Century Paris', *Journal of Design History* 17 (2004): 71–89.
27 See for instance Danielle van den Heuvel, *Women & Entrepreneurship: Female Traders in the Northern Netherlands, c. 1580–1815* (Amsterdam: Aksant, 2007); Deborah Simonton, *A History of European Women's Work, 1700 to the Present* (London: Routledge, 1998).
28 Scarlett Beauvalet-Boutouyrie, *Etre veuve sous l'Ancien Régime* (Paris: Belin, 2001), 276–77.
29 Coquery, *L'hôtel aristocratique*.
30 Philippe Meyzie, 'La noblesse provinciale à table: les dépenses alimentaires de Joséphine de Galatheau (Bordeaux 1754–1763)', *Revue d'histoire moderne et contemporaine* 2 (2007): 32–54; Coquery, *L'hôtel aristocratique*, 139.
31 Elias, *La société de cour*, 49.
32 Coquery, *L'hôtel aristocratique*, 195.
33 Bruno Pons, 'L'hôtel du Lude', in *La rue Saint-Dominique: hôtels et amateurs*, ed. Délégation à l'action artistique de la Ville de Paris (Paris: Délégation à l'action artistique, 1984).
34 Jean-François Blondel, *Architecture française* (Paris: Charles-Antoine Jombert, 1752–1757); A.N., O1/1578/302–319, the mansion's plans drawn in 1759.
35 Natacha Coquery, *L'espace du pouvoir, de la demeure privée à l'édifice public, Paris 1700–1780* (Paris: Seli-Arslan, 2000).
36 Colin Cunningham, '"An Italian House is my Lady", Some Aspects of the Definition of Women's Roles in the Architecture of Robert Adam', in *Femininity and Masculinity in Eighteenth-Century Art and Culture*, ed. Gill Perry and Michaël Rossington (Manchester: Manchester University Press, 1997), 63–78.
37 Daniel Roche, *La culture des apparences: une histoire du vêtement XVIIe–XVIIIe siècle* (Paris: Fayard, 1989).
38 Catherine Lanoë, *La poudre et le fard* (Seyssel: Champ Vallon, 2008), 274.
39 Mathieu Marraud notes about two hundred cases in Paris in 1788; Mathieu Marraud, *La noblesse de Paris au XVIIIe siècle* (Paris, Seuil, 2000), 147.
40 A.N., ET/LXXIII/1020, 5 May 1781.
41 A.N., ET/LXXI/78, 14 June 1787.
42 Jean Duma, *Les Bourbon-Penthièvre (1678–1793): une nébuleuse aristocratique au XVIIIe siècle* (Paris: Publications de la Sorbonne, 1995).

43 Laurence Fontaine has pointed out the importance of female lenders; Laurence Fontaine, *L'économie morale, pauvreté, crédit et confiance dans l'Europe pré-industrielle* (Paris: Gallimard, 2008).

44 *Dictionnaire de l'Académie* (1762), s.v. 'crédit'.

45 Coquery, *L'hôtel aristocratique*, 158–66.

46 Bibliothèque de Chantilly (Chantilly castle's library), 1-A-044, Thérèse-Bathilde d'Orléans, Duchess of Bourbon. In 1787 or in 1789, A.N., 35 300 AP, I, 76, the Duchess of Bourbon's succession.

47 Alexia Lebeurre, 'Le décor intérieur des demeures à la mode dans la deuxième moitié du XVIIIe siècle (Paris-Ile de France)'. PhD diss., Université de Paris Panthéon Sorbonne, 2006, 179.

48 English style dress: robe fitted and shaped to torso. Turkish style dress: tight-bodice gown with attached open-front outer robe, closed in front, with draped sash and funnel shape sleeves.

49 Joined to the Order of Malta in 1778.

50 A.N., 300 A.P., I, 82, Conti's Succession, pièce n 127, Princesse de Conti's inventory after death.

11 Favourites of Fortune: The Luxury Consumption of the Hackmans of Vyborg, 1790–1825

Ulla Ijäs

> They are very honoured in many ways, but they can hardly excuse the mania of copying the luxury of St Petersburg: they have the clubs, the concerts, the balls, the masquerades, the embroidered jackets and the beautiful carriages.[1]

A German traveller, Abel Burja, wrote these lines in the 1780s when he visited Vyborg, the hometown of the Hackmans. In these lines, he emphasises the inhabitants' desire to copy the luxurious lifestyle of St Petersburg. He also notes the typical male luxuries, such as waistcoats and equipage, and the new civility and social manners of the eighteenth century—all of which have been at the centre of the historical studies of luxury.

This chapter focuses on the gendered patterns of consumption which can be found by studying the merchant Johan Friedrich Hackman's luxury consumption when single, his family purchases once he was married with two sons, and, finally, the widowed Marie Hackman's luxury purchases. First, the chapter will illustrate what was considered luxury in nineteenth-century Finland, which at that time was part of Imperial Russia as the Grand Duchy of Finland. Among the high society of late eighteenth- and early nineteenth-century Vyborg, luxury was something that was bought from St Petersburg, or it was imported, often smuggled, from Britain, France or Germany. Many of the luxury products that were purchased from St Petersburg were called 'English' as they were imported usually from England, and sold in St Petersburg by British merchants.[2]

The Hackmans, as part of the Vyborg elite, preferred luxury goods that were fairly recent inventions, produced with new mass-production techniques, recently modish and good quality. Many of the luxury products were purchased from or with the help of friends and family members who lived in St Petersburg; officers, civil servants, lower nobility and wealthy merchants disseminated information about the latest fashion to Vyborg. These luxury products with elite backgrounds were affordable only for a small group of people in Vyborg.

Secondly, this chapter discusses what typical male or female luxury consumption was in this context. There is no evidence to suggest that people in Vyborg considered some luxuries as belonging to either men or women alone; instead it depended on the owner's position in the household, as well as his or her individual capabilities.[3] Furthermore, this chapter shows that it was not always men who travelled more and who would have been therefore able to make more luxury purchases. It seems that an individual's or household's social position among Vyborg high society was more of a determining factor than gendered consumption patterns, which were fairly flexible. Thus, this chapter reasserts the essence of luxury—it was socially constructed. For example, luxury goods that were seen as old-fashioned by the aristocracy in St Petersburg were still considered as luxury among the elite bourgeoisie in Vyborg.

The sources used to explore these issues were, primarily, letters. Mostly they were written for business purposes; however, they often also included private information such as notes about luxury goods that the Hackmans had asked for. Beside these letters, private accounts were also used. After the death of J. F. Hackman, such letters were written and accounts kept by a professional clerk, but Marie Hackman made her needs clear to this man whenever necessary. The Hackmans were a merchant family who lived in Vyborg, a small town of 3,000 to 4,000 inhabitants about 140 kilometres west from St Petersburg. The town closely resembled Tallinn or Lübeck, with its city walls and cobbled streets, and many of its inhabitants, especially merchants, had German roots; indeed, J. F. Hackman himself moved to Vyborg from Bremen, and Marie Hackman's parents also had German origins. Vyborg was a garrison town, originally established by the Swedes in the thirteenth century, and which became part of the Russian empire from 1710. From 1812 to 1917 Vyborg and the surrounding province were part of the Grand Duchy of Finland, and from 1917–1939 was part of Finland itself, being at that time Finland's second largest town.

The town had busy connections to St Petersburg over sea and land; the journey took two days, and when the weekly steamship route from St Petersburg to Helsinki via Vyborg was opened in the 1840s, travelling was even easier and more comfortable. Every summer ships from Britain, France, the Mediterranean and even as far as South America sailed to Vyborg, bringing salt, wines, coffee and tea, but also some fabrics, china, books and many other consumer goods. In Vyborg, luxury products were not widely available because:

> St. Petersburg and Helsingfors [Helsinki] are so close and our town is so small that the consumption of such goods is not big enough to cover all the charges and besides the importation of these goods is allowed only by Russian ships.[4]

However, as shipowners, the Hackmans could import luxury products for their own use; in fact, they often wrote to captains of ships they owned to ask if they could transport these luxury products in the captain's cabin to avoid the high taxes. The money to purchase luxury products came from selling timber, mainly to Britain, France and Spain, from their own sawmills. They also sold tar and ropes to Russian admiralty and ran a chicory coffee factory on their estates near Vyborg.

THE MANIA OF COPYING LUXURY

Previous Finnish studies about Hackman & Co and other trading houses have emphasised modesty and frugality as the main characteristics of merchants. For example, in the 1830s Marie Hackman wrote to her son, who was travelling in France, that their part in life would be only good housekeeping and frugality, and not the riches that her son was experiencing in Marseilles.[5] Yet modesty was only in words, not in actions. In business letters, wishes for great successes and good contracts were constantly repeated, and when it came to purchases like silverware, clothing, exotic animals or carriages, price was seldom an issue. More important than the cost were features such as 'modernity', a fashionable colour or the good quality of a product.

During the eighteenth century, St Petersburg grew massively and had a great impact on people's lives in eastern Finland. It was the place of cultural and economic interaction, where consumption possibilities were much greater than in the surrounding countryside. Until 1842, shopkeeping was prohibited in the countryside except during special market days, and therefore towns were crucial places for those who wanted to purchase something.[6] For those who sought luxury goods, St Petersburg was the place to go. At the end of the eighteenth century, it was competing with other European metropolises, and all modern luxuries as well as exquisite rarities were merchandised. From a Russian and Finnish point of view, luxury was not only a very urban phenomenon, but also very St Petersburgian.

The Russian aristocracy was renowned for its abundant luxury. Excessive luxury consumption was restricted by several edicts, but no consistent sumptuary legislation existed in eighteenth-century Russia. Many Russian emperors tried to prevent the country's money from disappearing abroad by setting high taxes on imported products as well as restricting the importing of luxury goods. Some scholars who have studied enlightened men in eighteenth- and nineteenth-century Russia have shown that the Russian provincial elite preferred domestic luxuries. However, as the Hackmans demonstrate, this was not the truth in reality, but instead an idealistic view of how people should consume. On the other hand, the provincial elite in Russia's heartlands did not have the financial or physical access to a similar lifestyle enjoyed by the elite in St Petersburg or Moscow, and therefore they might have preferred local goods more often than the Hackmans, who visited and did their shopping in St Petersburg regularly.[7]

The concept of luxury implies an idea of exclusiveness, however, which may have varied within different social categories, yet within the same social group both men and women shared similar impressions of what luxury was. It was often neighbours or fellow merchants whose taste was copied and relied on.[8] Modes, new styles and new consumer goods were immediately known and used in Vyborg because of the strong and vibrant contact with St Petersburg: 'But so small place like Vyborg which is so close to St Petersburg, so that anyone could bring his small needs from there', as the Hackmans wrote to Baron Rall in December 1820.[9] J. F. Hackman often trusted the taste of his friend, the postmaster of Vyborg, who stayed in St Petersburg, or fellow merchant Bruun, whose sister was married to the Marquis de Traversay and who at the time was the commander-in-chief of the Russian Black Sea Fleet. Marie Hackman's contact in St Petersburg was her second cousin, Baroness Steinheil. Her husband, Baron Steinheil, and her father, Baron von Engelhardt, were both high officers and governors of the Vyborg province.[10] The luxury consumption of the Vyborg elite thus follows the ideas of emulation and imitation. When the Hackmans were influenced by the lifestyle of St Petersburg, they imitated the bourgeoisie or lower nobility of the capital. The Vyborg-born merchants, officers and civil servants living in St Petersburg were those who dictated what was '*à la mode*' in their old hometown.[11]

The Hackmans and the Vyborg elite preferred British luxury products, as J. F. Hackman's letter to merchant Bruun in August 1802 shows. In this letter he asked Mr Bruun to purchase for Marie Hackman 'from the English shop a large [piece of] English damask silk', although it is impossible to know whether this fabric was actually made in England or not. However, French luxury products were mentioned only once in the letters, in 1823, when the clerk of the merchant house of Hackman & Co wrote to Lübeck and made it clear that 'there is no demand for the French products here'.[12] As this letter shows, it was possible to purchase French luxuries from several Finnish towns. In St Petersburg, these French products were very expensive because of the high taxes, which were higher than for British products and merchants, who had privileged status in Russia. Naturally, the aristocracy in St Petersburg had greater financial means to purchase these luxury goods. However, most of the Vyborg elite preferred British luxuries, which were by no means any less luxurious. Since the eighteenth century, 'anglomania' had stormed the European elite and reached Russia during Catherine II's reign. In Paris as well as in St Petersburg, the '*magasin anglais*' was the place to shop for the most fashionable luxury goods. Maxine Berg, who has studied the new semi-luxurious goods made in Britain, has shown that these products, made with new techniques, were especially popular among the middle classes. Both men and women of the urban bourgeoisie preferred these luxury goods, which imitated the French and Asian luxuries but were cheaper and more comfortable, but still fashionable.[13] The most important factor was, however, that British merchants and their products were familiar to the Vyborg elite, who had strong connections to Britain from trading timber with the British merchant houses since the early eighteenth century.

However, even the acquisition potential of St Petersburg was not enough for the Hackmans. It is possible that the variety of luxury goods in St Petersburg did not satisfy demanding customers like Marie Hackman. Moreover, it was also cheaper to import luxury products via ship captains, especially those who commanded a ship that the Hackmans owned. These ships sailed to Germany, Britain and France, but also to distant South America. Many of the luxury goods they imported were smuggled; high taxes and custom fees placed on luxury goods in Russia encouraged smuggling. The customhouse inspectors checked every arriving ship, so it was not wise to smuggle large items, but the Hackmans brought in illicit wines and fabrics, which were easy to hide in the captain's cabin.[14]

THE BACHELOR JOHAN FRIEDRICH HACKMAN AND HIS CONSUMPTION CHOICES

During his bachelor years, J. F. Hackman was a stereotypical eighteenth-century male consumer who wore a silk waistcoat and drove a four-horse carriage, although he was never impulsive, which several scholars have shown to been one of the most dominant features of male consumption.[15] Impulsiveness was difficult in a town where there were no high-quality shops and where everything had to be ordered in advance from overseas, or at least from St Petersburg. J. F. Hackman invested in himself. He lived with a man servant in rented rooms with his pet monkey; he had no need for a large set of china, nor vast numbers of tables and chairs.

The money spent on groceries comprised the biggest specific sum in J. F. Hackman's accounts, since he bought imported delicacies of all kinds. The letters that he sent to his business partners confirm that he was a real gourmand; for example, he ordered sausages and 'spa *wasser*' from Germany, which restored his health after eating too much.[16] In a country where most people ate dark rye bread and salted fish, exotic delicacies were expensive and luxurious. Exclusive delicacies and dinners were a sign of wealth and good connections, and an indicator of civilisation and politeness; J. F. Hackman was an educated man, and good manners could improve any flaws that his low birth may have inflicted.

Masculinity and concepts of masculine luxury were created and enforced at this time by men. For example, as he lived in a small apartment and was the president of a local gentlemen's club, it is possible that J. F. Hackman took the food to his club and dined there with his male friends. In 1800, on the Emperor's orders, all clubhouses in Russia were shut down, after which genteel men entertained guests in their homes, because local ale houses and taverns were crowded with common folk. Entertaining friends was an essential part of a merchant's lifestyle. Clubs, taverns and dinners at private homes were specifically urban phenomena; there were no clubs in the countryside and long distances constrained social gatherings in provincial

Finland and Russia. In these urban settings of male gatherings, good relationships with other merchants and ship captains were maintained.[17]

However, clothing was the most visible way to show respectability, wealth and social status. J. F. Hackman appreciated his appearance, and he was no exception among his contemporaries; both men and women were conscientious about their wardrobes. His '*garde-robe*' included exclusive silks, imported 'patent stockings' and frocks made by a tailor in St Petersburg. The Russian fashion historian Olga Vainshtein has also noted that in eighteenth-century Russia there was a 'culture of foppishness', which culminated during Catherine II's reign.[18] In early nineteenth-century Russia, civil and military personnel had to wear uniforms, at least for their public duties. This regulation had an impact on J. F. Hackman's dress. He held a post in the town council, and from 1802 onward he was the Prussian consul in Vyborg; the latter post required certain dress, which was not modest by any means. A consul's dress, for example, included a blue frock with red lapels, a red waistcoat and a stock with golden stitching, white breeches and a black hat with a cockade.[19] It is clear that J. F. Hackman indeed dressed according to his social position, at least when accomplishing his public duties. The uniform dress asserted group and gender identities, as previously outlined by Christine Ruane. The regulations concerning dressing enforced the nature of luxury and gender as social constructions, because these flamboyant uniforms were permitted only for a certain group of men.[20]

A few months before J. F. Hackman married, he invested in furniture. For example, he bought a mahogany table, a sofa and chairs, four golden mirrors, and later three more mirrors, and a toilet table with a mirror with brass fittings and locks. Some months after the wedding, he paid 150 roubles for a clavier, which was bought from Madame Steinheil. He also purchased china and portraits of Emperor Paul I.[21] The moment he purchased the mahogany furniture, the musical instrument and the tea service realised the gendered nature of these luxury goods. Feminine luxury was comfortable and it implied the idea of sociability, whereas masculine luxury purchases were aimed at public life in clubhouses and public duties in offices and the city streets.

MARRIED WITH CHILDREN

In April 1799, J. F. Hackman married twenty-three-year-old Marie Elisabeth Laube, the oldest child and only daughter of an ennobled civil servant, J. F. Laube, and a merchant's daughter, Helena Haveman. Following the latest fashion seems to have been important for Marie Hackman, which was motivated by her desire to show her taste, wealth and new position as a married lady. In April 1801, she was upset because her husband could not persuade his business associate to purchase for her some new accessories for a ball. The business associate was indignant at having been put upon to run

Marie's errands, and J. F. Hackman explained his wife's motives thus: '. . . she wanted to show her new clothes in high society, but now it is too late [because it was past the ball night]'.[22] Later that year J. F. Hackman made further apologies for his wife to his friend, Vyborg's recently ennobled postmaster Zagel. At the time, she was lying-in after giving birth to her eldest child. The letter Hackman wrote expresses the gender roles in the Hackman family; it was men who provided for daily life but women who managed it, as several scholars have previously shown.[23]

> My wife is especially content with the bolt of cloth which you sent. She is thanking you and *madame* Sievers for your taste! But she is impudent enough to bother you again. I follow her, but I have no choice. I have my burden to carry. She wants—and it is no less than 1) Leno [transparent fabric made from linen thread] for women's clothes. 2) 14 ells of white Atlas [silk] and one pair of long women's gloves made of silk. 3) One green garland, without flowers, made of oak, peach or other leafs, as the fashion is. . . . Because my wife wants to spend so much money, so I will open my purse too. That marble top table, which I mentioned to you earlier, I will have it.[24]

As a devoted husband, J. F. Hackman, motivated by his wife, wrote constant notes to his friends asking them to send items such as hats, shawls and gloves. Their accounts reveal that the mahogany table cost 35 roubles, 9 Russian ells (*arshins*, about 6.5 metres) of lino almost 50 roubles and 14 Russian ells (about 10 metres) of atlas silk about 20 roubles. The silk gloves cost 5 roubles and the garland 4.50.[25] This letter shows that women had the possibility to use more money and buy more expensive things than their husbands did, although the husbands might also have considered shopping unnecessary, as J. F. Hackman hinted when he wrote about his wife's urge to spend money. A husband might have thought that new silk curtains or a wife's new dress were unnecessary luxuries, but for the wife they were highly essential symbols of her social position and expressions of her identity.[26]

J. F. Hackman, nevertheless, wanted his own share of luxuries, and it was Hackman who was responsible for ordering furnishing items. British historians have discussed whether it was men or women who made the ultimate decisions when it came to refurbishing a house. Was it women who, with the increasing privatization of domestic culture, determined the decoration of the home, or was it men who furbished their houses as an extension of their public role? Berg has identified that furniture and decorative items marked both manhood and womanhood; usually men bought larger furniture while women purchased smaller decorative objects. However, Amanda Vickery has associated men with the refurbishing of houses, although she admits that negotiations, often invisible in sources, also took place between men and women.[27]

In the Hackman household, it seems that ultimately it was the wife who negotiated where furniture was purchased and what style and quality it should have been, because much of it was bought from or through Marie Hackman's second cousin, Baroness von Steinheil. There are no surviving letters concerning negotiations about purchases; Marie Hackman and Baroness von Steinheil conducted these negotiations face to face when visiting each other.[28] The noble origin of goods, or goods selected according to a noble taste, guaranteed not only the good quality of the products but also showed that the Hackmans had connections, mingled with the aristocracy and were able to bring St Petersburg-style luxury to Vyborg. When looking at the furniture purchases of the Hackman household, it is clear that they copied their superiors. However, it is not clear whether they were motivated by the desire to follow a noble lifestyle, were endeavouring to separate themselves from other merchants in Vyborg or were simply trying to improve their personal comfort whenever possible.

In one letter, Marie Hackman sent her thanks to Madame Sievers for her good taste. Madame Sievers was a merchant's daughter from Tallinn who was married to a German-born merchant in St Petersburg. She knew the latest fashion for new mothers and babies in St Petersburg, since she had given birth to her fifth child just three days later than Marie Hackman had her firstborn son. Jan de Vries, among others, combines 'taste' with 'the new luxuries', such as new types of fabrics, hot beverages and china, all new commodities that became fashionable in the eighteenth century. Good taste was negotiated within the same social group, and in this process superiors were emulated in the same way as in luxury purchases. In Vyborg, the noble and St Petersburgian tastes were more highly valued when choosing luxuries, as these people knew the latest fashions. According to Berg, the urban middle class preferred fashion to taste.[29] This is visible in J. F. Hackman's letter when he asked for a garland to be sent 'as the fashion is'. But here the fashion is not necessarily the crucial factor. By relying on noble taste of Mr Zagel, not only could the Hackmans ensure the luxury status of their purchases, but it also separated them from the petty merchants and craftsmen who did not have similar access to noble and St Petersburgian taste. This implies the very essence of luxury; it was socially constructed.

As we have seen, many of the luxuries were bought from St Petersburg. In genteel society, men often dominated the purchase of luxury goods, as shown by Vickery, partly because they had greater possibilities to travel and operate in public spaces. Berg echoes this assumption that it was men who travelled to cities to shop.[30] However, according to their accounts and letters, in the Hackman family it was Marie Hackman, not her husband, who more often travelled to St Petersburg to shop. J. F. Hackman was immobile for long periods of time because of his episodes of gout; if he wanted to purchase something from St Petersburg he would have used his commission agents in the imperial capital. Indeed, there is only one mention of his having had the opportunity to travel by himself.[31] Shopping requires knowledge, the skill to negotiate and bargain, and the ability to distinguish a good quality product, count money and measure. These skills were part of household management, which was part of women's everyday-life routines. However, these shopping skills were often limited to the everyday purchases which were within women's domain, and luxury shopping, conversely, was men's duty.[32] Yet Marie Hackman had all the capacities to qualify her as a competent shopper; she had visited St Petersburg since her youth, so she knew where to go or to whom to address when looking for luxury products. It is thus highly possible that in the Hackman household the person with the most capability to shop travelled to St Petersburg to do shopping; it was not so much about the gender of the shopper than her capabilities, and this also applied to shopping for luxury goods.

WIDOW, THE FAVOURITE OF FORTUNE

Marie Hackman's husband died after only eight years of marriage, and she lived for fifty-eight years after his death, never marrying again. The first few years after J. F. Hackman's death were difficult economically; Hackman's assets were confiscated because of an unclear inheritance, which was resolved in Marie Hackman's favour in 1811, and the Napoleonic wars made the timber trade challenging. Despite these hardships, Marie Hackman went shopping in St Petersburg at least once a year.

In 1818–1819 Hackman's sons began their training away from home: Fritz completed his merchant training in Germany and Carl enrolled in the military academy in St Petersburg. The sons' educations were expensive, but Marie Hackman still managed to make purchases while visiting Carl in St Petersburg. What she bought whilst there was usually unspecified, and after Fritz returned home in 1823 and started to take care of the bookkeeping the accounts became even more unspecified in relation to Marie Hackman's private expenditures. It is possible that her private luxury consumption is thus hidden in these figures; the accounts only sporadically mention jewellery, clothes or furniture. This suggests a 'masculinity' in Marie Hackman's consumption choices, since it was usually men who did not feel a need to inform anyone about their spending. Thus, Marie Hackman's social position emancipated her from detailed accounting of her private life. It also means that her consumption is far from Vickery's idea of typical eighteenth-century female consumption, which, according to Vickery, was visible and mundane while men's consumption was invisible; or, if it can be tracked, was expensive, impulsive and dynastic.[33]

Marie Hackman's position as the head of a merchant household allowed her the means, and assets, to consume. She was ready to use money when it came time to show that she had the ways and means to purchase the latest fashion items from St Petersburg or from Britain. For example, in September 1814 Marie Hackman bought a silver breadbasket and a fish spoon which cost over 200 roubles. Later the same year she bought a set of new china, worth over 500 roubles, and a tea service and cutlery, which totalled over 350 roubles. In 1823 she bought from her neighbouring merchant, Heyno, a crystal chandelier, which cost 400 roubles, and in 1826 she bought new lace curtains, which were made of Brabant lace.[34] These luxury purchases were far more expensive than those she made when her husband was still alive. These luxury goods were visible, so even her guests could enjoy them. A more intimate luxury purchase was the earrings that Marie Hackman bought in 1814. This was the first year that her businesses flourished after the hard years, and she provided herself with jewellery that cost 400 roubles.[35]

When ordering goods from overseas, Marie Hackman still used the same contacts as her late husband because she continued to trade with the same merchant houses in Britain, France, Germany and St Petersburg. What was different was the number of contacts in British port towns and the volume of smuggling. In 1817, for example, she did not declare the following goods to the custom in Vyborg: two dozen table knives and forks, two dozen candle snuffers, a dozen pen knives, four dozen pencils, one ream of letter paper, twenty-five yards of calico for women's clothes and twenty-five yards of other fabrics, an English dog 'of high race', a dozen men's cravats, six pairs of ladies' shoes and two pairs of ladies' boots.[36] However, this increase is mostly due to the end of the Napoleonic wars, when sailing was again easier in the Baltic and North Sea, and not her gender as a purchaser.

In her youth Marie Hackman invested in her appearance, just as her husband had done. However, most of the luxuries she bought were for the use of the household, such as the china, cutlery and fabrics. This became more important as the years passed. The luxuries she invested in showed the social status of the household; a new set of china or modish furniture were signs of respectability, good connections and polite manners. Marie Hackman also wanted to show her wealth. Her bookkeeper's memoirs reveal her attitude toward luxuries and affluence. The bookkeeper, who was born in Cassel and travelled in Europe, wrote that:

> She is likewise one of those favourites of fortune, completely spoiled by her good luck, and now setting so ridiculous a value on the advantages which wealth gives, despising everybody who is not either rich, or a man of a high rank.[37]

Throughout his memoirs, this bookkeeper made bitter comments about women, but his comments are not merely the bitterness of an ageing bachelor; he saw the parvenu in Marie Hackman. Perhaps she did not have the taste or the polished manners of the nobility, despite her noble friends in St Petersburg; maybe she went too far and bought luxury goods that were too showy and too expensive when she tried to display her prestige.

However, Marie Hackman was not a typical woman of her time; no other women in Vyborg had the same opportunities as she had. She was not the wealthiest woman or the highest in rank—there were some noble ladies whose husbands held a position in the imperial court—but she was the wealthiest woman in Vyborg who had control of her own property. In this untypical state lies the key to understanding gender in a wider context: It was not only her gender that affected her decisions in consumption, but also her social position, her age and the time and place in which she lived.[38]

GENDER AND LUXURY—SOCIAL CATEGORIES

Due to the nature of business letters, it would be easy to draw the conclusion that it was men who made the decisions, including those concerning luxury purchases. However, when reading these letters more closely, it seems that it was the lady of the house who made the major decisions when it came to the final decisions about furnishing or luxurious fabrics; men only took care of their own dress and some occasional furniture. Both men and women were motivated by the desire and the social obligation to show in public both wealth and status. Scholars who have studied the gender division of labour have found that women could participate in the daily routine of running a merchant house while their husband was away or ill.[39] This also seems to be true when it was time to make purchases for the household, even concerning luxury goods. Purchasing luxury goods required skills that both men and women were capable of possessing: both the men and women in the Vyborg elite used middlemen (and middle women) when shopping for luxuries, and especially popular were middlemen and middle women who belonged to the nobility. This guaranteed the taste, the quality and the luxury of the product. It is slightly more possible that men used middlemen and women turned to other women for such services, although women could also negotiate for purchases that were intended for men's use.

Among the elite of late eighteenth- and early nineteenth-century Vyborg, luxury was something that was purchased from St Petersburg or Britain, and many times even when it was purchased from St Petersburg it was still 'English'. These luxury goods were fairly recent inventions or had become recently modish, such as china or certain types of fabrics, and they were described as 'fashionable'. The quality and modernity of these products was essential, and in some cases luxury items had an exotic background. Luxury was something new, something that was affordable only for a certain group of people in Vyborg, and preferably something that had a noble or otherwise elite origin or had been selected with noble taste. Luxury goods were almost obligatory if a person wanted to climb the social ladder or maintain their position in local high society.

The shoppers of Vyborg were far from impulsive; the two-day journey to St Petersburg took its toll, and only those who were in good health or otherwise capable of enduring an uncomfortable wagon ride took the risk. In the Hackman family, it was typically the wife who travelled to St Petersburg to shop and meet friends. During these trips she bought fabrics, wines and colonial products that were not sold in Vyborg; she had the liberty to use her money on these journeys, and what she had bought was seldom recorded afterwards.

Gendered patterns of consumption were fairly flexible, yet an individual's or household's social position among Vyborg high society was important when it came to consumption choices. This is especially highlighted after Marie Hackman was widowed; then she had more money to use. At this stage of her life, her consumption is unspecified in the accounts, as she was at liberty to use money without any explanations. This type of extravagant consumption is often associated with men, but it was also possible that widows of adequate means were free to consume without any repercussions. This consumption pattern was not self-indulgent: For a merchant house manager like Marie Hackman, investing in her household was at the same time investing in the merchant house; the decorations and furniture in her private apartment were important for entertaining visiting fellow merchants.

Gender and social identity are interwoven concepts, which can be rewritten in the different stages of an individual's life. Luxury purchases depended on a person's social position and social identity more than biological gender. There is no evidence that people might have considered some luxuries as belonging solely to either men or women. Gender is a socially constructed category that seems to allow an individual to act quite liberally according to their needs and, moreover, according to the needs of their household.

NOTES

1 'Ils sont très estimables à bien des égards, mais on ne peut guère excuser la manie qu'ils ont de copier le luxe de Pétersbourg: il leur faut des clubs, des concerts, des bals, des mascarades, des vestes brodées, de beaux équipages'. Abel Burja, *Observations d'un voyageur sur la Russie, la Finlande, La Livonie, la Curlande et la Prusse*. Nouvelle édition, revue & corrigée (Maestricht: Dufour & Roux, 1837 [1787]), 77.

2 In St Petersburg, there were practically no French merchants, and the British merchants had more privileges than the others. The privileges of the British merchants dated back to the trade treaty of the sixteenth-century Muscovy Company, and the British had a primacy in Russian foreign trade. James Cracraft, *The Revolution of Peter the Great* (Harvard: Harvard University Press, 2003), 47.

3 Amanda Vickery, 'His and Hers: Gender, Consumption and Household Accounting in Eighteenth-Century England', *Past and Present* 192 (2006): 12–38; Lorna Weatherill, 'A Possession of One's Own: Women and Consumer Behaviour in England, 1660–1740', *The Journal of British Studies* 25 (1986): 131–56.

4 'Mit Französischen Produckten ist hier nicht zu machen so lange man sie aus St. Petersburg, Lowisa & Helsingfors so wohlfeil bezieht welche Stadte uns zu nähe umgeben, und dann ist die Consumption eines kleinen Ortes wie Wyburg ohne groβ genug um ganze Ladungen einzuversehen auch die Importation nur in Russischen Schiffen erlaubt', 21 July 1823, Woeniger, Lübeck, B 46 I, Hackman & Co, ELKA.

5 Örnulf Tigerstedt, *Kauppahuone Hackman. Erään vanhan Wiipurin kauppiassuvun vaiheet 1790–1879. Ensimmäinen osa* (Helsinki: Otava, 1940), 359.

6 In the Vyborg province, Swedish legislation and law of 1734 was used, at least in theory. From the 1780s to 1812, Russian institutions tried to introduce Russian legislation, sometimes successfully; for example, Russian merchant guilds were use in Vyborg province from 1785 to 1812. In the Grand Duchy of Finland, the senate did not meet until 1863, and therefore new laws were not settled until then. According to Swedish legislation, shopkeeping was allowed only in towns.

7 About non-existing sumptuary legislation and Catherine II's sumptuary edicts, see Christine Ruane, *The Empire's New Clothes: A History of the Russian Fashion Industry, 1700–1917* (New Haven: Yale University Press, 2009), 15; Paul Keenan, 'The Function of Fashion: Women and Clothing at the Russian Court (1700–1762)', in *Women in Russian Culture and Society, 1700–1825*, ed. Wendy Rosslyn and Alessandra Tosi (Basingstoke: Palgrave Macmillan, 2007), 138–39; Olga Vainshtein, 'Russian Dandyism: Construction a Man of Fashion', in *Russian Masculinities in History and Culture*, ed. Barbara Evans Clements, Rebecca Friedman and Dan Healey (Basingstoke: Palgrave Macmillan, 2002), 63; see also Katherine Pickering Antonova, *An Ordinary Marriage: The World of a Gentry Family in Provincial Russia* (Oxford: Oxford University Press, 2013), 38; Colum Leckey, *Patrons of Enlightenment: The Free Economic Society in Eighteenth-Century Russia* (Lanham and Plymouth: The Rowman & Littlefield Publishing Group and University of Delaware Press, 2011), 86.

8 Maxine Berg, *Luxury and Pleasure in Eighteenth-Century Britain* (Oxford: Oxford University Press 2005), 206–7.

9 ' . . . aber ist an einem so kleinen Orte wir Wyburg wenig zu nahen der so nahe an St Petersburg liegt daβ fast Jeder seine geringer Bedürfniβe won da mit bringt', 10 Dec.1820, Rall, St Petersburg, B 40 I, Hackman & Co, ELKA.

10 '. . . einen grüne Guirlande, ohne Blumen, won Eichen, Pfirschen oder andere Laub, wie es jezt Mode ist. . . . Wegen den Werzierungen der Füβe &ce werlaβe ich mich auf Ihren Geschmack', 29 Oct. 1801, Zagel, St Petersburg, B 14 I; 19 Aug. 1802, Bruun, St Petersburg, B 16 I, Hackman & Co, ELKA.

11 Berg, *Luxury and Pleasure*, 45; Jan de Vries, *The Industrious Revolution: Consumer Behaviour and the Household Economy, 1650 to the Present* (Cambridge: Cambridge University Press, 2008), 49–50. About copying the lifestyle of the elite in Russia, see Antonova, *An Ordinary Marriage*, 36–38.

12 'Meine Frau bittet Sie richt sehr ihr aus dem Englischen Magazin ein groβes Englisches damastenes seidenes Mode Tuch, am liebsten orange mit weiβ, oder orange mit Braun . . . ', 19 Aug. 1802, Bruun, St Petersburg, B 16 I, Hackman & Co, ELKA. See also note 4.

13 Carolyn Sargentson, *Merchants and Luxury Markets: The Marchands-Merciers of 18th Century Paris* (Oxford: Oxford University Press, 1996), 115; Berg, *Luxury and Pleasure*, 115, 195–204, 248 (about fashionable British luxury goods and national identity see especially 197).

14 'Nesseltüch zu einem damens Kleid won modernen Geschmack, 6 paar seidene damens Strümpfe, 3 paar weiβe u 3 paar Modefarbe, 1 Spencer won Tricot

wenn solche noch mode, sonst irgend was anders, 1 groβen seidene Mode Tuch. Incognito', 31 June 1803, Mackeprang, Lübeck, B 18 I; ' . . . and when he ships some trifling of Sugar, wine amounts &ce, we wish it to be lay'd in the Cabin and mentioned here in the custom house as ships provision, if moreover You get a green parrot from him you'll oblige Mrs. Hackman to bring this bird a living an well conditioned . . . ', 14 Jan. 1820, Captn. Runeberg, Christiansand, B 39 I, Hackman & Co, ELKA.

15 On impulsive masculine consumption patterns, see Amanda Vickery, *Behind Closed Doors: At Home in Georgian England* (New Haven: Yale University Press, 2009), 11–12; Vickery, 'His and Hers', 16, 33. See also David Hussey, 'Guns, Horses and Stylish Waistcoats? Male Consumer Activity and Domestic Shopping in Late-Eighteenth and Early Nineteenth-Century England', in *Buying for the Home. Shopping for the Domestic from the Seventeenth Century to the Present*, ed. David Hussey and Margaret Ponsonby (Aldershot: Ashgate, 2008), 48; Margot Finn, 'Men's Things: Masculine Possession in the Consumer Revolution', *Social History* 25 (2000): 133–55.

16 1797 wine 14.1 per cent, food 18.9 per cent; 1798 wine 2.9 per cent food 11.1 per cent; 1799 wine 5.2 per cent, food 11.4 per cent, of all his expenditures. See, for example, May 1798 '1 Kiste wersiegelt und gut wermahrt, mit 12 Stück beste Schlackwürste 14,50 . . . ein Kistchen Würste in Lübeck 1,59 . . . '; June 1798 'Unkosten für Würste &ce 5,83 . . . 5 Bouteillen Spa Wasser 3 Rub'; July 1798 '1/2 Fass Salz Fleisch aus Rewal 13 Rub . . . '. Particular memorial G 1 XV, Hackman & Co, ELKA.

17 According to David Hussey, male consumption moved from clubs and teahouses to the home in eighteenth-century England. Hussey 'Guns', 51; John Tosh, *A Man's Place, Masculinity and the Middle-Class Home in Victorian England* (New Haven: Yale University Press, 1999), 187; Berg, *Luxury and Pleasure*, 228–34.

18 Vainshtein, 'Russian Dandyism', 52, 54, 63–64.

19 'Ich brauche nun eine Uniform nebst Zubehör. Das ganze bestehet in folgenden: Ein blauer Rock mit rothen Unterfutter, desgleichen Kragen und Aufzügen, eine Rothe Weste und weiße Beinkleider; was zwar den Krägen, die Aufschläge, und die Weste mit Gold gestickt. Ein schwarzer Huth, ohne Tressen mit schwarzer Cocarde und goldenen Lor. . .s', 4 April 1802, Zagel, St Petersburg, B 15 I, Hackman & Co, ELKA.

20 Vickery, *Behind Closed Doors*, 13; Berg, *Luxury and Pleasure*, 238, 243; Vainshtein, 'Russian Dandyism', 52, 54, 63–64; Ruane, *The Empire's New Clothes*, 2, 8–10, 19–20.

21 'Januar 1799. . . . 1 dutz weiss Thetassen u. 1 Spülkummen, 1 Toilett Spiegel, . . . einen runden Mahony Tish . . . . Merz 1799. Kanaper u. Stuhle auf zu stopfen . . . einen Toilett Tisch und eine Toilett Spiegel . . . . Aprill 1799. . . . einen Toilett Spiegel . . . Schlösser, Schilder & aus St. Petebg zum Toilett Tisch . . . . September 1799. . . . 1 Clawier an die Generalin Steinheil . . . Kaffe Kanne & The Kanne, Glässer & diwerses, ein Portrait des Kaisers', G1XV, Hackman & Co, ELKA.

22 'Nehmen Sie liebster Freund doch ja nicht übel, dass wir wegen der Kleinigkeiten, zu dringlich waren. Wir schee wohl ein, dass Ihre Geschäfte Ihnen nicht immer erlauben dergleichen gleich zu besorgen, indes da Sie so nahe beÿ den Buden wohnen, so dachsten wir es würde augenblicklich geschehen können. Eigentlich ist meine Liebes Weibchen an allen Schuld, denn sie wollte gernen sich in einer gewissen Gesellschaft mit einem neuen Kleide produciren das nun aber wohl zu spät kommen wird', 5 April 1801, Bruun, St Petersburg, B 12 I, Hackman & Co, ELKA.

23 Antonova, *An Ordinary Marriage*, 74–78; Tosh, *A Man's Place*, 62–64; Deborah Simonton, *A History of European Women's Work: 1700 to the Present* (New York: Routledge, 1998), 21–26.

24 'Meine Frau ist mit dem gesandten Stück Zeuge außerordentlich zu frieden. Sie rühmt Ihren und der Madame Sievers ihren Geschmack! Aber sie ist auch ausgeschrieben genug, und Ihnen gleich wieder incommodiren zu wollen. Ich gehe zwar ungern daran aber was soll ich machen? Ich habe einmahl das Kreuz, und muss es also tragen. Sie werlangt wieder,—nicht eine Kleinigkeit sondern 1) Lino nach einl. Probe so weil als zu einem wollkommenen Damens Kleide erforderlich ist. 1 Paar weiße seidene lange Damens Handschuhe. 2) 14 ars. weißen ordinairen Atlas. 3) einen grüne Guirlande, ohne Blumen, won Eichen, Pfirsichen oder andere Laub, wie es jezt Mode ist', 29 Oct. 1801, Zagel, St Petersburg, B 14 I, Hackman & Co, ELKA.

25 '1 marmornen Tish auf feinen mit Mahogony und brons belegten [. . .] 35 Ro, 9 ars[chin]. Lino aller feinsten 49,50, 14 ars. Ord. Weißen Atlas 19,60. 1 pr weiße seidene handschuhe 5 Ro, 1 grüne Guirlande mit Emballage 4,50.' Nov. 1801, G 5 V, Hackman & Co, ELKA. A workman's daily wage was about one rouble, and Marie Hackman's clerk and gardener earned about 300 roubles per year.

26 Berg, *Luxury and Pleasure*, 238–39.

27 Vickery, *Behind Closed Doors*, 11–12, 124–25; Berg, *Luxury and Pleasure*, 196, 242–43; Hussey, 'Guns', 55–56; Vickery, 'His and Hers', 34; Finn, 'Men's Things'.

28 All these were bought via von Steinheils: a clavier, Sept. 1799; different fabrics and chairs, Feb. 1800; leather chairs and a sofa, a mirror and fabrics, July 1800, G1XV; chairs and a sofa, G 5 V, Hackman & Co, ELKA.

29 Berg, *Luxury and Pleasure*, 42–45, 196; Vickery, *Behind Closed Doors*, 18; De Vries, *The Industrious Revolution*, 44; Woodruff D. Smith, *Consumption and the Making of Respectability, 1600–1800* (London: Routledge, 2002), 81–82. Katherine Pickering Antonova considers the comfort and security of the product as the most important factor over luxury or status among the provincial gentry in Russia. Antonova, *An Ordinary Marriage*, 38.

30 Vickery, *Behind Closed Doors*, 10; Vickery 'His and Hers', 16; Berg, *Luxury and Pleasure*, 243. See also Antonova, *An Ordinary Marriage*, 35. According to her, only few had financial resources to travel comfortably enough in provincial Russia, therefore lower nobility refrained from travelling.

31 J. F. Hackman brought some goods with him from Bolshaja Izora. See Merz 1800, G5V, Hackman & Co, ELKA.

32 Berg, *Luxury and Pleasure*, 267.

33 Vickery, 'His and Hers', 16.

34 'September 1814. Per Haushaltung . . . Auf einen Brodkorb & Fishlöffel won Silber zugegeben 201,49 Rub.; December 1814. Per Haushaltung. 1 Blaues Tisch Service 500 Rub., 1 Thee Service 125 Rub., 2 Gedecke Tischmesser 230 Rub.' Private memorial 1808–1815; 'November 1823, Per J. F. Hackmans Wwe . . . eine neue Lüster durch Heyno 404 Rub.' G 22 V; '. . . 2 Garnituren modernster Brab. sptizen in zweÿ werschiedenen schönen dessins . . .'. 8 March 1826, Lüning, Gogel & Co, Antwerpen, B 54 I, Hackman & Co, ELKA.

35 'Aprill 1814. Per Haushaltung . . . An Lado's Erben für Ohr Gehänge . . . 400 Rub.' Private memorial 1808–1815. Hackman & Co, ELKA.

36 'We'll thank You to order the Captains to bring us. 2 Dozen of ordinary Table knifes & Forks 2 Dozen of ordinary Candle Snuffers of steel 1 Dozen of good pen knifes 4 Dozen of pencils, thicker ones 1 Ream of post paper the same as Your Letter was written on 25 Yards of thin Boy (light grey knap bearen

they call it) 25 Yards of the very finest white Callincort for Ladies Dressings if possible an English dog few months old and of an high race, 3 pairs of Ladies shoes 91/2 Inches long 1 do Ladies boots do 3 do do shoes 9 do 1 do do boots 9 do all of black and thin leather after the newest fashion and not broad, 1 Dozen of mans cravats of the finest musseline smaller ones and of new fashion. . . . The above different articles the Captain must lay out of the way and not mention them on arrival. . . . The Captn must address to us, all declaration on order being prohibited', 17 & 18 Feb. 1817, Barckworth & Spalding, Hull, B 34 I, Hackman & Co ELKA.

37 Hackman's bookkeeper's memoir, Handelshuset Hackmans arkiv, HH 33, ÅA.

38 See also Berg, *Luxury and Pleasure*, 234. Maxine Berg has noticed that class dictated luxury consumption as much as gender.

39 Antonova, *An Ordinary Family*, 75; Deborah Simonton, 'Women Workers; Working Women', in *The Routledge History of Women in Europe since 1700*, ed. Deborah Simonton (London: Routledge, 2006), 151; Simonton, *A History of European Women's Work*, 5, 156. See also Carol Gold's chapter in this volume.

12 The '*Díszmagyar*' as Representation in the Andrássy Family in Late Nineteenth-Century Budapest

Zsuzsa Sidó

The aim of this chapter is to examine and contextualise the concept of luxury in a Hungarian aristocratic family in late nineteenth-century Budapest and to investigate the ways and mechanisms in which luxury intersected with social representation. The chapter analyses the festive outfits of the Count Andrássy family, which were used as tools by the aristocracy in the construction of their self-image and in legitimising their social position. The analysis is based on the Hungarian gala dress, the *díszmagyar*, and other festive garments, which operated as costumes in their 'social theatre'. The chapter examines the aristocracy's preference for the Hungarian gala dress or the European festive dress and sheds light on the questions of group identity and self-perception of the male and female aristocrats. The interconnectedness of the urban economy of Budapest, especially of the tailors and dressmakers, and of aristocratic luxury consumption provides the framework for the analysis.

THE MEANING OF LUXURY FOR THE ARISTOCRACY

From the categories of luxury goods listed by Christopher J. Berry in *The Idea of Luxury: A Conceptual and Historical Investigation*, the chapter examines clothing.[1] Clothing has long been a means of communication with society, conveying symbolic values. Expensive, fine textiles and rare and exclusive jewellery are traditionally marks of luxury and status. As Berry argues, approaching luxury from a moralising perspective does not give the best results since luxury is 'ineliminable'; it is the embodiment of both human desire and needs. He also points out that it is more fruitful to understand luxury in relational terms, because what is a necessity for one person or one social group might be a luxury for another.[2] In this understanding, the official garments, the *díszmagyar*, and the jewellery used by the Hungarian aristocracy can be interpreted as a social necessity, since they were vital for communicating and maintaining their position in society. The question Berry asks is how does luxury and necessity bear more specifically on the rules which constitute social identity. One way of looking at luxury—in the present case the gala dress—as a tool for examining social identity is seeing it as a categorical continuity with a substantive discontinuity.[3] The outfits in general are timeless, continuous artefacts, tools for sending certain messages about one's position. However, the individual pieces of the garment change over time, shaped by the contemporary structures of meaning. The *díszmagyar* then becomes a representation of the self-perception of the Hungarian aristocracy and also a signifier of the social structures.[4] It is especially interesting to see how the sign system of the *díszmagyar* worked in the late nineteenth-century urban setting, and how individual, personal aspirations surfaced or were suppressed by the concept of *noblesse oblige*. In line with Maxine Berg and going back to Norbert Elias, focusing on the behaviour surrounding luxuries, rather than on the goods themselves, helps us interpret the mechanisms of the unfolding 'social drama'.[5] The Braudelian 'choice spectacle' unfolds with the help of the *díszmagyar*.[6]

In this analysis the focus is on three aspects: the *díszmagyar* as a luxurious dress with added symbolic value based on the idea of historicism; the investigation of gender aspects by looking at the choices made by male and female aristocrats; and finally, the impact of the consumption practices of the aristocracy on the urban economy, more specifically the ways in which their choice for the special festive dress influenced the business of dressmaking and the formation of the 'magnate tailors'.

SOURCES AND METHODOLOGY

Because the activities of the members of the Hungarian aristocracy were acted out in public, there are numerous sources about their lives. Newspapers described their whereabouts in great detail, and the aristocracy often left behind personal notes in letters, diaries or memoirs. In the late nineteenth century, with the emergence of photography, the outfits, especially the ceremonial ones, were well documented, making research on clothes easier. In addition, there are account books and inventories. These sources combine to give a detailed picture of the relationship between luxury and representation of the aristocracy. However, this rich material has not been studied from the point of view of gender and luxury in the city. Thus, this chapter investigates, in the context of the rapid urban development of Budapest, the understanding of the notion of luxury through the example of one of the most important Hungarian aristocratic families of the nineteenth century.

The chapter builds on contemporary newspapers, fashion magazines, memoirs of aristocrats and foreign, mostly English, accounts of their Hungarian experience. The letters of Miss Mary Elizabeth Stevens, the family's English governess, provides an additional layer of information for the present research.[7] She stayed in Hungary for five years (1864–1869), and wrote long and detailed letters to her family about her experiences in the Andrássy households. Her letters, as a source, are special in many ways in the context of luxury in the city and its connections to gender. In addition, her letters provide an English perspective of the anglophile Hungarian society. It is a well-known fact that the Hungarian aristocracy often imitated the English, not only in terms of fashion but also in terms of urban and social development. Next to Paris, London was the inspiration for the Hungarian modernising metropolis. Mary had experience of living in France and England, having moved to France with her mother and sister after her father's early death. Because she was acquainted with both countries, she could compare not only the capital cities and their urban developments, but the social life of each city as well. The comparative perspective Mary's letters bring is particularly pronounced for the private spheres of life, especially clothing and daily family activities.

For most nineteenth-century English travellers, Hungary fell largely in the realm of exotic.[8] What is special about the letters of Miss Stevens, in comparison with other British accounts from travellers, is that she lived with the family, took part in various social activities and used the infrastructure and services of the city for years. Her accounts add a more nuanced, gendered perspective to the pre-existing narrative about the role of luxury in shaping and representing social positions.

SETTING THE SCENE: THE URBANIZATION OF BUDAPEST

The history of the Hungarian nation in the nineteenth century revolved around the struggle for independence from the Habsburg Monarchy. The aim was to achieve the same independence that they had had in the Middle Ages. Because of this, an idealization and glorification of that historic period appeared in all spheres of cultural life. In 1867, when the Austro-Hungarian Compromise came about and Hungary again had a king and independent governance, they used references to the past which became a legitimiser for their achievements. In this way, the medieval became the modern, and the aristocracy, a 'feudal' group, became the facilitator of a modern institutional system. The two were not mutually exclusive; it was instead a peculiar continuity that manifested itself in their representative, festive garments as well. As Christopher Breward points out in *The Culture of Fashion*, one cannot argue against the unprecedented innovation in the field of consumption and dressmaking; however, the nineteenth century was equally preoccupied with values of the past and moral certainties.[9]

This is why, even though the second part of the nineteenth century is known as the century of the bourgeoisie, especially in Britain, France and Germany, in the Central European countries, and particularly in Hungary, the social dynamic took a different trajectory. Social-political life was still very much organised around and directed by the estates, in which the aristocracy had a central role. As in Poland, the Hungarian nobility made up more than five per cent of the population and held fifty per cent of the land.[10] Although change was inevitable, until the turn of the century the aristocracy mostly made the political decisions. This political role imposed a special responsibility on them, meaning they had to follow symbolic rituals, as their political capital was demonstrated by their consumption and behaviour. The so-called 'aristocratic life' was marked by a sense of social duty, what Miss Stevens mentioned repeatedly in her letters as '*noblesse oblige*'. It was an obligation to host balls and receptions and to build luxurious houses in the city. Before turning to the analysis of the *díszmagyar* and its political character, it is important to sketch out the urban historical setting where the performance took place.

In common with other European cities, Budapest went through remarkable urban development in the second part of the nineteenth century. It was the fastest growing city in Europe, reaching one million by the First World War.[11] An important date in the history of the city was 1873, when Budapest was officially born from the unification of Buda, Pest and Óbuda. Prior to 1873, these three settlements had separate administrations. Buda was a royal free town with a castle and medieval street system surrounded by hills and vineyards. Pest had been the economic centre of the country since the Napoleonic times, but in spite of this it resembled more a market place than a modern trade centre. The most important factor in the modernization of Buda and Pest, from both a symbolic and an urban point of view, was the construction of the Chain Bridge over the Danube in 1849. The Chain Bridge connected not only the two sides of the city, but the eastern and western part of the country as well. As a result, Buda and Pest became the commercial and administrative centre of the country. It also became the centre of the national economy thanks to economic and political developments in the Reform Era.[12] Naturally, the role of the trade was significant in the circulation of luxury goods as well.

Population growth was most pronounced in the 1850s, and by the late 1860s every third inhabitant was a newcomer.[13] The developing city attracted not just people from rural areas or foreigners searching for employment, but the aristocracy as well. Due to the seasonal character of their life, the aristocracy still divided their time between Pest, a country house and a hunting lodge somewhere in the mountains, Karlsbad or some other spa resort. From the 1860s on, however, more and more time was spent in Pest, especially after the 1867 Austro-Hungarian Compromise when it became the chosen location for numerous social and political events. This put a mark on the capitalist development of the city and contributed largely to the restructuring of the urban space and urban economy. As the location of the new capital, it became more and more common for the aristocracy to stay in Budapest for longer periods. Count

István Széchenyi, a prominent reform figure, already had a plan linking the development of the city with the residences of the aristocracy. He thought that if aristocratic families would build palaces and move to Pest, then manufacture, commerce and trade would get a boost since their consumption would improve the urban economy.[14] Széchenyi's initiative was echoed three decades later by the press when reacting to the constructions initiated by Count György Festetics, Count Lajos Károlyi and Count Pál Esterházy. One contemporary newspaper account praised the palaces and the initiative, saying that 'it is a generous gesture from the aristocracy that they devote part of their wealth to the beautification of the city and thus to the dissemination of taste'; the journalist also expressed his hope that once the palaces were furnished with all the necessary equipment, the family would settle permanently and have a positive effect not only on the social but also on the literary and artistic life, and on the industrial development of the city.[15] The aristocracy's agency in the transformation of the urban landscape, especially the construction of the so-called Palace District helped the development of the service sector, attracted craftsmen, shaped the urban landscape and most importantly influenced the development of the urban infrastructure. Furthermore, the imperial court stayed in the city from time to time, which had an enormous impact on the economy of the city. Budapest, the newly emerging capital city next to Vienna, became a stage for official court ceremonies and festivities, and for various social events for which the *díszmagyar* was the costume of the Hungarian aristocracy.

'NOBLESSE OBLIGE': THE DÍSZMAGYAR AS A NECESSARY LUXURY

The following is an analysis of the *díszmagyar* as a manifestation of the obligatory luxury or functional luxury as was suggested by Berry and discussed above. Given the premise that consumption is an exercise in identity construction, this section will explore the ways in which garments enabled the aristocrats to construct social identities.[16] Mary Stevens' comments about the everyday activities of the Andrássy family reveal nuances in the connection between the concept of luxury and social representation. Mary repeatedly commented on balls, dinners and afternoon teas as a noble obligation. Similarly, Countess Maria Festetics noted in her diary that Count Gyula Andrássy took part in political life motivated by a feeling of duty towards his country and emperor, and he was not getting any material reward for it.[17] He and his wife were the centre of society, especially after the Austro-Hungarian Compromise. The court ball, held every two or three years in Buda, was where the Hungarian peerage appeared in their best (see Figure 12.1 and Figure 12.2). These balls were important for the urban economy, from confectioneries to tailors and dressmakers.

Figure 12.1 Count Gyula Andrássy.

The Hungarian gala dress, the *díszmagyar*, was the most luxurious; tailors perceived it as a masterpiece. Mary described it in 1866:

> The elegance here is really wonderful, I never saw anything to equal it. You asked me about costumes. I think I have told you about the Hungarian ones. The court dress must be most rich, especially for gentlemen. They wear suits with tight trousers of dark velvet embroidered with gold; a small Spanish cloak over one shoulder, also of velvet, trimmed with fur and clasps of gold and precious stones; small toques of velvet with plumes fastened in aigrettes of diamonds and other gems. The ladies wear long trained dresses of all sorts of rich stuff, the body laced across like a stomacher; a wide apron of beautiful lace; white lace short sleeves to match.[18]

What Mary calls a Spanish cloak on one shoulder is nothing other than the so-called '*mente*', a special overcoat or pelisse worn as a sleeveless cloak, which is the mandatory component of the *díszmagyar.* Under it, but over the shirt, men wore the '*attila*', which was a waist-cut 'dolman' with a stand-up collar decorated with metal lace cording and trimming.[19] These were made of velvet or silk and worn with tight trousers and long embroidered boots. In the case of the ladies, the skirt followed European trends, having a lace apron, but the upper part was also composed of a white shirt and a corded, laced bodice, with similar elements as the men's '*attila*'.

This type of dress was designed by Ádám Kostyál in the late 1820s and became popular for the 1830 coronation of Ferdinand V.[20] Ádám Kostyál was a tailor who made costumes for the theatre as well.[21] In the patriotic atmosphere of Romanticism, he designed the Hungarian gala dress inspired by historical dress, especially by the seventeenth-century outfit with a *dolmány* and *mente*. This type of gala dress became popular because it helped Hungarians to distinguish themselves in a visible way from the Austrians, and because the cut of the *dolmány* followed the line of European fashion.[22] Lesser nobles wore similarly cut attire as well—the richly decorated gala dress was reserved as the hallmark of aristocracy; the bourgeoisie were advised not to wear it.[23] Worn only by the aristocracy, and constructed from exquisite textiles with lavish decorations such as family jewels, buttons and silver or gold cording, this form of díszmagyar clearly fell into the category of luxury.[24] It not only showed the wealth and power of the wearer; it also communicated the separate social and national identity of the Hungarian aristocracy *vis-à-vis* the Habsburg court. Although there are arguments for the *díszmagyar* as a symbol of wealth regardless of national origin, the elaborately embellished versions made a clear distinction between aristocracy and lesser nobles of various nationalities within the monarchy.[25] Thus, by the *fin-de-siècle*, this type of clothing became an evident signifier of status. In the 1830s the *díszmagyar* was used widely, but in the dualist period it was kept for state occasions, weddings and other festive occasions, which are discussed later in this chapter.

In the context of luxury, another aspect of the *díszmagyar* is the combination of old and new. Depending on the context, luxury can be viewed as something old and antique, or something that follows the latest trend, something innovative. The gala dress combined the two by taking advantage of a new European style cut, making it easier to fit in the court, but essentially referring back to a traditional Hungarian item of clothing. This combination also reflects the dual identity of the Hungarian aristocracy. Culturally they were part of Viennese court society, part of the aristocracy of a multinational empire, but historically they were members of the Hungarian nation.[26] Although Budapest was on the way to becoming a modern metropolis, Vienna remained the place for the 'social theatre'. The dress became very popular in the 1860s, and it essentially replaced the French or German style dress in the wardrobe of the Hungarian aristocracy. As the press covered the various state and court events, the *díszmagyar* made its way not only into Hungarian newspapers, but also into Viennese newspapers, and the French *Journal des dames* as well. The first international success of the dress was in 1829 in Paris, when Count Rudolf Apponyi wore a design made by Kostyál at a ball.[27] The *díszmagyar* received publicity in the contemporary fashion press and its various elements, especially the cording and the cut of the *mente*, were introduced into the latest fashion. Viennese fashion magazines regularly chose Hungarian aristocratic ladies for their front page, further enhancing the spread of Hungarian fashion.[28] However, this did not dilute the exclusive aspect of the dress, since only particular elements were taken over. The essence of the *díszmagyar* is complex. In keeping with Berry's theory of categorical continuity with substantive discontinuity, it was a luxury item that contained decoration or fabric that came from the family's treasury, but it was applied on or combined with new attire. In this way, the garment was also historicised and transformed into a traditional marker of ancestry, past glory and legitimacy in the contemporary social system.

Countess Katinka Andrássy was one of the most frequently mentioned ladies in the press, second only to the shy Empress Elisabeth. Not only was she beautiful, but she was also the wife of Gyula Andrássy, the first prime minister of the Austro-Hungarian Monarchy. Her social position required her to pay special attention to her outfits, although, as we know from the letters of Mary Stevens, she was not very keen on ceremonial dresses and spectacle. Katinka rather preferred to stay at home and read. Mary's description of the dress the countess wore at the court presentation in Buda in 1865 explains the enthusiasm of the press:

> There were 90 ladies in fullest court dress. My Countess looked most lovely, she had on a white moiré-antique dress trimmed with a superb black lace, a train four yards long (that was the regulation length), a black lace apron (that belongs to the costume), the body made rather like a stomacher in front, laced across and across, with large clasps of diamonds down to the waist; a coronet of diamonds with three magnificent emeralds, pendants, ditto earrings, ditto necklace and bracelet; from one side of the coronet fell the black veil shading with one end the right shoulder, the other falling almost to the feet behind; she looked lovely, so glittering with diamonds that she was quite dazzling.[29]

The exclusivity and richness was not unlike that of her husband, Gyula Andrássy:

> Our Count was in maroon velvet with a beautiful belt of gold, pearls and emeralds and other precious stones, his cap was decorated with a beautiful clasp matching his belt and an eagle's feather. He looked very well though his dress is not quite new, as of course lately there has been no necessity for court dress; he is going to get one of black velvet.[30]

The outfits of the male aristocrats were as richly decorated as that of the ladies, if not more so. The gender division in the public performances of the Hungarian aristocracy was less pronounced, and both sexes participated

Figure 12.2 Katinka Kendeffy, Countess Andrássy.

equally in the 'social theatre', with the *díszmagyar* as exclusive accessories. The coronation of Franz Joseph with the Hungarian crown on 8 June 1867 marked the establishment of the Austro-Hungarian Monarchy, providing an important occasion for the aristocracy to wear the family armour and jewels. They marched through the city with pride, imagining themselves copies of their glorious ancestors. The political character of the *díszmagyar* was evident, since throughout the neo-absolutist period, after the defeat of the 1848 revolution, the court had banned everything that had reference to national character.[31] At the top of the list was the Hungarian gala dress. It was especially important for the aristocracy to pick up on these elements and refer back to history as a signifier of their political success. The sight of the coronation procession astonished Mary:

> The magnates, with more sense than I should have given them credit for, ranged and marshalled themselves just under our balcony . . . There

> was scarcely one who had not something distinguished in the shape of jewels, furs, etc. The Baron Wenckheim has a magnificent ornament shaped like a plume from which hung several immense emeralds; the trappings and saddle-cloth of the Prince Esterhazy were one mass of precious stones; and then their costumes! There was cloth of gold and of silver, velvet of every shade and colour.[32]

For this occasion Count Andrássy wore a new *díszmagyar* with a set of jewels adorned with gems from the family heirlooms including gold buttons of three different sizes. The *mente*/pelisse had the largest, medium-sized one on the '*attila*' and the smallest one decorated the vent of the sleeves and the side of the pelisse. A gold chain fastened the *mente* decorated with an ivory portrait of Medusa, and the outfit included a belt, a sword-ling, spurs and *agraffe*.[33] Ludwig Ritter von Przibram compared the magnificent sight of the horse tackle, jewelled swords and old guns embellished with turquoise, ruby and pearl with Eastern pomp. Characterising the whole scene, however, he wrote that the procession taken as a whole seemed rather like a muster of feudal aristocrats: 'Seeing all the well-dressed barons and flagmen of the country, escorted by a silent humility of their armed henchmen and vassals, one really felt to be again in the Middle Ages'.[34] The analogy to Eastern pomp appears because, indeed, the male gala dress with its fur trimmed velvet *mente*, colourful silk *dolmány* and tight-corded boot trousers reminded the onlookers of Oriental traditions. Historicising as well, the ladies' dresses preserved the laced bodice and aproned skirt of the sixteenth and seventeenth centuries. Two English ladies who travelled through Austro-Hungary also noted the anachronistic character of the gala dress in 1891. One of their hosts, 'Count F.' impressed them with his *díszmagyar*:

> He seemed to have gained several inches in the dress, and looked like some majestic creature who had suddenly stepped from the middle ages. . . . The dress seemed to have called to life all the pride and fire latent in his easy-going face, to have suddenly aroused the reverse side of the Magyars. . . . The form never changes but the colour and jewels vary with the family. I can hardly imagine a finer sight than a regiment of nobles, mounted on horses draped in their respective colours, riding along in the sunlight; and such a spectacle, . . . is still to be seen on royal occasions.[35]

This passage not only resonates with the same theatrical aspect as in the foreign accounts above; it also gives an insight into the role and significance of the *díszmagyar* for the aristocracy in their identity construction and preservation process. As a hallmark of continuity, this luxurious and unique ceremonial ensemble was kept and handed down to generations. This is the reason why we know about the silk and velvet festive dress of Countess Stefánia Majláth, *née* Pradau, who wore the gown for the 1867 coronation and with little modification for the 1896 millennial festivities. In 1916 her daughter-in-law wore the same outfit in at the coronation of Charles IV.[36]

By the nineteenth century throughout Europe, the male outfit became simple, less colourful and with fewer decorations, yet the ladies' dresses compensated for this.[37] The latter became the outlet for representing the social status of the family. Especially in the 1860s, with the introduction of the crinoline, skirts became bigger, lace and flounces covered the ladies, more precious stones were applied and the colour scheme enriched.[38] While in French, English or German courts men wore black frock tails for official events, in Hungary they had various types of colourful velvet and silk garments. Especially on state occasions, both men and women wore very colourful clothes, with various precious stones and pearls applied to them or worn on their headdresses and hats. In this way men shared the representational role of the women, through wearing similar exclusive textiles and rich decorations. The Swiss ambassador commented that the 1867 coronation looked rather like a *carnavalesque* procession with all the vivid colours worn by both men and women. In comparison with other Western European men's outfits, which were only black and white, with colour restricted only to the bowtie or waistcoat, Hungarian aristocrats in their colourful attire seemed entirely anachronistic.[39] The use of old-fashioned dress was a deliberate choice, not because they were ignorant of Parisian or London fashion trends, but also because of the special significance of the outfits for their national and political cause.

'TAILOR MAGNATES' IN THE CITY

In spite of the fact that the city was growing and numerous types of goods were accessible, the goods used in creating the *díszmagyar* were often more expensive or were not of a high enough quality. Mary was constantly complaining about the prices of clothing and textiles in general:

> My silk jacket is sadly worn out, . . . and I do so dread buying one it will, I fear, cost so much. I thought, if I am obliged to purchase, of begging Aunt Amalie to get me something very nice in Vienna where they are not too high a price.[40]

Her commentary on housing was similar, and prices compared to England were much higher, but living conditions were worse. Food and basic goods were widely available; however, finer products and luxury could be had in Vienna or other European cities. According to Mary, only the gloves seem to be of better quality and cheaper than in London.[41] Not surprisingly, Countess Andrássy bought the furniture for the Sándor Palace, the official residence of the prime minister, in Vienna.[42] In spite of the scarcity and low quality of available services, organising dinners and other events by the aristocracy was a social obligation, and this began to have a growing impact on the economy of the city. The great scale of these events reminds us of the dream of Széchenyi about the beneficial aspects of aristocratic consumption on the urban economy.

> There is going to be a gigantic soirée tonight, nearly 700 people are to be here. . . . Why, the confectioner alone who had the refreshments to provide must have at least 700 florins; and then the wax candles for all those large rooms, and all the numerous other things—it must be a dreadful expense. But nobility obliges, you know, and the Count must pay the price of his grandeur.[43]

The phrase *noblesse oblige* appears several times in Mary's letters referring to the justification for all the spending and luxury. These activities, just like the festive garments, were players in their social theatre in the city. Even though the Countess, a person with simple tastes, was not fond of balls and ceremonies, being the wife of the prime minister forced her to fulfil certain social obligations, especially in the city. On one occasion Mary was witness to the Countess voicing her opinion, and she comments:

> I like her much, . . . [she is] so straight forward, honourable and sincere—and not the slightest pride or vanity about her, indeed if anything she has too little vanity; the Count often scolds her when she neglects to dress for dinner and she always says, 'provided one be clean and neat what does it signify in the country?[44]

If we accept that goods give as much information about status as about personality, then the above quotation underlines even more the reinforcing character of the festive dresses. They also support the rural and urban divide in the choice of clothing, with a preference for sophistication and quality in the latter. In the city, a lady could not appear twice in the same dress, so they either modified the previous one or ordered a new one. All this made a substantial impact on the urban economy, and more precisely on the dressmaking industry.

In spite of rapid modernization, the industries were organised into guilds until the late nineteenth century. The tailors' guild was abolished only in 1872, making space for the Trade Association in 1885.[45] In 1803, the guild of Hungarian tailors in Pest making Hungarian clothing had 33 members; the German guild, which specialised in European fashion, had 79 members. The numbers changed radically by 1827, when the first one had 32 members and the latter 207 members.[46] Textile factories however, were producing low-quality fabric, not suitable for the festive dresses. The Valero silk factory, established in 1839, functioned only until 1849 despite the fact that it was copying Parisian models in better quality fabric. The period of the Protective Association was the only time when locally produced textiles were in use.[47] One noted example was the ball of 1845, where ladies were required to make their dresses from the blue-dyed calico favoured by the peasantry.[48] This general development, or 'non-development' of the textile industry, however was only indirectly connected to the consumption of the aristocracy, who bought most of their clothing abroad. Because they could not find goods that satisfied their needs in Pest-Buda, London was the preferred shopping venue for men, while Paris or Vienna was for the ladies. Already by the 1820s, Széchenyi wore the English dress, which was associated with good quality textiles, practicality and comfort. 'Oscar Wilde dandyism' and especially sportswear became very popular in the 1850s–1860s, because the masculine ideal had become the English gentleman. The centre of fashion for the ladies between 1814 and the 1830s was Vienna, but after 1850 they shopped in or ordered from Paris. In 1869, before the social season, Katinka Andrássy ordered her dresses from Paris:

> The Countess has had a heap of French letters that of course were shuffled on to my unfortunate shoulders, and I had to go to Pest to buy French money to send to a woman in Paris who is making her a dress for a costume ball in Vienna; she is going there for a week or two for the Court balls. She will be the Sea, and very elegant, the dress will cost 600 *francs*.[49]

Even Mary bought a dress through the shopping network of the aristocracy:

> I have just bought a dress for four florins—one from Paris and such a nice one. It happened that the Pejacsovichs were sending to Paris for some dresses and their governess sent for one and did not like it when it arrived because it was a washing material, so I took it off her hands. And I like it so much, and of course I can get it washed as often as I like here.[50]

Although most ball gowns and other exclusive garments were made abroad, the gala Hungarian costume was a speciality of Pest tailors. In the context of the urban economy—especially linked to the tailors' and dressmakers' association—the *díszmagyar* had a special role. This was the garment that was made by local tailors, but from imported materials. In the 1840s and 1850s, three names were associated with making them: Ádám Kostyál, the inventor of the *díszmagyar*, Vencel Klasszy and Gáspár Tóth.[51] After 1830, more and more tailors moved to Pest from Vienna. In spite of a weak textile industry, a rise in the general demand for dressmaking, caused by an increase in population, brought an increased number of tailors, especially from Germany.

However, it was not just any tailor who could make the *díszmagyar* or make festive dresses for the aristocracy. There was a separate group of tailors who produced clothing exclusively for the aristocracy, the so-called 'magnate tailors'. These tailors did not advertise in newspapers; they served an exclusively aristocratic clientele on the basis of recommendations. Countess Katinka Károlyi, the granddaughter of Katinka Andrássy, wrote in her memoirs that during the ball season the doorknob was passed from tailor to seamstress without interruption. There was a long queue on the corridor from the representatives of the fashion saloons who lined up with boxes and models. When the tailor Herr König was announced, she as a child always thought that Emperor Franz Joseph was arriving, because everybody was behaving in an exalted way.[52] This example illustrates the high prestige of the 'magnate tailors'. Alter and Kiss, Monaszterly and Kuzmik and later Girardi were the most well-known female dressmakers, producing both European-style festive dresses and the *díszmagyar*. For men, János Schäffer was considered not only a star tailor, but also a fashion dictator. All the aristocratic names appear in his size-book, earning him the honorary title of the 'Permanent Tailor of Magnates'.[53]

By the turn of the century, thanks to the development of industry and manufacture and, in general, to Budapest becoming a European metropolis, a proliferation of luxury tailors can be observed. In addition, numerous Viennese companies moved or opened agencies and warehouses in the city. Skriván hatmaker, Tiller uniform and gala dressmaker and Neumann's shop for gentlemen were originally in Vienna, but transferred altogether to Pest during this period. Rothberger, Ebenstein and Rosenthal, although opening stores in Pest, kept their head office in Vienna and shipped ready-made clothes to the city.[54] As the fashion of the *díszmagyar* was spreading all over, and to Paris thanks to the fashion magazines, tailors in Vienna realised the potential in learning the cut of the gala dress and began producing it. Following this trend, the Viennese Breyer Company made Empress Elisabeth's Hungarian dress for the millennial celebrations in 1896. More aristocratic ladies commissioned their gala dresses from Viennese companies than men; the *díszmagyar* of the latter was almost exclusively made in Budapest. This is how we know about the Laufer Company, who made the dresses of Countess Eszterházy-Andrássy, although most others were made by the Spitzer Fashion House, including those for Lady Mary-Victoria Douglas-Hamilton, wife of Count Tasziló Festetics, and for the wife of Count Géza Andrássy. An interesting and significant detail regarding the *díszmagyar* is the fact that the Spitzer Fashion House at the 1898 fashion exhibition was represented with an '*ungarische Nationalcostüm*'.[55]

The group of Hungarian aristocrats dressed in their red-, green-, blue-coloured, etc., *díszmagyar* at the 1989 funeral of Zita, the last Hungarian Queen, was a curious sight. As in other European countries, the colour of the mourning was black, yet for this occasion the Hungarian aristocrats chose to make a symbolic gesture by putting on their festive Hungarian gala dress in honour of the queen, in spite of its anachronistic and unsuitable look. This act underlines the symbolic importance and the continuity of the *díszmagyar* for their public and group identity.

CONCLUSIONS

This chapter aimed at explaining the development and use of the *díszmagyar* by the aristocracy for ideological purposes in the context of nineteenth-century urban development of Budapest. The case of the Andrássy family offers fruitful material for analysing the subtle nuances of status and the organization of shopping in the city. The premise is that the *díszmagyar* was a luxurious item with a complex symbolic value, with layers of meaning, combining family history with contemporary aspirations for power. Similar to other luxury goods, only the top layer of the society—the aristocracy—used the díszmagyar.

The establishment of the Austro-Hungarian Monarchy transformed Budapest into a metropolis. For the rural masses this meant employment opportunities, while for the aristocracy it became a new scene for politics and representation. This chapter has built on the concept of social theatre, in which the use of distinctive external characteristics was strongly connected to preserving social hierarchies. In this framework the *díszmagyar* was a tool in the urban performance of the aristocracy. The insistence of the aristocracy on the use of the *díszmagyar* made an impact on the dressmaking industry of Budapest by driving the formation of the 'magnate tailors'. However, this impact only had a limited effect on the overall urban economy, because the Hungarian textile industry was incapable of producing the fine quality fabrics required for these exclusive garments. Thus, the tailors or the aristocracy had to buy them from abroad. The analysis has also showed that although local tailors made most of the Hungarian festive dresses, the ladies' dresses were often produced in Vienna.

The investigation has revealed interesting results about the relation between gender and luxury in comparison to other European societies. While in other European courts the black and white outfit was considered the model for the modern man, Hungarian noblemen wore red, green, blue, purple, yellow, etc., outfits for festive occasions. The explanation for this can be found in the historicist character of the *díszmagyar* and in the different understanding of what was considered masculine and powerful. While on festive and political occasions, the Hungarian aristocrats wore their ancestor's colourful garments; for everyday life, and especially for sport, they followed the English gentleman's model. This aspect links to the question of the circulation of goods and demonstrates that they relied on the international luxury market, for either ordering or direct shopping. While the men preferred London, the ladies purchased their exclusive garments in Vienna, and from the 1860s in Paris.

Overall, this chapter has contributed to the understanding of Christopher Berry's theoretical frame of analysing luxury as a categorical continuity with substantive discontinuity. By looking at the festive outfits of Hungarian aristocrats as a tool in their urban performance, the analysis has highlighted the dual character of their identity. Combining the old and new, the traditional and the modern, the public activity of the aristocracy contributed to the forces of development of nineteenth century modernity, which was built on this dichotomy.

NOTES

1 Christopher J. Berry, *The Idea of Luxury: A Conceptual and Historical Investigation* (Cambridge: Cambridge University Press, 1994), 5.
2 Ibid., 231–32.
3 Ibid., 242.
4 'Luxury Trades', in *The Oxford Encyclopedia of Economic History*, ed. Joel Mokyr (Oxford: Oxford University Press, 2003), 401.
5 Maxine Berg, 'Luxury, the Luxury Trade, and Industrial Growth', in *The Oxford Handbook of the History of Consumption*, ed. Frank Trentmann (Oxford: Oxford University Press, 2012), 179.
6 Fernand Braudel, *The Structures of Everyday Life: The Limits of the Possible* (Los Angeles: University of California Press, 1981), 184.
7 A selection of her letters was published under the title *Letters from Hungary 1864–1869: Written by Mary Elizabeth Stevens to Her Mother and Sister* (London: DRP, 1999). A Hungarian translation, including a few more letters than the original was published in András Cieger, ed., *Levelek az Andrássy házból: egy angol nevelőnő levelei, 1864–1869* [Letters from the Andrássy house: The letters of an English governess, 1864–1869], trans. Vera Bánki (Budapest: General Press, 2007). A presentation of the source in András Cieger, '"We are Now the First People in Hungary"; Count Andrássy's Family and Friends through the Eyes of an English Governess', *New Hungarian Quarterly* 3 (2008): 133–42. I would like to take this opportunity to thank András Cieger for giving me the original publication of the letters and his valuable advice. In this chapter I refer to the English publication.
8 Tibor Frank, *Picturing Austria-Hungary: The British Perception of the Habsburg Monarchy, 1865–1870*, (Boulder, CO: Social Science Monographs, 2005), 178.
9 Christopher Breward, *The Culture of Fashion* (Manchester: Manchester University Press, 1995), 176–78.
10 László Péter, 'The Aristocracy, the Gentry and Their Parliamentary Tradition in Nineteenth-Century Hungary', *The Slavonic and East European Review* 1 (1992): 79; Iván T. Berend and György Ránki, *Hungary*, a *Century of Economic Development* (Newton Abbot: David & Charles, 1974), 41–42; Gábor Gyáni and György Kövér, *Magyarország társadalomtörténete a reformkortól a II. világháborúig* [The social history of Hungary from the Age of Reforms until World War II] (Budapest: Osiris, 2006), 118.
11 András Gerő and Poór János, eds, *Budapest: A History from its Beginnings to 1998* (New York: Columbia University Press, 1997), 3–4.
12 László Csorba, 'Transition from Pest-Buda to Budapest, 1815–1873', in András Gerő and Poór János, *Budapest: A History*, 84.
13 Ibid., 71.
14 István Széchenyi, *Buda-pesti por és sár* [Dust and mud in Buda-Pest], ed. Ervin Fenyő (Budapest: Balassi, 1995), 5, 16. Written between 1837–1840, first published in 1866.
15 *Vasárnapi Újság*, 1864, 345. Similar ideas were expressed in *Az Ország Tükre*, 1863, 402.

16 Ann Bermingham and John Brewer, *The Consumption of Culture, 1600–1800: Image, Object, Text* (London: Routledge, 1995), 15.
17 Mária Festetics, *Egy udvarhölgy naplójából: Festetics Mária grófnő, udvarhölgy naplójának Budán és Gödöllőn papírra vetett részei* [From the diary of a lady in waiting: Sections from the diary of Countess Mária Festetics written in Buda and Gödöllő] (Gödöllő: Gödöllő Királyi Kastély Múzeum, 2009), 71. See also Max Weber, 'Politics as Vocation', in *The Vocation Lectures* (Indianapolis, IN: Hackett Pub., 2004), 32.
18 Stevens, *Letters from Hungary*, 55.
19 The word 'dolmány' comes from the Turkish 'doloman' and it is a front-buttoned coat whose origin goes back to the caftan.
20 Katalin F. Dózsa, 'Court and City Costume in the 18th to 20th Centuries', in *Historic Costume from Budapest*, Exhibition catalogue (Manchester: Whitworth Art Gallery, 1979), 17.
21 Katalin F. Dózsa, ed., *1116 Years of Hungarian Fashion* (Budapest: Absolut Media Zrt, 2012), 83. I wish to thank Katalin F. Dózsa for her suggestions.
22 Anikó Lukács, 'Nemzeti divat a pesti magyar nyelvű sajtóban az 1850-es, 60-as években' [National fashion in the Hungarian press of the 1850–60s], in *Nemzeti látószögek a 19. századi Magyarországon* (Budapest: Atelier, 2010), 277–83.
23 Katalin F. Dózsa, 'A rendi nemzettudat szimbóluma, a díszmagyar' [The díszmagyar: Symbol of national consciousness of the estates], in *Magyarok Kelet és Nyugat között*, ed. Tamás Hofer (Budapest: Néprajzi Múzeum, 1996), 161.
24 Lukács, 'Nemzeti divat', 284, 297–8.
25 Ibid., 161; Anikó Lukács, 'Átöltözések. A 19. századi magyar nemzeti divat emlékiratok és naplók türkében' [Changing clothes. Hungarian national fashion in the nineteenth century in the mirror of diaries and memoirs], *Aetas* 3 (2008): 46–64.
26 Hungarian 'nation' until the First World War basically meant the nobility. This is due to the peculiar composition of the Hungarian society and to the fact that the initiators of modernization were the nobles.
27 Dózsa, *1116 Years*, 82.
28 Katalin F. Dózsa, 'Osztrák-magyar kapcsolatok és kölcsönhatások a divat területén 1850 és 1916 közöt' [Austro-Hungarian relations and interferences in the field of fashion between 1850 and 1916], *Folia Historica 5* (1977): 184.
29 Stevens, *Letters from Hungary*, 108.
30 Ibid., 106.
31 Robert Nemes, 'The Politics of the Dance Floor: Culture and Civil Society in Nineteenth-Century Hungary', *Slavic Review* 4 (2001): 802–23.
32 Stevens, *Letters From Hungary*, 124–25.
33 Katalin F. Dózsa,'How the Hungarian National Costume Evolved', in Polly Cone, ed., *The Imperial Style: Fashion of the Habsburg Era* (New York: The Metropolitan Museum of Arts, 1980), 74–99.
34 Ludwig Ritter von Przibram, *Erinerung eines alten Österreichers* (Stuttgart, 1910), I. 187; quoted in Brigitte Hamann, *Erzsébet királyné* (Budapest: Európa, 2012), 284.
35 Margaret Fletcher, *Sketches of Life and Character in Hungary* (London: Swan Sonnenschein & Co., 1892), 71–72.
36 Dózsa, *1116 Years*, 117.
37 Christopher Breward, *The Hidden Consumer: Masculinities, Fashion and City Life 1860–1914* (London: Manchester University Press, 1999), 24–27.
38 Cally Blackman, *100 Years of Fashion Illustration* (London: Laurence King Publishing, 2007), 8.

39 Quoted in Katalin F. Dózsa, 'Királynék díszmagyarban. Magyar női díszruhák' [Queens in 'díszmagyar.' Ladies' Hungarian festive dresses], *Rubicon* 6 (1990). http://www.rubicon.hu/magyar/oldalak/kiralynek_diszmagyarban_magyar_noi_diszruhak/ (Accessed 25 October, 2013).
40 Stevens, *Letters from Hungary*, 171.
41 Ibid., 188.
42 Ibid., 119.
43 Ibid., 165–66.
44 Ibid., 96.
45 Katalin Dózsa, 'A szabóipar helyzete a századfordulón' [The situation of the tailors at the turn of the century], in *VII. Kézművesipartörténeti Szimpózium* (Budapest: MTA, 1991), 55.
46 Dózsa, *1116 Years*, 74.
47 The Protective Association was founded in 1844 as a union whose members agreed not to buy foreign goods if they existed in Hungary and to support local industry. However, despite six years of existence, only until 1846 were they actively involved in this aim, 1846 being the best year.
48 Terézia Pulszky, *Egy magyar hölgy emlékiratai* [Memoirs of a Hungarian lady] (Budapest: Magvető, 1986), 10.
49 Stevens, *Letters from Hungary*, 200.
50 Ibid., 174.
51 Lilla Tompos, *A díszmagyar: a magyar díszöltözet története* [The gala Hungarian: History of the Hungarian festive dress] (Budapest: M. Mercurius, 2005), 113–15.
52 Katinka Károlyi, *Együtt a forradalommal* [Together with the revolution] (Budapest: Európa Könyvkiadó, 2011), 19.
53 Szabó Hírlap, 1910, 23–24, 64. Quoted in Tompos, *A díszmagyar*, 116.
54 Dózsa, 'Osztrák-magyar kapcsolatok', 178.
55 Ibid., 186–87.

13 The Luxury They Could Not Afford? Households of Workers in the Industrial Town of Drammen, Norway c. 1900

Hanne Marie Johansen

The study of working-class history became an important field of interest in the 1960s. Scholars explored the rise of class consciousness, unions and how labour politics became an important factor in the formation of the modern Western state. The study of poverty was also a topic in working-class history. Another approach was to study changing patterns of consumption among workers and how the working class viewed and appreciated their world of consumer products, including luxury items. Scholars that dealt with consumption habits highlighted how new consumer goods in the Western world became important both to the middle and working classes. They often linked their studies to gender, the family and the modern city. In drawing attention to how different the idea of luxury was in the past, and in pointing out how luxury as a concept is highly variable depending on historical and social circumstances, these scholars have made major research contributions.[1] This chapter about working-class families is inspired by the consumer-history approach in working-class history and in urban history.[2] It presents a case study of the town of Drammen, the fifth largest town in Norway in 1900, illustrating how members of working-class families used their income in order to understand what kind of buying and spending was considered a luxury. It explores which consumer goods were considered commonly affordable and which goods were considered luxuries, which kinds of eating, drinking, and smoking habits were seen as luxuries by workers and what was regarded as luxurious in housing arrangements. It also asks whether hard-working families could pay for cultural activities, sports and entertainment when they had to spend nearly half their income on food. The concept of luxury was relevant to so many everyday situations, and the concept was gendered in Drammen, in Norway and among the working classes, as elsewhere.

The household economy was based on gender division. Indeed, working-class women (like women in other classes) experienced financial marginalisation in both the private and the public sphere. Working-class women were restrained financially, both by gender and class. Gendered ideals expected these wives to forget about their own (luxury) needs and to give priority to husbands' and children's well-being. They were obliged to look after their families, to feed and to clothe them. There were no housemaids to do the job. When shopping for groceries, meat, milk and bread, working-class wives had to decide what was really necessary to buy in order to make ends meet. They also had to take care of their children's health.[3] Special occasions such as Christmas or vacations were the most probable occasions for extra spending. Husbands and fathers had special consumer rights and needs versus those of the wife and children. Smoking and drinking alcohol were considered the norm for men, and were seen as less relevant for women. Hilde Sandvik comments on the development of the Norwegian working-class family in the interwar period, pointing out that the Marriage Law of 1927 stressed that unpaid housework was just as valuable as paid work outside the home. This was to make sure women had rights in case of a marriage breakdown. But while the couple lived together, the husband was usually in charge of the family economy, and a wife was economically dependent on her husband. She usually received a certain part of her husbands' weekly salary as housekeeping money (*husholdningspenger*).[4]

In the twenty-first century, rent, lighting and heating represent huge elements in most families' budgets.[5] To live in a comfortable home is seen as a necessity. Working-class families in earlier generations perhaps thought differently about housing arrangements, or they had to choose between putting food on the table or heating up their home. This study examines the portions of family incomes spent on food and what was left for other purposes, such as housing, transportation and leisure activities; in addition it explores the distinct gender differences in these purchases.

Both quantitative and qualitative sources are important to this study. In 1912–1913 the Municipality of Kristiania (today Oslo) organised a pioneering study of consumer habits in Norwegian towns, and a sample of working-class families were invited to produce complete family budgets for a whole year. Participants were given account books with printed forms, and they were expected to keep a record of their private consumer expenditures over a twelve-month period.[6] It is not recorded who wrote the account books, wife or husband. Since in most families women took care of every day shopping and expenses, the account books may well have been the women's sole responsibility. Some families, among them twelve from Drammen, were able to fulfil their task and deliver an account book by the end of the study, October 1913. The project had a comparative perspective; therefore people from different towns were involved. The aim was to study how working-class families were able to manage their finances and what their consumer habits were. The accounts give information on incomes of every sort, and how the family's income was spent or saved. Families that kept accounts of their private consumer expenditures were well organised. Families with social problems were probably underrepresented. Several more families from Drammen tried but gave up during that year, or their book was not accepted for statistical analysis. This situation occurred in all the participating towns. The Statistical Office in Kristiania published a report on how Norwegian families, who had taken part in the project, had earned and used their money.[7] This chapter is also based on papers collected by the Norwegian Folk Museum in 1950. Workers from all over the country, born in the 1870s and 1880s, were invited to write down their memories. Eleven men and one woman from Drammen, mostly factory, sawmill and paper-mill workers responded. They described the living conditions in their childhood hometown, and their stories provide vivid pictures of everyday life, consumer habits and what was considered luxury goods.[8]

DEVELOPMENT FROM A SURVIVAL SOCIETY TO A CONSUMER SOCIETY

After Norway broke away from the Union with Sweden in 1905, optimism was strong in many ways. Political freedom came at the same time as the economy boomed. Norway's economic growth was based on the development of natural resources, fisheries, timber and minerals. The process of industrialization that had begun from about 1850 continued, faster than ever before. From about 1905, factories benefitted from cheap electric power, produced by the many waterfalls in Norway: Norwegian White Gold. Local manufacturing and construction industries all over Norway expanded to meet the immediate needs of growing markets and populations in Europe and within the country.[9] Both women and men experienced new work opportunities, and many had increases in real wages, despite reductions in working hours.[10] It looked as if progress was under way, and that the time had come for labourers to reap their reward. Christian Michelsen (1857–1925), the first Norwegian prime minister in the new era, spoke on behalf of many when he described the situation as 'The New Working Day' for the nation and its people.[11]

Generally, wage earners had 2 to 3.5 times more purchasing power in 1920 than they had had in 1850. This applied to both sexes. But women as a group did not catch up with men financially. The gender system trapped them in low-paid, low-skilled jobs. Norwegian historians state that right up to the Second World War, the most common occupation for women was domestic service. Men had escaped from low-income occupations, while women were left behind. Thus Norwegian women's work opportunities were rather limited, in spite of the Industrial Revolution and the growth in the economy.[12] Industrial workers and wage earners in the civil service occupations, such as police officers and office workers, benefited more than other wage earners in that period. At the same time, society witnessed ongoing wage equalization between the classes.[13] This is rather surprising and contradicts what the findings from, for example, Great Britain have uncovered. A number of British historians mention that income distribution moved in favour of those who were already better off in Great Britain in the first half of the twentieth century. This resulted in a growing bourgeois consumption. This was not the case in Norway. Rather the opposite was true, as incomes became more equally distributed in Norway.[14]

Economic historians describe the development in Norway as a progression from a 'survival society' to a 'consumer society', and indicate that consumerism showed a steady upward trend even in the working classes.[15] What had been considered luxuries gradually became everyday experiences and goods. Both men and women in the Norwegian working class benefitted from this development, women perhaps more indirectly than men, since in many cases they did not have incomes of their own and were not heads of households. Generally, a head of household was in the best position to decide on the family's consumption patterns, as well as approving the use of luxuries.[16]

Consumption expectations probably changed between 1850 and the early twentieth century. In the early twentieth century people could dream of a new, modern and comfortable lifestyle. As 'The New Working Day' came about, new commodities for everyday use were imported and displayed in shop windows. There were items like elegant furniture and carpets, porcelain, china and textiles, cotton, silk and wool for cloth production. In addition, the modern Norwegian textile and fashion industries could offer a large amount of ready-made clothing. New foodstuffs were introduced, including, among other things, exotic fruits from Southern Europe. The Norwegian food industry boomed, and families with spare money had hitherto unknown possibilities. For example, mothers who did not want to breastfeed (or pay someone to do it) could buy sweetened Viking Milk and Viking Milk powder, designed for infants, in cans. The Swiss company Nestlé, which started food production in Norway as early as 1898, manufactured these products in Norway.[17] During the First World War (1914–1918), supply lines were difficult to keep open, even in neutral Norway. The authorities were obliged to regulate production, prices and conditions of sale. People had money, but store shelves were often empty and the black market flourished.[18] After the war the situation for ordinary wages earners and consumers improved again.[19]

Economic theory and both historical and contemporary empirical studies usually state that an increase in prosperity will lead to a smaller proportion of income being spent on food. However, economic historians have concluded that this 'law' does not apply to Norway in the period 1850–1920. In spite of a general increase in real wages, most families did not stop spending a very large proportion of their income on food. An average Norwegian family used 46.6 per cent of its income on food in 1865, and 42.2 per cent in 1910.[20] In other worlds, the consumer pattern was surprisingly traditional (and poor) in 1910. This indicates that people in Norway with moderate incomes must have experienced a great deal of economic and social difficulty in spite of the 'optimism in economy', the rise in wages and the longed-for consumer revolution. [21]

THE TOWN: DRAMMEN IN SOUTH–EASTERN NORWAY

Drammen is situated just forty kilometres southwest of the capital Kristiania.[22] The part of Drammen north of the river is named Bragernes, and the part south is Strømsø. Drammen is located at the junction of where the river meets the fjord. That made the town an important harbour. Right up to the 1950s, both Bragernes and Strømsø were centres of seafaring, shipbuilding and log driving. The size of the population in Drammen was 23,600 in 1900 and by 1910 it had grown to 26,000. Only Kristiania, Bergen, Trondheim and Kristiansand were larger. Demographic growth was a result of both a birth surplus, due to a fall in mortality rate, and migration. Rural migrants from Norway and Sweden settled in great numbers. Workers were needed. Drammen, like other Norwegian towns, was beginning to industrialise from about 1850, when steam-powered sawmills were established along the lower section of the river. In the course of the twentieth century these sawmills disappeared as the paper and cellulose industries boomed. Drammen was an important national centre of the Norwegian timber industry, as well as for other kinds of industries, such as textile and shoe factories and breweries, to mention a few. People who settled in towns like Drammen and elsewhere in Norway could find work not only in factories, but also in the growing commercial arena, in the communication sector and within the expanding public sector (see Figure 13.1). By 1900 the town was

Figure 13.1 Streets and homes—Gulskogen, Drammen, c. 1900. Eiker Arkiv, Norway.

an important regional centre of the province of Buskerud, both in trade and in regional administration. When the Norwegian railway system developed in the nineteenth century, Drammen Station became a centre of regional and national importance.[23]

INCOME

Domestic accounts from Drammen and Kristiania in 1912–1913 indicate that the male breadwinner's health and ability and willingness to work determined a family's welfare (Table 13.1). A husband's income was the family's main source of income, while the wife and children barely earned any money at all. This was a surprise. We know from other sources that many wives in Drammen and other Norwegian towns used to take part-time work in private homes, doing laundry and housekeeping. Or they took seasonal and part-time jobs in industry, or produced goods for sale at home. Handicrafts were an important source of income. Even children contributed to the family economy by earning wages. Law prohibited child labour in Norwegian factories by the Factory Supervision Law of 1898. But this law was not always respected, and children could legally find work in the service sector, as delivery boys and paperboys and girls, for example.[24] Widows and unmarried mothers were, of course, entirely dependent on their own industriousness and enterprising children in order to be able to eat and live reasonably well. Therefore, account books produced in 1912–1913 and later do not necessarily give a complete picture of the sources of women and children's incomes and certainly do not give a representative picture of sources of women's and children's work effort. It is possible women who wrote account books deliberately under-reported their own and children's paid work out of pride. The middle-class idea that the husband should be able to support his family alone was starting to spread among workers. And workers with social ambitions, willing to sign up for account recording for a whole year, were probably more 'middle class' in attitude than the average worker, and were eager to demonstrate that they had social ambitions.

However, information on family incomes in these account books corresponds with other sources informing our historical knowledge in many respects. For example, they show that people's homes were sources of income in many ways. Taking in lodgers or relatives or other people supported by the municipality, paupers, was a quite common solution to the money problems of working-class families. Four out of twelve families from Drammen who completed their family budgets in 1912–1913 indicated lodgers as a source of income. This was perhaps a way to compensate for the lack of income from wives and children, since historically women turned their domestic expectations into income earning in this way.

Table 13.1 The average total income and expenditure for a group of working-class families from Drammen and Kristiania, Norway. October 1912–October 1913.

	Drammen—12 families Average numbers				Kristiania—103 Families Average numbers			
	NOK 1913	NOK 2013	Euro 2013	Pound 2013	NOK 1913	NOK 2013	Euro 2013	Pound 2013
Total expenditures	1,798	90,868	11,876	8,632	2,056	103,907	13,799	9,871
Total income	1,796	90,767	12,054	8,623	2,101	106,181	14,101	10,087
Total income from work	1,633	82,529	10,960	7,840	1,878	94,911	12,604	9,017
Husbands' main source of income	1,498	75,706	10,053	7,192	1,693	85,562	11,363	8,128
Husbands' secondary source of income	44	2,224	295	211	51	2,577	342	245
The wives' and children's income	9	455	60	43	133	6,722	893	639
Lodgers—source of income	86	4,346	577	413	91	4,599	611	437
Other income	77	3,891	517	369	132	6,671	886	634

Source: Domestic (Household) accounts from lower income families in Christiania, Bergen, Trondhjem, Kristiansand and Hamar in 1912–1913. Special studies. IV Christiania Municipality Statistics. (1915). Table 3, pp. 84–93.

Note: Amounts are rounded. The calculations show the development in the value of the Norwegian crown when based on the Consumer Price Index. The calculations do not show what the individual items ought to cost or will cost when the price is adjusted by the Consumer Price Index.

A surprising feature of the families that kept household accounts was that so many of them were registered as having a small income from lodgers, since their homes were already so small. Thus there were 'roommates' in their small apartments. A blacksmith, who kept accounts in Drammen in 1912–1913, had his mother-in-law living in a one-bedroom apartment. He also needed accommodation for himself, his wife and three children. 'His wife's mother' had 'full board and lodging at government expense'. One entry that was often recorded was 'Kristiania Municipality'. This may mean that the Kristiania Municipality supported the mother-in-law so she could pay her own way at her daughter and son-in-law's home. Others, who had income from lodgers and who had two-bedroom apartments, often set it up so the family could stay in one room and the lodgers could have the other room for themselves. In Drammen in 1912–1913, a municipal worker, with a wife and three children, had two adult male lodgers with 'full room and board' (see Table 13.2). A masonry worker and his wife and their three children had three grown men living in one room inside the apartment. This family had a contract stating 'room with coffee and eggs in the morning'. Having eggs for breakfast on weekdays was not common, and indicates that the family kept chickens in the backyard or garden. A typesetter with his wife and two children also had a spare room for a lodger, a woman aged

Table 13.2 Expenditure of a municipal worker from Drammen, 1912–1913, his wife and three children.

		NOK 1913	NOK 2013	Euro 2013	Pound 2013/14
A	Total Income	1,595	80,609	10,705	7,658
I	Total Income from Work	1,482	74,898	9,947	7,115
1.	Husband's main source of income	1,224	61,859	8,215	5,877
2.	Husband's secondary source	194	9,804	1,302	931
3.	The wife's and children's total income	63	3,184	423	302
4.	Children's income	0	0	0	0
II	Lodger – source of income	113	5,710	758	542
III	Insurance	0	0	0	0
IV	Gifts	0	0	0	0
V	Additional income	0	0	0	0
B	Total expenditures	1,551	78,385	10,410	7,447
I	Food	1,030	52,054	6,913	4,945

(*Continued*)

		NOK 1913	NOK 2013	Euro 2013	Pound 2013/14
II	Alcohol and tobacco	23	1,162	154	110
III	Clothing and shoes	212	10,714	1,423	1,018
IV	Housing	132	6,671	886	634
V	Electricity and heating	26	1,314	175	125
VI	Cleanliness and hygiene	18	910	121	86
VII	Expenses for in-house contents	4	202	27	19
VIII	Doctor and medical expences	2	102	14	10
IX	Servants	0	0	0	0
X	Club dues and insurance expenses	71	3,588	476	341
XI	Taxes	30	1,616	201	154
XII	Gifts	0	0	0	0
XIII	Intelectual pursuits, books and papers etc.	2	102	14	10
XIV	Recreation	1	50	8	5
XV	Gambling	0	0	0	0
XVI	Travelling	1	50	8	5
XVII	Miscellaneous expenses	1	50	8	5

Source: Domestic (household) accounts from lower income families in Christiania, Bergen, Trondhjem, Kristiansand and Hamar in 1912–1913. Special studies. IV Christiania Municipality Statistics. (1915). Table 3, pp. 84–93.

Note: In 2013, 1 EURO = 7,53 NOK. In 2013, 1 Pound = 10.56 NKR. Amounts are rounded.

thirty-five. She had ‘room with coffee in the morning, milk in the evening’. One month in the year 1912–1913, the woman shared her room with a visiting woman aged seventy-two. It was perhaps the family’s grandmother. And of course, much of the work of accommodating lodgers fell on the women.

A few urban families in Norway around 1900 received support from their trades unions if the male breadwinner died, became ill or had an accident in the workplace. A law from 1899 decreed that workers should have workman’s compensation insurance from their employers if they had an accident in the workplace. However, these funds were not sufficient to support a family, and for most people there was virtually no welfare system to rely on, only family support. Unemployment, illness and death were serious threats to the family’s economy and security. The fear was that the family might fall apart, and that family members would end up as paupers, dependent on the municipality. This was regarded as a shame. Also, parents and children risked being separated if poverty struck.

EXPENDITURES

The report from Drammen shows the families involved in the study had a typical Norwegian consumer pattern, a pattern that indicates poverty. They used fifty to seventy per cent of their income on food, and only ten per cent on housing. Very little was left for other needs. To set aside money for savings was very difficult; hardly anything was ever put aside. This was a surprise, because saving was an ideal in the society. Generally, people were expected to save money in order to have some security in case of sickness, loss of the breadwinner and old age. Thus, this suggests that there was little or no 'extra' for saving.

There were many simple things people could do in order to save money or stretch the family budget, and it was probably first and foremost wives' responsibility. Husbands who took part in the Drammen study worked full-time, and spent about ten to twelve hours a day in the work place. Their wives hardly earned anything, as indicated above. They stayed at home most of the time, occupied with household work, including shopping. People who came and knocked at the doors offered fresh fish and other commodities for sale. When women left the house it was to do the shopping in the nearby dairy, bakery or the small grocery store in the neighbourhood. Wives and mothers had to find ways to save on everything from bread to soap. This meant there was little left for real luxuries in the family budgets.[25] Women who wasted their families' money on 'nothing', not to say on tobacco and alcohol, were criticised. The man in the house usually had greater 'consumer freedom'. He was at least in theory the main person in the household, hard working, and he could argue that he 'deserved' something extra.

Housing conditions were especially bad in Drammen. Cramped family homes with or without lodgers were common in the town at the beginning of the twentieth century, due to people's low income. To have an extra room for the children to sleep in, for example, was regarded as a luxury one could not afford. One-bedroom apartments with no kitchen or with a shared kitchen had price increases of, respectively, 120 and 97 per cent in Drammen from 1910 to 1920. Typical middle-class apartments, with three rooms and a kitchen, rose only by fifty-six per cent during the same period, and two-bedroom apartments with kitchens rose by sixty-seven per cent. There was an especially short supply and great demand for small and cheap apartments in the city. Thus, homeowners could increase the rent substantially for this kind of apartment. Around 1900, a great number of the town's apartments were overcrowded, meaning that three or more people shared one room. It was quite common for two working-class families to share a kitchen. One in ten families had to share a kitchen with another family. As late as 1939, only ten to fifteen per cent of the town's homes had a bathroom. Indeed, bathrooms in private homes were nearly unknown outside the social elite. Even bedrooms were an unknown luxury. The kitchen and the living room were filled with mattresses and beds in the evenings, family members slept on sofas and children even slept in the kitchen drawers. [26]

In memories of workers born in the 1870s and 1880s, and collected by the Norwegian Folk Museum in 1950, the eleven men and one woman from Drammen described living conditions in their childhood. Sigurd Johansen, born in 1870, wrote:

> There were some individual families that had two rooms and a kitchen, but they used only one living room. The second was used 'only for company' as it was called. One should be able to get by with just one room; anything else was considered a luxury. I mentioned to Mother that we lived so poorly and that we should think about getting something better. She replied that what we have is good compared to what she and my father had when they moved into together after their wedding. They had only one room with a dirt floor.[27]

And Johannes Halvorsen (born 1874) wrote: 'We were a family with 12 members who lived in one room and a kitchen, and that was often not very easy for those who worked at night and had to sleep during the day'.[28]

Electricity was installed in Drammen from 1903, yet it was not until after the First World War that it was common for working-class families to have access to it. As a general rule, electricity in private homes was only used for illuminating up to the First World War. Ordinary people cooked their food on a traditional oven fired by wood, and heating was also done by wood or 'coke'. As can be seen from the twelve domestic accounts from Drammen 1912–1913, electricity and heating did not represent great sums of money because the families went to bed early in the dark and cold winter evenings. During the winter months, at times the temperature in Drammen goes down to minus twenty degrees centigrade; in December and January days are very short and it gets dark by four o'clock in the afternoon.

Supplies of freshwater were a problem. Drammen had a modern waterworks built in the 1860s, but this did not serve every part of the town. Many, but not all, had hand-powered water pumps in the street where they lived and could go out and fetch water from there. The water pump was free to use for people in the neighbourhood; others had access to wells. Some people had to find water in the river, even though this was polluted and not suitable for drinking or food preparation. People did not spend money on fresh water, but being able to buy milk was important.

MILK AND FOOD

Domestic budgets indicate that fresh milk was common among better-off working-class families. Yet even if families prioritised fresh milk, it was far from certain that it was available for sale in the vicinity. Often a neighbour with a barn and a few cows provided fresh milk for daily use for those who could afford it. On Konggata (The King's Road) in Drammen, a widow made her living by having a barn and a few cows in the backyard, which she would graze in the nearby hills. This barn on Konggata was in use until 1934, and the neighbourhood residents would show up at her fence, bucket in hand, to purchase the sought-after milk.[29]

Milk was a luxury for the urban poor. From the end of the nineteenth century, middle-class women supported the organization known as The Norwegian Women's Public Health Association (Norske Kvinners Sanitetsforening, NKS). In Drammen, as in other Norwegian towns, these women took a special interest in preventative healthcare. They emphasised the importance of a healthy diet and tried to help poor families get the health benefits of fresh milk. Their method was to visit poor families in their homes; lay workers were recruited to visit homes, or they paid professional nurses to do the job. The aim was the same: not only to inspect and to educate families about the benefits of drinking milk, but also to give vouchers for fresh milk so that people who lacked cash could purchase that sought-after nutrient at their local milk exchange.[30] People liked fat, not only milk fat, and it was important in their diet. Memories from workers in 1950 often mentioned using margarine and fat from whales for daily use and serving butter for special occasions. The whale-fat margarine was spread on bread, and it took away their appetite. In their reminiscences, many workers from Drammen mentioned the difficulty they had in swallowing whale-fat sandwiches, because it tasted awful and its consistency was unpleasant.[31]

Ice was a rare commodity for working-class families. Aase Johansen (born 1926), daughter of the sausage-maker Braathen from Strømsø, reminisced about the day-to-day life in her childhood home—for example, how blocks of ice were delivered and placed in ice boxes in their basement. Ice production and delivery was an important industry in Drammen from 1900 through the interwar years. Ice from the river and lakes was cut into blocks during the winter. In the summer, it was stored in icehouses, covered with sawdust that would keep it from melting. Both private homes and businesses used iceboxes in the summer for storage of milk, among other things. However, working-class families would probably not be able to afford to buy it, so having ice in the summertime was a luxury. This lack of refrigeration may have contributed to potentially harmful food storage practices in workers' homes and may have been a source of disease and contamination in the summer months.[32]

Purchases of fruit and vegetables also were relatively rare in working-class budgets, while exotic fruits were an exceptional luxury. Drammen was a green town in the early twentieth century, and many families had a small garden and chose to use it as a potato field. However, potatoes represented a solid sum of money in working families' budgets. On average, the twelve families from Drammen used about five or six per cent of their food money on potatoes, and very little on fruits and vegetables. Fruits and vegetables usually came from people's gardens or from the woods. Potatoes were their main source of vitamin C, along with berries from the woods. A closer look at the domestic accounts from Drammen (and other Norwegian towns) in 1912–1913 reveals that families spent perhaps three or four crowns, that is, very little, each year on exotic fruits, mostly oranges. Children could expect to taste an orange during Christmas celebrations.[33] Oranges were first imported to Norway from the 1860s and 1870s onwards. A woman who grew up as the daughter of the richest man in Drammen in the second half of the nineteenth century wrote in her memoirs that in her childhood town people were quite unfamiliar with exotic fruits. 'When father occasionally bought tropical fruits for his customers, once in a while a couple of grapes or orange slices would fall off and be given to us'. She remembered quite clearly that even for the wealthy this was a luxury in the 1860s and 1870s, and writes also: 'In those times, no child—to say nothing of an adult—aspired to have a whole orange for themselves'.[34]

Average figures for the participating families in Drammen in 1912 and 1913, show that a relatively large part of the cost of meals, approximately one-fifth, went on meat and pork. Family men who worked ten to twelve hours a day needed substantial food, fats and proteins. The members of the family also ate at different times because the man of the house had such a long day at work and, in many cases, shift work. It is not certain whether the mother and the children had the same hearty fare as the father; the food budget was very tight. Women who wanted to save a little on food devoted perhaps some of their own food allocation in order to serve something tasty and hearty to their husband. Adult children living at home also had to work hard and often full-time at the factory, giving their salaries to their parents. One way or another all family members had to contribute, earn money and bring food to the common table.[35]

Household accounts show that groceries in the years before the First World War and up to the end of the 1920s consisted mostly of sugar and coffee, and some spices.[36] Collectively grocery goods usually accounted for no more than about ten per cent of food expenditures. A municipal worker from Drammen and his wife and three children had a typical food consumer pattern (Table 13.2). The family's total income was 1,595 Norwegian *kroner* (NOK). Their total expenditure on food in the fiscal year 1912–1913 was 1,030 NOK. But they spent only 118 NOK for groceries in the general store. Of this 74.63 NOK went for coffee, 55.20 for sugar (brown sugar lumps and regular sugar), 0.43 NOK on candy and 0.20 NOK for cocoa. They did not buy chocolate! Perhaps the children in this family had only tasted chocolate once or twice during their entire childhoods. Sugar was used for baking, tea and coffee, as well as to put on bread instead of jam. Some of the families purchased honey and syrup in small amounts. Sugar was part of the diet, but regular tooth brushing was not a usual habit. Thus, dental health was a big problem in the first part of the 1900s; not least, the children had problems with tooth decay because of improper diet and poor oral hygiene. Problems with dental care could also result in problems for ones finances.

In Drammen most people's diet was poor. But it did not mean starvation, only little variation. A worker born in Drammen around 1880 described his family's standard of living around 1900: 'The standard of living was not good at that time; I remember clearly that we ate lots of porridge, potatoes and herring. All the money that one could scrape together went almost entirely to food'.[37] In the beginning of the twentieth century, the situation was probably much the same in many working-class families in Drammen. Household accounts do not give the full picture of how working-class people were able to feed their families and get food on the table every day. We know it was common to go fishing in the river or in the fjord, or to grow potatoes, vegetables and fruit in the garden. People in Drammen also kept a family pig, rabbits or hens. Hans Johansen, with his wife Amagda, wrote their childhood memories and presented them to the Norwegian Folk Museum in the 1950s.[38] Hans sometimes wrote for a local newspaper as well. He described how his family ran a successful food production business at 'Halvorstua', their home, a small house or cottage in Drammen. The Johansen family was concerned about whether it was profitable to raise chickens. Having hens meant, of course, eggs in addition to chickens to cook in one's own kitchen as well as to sell at Bragernes Square. On 23 February 1914, Hans wrote an article in the local newspaper *Fremtiden*, where he described the expenditures and income obtained from raising chickens in his garden during the calendar year 1913. Though it cost money to purchase chickens, feed them and build their roosts, the business was in the black. Twenty-two young chickens were sold for a crown piece at Bragernes Square. Also, twelve older hens were slaughtered in the autumn, and the family earned 34 crowns from selling the meat. Furthermore the chickens at Halvorstua laid 1,650 eggs during the year. This resulted in an income of 132 crowns. After expenses were deducted, the family was left with a net income of 73 crowns from this activity, and they had extra eggs in their diet as well. 'The wife', that is, Amagda Johansen, told her husband to say that there is much joy to be had in raising chickens. She believed this kind of work was better than the useless Hardanger Sewing and other things that so many women occupied their time with. At that time, just before World War I, there was also a need for major repairs at Halvorstua, where Hans Johansen's mother lived alone. Expenses for timber in 1912–1913 were covered by the family breeding a pig, which they later sold to slaughter so that their grandmother could get the materials she needed. It said nothing about who did the repairs, but there is probably little doubt that her adult sons carried out the work for her, among them Hans Johansen himself.[39]

ADDITIONAL EXPENSES

The tradition of free public schools for the common people in Norway goes back to the year 1739, when the King made confirmation compulsory; thus every child had to learn to read in order to understand the Bible and the Lutheran tradition.[40] Parents who could not afford textbooks for their children could turn to *Drammen's Poor Relief Fund* for help. Those who were deemed to be both worthy and needy received free books for their children; however, they had to be registered and labelled as one of 'Drammen's Poor'. Schoolbooks without the 'poor stamp' were a luxury in Drammen after 1900. In 1911, the Municipality of Drammen voted that all school children in Drammen should have free school supplies and books, and the problem of the 'poor stamp' in schoolbooks was brought to an end.

As can be seen from Table 13.2, the family of a municipal worker spent 212 Norwegian *kroner* on clothing and shoes. This was a large amount of money, much more than was spent on housing. This pattern was surprising in such a tight budget. His family was not the only one in Drammen that had relatively high costs for shoes, clothing and housing. Many sources indicate that people worried about clothing and shoes. During the winter the whole family needed solid shoes and warm clothing. When another worker from Drammen, born in 1882, was asked to describe his family home, he wrote,

> There was little or nothing in way of clothing or shoes. The youngest children wore hand-me-downs from the older children. I myself am one of those who had to use and wear clothes and shoes after my older brothers. I was in fact the youngest of 6 children. The first new suit I received was for my confirmation, and it cost 17,—*kroner*. A pair of leather shoes for 6,—*kroner*. Yet, at the time the joy was in getting something new, even if it was rough and simple; the joy was greater than those today who now receive silk and designer clothes.[41]

The families who had kept household budgets were not given to drink, nor could they have been heavy smokers, either. In 1912–1913, nine of the twelve families listed tobacco costs, but this came to only two or three *kroner* a year. In 1927–1928, the fifteen families from Drammen that kept records used, on average, about fifty *kroner* for alcohol. Those who were recruited to keep household accounts in these two periods were 'model families', who were more economical than most, and they were not afraid to show off where their money went. Drunkards, or also those with wild or impulsive lifestyles did not maintain household accounts (see Figure 13.2). Several who tried had to give up. Therefore, it becomes difficult to argue that working-class families before and after World War I used to spend little money for alcohol and tobacco, as the numbers in the household accounts seem to indicate, since the data represents 'thrifty' and 'responsible' families.

Drammen's locally produced beer from Aass Brewery was very popular, though misuse of alcohol damaged many working-class families. Prohibition in Norway lasted from 1916 to 1927, but beer was allowed to be produced and sold.

Figure 13.2 To spend money on beer was a male privilege? Eiker Arkiv, Norway.

At the beginning of the twentieth century, every additional expense was burdensome to working families. A worker's wages did not cover much more than daily living expenses. Drammen Electric Court AS established the Drammen Tram Company, not a tram on rails, but electric powered trolley buses with an antenna on the roof, in 1909. It was one of the first of its kind in Norway (the word 'tram'—*trikk*—was used as an abbreviation for electric transportation). Despite the train and trams, working families did not travel far, not for holidays nor day trips with local trams. Tram tickets cost a few cents, but these costs did not appear in most household accounts (see Figure 13.3). Transportation costs appeared to be incredibly low for the families in the study. The municipal worker and his family, for example, spent 0.60 crowns on the tram in 1912–1913 and nothing for out-of-town travel that year.[42]

As can be seen from the municipal workers' family budget, very little money was spent on recreation and travelling. Workers' memoirs often mention that young people did not have money for cinema, theatre and other cultural activities that went on in the town. People worked long hours, twelve hours a day, as late as in the 1890s and the first years of the twentieth century. The eight-hour workday came into law in 1918, and it wasn't until 1920 that industrial workers had a legal right to take a holiday for one or two weeks a year.[43] Young people longed to have some recreation, but this was expensive. One older worker from Drammen wrote in 1950 about this

Figure 13.3 Strømsø torg: To be able to buy tickets for the 'tram' was considered a luxury. Drammen was a pioneer when the trolleybus company was established in 1909; however, working-class families usually walked around the town. Eiker Arkiv, Norway.

youth in Drammen just after 1900: 'For young people at that time there was not so much to choose from regarding entertainment or leisure time activities. Admittedly, we had the town Drammen to go to on Sundays, but everything there cost money'.[44] And another explained:

> It was important to use one's leisure time on something that did not cost money. Thus it was nice to have the Drammen Recreation Area. Many talked about trips to the woods. Otherwise, recreational activities depended on the seasons of course. In the summer, leisure activities consisted in rowing down the river and in the bay, and we hear, in the winter there was ice-skating and skiing.[45]

FINAL REMARKS

Norwegian wage earners experienced remarkable rises in purchasing power between 1850 and 1920, and statistical material suggests the working classes benefitted the most. However, in this case study of the town of Drammen, household budgets show that this did not lead to luxury consumption or the opportunity for saving money for sickness and old age. Food made up fifty to seventy per cent of their household expenditures, even when the family was careful: baking their own bread, fishing in the river and fjord and collecting berries in the woods. People did not starve, but the diet was meagre and marked by very little variation. To have plenty of milk for the children was considered a luxury. Household accounts and collections of labourers' reminiscences give little direct information on how family members, husband and wife, negotiated the use of the families' food resources. In Norway the norm was for husband and wife to eat together. The wife did not serve at the table while her husband was eating. She sat down with him. Still one must assume that the male head of household was given priority at the table. He was in control of the money in the family, worked twelve-hour shifts and had to eat more than the wife and the children. In the beginning of the nineteenth century, smoking and drinking were male habits, so non-essential items in the household budget, such as tobacco and alcohol, were in many cases reserved for men only.

The climatic situation with a long, cold and dark winter forced people in Drammen to spend a relatively high percentage of their income on clothing, footwear, lighting and heating. Siblings used each other's clothes and shoes, and everything was worn out. Housewives made important contributions to the family economy in stretching the clothing budget. Women knitted and sewed clothes for themselves and the children, but the man in the house needed a suit for Sunday and for work. He had to buy clothes, whether new or second hand. Ready-made clothing was a real luxury, especially for women and children. Surprisingly, little money was spent on housing. Working-class families in Drammen lived in crowded apartments. They must have had problems in paying the weekly or monthly rent, since it was not unusual to take in lodgers in just a two-room apartment. Lodgers paid for both housing and food. The housewife had to do the lodger's washing too, and the family lost their privacy. Working-class families in Drammen had hardly any money to use for transport and recreation. The household budgets from Drammen and other Norwegian towns during 1912–1913 indicate that even though wages improved, workers could spend very little on luxuries. In the early twentieth century, people in Drammen and other Norwegian towns had just started to rise out of deep poverty. They had just started on their way to welfare and social security. The conclusion is that consumer goods and a little everyday luxury were very difficult to obtain. Wives were economically dependent. Together with hard-working and sober husbands, they tried hard not only to make ends meet, but also to secure for the household a little everyday luxury and money for great occasions.

NOTES

1 Ida Zweiniger-Bargielowska, 'Living Standards and Consumption', in *A Companion to Contemporary Britain, 1939–2000*, ed. Paul Addison and Harriet Jones (Oxford: Blackwell Publishing, 2005), 228–41. See also the introduction to this volume.

2 This article is based on the author's monograph published in 2011, when the town of Drammen celebrated its 200th anniversary: Hanne Marie Johansen, *Slik levde de da. Familie- og hverdagsliv i Drammen gjennom 200 år* (Oslo: Spartacus, 2011), 221–40.

3 Gro Hagemann, 'Del III. De stummes leir?', in *Med kjønnsperspektiv på norsk historie*, ed. Ida Blom and Sølvi Sogner (Oslo: Cappelen Akademiske forlag, 2005), 179–85.

4 Hilde Sandvik, 'Kapittel 3; Det økonomiske fellesskapet,' in *I gode og vonde dagar. Familielivet i Noreg frå reformasjonen til vår tid* (Oslo: Det Norske Samlaget, 2003), 107.

5 Ibid.

6 *Husholdningsregnskaper ført av endel mindre bemidlede familier i Kristiania, Bergen, Trondhjem, Drammen, Kristianssand og Hamar i aaret 1912/13*. Spesialstudier IV, [Domestic (household) accounts from lower income families in Kristiania, Bergen, Trondhjem, Kristiansand and Hamar in 1912–1913. Special studies. IV] (Kristiania: Kristiania kommunes statistiske kontor, 1915). Tabell 3, 84–93.

7 Kristianias kommunes statistiske kontor. *Husholdningsregnskaper ført af en del mindre bemidlede familier i Kristiania, Bergen, Trondhjem, Drammen, Kristiansand og Hamar i Aaret 1912–1913* (1915, Kristiania); *Husholdningsregnskap Septembe. 1918–September 1919*. Norges Offisielle Statistikk, rekke VII, nr. 13.

8 Norwegian historian Edvard Bull collected workers' memories in the 1950s. This made him a pioneering researcher in Norwegian social history and in the history of the working classes. His program was to study 'history from below'. About his use of oral sources and research program, see, for example, Edvard Bull, *Arbeidsfolk forteller: Fra papirindustrien* (Oslo: Tiden, 1953).

9 Ola Honningdal Grytten and Kjell Bjoern Minde, 'The Demand for Consumer Goods in the Modernization of the Norwegian Economy, 1850–1920', *Scandinavian Economic History Review* 46 (1998): 49–54.

10 Fritz Hodne, Ole Grytten and Joerund Alme, 'Norwegian Real Wages: Trends in Prices and Wages, 1850–1950', in *Labour's Reward: Real Wages and Economic Change in Nineteenth and Twentieth Century Europe*, ed. Peter Scholliers and Vera Zamagni (London: Aldershot, 1995), 63.

11 Rolf Danielsen, Stale Dyrvik, Tore Gronlie, Knut Helie and Edgar Hovland, *Norway: A History from the Vikings to Our Own Times* (Oslo: Scandinavian University Press, 1995), 316–17.

12 Grytten and Bjoern Minde, 'The Demand for Consumer Goods', 52. For an overview of the history of Norwegian women in domestic service, see Sølvi Sogner and Kari Telste, *Ut og søkje teneste. Historia om tenestejentene* (Oslo: Det Norske Samlaget, 2005).

13 The real wages for groups of industrial workers increased up to 250 per cent between 1850 and 1920 and doubled between 1890 and 1920. Hodne, Grytten and Alme, 'Norwegian Real Wages'. See also Norges Offentlige Statistikk (NOU), Statistisk årbok 1880–1921 [Statistics Norway, 1881–1921].

14 Grytten and Bjoern Minde, 'The Demand for Consumer Goods', 50.

15 To understand the historic use of the terms 'survival society' and 'consumer society', see, for example, Hans Chr. Johansen, 'Food Consumption in the Pre-industrial Nordic Societies', *Scandinavian Economic History Review* 46 (1998): 11–23.

16 See Sandvik, Det økonomiske fellesskapet.

17 Nestlé started a factory abroad for the first time in 1898, and it was in Norway. Jean Heer, *World Events 1866–1966: The First Hundred Years of Nestlé* (Zurich: Vevey Nestlè, 1991).

18 Danielsen et al., *Norway: A History*, 316–17.
19 Ibid., 271–96, 316–18.
20 For example, in 1996–1997 Statistics Norway found Norwegian households on average used thirteen per cent of yearly income food. See Statistisk Årbok 2000. Tabell 2020. Utgifter pr. Husholdning pr år, etter vare- og tjenestegruppe.
21 Grytten and Bjoern Minde, 'The Demand for Consumer Goods', 42–58.
22 The name of the Norwegian capital was spelled Christiania till 1897 and then Kristiania. The name of the city was changed to Oslo in 1925, the original medieval name.
23 Johansen, *Slik levde de da*, 221–40.
24 Øyvind Bjørnson and Inger Elisabeth Haavet, *Langsomt ble landet et velferdssamfunn: Trygdens historie 1894–1994* (Oslo: Ad notam Gyldendal, 1994).
25 See for example Hodne, Grytten and Alme, 'Norwegian Real Wages', 72.
26 NOS [Statistics Norway] VII nr 98. *Folketellingen i Norge. 1920*. Syvende hefte. Boligstatistikken, s. 19.
27 Norsk folkemuseum. Arbeiderminner. Treforedlingsindustrien. [Norwegian Folk Museum. Workers memories. Pulp and Paper Industry, hereafter cited as NFM], Sigurd Johansen, born in 1870.
28 NFM, Johannes Halvorsen, born in 1874.
29 Johansen, *Slik levde de da*, 241–84.
30 Ibid.
31 NFM, various entries.
32 Johansen, *Slik levde de da*, 257.
33 Ibid., 248–54.
34 The woman was Christiane Milborg, maiden name Solberg. Her relative, Sven Adolf Solberg, collected family documents, among them Christiane's childhood memories: Sven A. Solberg, *Kort familiekrønike og barndoms- og ungdomserindringer* (Oslo: Privat forlag, 1974), 56–93.
35 Husholdningsregnskaper ført av endel mindre bemidlede familier, 1915. Tabell 3, 84–93.
36 See for example, Norges Offisielle Statistikk VIII. 103. Husholdningsregnskap 1927–1928. (Oslo, Det Statistiske Centralbyrå [Statistics Norway], 1929). Table 3, 102–13.
37 NFM, Jens Johannessen, born in 1887.
38 NFM, Hans Johansen, born in 1887. See also Amagda and Hans Johansen, *De er med oss. Barndomsminner* (Oslo: Privat forlag, 1967), 45.
39 Hans Johansen, 'Lønner det sig at ha høns?', *Fremtiden*, 23 February 1914.
40 Danielsen, et al., *Norway; A History*, 189.
41 NFM, Jens Johannessen, born in 1887.
42 Husholdningsregnskaper ført av endel mindre bemidlede familier, 1915. Tabell 3, 84–93.
43 Bjørnson and Haavet, *Langsomt ble landet et velferdssamfunn*.
44 NFM, Torleif Andresen, born in 1888.
45 NFM, Oscar Svendsen, born in 1879.

Afterword

Gender, Luxury and Towns Revisited

Anne Montenach, Marjo Kaartinen and Deborah Simonton

'But what is this luxury that we so infallibly attribute to so many objects?'[1] This book, which is the product of a collaborative network studying gender in the European town, has demonstrated that luxury, far from being only a concept—as eighteenth-century debates might make us believe—was also a very concrete, individual and universal experience shared by many men and women in eighteenth- and nineteenth-century urban, and even rural, Europe.[2] As a social and historical construct, luxury cannot be universally or simply defined as an absolute category, since its meaning changes over time, place, political or cultural context, social groups or individuals. However, these chapters have contributed to enriching and developing the complexity of how luxury is defined and perceived, whether they have taken into account material objects or social behaviours. Moreover, they have shown that luxury can be usefully employed as a heuristic tool in order to analyse the operation of gender within eighteenth- and nineteenth-century European urban life.

Among the numerous characteristics that can define luxury, the authors in this book have scrutinised some more specifically, such as exoticism, creativity, quality and rarity. Along with other goods originally imported from the East and afterwards manufactured in Europe, calicos have offered an emblematic example of the market's segmentation between luxury, semi-luxury or even popular goods which benefited, among other attractive qualities, from the prestige conferred by their real or supposed foreignness.[3] Tea, coffee or sugar traded into Denmark from overseas in the late eighteenth century and peddled in Copenhagen streets, as well as Indian textiles displayed at a Scottish international exhibition one century later, presented similar characteristics. But exoticism could also refer to a chimerical vision of 'traditional' rural life, as in the latter case and within the particular context of rapid urbanisation and industrial modernisation. In this sense, luxury has something to do with illusion or, more precisely, with the recreation of the past, and for recent or experienced urban citizens, the recreation of a more or less familiar kind of 'otherness'.

Creation, imagination and invention were also constitutive of the skills of eighteenth-century milliners, who were at the forefront of setting fashion and fostering luxury in European medium-sized or large towns of the time, like Aberdeen; style and 'modishness' thus played a crucial role in their advertising strategies. As shown, for instance in the case of Grenoble, millinery shops represented only a small part of the various distributive circuits which contributed to the supply of luxury or semi-luxury goods, from itinerant merchant and pedlars to lively second-hand and black markets facilitating the social redistribution of objects. Fashion accelerated these circulations by promoting the obsolescence of things.[4] From that perspective, up-to-date information and specialised knowledge about the best place to shop, the right thing to buy or good suppliers to trust were decisive factors to achieve an appropriate consumption, as shown by the cases of the eighteenth-century Swedish diplomats, English aristocrats and early nineteenth-century Finnish bourgeoisie. In this sense, changes in commercialization and consumerism went hand in hand throughout the two hundred years under scrutiny, with a developing '*économie des connaisseurs*' [economy of connoisseurs], who relied on a specific knowledge about luxury and the transmission of purchasing skills.[5]

Due to the acceleration and social diffusion of consumption, some goods, such as shawls, which a hundred years ago were the prerogative of elite women, became widely diffused among female peasants at the end of the nineteenth century. This 'democratisation of luxury'—an expression which sounds like an oxymoron—encouraged the recreation or the invention of new criteria, allowing the elite to distinguish themselves from the working classes.[6] High quality—which only a handful of 'initiated' people were able to identify—was one of these criteria, as demonstrated for example by the emblematic case of the Shetland bridal shawls displayed at the Edinburgh International Exhibition in 1886, which were so delicate that the best could pass through a wedding ring. Rarity, or indeed, uniqueness, was another distinctive criterion of luxury: Work of art produced by female artists in the London West End in the latter half of the nineteenth century offer a perfect illustration of these kinds of goods, appealing to the taste of an educated *amateur*, while the neighbourhood itself offered these female painters an inviting and stimulating environment—in other words, a luxurious space.

As shown by this brief overview, luxury goods integrated different sorts of value, which this book, as others before it, cannot discuss exhaustively. From this point of view, it was more fruitful—as the authors of these chapters have done—to consider luxury not as a 'special class of things' but instead, following Appadurai's suggestion, as a special 'register' of consumption.[7] Therefore, a major result of this book is to have illuminated how not only consumption but also production and marketing of luxury goods challenged gender roles. Beyond the stereotypical distinction between the producing man and the consuming woman, which has long been contested, the alleged differences between male and female consumption practices still deserved closer examination.[8] Case studies of the Hackmans, a Finnish merchant family in Vyborg, or of Edward and Mary Leigh, successive owners of

Stoneleigh Abbey in Warwickshire, have challenged the classical stereotypes of gender-based consumption by highlighting the flexibility and complexities of consumption patterns, according to the position of an individual in the household or reflecting the stage of his or her life. Whereas the wealthy widow Marie Hackman, like the independent landowner Mary Leigh, conformed to a 'masculine' model in her purchases, in eighteenth-century Barcelona *petimetre* and *petimetra* were perceived as 'crazed' for fashion and superfluous goods; moreover, the same object, such as a golden watch, could be equally praised by urban aristocratic women and by elite men in rural Catalan areas.

More generally, as shown by the different approaches developed in these chapters—whether individual or quantitative—room for *manœuvre* as consumers, as well as producers and distributors of luxury goods, could vary considerably across time and place and according to age, marital status or social position: Catalan married women, for instance, had very little autonomy in spending the family income, whereas they were the shop windows of their husband's status. Here the concept of agency, which has been widely discussed in a previous book from the Gender in the European Town network, appears as a pertinent tool to analyse the relationship between gender, luxury and town.[9] If we look at the process of production, several chapters have analysed in detail how in eighteenth-century towns significant changes in female fashion created opportunities for women, despite their lower legal status, to play a much larger role as makers, agents and subjects of fashion. Whether in the legal trade of millinery, or in the underground economy of calicos during the French prohibition, women developed businesses and partnerships, challenging the traditional male monopoly in the clothing industry; from this point view the 'frivolity' they were incarnating was 'subversive' in multiple ways.[10] One of these ways was to bypass royal laws by flouting the embargo to satisfy all categories of clients: an attitude that was also observed among the Swedish aristocracy or the Finnish merchants, for whom taste for fashion or an aristocratic lifestyle made it *necessary* to transgress sumptuary and protectionist legislation. Some of the women mentioned above, who were engaged in fashion trades, could become very successful and achieve the same visibility as men on the urban stage, as did Copenhagen business women engaged in the risky but lucrative overseas luxury trade: Their experience as active merchants demonstrates that being at the top of the economic structure with a large and dynamic capital enterprise was part of the *possible*, even in a female life trajectory.

Other chapters in this book have explored, more or less explicitly, the agency of the male or female consumer and the ways in which consumption 'choices' were both the result of social constraints and a key element in the construction of individuals' or groups' identity, especially when they related to socially highly valued items such as luxuries.[11] In early twentieth Norway, household budgets have shown that this agency was very limited among working-class families, especially mothers, unless we consider that eating less to offer her children or husband a little treat—such as a Christmas orange or some butter—can still be considered as a form of agency. Far away from this survival society and at the opposite end of the social scale, Edward Leigh's consumption patterns reveal the multifaceted personality of a young educated aristocrat. Not surprisingly, Edward, fifth Lord Leigh, spent handsome sums on building, decorating and furnishing his impressive residence (an important aspect of elite male spending), but was relatively uninterested, on the other hand, in conforming to the stereotype of polite gentleman, with its concern for display and sociability. His sister Mary, as well as the French princess of blood Marie Fortunée d'Este, developed more complex consumption practices during their life-courses: In both cases, their agency as independent female buyers was in fact tempered by the social and familial responsibilities attached to their aristocratic status.

The case of the Hungarian gala dress, the *díszmagyar*, opportunely and ultimately reminds us that things themselves, as suggested by anthropologists, not only have a 'social life' but also an agency, which enables them to produce changes through their material, social or symbolic proprieties.[12] The luxury of this festive garment served, on one hand, to foster the construction of Hungarian aristocratic families' self-image and the legitimisation of their social position. From that perspective, the *díszmagyar* was not fundamentally different from other items of clothing worn by the eighteenth- and nineteenth-century European elite—except the fact that its colours distinguished it from the black and white 'masculine' fashion prevailing in other European courts at the same time. On the other hand, the *díszmagyar* was much more than a simple tool in symbolic rituals and in the urban performance of the aristocracy. By referring back to a traditional Hungarian item of clothing, it contributed to the struggle for independence from the Habsburg monarchy by communicating the separate national identity of the Hungarian aristocracy *vis-à-vis* the Habsburg court.

Finally, the book has given us access to the ways in which gender, town and luxury interacted on different scales and in various national or local contexts, from the already well-studied French and British kingdoms to less well-known parts of Central, Mediterranean or Scandinavian Europe. Men and women who were engaged in many aspects of the luxury trade and consumption in eighteenth- and nineteenth-century European towns not only benefited from their urban setting, but also played a crucial role in the transformation of cities: Women artists thus contributed to the feminisation of the London West End, while using the resources of the neighbourhood to move beyond the traditional confines of their sort; the flow of commerce and information helped eighteenth-century La Rochelle milliners, Grenoble pedlars or Copenhagen female entrepreneurs to engage in various forms of luxury trades which shaped the urban commercial landscape. On the other hand, the choices of Marie Fortunée d'Este contributed to defining the geography of luxury shops and suppliers in eighteenth-century Paris; one hundred years later, the consumption practices of the Hungarian aristocratic families influenced the formation of the 'magnate tailors' group in Budapest. Chapters have also explored the dynamic relationship created between town and country by the exchange and circulation of luxury goods, and thus challenged any simple dichotomy of urban supply and rural consumption—a quite recent research field that still deserves further exploration. If capital cities such as London and Paris clearly dominated the supply system and dictated fashion, smaller towns and the countryside offered a variety of producing and consuming patterns, according less to their urban or rural character than to their global environment.[13] The proximity of Stoneleigh Abbey thus stimulated artisans' work in towns and villages of Warwickshire, while luxury or semi-luxury goods progressively penetrated urban surroundings in eighteenth-century Dauphiné or Catalonia.

By interrogating together the role of gender and the modern town as crucial sites in the creation and circulation of luxury during a critical period of historical change, these chapters have filled a gap in the rich historiography of consumption and added to our knowledge of urban European societies and economies. This book has also opened new and stimulating fields of research in encouraging us to challenge stereotypes defining *a priori* male and female roles as producers or consumers, to look beyond any simple dichotomy of tradition and modernity, town and country, legal and illicit commerce, and to rethink our tendency to categorise.

NOTES

1 'Mais qu'est-ce que ce luxe que nous attribuons si infailliblement à tant d'objets?', Denis Diderot, 'Encyclopédie', in *Œuvres de Denis Diderot. Dictionnaire encyclopédique*, vol. 3 (Paris: J.L.J. Brière, 1821), 243. English quotation from Maxine Berg and Elisabeth Eger, 'The Rise and Fall of the Luxury Debates', in *Luxury in the Eighteenth Century: Debates, Desires and Delectable Goods*, ed. Maxine Berg and Elisabeth Eger (Basingstoke: Palgrave Macmillan, 2003), 11.

2 Pierre Rétat, 'Luxe', *XVIIIe siècle* 26 (1994): 79–88.

3 Gilles Lipovetsky, *The Empire of Fashion: Dressing Modern Democracy* (Princeton, NJ: Princeton University Press, 1994); Georg Simmel, 'Fashion', *International Quarterly* 10 (1904): 136, quoted by Beverly Lemire and Giorgio Riello, 'East & West: Textiles and Fashion in Early Modern Europe', *Journal of Social History* 41 (2008): 887–916. On the adaptation of Asian commodities to the European consumer's taste, see Maxine Berg, 'Manufacturing the Orient. Asian Commodities and European Industries', in *Prodotti e tecniche d'oltremare nelle economie europee secc. XIII–XVIII*, ed. Simonetta Cavaciocchi (Florence: Le Monnier, 1998), 385–419.

4 Daniel Roche, 'Between a Moral Economy and a Consumer Economy: Clothes and their Function in the Seventeenth and Eighteenth Centuries', in *Luxury Trades and Consumerism in Ancien Régime Paris*, ed. Robert Fox and Anthony Turner (Aldershot: Ashgate, 1998), 221.

5 Jean-Yves Grenier, 'Une économie de l'identification', in *La qualité des produits en France (XVIIIe–XIXe siècles)*, ed. Alessandro Stanziani (Paris: Belin, 2003), 25–54; Daniel Roche, 'Préface. La magie du luxe. Réflexions sur

les luxes et leur internationalisation', in *Luxes et internationalisation (XVIe–XIXe siècles)*, ed. Nadège Sougy (Neuchâtel: Editions Alphil-Presses universitaires suisses, 2013), 7–18.

6 Patrick Verley, 'Essor et déclin des industries de luxe et de demi-luxe au XIXe siècle', in *Le luxe en France du siècle des Lumières à nos jours*, ed. Jacques Marseille (Paris: Association pour le développement de l'histoire économique, 1999), 107–23.

7 Arjun Appadurai, 'Introduction: Commodities and the Politics of Value', in *The Social Life of Things*, ed. Arjun Appadurai (Cambridge: Cambridge University Press, 1986), 38.

8 Amanda Vickery, 'Women and the World of Goods: A Lancashire Consumer and Her Possessions, 1751–1781', in *Consumption and the World of Goods*, ed. John Brewer and Roy Porter (London: Routledge, 1993), 274–301; Maxine Berg, *Luxury and Pleasure in Eighteenth-Century Britain* (Oxford: Oxford University Press, 2005), 234–37; Beverly Lemire, *The Business of Everyday Life: Gender, Practice and Social Politics in England* (Manchester: Manchester University Press, 2005), 127.

9 Deborah Simonton and Anne Montenach, eds, *Female Agency in the Urban Economy: Gender in European Towns, 1640–1830* (New York: Routledge, 2013).

10 Roche, 'Between a Moral Economy', 221.

11 Mary Douglas and Baron Isherwood, *The Worlds of Goods: Toward an Anthropology of Consumption* (New York: Basic Books, 1979); Maxine Berg, 'Luxury, the Luxury Trades, and the Roots of Industrial Growth: A Global Perspective', in *The Oxford Handbook of the History of Consumption*, ed. Frank Trentmann (Oxford: Oxford University Press, 2012), 173–91.

12 Appadurai, *The Social Life of Things*; Alfred Gell, *Art and Agency: An Anthropological Theory* (Oxford: Clarendon Press, 1998); Beverly Lemire, 'Le goût du coton: culture matérielle, politique et consommation dans le Japon des Tokugawa et l'Angleterre moderne', *Revue d'histoire moderne et contemporaine* 60 (2013): 71–105.

13 Dominique Margairaz, 'City and Country: Home, Possessions, and Diet, Western Europe 1600–1800', in *The Oxford Handbook of the History of Consumption*, 192–210; Belén Moreno Claverías, 'Lugar de residencia y pautas de consumo: El penedes y Barcelona, 1770–1790', *Revista de Historia Industrial*, 15 (2006): 139–66.

Contributors

Marjo Kaartinen is a professor of cultural history at the University of Turku. She is also the director of the Turku Centre for Medieval and Early Modern Studies. She is the author of *Religious Life and English Culture in the Reformation* (2002), and was until 2013 editor-in-chief of *Cultural History*, the journal of the International Society for Cultural History published by Edinburgh University Press. She has published several monographs in Finnish, and lately has focused on the issues of gender, space and the body. Her book, *Breast Cancer in the Eighteenth Century,* was published in 2013 by Pickering and Chatto.

Anne Montenach is an associate professor of early modern history at Aix-Marseille University, CNRS, UMR 7303 TELEMME (13094 Aix-en-Provence, France). In Aix, she is co-responsible for a research group on Women and Gender History located at the Maison Méditerranéenne des Sciences de l'Homme. Her PhD was defended at the European University Institute in Florence and published as *L'économie du quotidien. Espaces et pratiques du commerce alimentaire à Lyon au XVIIe siècle* (2009). Following research on the early modern urban economy with a special emphasis on informal circulations and exchange, she has turned to working on female economic territories in early modern Europe, and is identifying how women were pivotal to urban economies, both illicit and legitimate. She is currently working on a monograph on this topic and has published several articles in different European journals. She has co-edited with Deborah Simonton a collection of essays, *Gender in the European Town: Female Agency in the Urban Economy, 1640–1830* (2013).

Deborah Simonton is an associate professor of British history at the University of Southern Denmark and visiting professor at the University of Turku, and leads the Gender in the European Town Network. Her research interests lie in issues of gender, work and education in the eighteenth century and the development of gender and urban identity in Europe. She edited *Female Agency in the Urban Economy: Gender* *in European Towns, 1640–1830* (2013) with Anne Montenach, and her book, *Women in European Culture and Society, Gender, Skill and Identity,* was published in January 2011, and the companion *Sourcebook* was published in November 2013. Other publications include *The Routledge History of Women in Modern Europe* (2006), *A History of European Women's Work, 1700 to the Present* (1998), *Gender in Scottish History* (2006) (co-editor), *Women in Eighteenth-Century Scotland* (2013) (co-editor) and articles on eighteenth-century towns, gender, childhood and work.

Aurélie Chatenet-Calyste is an associate professor in Early Modern History, University of Lorraine, and fellow of the CRULH. In 2010 she defended a PhD 'Une consommation aristocratique et féminine à la fin du XVIIIe siècle: Marie-Fortunée d'Este (1731–1803)' (*Une consommation aristocratique fin de siècle: Marie-Fortunée d'Este, princesse de Conti*, Limoges, Presses Universitaires de Limoges, 2013). She continues to research on early modern aristocratic consumption and on the princesses of blood in the eighteenth century. She also works on female body spending and has published several articles on this topic.

Carol Gold retired as Arthur T. Fathauer Professor of History from the University of Alaska Fairbanks in 2011. She received her PhD in modern European history from the University of Wisconsin-Madison in 1975 and has taught at the Universities of Minnesota, Odense (Denmark) and Alaska. Specializing in eighteenth- and nineteenth-century Danish history, she has published two books in this field—*Educating Middle Class Daughters: Private Girls Schools in Copenhagen, 1790–1820* (1996) and *Danish Cookbooks: Domesticity and National Identity, 1616–1901* (2007). The latter won an award from Gourmand for Best Culinary History in 2007. Gold's current research deals with women in pre-industrial Copenhagen who earned money on their own. Using traditional archival sources and official records, she has identified approximately 3,000 women from roughly 1740 to 1830 who had official interaction with government authorities in their own names. Gold currently lives in Alaska, Hawai'i and Copenhagen.

Ulla Ijäs is a member of the network Gender in the European Town. She is a PhD student in Finnish History in the School of History, Culture and Arts Studies at the University of Turku, Finland. In 2009, she graduated (MA in History) at the Department of History and Philosophy at the University of Tampere, Finland. In her thesis she is focusing on a merchant widow called Marie Hackman (1776–1865), her places of consumption and female agency. Ijäs's interests are the gender history and history of Old Finland (eastern Finland, Karelia) in the eighteenth and nineteenth centuries.

Johanna Ilmakunnas is a postdoctoral research fellow at the University of Helsinki and visiting research fellow at the University of Northampton. She gained her PhD from the University of Helsinki in 2009, and her research has concerned aristocracy, elites, material culture, consumption, credit and lifestyle in eighteenth-century Sweden and France. Her publications include a major study of the lifestyle of Swedish eighteenth-century aristocracy: *Ett ståndsmässigt liv: Familjen von Fersens livsstil på 1700-talet* (2012) and 'Aristocratic Townhouse as Urban Space: The Fersen Palace in Eighteenth-Century Stockholm' in *Gendering Spaces in Early Modern Towns, 1700–1914*, edited by Marjo Kaartinen and Elaine Chalus (2014). In 2012 she won an award from the Swedish Academy for her work on eighteenth-century Sweden. Ilmakunnas's current research project, 'Diligent aristocracy: Nobility, Service and Work in Sweden, from the Great Northern War to the Napoleonic Wars' is funded by the Academy of Finland.

Hanne Marie Johansen is an associate professor, Centre for Women's and Gender Research (SKOK), and research librarian in History, University of Bergen. Dr Johansen's main research background is in Norwegian and Nordic history: gender history, family history and urban history. Her doctorate thesis examined the history of divorce in Denmark-Norway, from the reformation to 1900. In 2011 she published a monograph on the urban history of Drammen 1811–2011, focusing on everyday life and family networks within the social elite, the middle classes and the working classes. In a textbook on family history, she published 'Family and care', *I gode og vonde dagar. Familiehistorie i Norge 1500–2000.* (Oslo: Det Norske Samlaget, 2003). She publishes both in Norwegian and English. in *Scandinavian Journal of History*, Vol. 29, No. 3–4, 2004. Johansen is a member of the network Gender in the European Town. She is involved in a research project initiated by Dr Therese Andrews, Nordland Research Institute: 'Infant feeding, Policy and Practice'. Ongoing research is directed towards the problems of gender and religion in Scandinavian society in the nineteenth century, including the emigration of religious dissenters, from Scandinavia to the United States.

Kemille Moore is an associate professor of Art History at the University of North Carolina, Wilmington, and for the last ten years has been Dean of the University College responsible for the first-year experience at the University and 'Learning Communities'. Her PhD thesis was on 'The Revival of Artistic Lithography in England, 1890–1913' (University of Washington, 1990). Her teaching and research interests lie in late nineteenth-century European art history, primarily British printmaking and photography. Her current research projects include an examination of the print market during late Victorian London and the role of women in the etching revival in England and America. She has published *Quintet:*

Five Print Suites by Donald Furst (2000), and 'Lithography from c. 1875 to the 1920s', in *British Printmakers 1855–1955*, edited by Robin Garton (1992).

Belen Moreno Claverías is a Doctor of History (2002) from the European University Institute (Florence), and she was a postdoctoral researcher (2003–2004) at the École des Hautes Etudes en Sciences Sociales (Paris). Since 2004, she has been a professor of Economic History at the Universidad Autónoma de Madrid (Spain). She has worked on the consumption patterns in pre-industrial Catalonia, especially on the introduction of new objects in the rural areas and the rise of social inequality between 1670 and 1790. In relation to this line of research, she has also investigated the social differentiation among the peasants taking into account other indicators, apart from consumption, such as the ways to accede to the land and the different agrarian contracts that existed in this period. Her research currently focuses on the figure of the apprentice in eighteenth-century Catalonia.

Stana Nenadic is a professor of Social and Cultural History at the University of Edinburgh. Her research is on the middle classes and elites since c. 1700 and material and visual cultures of the past. Recent publications include *Lairds and Luxury: the Highland Gentry in Eighteenth Century Scotland* (2007); as editor, *Scots in London in the Eighteenth Century* (2010); *Colouring the Nation: Scotland's Nineteenth-Century Printed Cotton Textiles* (2013) (with S. Tuckett). She is Principal Investigator for a current three-year research project, with funding from the Leverhulme Trust, titled 'Artisans and the Craft Economy in Scotland, c.1780–1914'.

Mark Rothery is a senior lecturer in Modern History at the University of Northampton. He has published widely in the area of landed elites and worked on various collaborative projects in the recent past, including a longitudinal study of the masculine identities of landed gentry men with Professor Henry French of the University of Exeter. This culminated in the publication of a monograph entitled *Man's Estate: Landed Gentry Masculinities 1660–1900* (2012). He is currently completing a project with Professor Jon Stobart of the University of Northampton on the consumption habits of the aristocracy entitled 'Consumption and the Country House'.

Zsuzsa Sidó is a PhD candidate in history at the Central European University in Budapest. She has received her BA degree in history and art history from the Babeç-Bolyai University, Cluj Napoca. Her MA thesis at CEU, entitled *The Symbolic Role of Hungarian Noble Architecture in the Late Nineteenth Century: A Case Study of the Andrássy and Károlyi Families' Country Houses (Betlér and Nagykároly)*, was awarded the Péter Hanák

Prize for the best MA thesis in 2010. Based on this research she published 'Ancestry in Stone and Brick: The Count Károlyi Family's Country Houses, with a Focus on Nagykároly' in *Centropa* 13, no. 2 (2013): 187–99. She has completed several courses on comparative urban history and has investigated the influence of aristocratic building activity in the modernization of Budapest; these findings were presented at international conferences. Her doctoral research focuses on the social-cultural history of nineteenth-century aristocracy, with a focus on aristocratic art patronage, country house culture and material culture.

Jon Stobart is a professor of History at the University of Northampton. His research interests encompass various aspects of retailing, consumption and material culture in eighteenth-century England. Recent projects include a study of the provincial grocery trade, published as *Sugar and Spice: Grocers and Groceries in Provincial England, 1650–1830* (2013), and a collection of essays on the textiles trade, soon to be published as *Selling Textiles in the Long Eighteenth Century: Comparative Perspectives from Western Europe* (2014; co-edited with Bruno Blondé). He is currently working on a major study of consumption and the English country house, which explores the complex relationships between supply networks, material culture, everyday life and elite identity in the eighteenth-century country house. Alongside this, he is continuing his long-standing interest in the second-hand trade and the reuse of goods within the home—see *Modernity and the Second-Hand Trade* (2010; co-edited with Ilja Van Damme).

Guide to Further Reading

Adburgham, Alison. *Shopping in Style, London from the Restoration to Edwardian Elegance*. London: Thames and Hudson, 1979.
———. *Shops and Shopping, 1800–1914: Where and in What Manner the Well-Dressed Englishwoman Bought Her Clothes*. London: Faber and Faber, 2012. First printed 1964.
Ago, Renata. 'Le genre de la consommation à l'époque moderne'. In *Genre, femmes, histoire en Europe*, edited by Anna Bellavitis and Nicole Edelman, 37–50. Paris: Presses universitaires de Paris Ouest, 2011.
Alexander, D. *Retailing in England During the Industrial Revolution*. London: Athlone Press, 1970.
Antonova, Katherine Pickering. *An Ordinary Marriage: The World of a Gentry Family in Provincial Russia*. Oxford: Oxford University Press, 2013.
Appadurai, Arjun, ed. *The Social Life of Things: Commodities in Cultural Perspective*. Cambridge: Cambridge University Press, 1986.
Assouly, Olivier, ed. *Le luxe: essais sur la fabricaion de l'ostentation*. Paris: Institut français de la mode, 2005.
Auslander, Leora. *Taste and Power: Furnishing Modern France*. Berkeley, CA: University of California, 1996.
Barker, Hannah. *The Business of Women: Female Enterprise and Urban Development in Northern England 1760–1830*. Oxford: Oxford University Press, 2006.
Barnes, Ruth, and Joanne B. Eicher, eds. *Dress and Gender: Making and Meaning in Cultural Contexts*. New York: Berg, 1992.
Barry, Jonathan, 'Consumers Passions—The Middle-Class In 18th-Century England'. *Historical Journal* 34 (1991): 207–16.
Beckett, John, and Catherine Smith. 'Urban Renaissance and Consumer Revolution in Nottingham, 1688–1750'. *Urban History* 27 (2000): 31–50.
Belfanti, Marco. *Civiltà della moda*. Bologne: Il Mulino, 2008.
Belfanti, Marco, and Fabio Giusberti. 'Clothing and Social Inequality in Early Modern Europe: Introductory Remarks'. *Continuity and Change* 15 (2000): 359–65.
Berg, Maxine. *Luxury and Pleasure in Eighteenth-Century Britain*. Oxford: Oxford University Press, 2005.
———. 'Manufacturing the Orient. Asian Commodities and European Industries'. In *Prodotti e tecniche d'oltremare nelle economie europee secc. XIII–XVIII*, edited by Simonetta Cavaciocchi, 385–419. Florence: Le Monnier, 1998.
Berg, Maxine, and Helen Clifford, eds. *Consumers and Luxury: Consumer Culture in Europe 1650–1850*. Manchester: Manchester University Press, 1999.
Berg, Maxine, and Elizabeth Eger, eds. *Luxury in the Eighteenth Century: Debates, Desires and Delectable Goods*. Basingstoke: Palgrave, 2003.

Bermingham, Ann, and John Brewer, eds. *The Consumption of Culture, 1600–1800: Image, Object, Text*. London: Routledge, 1997.

Berry, Christopher J. *The Idea of Luxury: A Conceptual and Historical Investigation*. Cambridge: Cambridge University Press, 1994.

Berry, Helen. 'Polite Consumption: Shopping in Eighteenth-Century England'. *Transactions of the Royal Historical Society* 12 (2002): 375–94.

Berry, Helen, and Jeremy Gregory, eds. *Creating and Consuming Culture in North-East England, 1660–1830*. Aldershot: Ashgate, 2004.

Bjoernson, Oeyvind, and Inger Elisabeth Haavet. *Langsomt ble landet et velferdssamfunn: Trygdens historie 1894–1994*. Oslo: Ad Notam Gyldendal, 1994.

Borsay, Peter. *The English Urban Renaissance: Culture and Society in the Provincial Town, 1660–1770*. Oxford: Oxford University Press, 1991.

Bourdieu, Pierre. *Distinction: A Social Critique of the Judgement of Taste*. Cambridge, MA: Harvard University Press, 1979.

Breward, Christopher. *The Culture of Fashion: A New History of Fashionable Dress*. Manchester: Manchester University Press, 1995.

———. *The Hidden Consumers: Masculinities, Fashion, and City Life, 1860–1914*. Manchester: Manchester University Press, 1999.

Brewer, John. *The Pleasures of the Imagination*. London: Harper Collins, 1997.

Brewer, John, and Roy Porter, eds. *Consumption and the World of Goods*. London: Routledge, 1993.

Brewer, John, and Frank Trentmann, eds. *Consuming Cultures, Global Perspectives: Historical Trajectories, Transnational Exchanges*. Oxford: Berg Publishers, 2006.

Briggs Asa, and Daniel Snowman, eds. *Fins De Siècle: How Centuries End, 1400–2000*. New Haven, CT: Yale University Press, 1996.

Bull, Edvard. *Arbeidsfolk forteller: Fra papirindustrien*. Oslo: Tiden, 1953.

Campbell, Kimberly Chrisman. 'The Face of Fashion: Milliners in Eighteenth-Century Visual Culture'. *British Society for Eighteenth-Century Studies Journal* 25 (2002): 157–71.

Carter, Philip. *Men and the Emergence of Polite Society: Britain 1660–1800*. Harlow: Longman, 2000.

Casteras, Susan, and Colleen Denney. *The Grosvenor Gallery: A Palace of Art in Victorian England*. New Haven and London: Yale University Press, 1996.

Cherry, Deborah. *Painting Women: Victorian Women Artists*. London and New York: Routledge, 1993.

Coquery, Natacha. 'La diffusion des biens à l'époque moderne. Une histoire connectée de la consommation'. *Histoire urbaine* 30 (2011): 5–20.

———. *L'hôtel aristocratique: le marché du luxe à Paris au XVIIIe siècle*. Paris: Publications de la Sorbonne, 1998.

———. *Tenir boutique à Paris au XVIIIe siècle. Luxe et demi-luxe*. Paris: Éditions du Comité des travaux historiques et scientifiques, 2012.

———. 'The Semi-Luxury Market, Shopkeepers and Social Diffusion: Marketing Chinoiseries in Eighteenth-Century Paris'. In *Fashioning Old and New. Changing Consumer Patterns in Western Europe (1650–1900)*, edited by Bruno Blondé, Natacha Coquery, Jon Stobart, and Ilja Van Damme, 121–31. Turnhout: Brepols, 2009.

Corfield, Penelope J. 'Walking the City Streets: The Urban Odyssey in Eighteenth-Century England'. *Journal of Urban History* 16 (1990): 132–74.

Corfield, Penelope J., and Serena Kelly, 'Giving Directions to the Town: The Early Town Directories'. *Urban History Yearbook* (1984): 22–34.

Corfield, Penny. 'Dress for Deference and Dissent: The Decline of Hat Honour'. *Costume* 23 (1989): 64–79.

Cowan, Alex, and Jill Steward, eds. *The City and the Senses: European Urban Culture from 1500*. Aldershot: Ashgate, 2006.

Cowan, Brian. 'What Was Masculine about the Public Sphere? Gender and the Coffee House Milieu in Post-Restoration England'. *History Workshop Journal* 51 (2001): 127–57.
Cox, Nancy. *The Complete Tradesman: A Study of Retailing, 1550–1820*. Burlington, VT: Ashgate, 2000.
Cross, Louisa. 'The Display and Trading of Fashionable Dress and Its Impact on Women in Scotland's Growing Urban Centres, c. 1780–1825'. In *Women in Eighteenth-Century Scotland, Intimate, Intellectual and Public Lives*, edited by Katie Barclay and Deborah Simonton, 233–52. Farnham: Ashgate, 2013.
Crossick, Geoffrey, ed. *The Artisan and the European Town, 1500–1900*. Aldershot: Scolar Press, 1997.
Crossick, Geoffrey, and Heinz-Gerhard Haupt, eds. *The Petite Bourgeoisie in Europe, 1780–1914, Enterprise, Family and Independence*. London: Routledge, 1995.
Crossick, Geoffrey, and Serge Jaumain, eds. *Cathedrals of Consumption: The European Department Store, 1850–1939*. Aldershot: Ashgate, 1999.
Crowston, Clare Haru. *Fabricating Women: The Seamstresses of Old Regime France, 1675–1791*. Durham, NC: Duke University Press, 2001.
Crowston, Clare. 'Women, Gender and Guilds in Early Modern Europe'. Supplement. *IRSH 53* (2008): 19–44.
Davies, Andrew. *Leisure, Gender and Poverty: Working-Class Culture in Salford and Manchester, 1900–1939*. Buckingham, UK: Open University Press, 1992.
Davis, Dorothy. *A History of Shopping*. London: Routledge & Kegan Paul, 1966.
D'Cruze, Shani. *A Pleasing Prospect. Social Change and Urban Culture in Eighteenth-Century Colchester*. Hatfield: University of Hertfordshire Press, 2008.
De Grazia, Victoria, and Ellen Furlough, eds. *The Sex of Things: Gender and Consumption in Historical Perspective*. Berkley, CA: University of California Press, 1996.
Denby, Elaine. *Grand Hotels: Reality & Illusion; An Architectural and Social History*. London: Reaktion Books, 1998.
De Vries, Jan. *The Industrious Revolution: Consumer Behaviour and Household Economy, 1650 to the Present*. Cambridge: Cambridge University Press, 2008.
De Vries, Joyce. 'Fashioning the Self in Early Modern Europe: Gender, Consumption, and Material Culture'. *Journal of Women's History* 23 (2011): 187–97.
Dolan, Brian. *Ladies of the Grand Tour: British Women in Pursuit of Enlightenment and Adventure in Eighteenth-Century Europe*. London: HarperCollins, 2001.
Douglas, Mary. *Thought Styles: Critical Essays on Good Taste*. London: Sage, 1996.
Douglas, Mary, and Baron Isherwood. *The World of Goods: Towards an Anthropology of Consumerism*. Harmondsworth: Penguin, 1978.
Dübeck, Inger. *Kvinder, familie og formue*. Copenhagen: Museum Tusculanums Forlag, 2003.
Dumont, Dora. 'Women and Guilds in Bologna: The Ambiguities of "Marginality"'. *Radical History Review* 70 (1998): 4–25.
Dwyer, John, and Richard B. Sher, eds. *Sociability and Society in Eighteenth-Century Scotland*. Edinburgh: Mercat Press, 1993.
Elliott, Paul. 'The Birth of Public Science in the English Provinces: Natural Philosophy in Derby, c.1690–1760'. *Annals of Science* 57 (2000): 61–100.
Ellis, Joyce. 'Consumption and Wealth'. In *The Reigns of Charles II and James VII and II*, edited by Lionel Glassey, 191–210. Basingstoke: Palgrave, 1997.
Epstein, Stephen R. *Town and Country in Europe, 1300–1800*. Cambridge: Cambridge University Press, 2001.
Erickson, Amy Louise. 'Eleanor Mosley and Other Milliners in the City of London Companies, 1700–1750'. *History Workshop Journal* 71 (2011): 147–72.
Farrant, Sue. *Georgian Brighton 1740–1820*. Brighton: University of Sussex Centre for Continuing Education, 1980.

Favier, René. '"Faiseurs de rien, vendeurs de tout". Les merciers de Grenoble au XVIIIe siècle'. In *La boutique et la ville. Commerces, commerçants, espaces et clientèles XVIe–XXe siècle*, edited by Natacha Coquery, 99–112. Tours: Publications de l'Université François Rabelais, 2000.

———. *Les villes du Dauphiné aux XVIIe et XVIIIe siècles*. Grenoble: Presses universitaires de Grenoble, 1993.

Fawcett, Trevor. 'Measuring the Provincial Enlightenment: The Case of Norwich'. *Eighteenth-Century Life* 8 (1982): 13–27.

Feather, John. 'The Power of Print: Word and Image in 18th Century England'. In *Culture and Society in Britain, 1660–1800*, edited by Jeremy Black, 51–68. Manchester: Manchester University Press, 1997.

———. *The Provincial Book Trade in Eighteenth-Century England*. Cambridge: Cambridge University Press, 1985.

Finn, Margot, 'Men's Things: Masculine Possession in the Consumer Revolution'. *Social History* 25 (2000): 133–55.

Fletcher, Pamela, and David Israel. *London Gallery Project*. Bowdoin College, 2007. Revised September 2012. Accessed 25 March 2014. http://learn.bowdoin.edu/fletcher/london-gallery/

Fontaine, Laurence, ed. *Alternative Exchanges: Second-Hand Circulations from the Sixteenth Century to the Present*. New York: Berghahn Books, 2008.

———. *History of Pedlars in Europe*. Cambridge: Cambridge University Press, 1996.

———. *L'économie morale. Pauvreté, crédit et confiance dans l'Europe préindustrielle*. Paris: Gallimard, 2008.

———. 'Les imbrications du formel et de l'informel dans la circulation des objets de luxe dans le Paris du XVIIIe siècle'. *Les Cahiers du Centre de Recherche Historique* 42 (2008): 49–65.

Fowler, Christina. 'Changes in Provincial Retail Practice during the Eighteenth Century'. *Business History* 40 (1998): 37–54.

Fox, Robert, and Anthony Turner, eds. *Luxury Trades and Consumerism in* Ancien Régime *Paris: Studies in the History of the Skilled Workforce*. Aldershot: Ashgate, 1998.

Gell, Alfred. *Art and Agency: An Anthropological Theory*. Oxford: Clarendon Press, 1998.

George, Dorothy. *London Life in the Eighteenth Century*. Harmondsworth: Penguin, 1966.

Girouard, Mark. *Life in the English Country House: A Social and Architectural History*. London: Yale University Press, 1978.

Gold, Carol. *Danish Cookbooks—Domesticity and National Identity, 1616–1901*. Seattle and Copenhagen: University of Washington Press and Museum Tusculanums Press, 2007.

———. *Educating Middle-Class Daughters—Private Girls Schools in Copenhagen, 1790–1820*. Copenhagen: Museum Tusculanums Press, 1996.

Greig, Hannah. *The Beau Monde: Fashionable Society in Georgian London*. Oxford: Oxford University Press, 2013.

Grenier, Jean-Yves. 'Une économie de l'identification'. In *La qualité des produits en France (XVIIIe–XIXe siècles)*, edited by Alessandro Stanziani, 25–54. Paris: Belin, 2003.

Grytten, Ola Honningdal, and Kjell Bjoern Minde. 'The Demand for Consumer Goods in the Modernization of the Norwegian Economy, 1850–1920'. *Scandinavian Economic History Review* 46 (1998): 49–54.

Hafter, Daryl M. *European Women and Preindustrial Craft*. Bloomington: Indiana University Press, 1995.

———. 'Stratégies pour un emploi: Travail féminin et corporations à Rouen et à Lyon, 1650–1791'. *Revue d'histoire moderne et contemporaine* 54 (2007): 98–115.
———. *Women and Work in Preindustrial France*. University Park: The Pennsylvania State University Press, 2007.
———. 'Women in the Underground Business of Eighteenth-Century Lyon'. *Enterprise & Society* 2 (2001): 11–40.
Hagemann, Gro. 'Del III. De stummes leir?'. In *Med kjønnsperspektiv på norsk historie*, edited by Ida Blom and Sølvi Sogner, 159–253. Oslo: Cappelen akademiske forlag, 2005.
Hann, Andrew, and Jon Stobart. 'Sites of Consumption: The Display of Goods in Provincial Shops in Eighteenth–Century England'. *Cultural and Social History* 2 (2005): 165–87.
Harris, Tim, ed. *Popular Culture in England, c. 1500–1850*. New York: St. Martin's Press, 1995.
Hart, Avril. 'The Mantua: Its Evolution and Fashionable Significance in the Seventeenth and Eighteenth Centuries'. In *Defining Dress as Object, Meaning and Identity*, edited by Amy de la Haye and Elizabeth Wilson, 93–103. Manchester: Manchester University Press, 1999.
Haupt, Heinz-Gerhard. *Konsum und Handel: Europa Im 19. Und 20. Jahrhundert*. Göttingen: Vandenhoeck & Ruprecht, 2002.
Hilton, Matthew. 'The Legacy of Luxury. Moralities of Consumption since the Eighteenth Century'. *Journal of Consumer Culture* 4 (2004): 101–23.
Hoden, Fritz, Ole Grytten, and Joerund Alme, 'Norwegian Real Wages: Trends in Prices and Wages, 1850–1950'. In *Labour's Reward: Real Wages and Economic Change in Nineteenth and Twentieth Century Europe*, edited by Peter Scholliers and Vera Zamagni, 60–84. Aldershot: Ashgate, 1995.
Honeyman, Katrina. *Well Suited: A History of the Leeds Clothing Industry, 1850–1990*. Oxford: Oxford University Press, 2000.
Hoppit, Julian. 'Attitudes to Credit in Britain, 1680–1790'. *Historical Journal* 33 (1990): 305–22.
Houston, Rab. 'Literacy, Education and the Culture of Print in Enlightenment Edinburgh'. *History* 254 (1993): 373–92.
Hunt, Margaret. *The Middling Sort: Commerce, Gender and the Family in England 1680–1780*. Berkeley, CA: University of California Press, 1996.
Hussey, David, and Margaret Ponsonby, eds. *Buying for the Home: Shopping for the Domestic from the Seventeenth Century to the Present*. Aldershot: Ashgate, 2008.
———. *The Single Homemaker and Material Culture in the Long Eighteenth Century*. Farnham: Ashgate 2012.
Hyldtoft, Ole. *Mad, drikke og tobak, 1800–35*. Copenhagen, Denmark: Museum Tusculanums Forlag, 2012.
Jacobsen, Helen. *Luxury and Power: The Material World of the Stuart Diplomat, 1660–1714*. Oxford: Oxford University Press, 2012.
Jianu, Angela. 'Women, Fashion, and Europeanization: The Romanian Principalities, 1750–1830'. In *Women in the Ottoman Balkans: Gender, Culture and History*, edited by Amila Buturović and İrvin Cemil Schick, 201–30. New York: I. B. Tauris, 2007.
Johansen, Amanda, and Hans Johansen. *De er med oss: Barndomsminner*. Oslo: Privat forlag, 1967.
Johansen, Hanne Marie. *Slik levde de da. Familie- og hverdagsliv i Drammen gjennom 200 år*. Oslo: Spartacus, 2011.
Johansen, Hans Chr., 'Food Consumption in the Pre-Industrial Nordic Societies'. *Scandinavian Economic History Review* 46 (1998): 11–23.

Jones, Jennifer. *Sexing La Mode: Gender, Fashion and Commercial Culture in Old Regime France*. Oxford: Berg, 2004.

Jordan, David P. *Transforming Paris: The Life and Labors of Baron Haussmann*. New York: Free Press, 1995.

Kaartinen, Marjo. *Arjesta ihmeisiin. Eliitin kulttuurihistoriaa 1500–1800-luvun Euroopassa*. Helsinki: Tammi, 2006.

———. 'Women's Metropolis—Elite Women in Early Modern London'. *Women's History Magazine* 53 (2006): 4–12.

Keeble, Trevor, '"Everything Whispers of Wealth and Luxury": Observation, Emulation, and Display in the Well-To-Do Late-Victorian Home'. In *Women and the Making of Built Space in England, 1870–1950*, edited by Elizabeth Darling and Lesley Whitworth, 69–86. Aldershot: Ashgate, 2007.

Klein, Lawrence. 'Gender and the Public/Private Distinction in the Eighteenth Century: Some Questions About Evidence and Analytic Procedure'. *Eighteenth-Century Studies* 29 (1995): 97–109.

König, Wolfgang. *Kleine Geschichte der Konsumgesellschaft: Konsum als Lebensform der Moderne*. Stuttgart: Franz Steiner Verlag, 2013.

———. *Consuming Subjects: Women, Shopping, and Business in the Eighteenth Century*. New York: Columbia University Press, 1997.

Kowaleski-Wallace, Elizabeth. 'Women, China and Consumer Culture in Eighteenth-Century England'. *Eighteenth-Century Studies* 29 (Winter 1995–96): 153–67.

Lancaster, Bill. *The Department Store: A Social History*. London: Leicester University Press, 1995.

Larrère, Catherine. 'Le sexe ou le rang ? La condition des femmes selon la philosophie des Lumières'. In *Nouvelle encyclopédie politique et historique des femmes*, edited by Christine Fauré, 168–207. Paris: Les Belles Lettres, 2010.

'Le luxe'. Special issue, *Entreprises et histoire* 46 (2007).

Lemire, Beverly. 'Consumerism in Preindustrial and Early Industrial England: The Trade in Secondhand Clothes'. *The Journal of British Studies* 27 (1988): 1–24.

———. *Cotton*. Oxford: Berg, 2011.

———. *Fashion's Favourite: The Cotton Trade and the Consumer in Britain, 1660–1800*. Oxford: Oxford University Press, 1991.

———. 'Le goût du coton: culture matérielle, politique et consommation dans le Japon des Tokugawa et l'Angleterre moderne'. *Revue d'histoire moderne et contemporaine* 60 (2013): 71–105.

———. *The Business of Everyday Life: Gender, Practice and Social Politics in England*. Manchester: Manchester University Press, 2005.

———, ed. *The Force of Fashion in Politics and Society: Global Perspectives from Early Modern to Contemporary Times*. Burlington, VT and Farnham, Surrey, UK: Ashgate, 2010.

Lemire, Beverly, and Giorgio Riello. 'East & West: Textiles and Fashion in Early Modern Europe'. *Journal of Social History* 41 (2008): 887–916.

Lepetit, Bernard. *Les villes dans la France moderne*. Paris: Albin Michel, 1988.

Lipovetsky, Gilles. *The Empire of Fashion: Dressing Modern Democracy*. Princeton, NJ: Princeton University Press, 1994.

Loeb, Lori. *Consuming Angels: Advertising and Victorian Women*. Oxford: Oxford University Press, 1994.

Lowerson, John. 'Leisure, Consumption and the European City'. *Urban History* 30 (2003): 92–7.

Lummis, Trevor, and Jan Marsh. *The Woman's Domain: Women and the English Country House*. London: Viking Press, 1990.

Lyna, Dries, and Ilja Van Damme. 'A Strategy of Seduction? The Role of Commercial Advertisements in the Eighteenth-Century Retailing Business of Antwerp'. *Business History* 51 (2009): 100–21.

Mackie, Erin S. *The Commerce of Everyday Life: Selections from 'The Tatler' and 'The Spectator'*. Boston: Bedford/St. Martin's, 1998.
Malanima, Paolo. *Il Lusso dei Contadini: Consumi e industrie nelle campagne toscane del Sei e Settecento*. Bologna: Il Mulino, 1990.
Margairaz, Dominique. 'Luxe'. In *Dictionnaire européen des Lumières*, edited by Michel Delon, 662–66. Paris: Presses universitaires de France, 1997.
Marseille, Jacques. *Le luxe en France du siècle des Lumières à nos jours*. Paris: Association pour le développement de l'histoire économique, 1999.
Maza, Sara. *The Myth of the French Bourgeoisie: An Essay on the Social Imaginary 1750–1850*. Cambridge, MA: Harvard University Press, 2003.
McCants, Anne E. C. 'Exotic Goods, Popular Consumption, and the Standard of Living: Thinking about Globalization in the Early Modern World'. *Journal of World History* 17 (2007): 433–62.
McKendrick, Neil, John Brewer, and J. H. Plumb, eds. *The Birth of a Consumer Society: The Commercialization of Eighteenth Century England*. London: Routledge, 1993.
Miller, Michael. *The Bon Marché, Bourgeois Culture and the Department Store, 1869–1920*. Princeton, NJ: Princeton University Press, 1981.
Mitchell, Ian. 'The Development of Urban Retailing, 1700–1815'. In *The Transformation of English Provincial Towns, 1600–1800*, edited by Peter Clark, 259–83. London: Hutchinson Educational, 1984.
Montenach, Anne. '"Uncontrolled Crossings": Gender and Illicit Economic Territories in Eighteenth-Century French Towns'. In *Gendering Spaces in European Towns, 1600–1914*, edited by Elaine Chalus and Marjo Kaartinen. London: Routledge, forthcoming.
———. 'Vendre le luxe en province: circuits officiels et réseaux parallèles dans le Dauphiné du XVIIIe siècle'. In *Le commerce du luxe, le luxe du commerce*, edited by Alain Bonnet and Natacha Coquery. Paris: Mare & Martin, 2014.
Moreno Claverías, Belén. 'Lugar de residencia y pautas de consumo: El penedes y Barcelona, 1770–1790'. *Revista de Historia Industrial* 15 (2006): 139–66.
———. 'Révolution de la consommation paysanne ? Modes de consommation et différentiation sociale de la paysannerie catalane, 1670–1790'. *Histoire et Mesure* 21 (2006): 141–83.
Mui, Hoh-Cheung, and Lorna H. Mui. *Shops and Shopkeeping in Eighteenth-Century England*. London: Routledge, 1987.
Nead, Lynda. *Victorian Babylon: People Streets and Images in Nineteenth-Century London*. New Haven, CT: Yale University Press, 2000.
North, Michael, ed. *Artistic and Cultural Exchanges Between Europe and Asia, 1400–1900: Rethinking Markets, Workshops and Collections*. Farnham: Ashgate, 2010.
Pardailhé-Galabrun, Annick. *The Birth of Intimacy: Privacy and Domestic Life in Early Modern Paris*. Philadelphia: University of Pennsylvania Press, 1991.
Peck, Linda Levy. *Consuming Splendor: Society and Culture in Seventeenth-Century England*. Cambridge: Cambridge University Press, 2005.
Pedersen, Mikkel Venborg. *Luksus—Forbrug og kolonier i Danmark i det 18. århundrede*. Copenhagen: Museum Tusculanums Forlag, 2013.
Perrot, Philippe. *Le luxe: une richesse entre faste et confort (XVIIIe–XIXe siècles)*. Paris: Seuil, 1995.
Phillips, Nicola. *Women in Business, 1700–1850*. Woodbridge: Boydell, 2006.
Plumb, J. H. 'The New World of Children in Eighteenth-Century England'. *Past and Present* 67 (1975): 64–95.
Porter, Roy, and Marie M. Roberts, eds. *Pleasure in the Eighteenth Century*. London: Macmillan, 1966.

Prior, Mary. 'Women and the Urban Economy: Oxford, 1500–1800'. In *Women in English Society, 1500–1800*, edited by Mary Prior, 93–117. London: Methuen, 1985.

Quataert, Jean. 'The Shaping of Women's Work in Manufacturing Guilds, Households and the State in Central Europe, 1648–1870'. *American Historical Review* 90 (1985): 1122–48.

Rabuzzi, David A. 'Fading Images, Fading Realities? Female Merchants in Scandinavia and the Baltic'. *Social History/Histoire Sociale* 34, 68 (2001): 355–70.

Rappaport, Erika. *Shopping for Pleasure: Women in the Making of London's West End*. Princeton, NJ: Princeton University Press, 2000.

Raven, James. *Judging New Wealth: Popular Publishing and Responses to Commerce in England, 1750–1850*. Oxford: Oxford University Press, 1992.

Reiht, Reinhold, and Torsten Meyer, eds. *Luxus und Konsum. Eine Historische Annäherung*. Münster: Waxmann, 2003.

Rétat, Pierre. 'Luxe'. *XVIIIe siècle* 26 (1994): 79–88.

Richards, Thomas. *The Commodity Culture of Victorian England: Advertising and Spectacle, 1851–1914*. Stanford, CA: Stanford University Press, 1990.

Riello, Giorgio. *Cotton: The Fabric that Made the Modern World*. Cambridge: Cambridge University Press, 2013.

———, ed. *Moda. Storia e storie*. Milan: Bruno Mondadori, 2010.

Riello, Giorgio, and Peter McNeil, eds. *The Fashion History Reader: Global Perspectives*. New York: Routledge, 2010.

Rivers, Isabel, ed. *Books and Their Readers in Eighteenth-Century England*. Leicester: Leicester University Press, 1982.

Robinson, Eric. 'Eighteenth-Century Commerce and Fashion: Matthew Boulton's Marketing Techniques'. *Economic History Review* 16 (1963): 39–60.

Roche, Daniel. *A History of Everyday Things: The Birth of Consumption in France, 1600–1800*. Cambridge: Cambridge University Press, 2000.

———. *The Culture of Clothing: Dress and Fashion in the Ancien Régime*. Cambridge: Cambridge University Press, 1994.

Ruane Christine. *The Empire's New Clothes: A History of the Russian Fashion Industry, 1700–1917*. New Haven, CT: Yale University Press, 2009.

Rydén, Göran, ed. *Sweden in the Eighteenth-Century World: Provincial Cosmopolitans*. Aldershot: Ashgate, 2013.

Saisselin, Rémy G. *The Enlightenment Against the Baroque: Economics and Aesthetics in the Eighteenth Century*. Berkeley, CA: University of California Press, 1992.

Sanderson, Elizabeth C. *Women and Work in Eighteenth-Century Edinburgh*. London: Macmillan, 1996.

Sandvik, Hilde, 'Kapittel 3; Det økonomiske fellesskapet'. In *I gode og vonde dagar. Familielivet i Noreg frå reformasjonen til vår tid*, edited by Sølvi Sogner, Hilde Sandvik, Beate Homlong, Kari Telste, and Hanne Marie Johansen, 72–118. Oslo: Det Norske Samlaget, 2003.

Sarti, Raffaella. *Europe at Home: Family and Material Culture, 1500–1800*. Translated by Allan Cameron. New Haven and London: Yale University Press, 2002.

Saurma-Jeltsch, E. Lieselotte, and Anja Eisenbeiss, eds. *The Power of Things and the Flow of Cultural Transformations: Art and Culture Between Europe and Asia*. Berlin: Deutscher Kunstverlag, 2010.

Sekora, John. *Luxury: The Concept in Western Thought, Eden to Smollett*. Baltimore, MD: John Hopkins University Press, 1977.

Shammas, Carole. *The Pre-Industrial Consumer in England and America*. Oxford: Oxford University Press, 1990.

Shannon, Brent. 'Refashioning Men: Fashion, Masculinity, and the Cultivation of the Male Consumer in Britain, 1860–1914.' *Victorian Studies* 46 (2004): 597–630.
Shovlin, John. 'The Cultural Politics of Luxury in Eighteenth-Century France'. *French Historical Studies* 33 (2000): 578–603.
Simmel, George. 'Fashion'. *International Quarterly* 10 (1904): 130–55.
Simonton, Deborah. *A History of European Women's Work, 1700 to the Present.* London: Routledge, 1998.
———. 'Apprenticeship: Training and Gender in Eighteenth-Century England'. In *Markets and Manufactures in Early Industrial Europe*, edited by Maxine Berg, 227–58. London: Routledge, 1991.
———. 'Gendering Labour in Eighteenth-Century Towns'. In *Working out Gender: Perspectives from Labour History*, edited by Margaret Walsh, 29–47. Aldershot: Ashgate, 1999.
———. 'Threading the Needle, Pulling the Press: Gender, Skill and the Tools of the Trade in Eighteenth-Century European Towns'. *Cultural History* 1–2 (2012): 180–204.
———. *Women in European Culture and Society*. London: Routledge, 2011.
Simonton, Deborah, and Anne Montenach, eds. *Female Agency in the Urban Economy: Gender in European Towns, 1640–1830*. New York: Routledge, 2013.
Smith, Chloe Wigston. '"Calico Madams": Servants, Consumption, and the Calico Crisis', *Eighteenth-Century Life* 31 (2007): 29–55.
Smith, S. D. 'Women's Admission to Guilds in Early-Modern England: The Case of the York Merchant Tailors' Company, 1693–1776'. *Gender & History* 17 (2005): 99–126.
Smith, Woodruff D. *Consumption and the Making of Respectability, 1600–1800*. New York: Routledge, 2002.
Sogner, Sølvi, and Kari Telste. *Ut og søkje teneste. Historia om tenestejentene*. Oslo: Det Norske Samlaget, 2005.
Solberg, Sven A. *Kort Familiekrønike og Barndoms- ogUungdomserindringer*. Oslo: Privat forlag, 1974.
Solkin, David. *Painting for Money: The Visual Arts and the Public Sphere in Eighteenth-Century England*. New Haven, CT: Yale University Press, 1992.
Sombart, Werner. *Luxus und Kapitalismus*. Munich: Duncker & Humblot, 1922.
Sougy, Nadège, ed. *Luxes et internationalisation (XVIe–XIXe siècles)*. Neuchâtel: Editions Alphil-Presses universitaires suisses, 2013.
Stobart, Jon. 'Gentlemen and shopkeepers: Supplying the Country House in Eighteenth-Century England'. *The Economic History Review* 64 (2011): 885–904.
———. 'Shopping Streets as Social Space: Consumerism, Improvement and Leisure in an Eighteenth-Century Country Town'. *Urban History* 25 (1998): 3–21.
———. *Spend, Spend, Spend! A History of Shopping*. Stroud: The History Press, 2008.
Stobart, Jon, Andrew Hann, and Victoria Morgan. *Spaces of Consumption: Shopping and Leisure in the English Town, 1680–1830*. London: Routledge, 2007.
Stobart, Jon, and Leonard Schwarz. 'Leisure, Luxury and Urban Specialization in the Eighteenth Century'. *Urban History*, 35 (2008): 216–36.
Strasser, Susan, Charles McGovern, and Matthias Judt, eds. *Getting and Spending: European and American Consumer Societies in the Twentieth Century*. Cambridge: Cambridge University Press, 1998.
Styles, John. 'Product Innovation in Early Modern London'. *Past & Present* 168 (2000): 124–69.
Styles, John, and Amanda Vickery, eds. *Gender, Taste, and Material Culture in Britain and North America, 1700–1830*. New Haven, CT: Yale University Press, 2006.

Sweet, Rosemary, and Penelope Lane, eds. *On the Town: Women and Urban Life in Eighteenth-Century England*. Aldershot: Ashgate, 2003.

Thirsk, Joan. *Economic Policy and Projects: The Development of a Consumer Society in Early Modern England*. Oxford: Clarendon Press, 1978.

Tiersten, Lisa. *Marianne in the Market: Envisioning Consumer Society in Fin-De-Siècle France*. Berkeley, CA: University of California Press, 2002.

Tilley, Christopher, Webb Keane, Susanne Küchler, Mike Rowlands, and Patricia Spyer, eds. *Handbook of Material Culture*. London: Sage, 2006.

Tosh, John. *A Man's Place: Masculinity and the Middle-Class Home in Victorian England*. New Haven, CT: Yale University Press, 1999.

Trentmann, Frank, ed. *The Oxford Handbook of the History of Consumption*. Oxford: Oxford University Press, 2013.

Ugolini, Laura. *Men and Menswear: Sartorial Consumption in Britain, 1880–1939*. Aldershot: Ashgate, 2007.

———. 'Men, Masculinities, and Menswear Advertising, c. 1890–1914'. In *A Nation of Shopkeepers: Five Centuries of British Retailing*, edited by John Benson and Laura Ugolini, 80–104. London: I. B. Tauris, 2003.

University of Glasgow. *Exhibition Culture in London 1878–1908*. Database. Accessed 25 March 2014. www.exhibitionculture.arts.gla.ac.uk/

Veblen, Thorstein. *The Theory of the Leisure Class: An Economic Study of Institutions*. New York: The Macmillan Company, 1899.

Verley, Patrick. *L'échelle du monde. Essai sur l'industrialisation de l'Occident*. Paris: Gallimard, 1997.

Vickery, Amanda. *Behind Closed Doors: At Home in Georgian England*. Yale University Press: New Haven and London, 2009.

———. 'His and Hers: Gender, Consumption and Household Accounting in Eighteenth-Century England'. Supplement. *Past and Present* 1 (2006): 12–38.

———. *The Gentleman's Daughter: Women's Lives in Georgian England*. New Haven, CT: Yale University Press, 1998.

Wahnbaeck, Till. *Luxury and Public Happiness: Political Economy in the Italian Enlightenment*. Oxford: Oxford University Press, 2004.

Walker, Lynne. 'Vistas of Pleasure: Women Consumers of Urban Space in the West End of London 1850–1900'. In *Women in the Victorian Art World*, edited by Clarissa Campbell Orr, 70–85. Manchester: Manchester University Press, 1995.

Weatherill, Lorna. 'A Possession of One's Own: Women and Consumer Behaviour in England, 1660–1740'. *Journal of British Studies* 25 (1986): 131–56.

———. *Consumer Behaviour and Material Culture in Britain 1660–1760*. 2nd ed. London: Routledge, 1996.

Welch, Evelyn. *Shopping in the Renaissance: Consumer Cultures in Italy 1400–1600*. New Haven, CT: Yale University Press, 2005.

Whittle, Jane, and Elizabeth Griffith. *Consumption and Gender in the Early Seventeenth-Century Household: The World of Alice Le Strange*. Oxford: Oxford University Press, 2012.

Williams, Rosalind. *Dream Worlds: Mass Consumption in Late Nineteenth-Century France*. Berkeley, CA: University of California Press, 1982.

Wischermann, Clemens, and Elliott Shore, eds. *Advertising and the European City: Historical Perspectives*. Aldershot: Ashgate, 2000.

Zweiniger-Bargielowska, Ida. 'Living Standards and Consumption'. In *A Companion to Contemporary Britain, 1939–2000*, edited by Paul Addison and Harriet Jones, 260–93. Oxford: Blackwell Publishing, 2005.

Index